Fuzzy Logic, Systems and Engineering Applications

Fuzzy Logic, Systems and Engineering Applications

Editor: Hubert Parks

MURPHY & MOORE

www.murphy-moorepublishing.com

Published by Murphy & Moore Publishing
1 Rockefeller Plaza,
New York City, NY 10020, USA
www.murphy-moorepublishing.com

Fuzzy Logic, Systems and Engineering Applications
Edited by Hubert Parks

International Standard Book Number: 978-1-63987-252-7 (Hardback)

Cataloging-in-Publication Data

Fuzzy logic, systems and engineering applications / edited by Hubert Parks.
    p. cm.
Includes bibliographical references and index.
ISBN 978-1-63987-252-7
1. Fuzzy logic. 2. Fuzzy systems. 3. Engineering mathematics. 4. Fuzzy mathematics.
5. Logic, Symbolic and mathematical. I. Parks, Hubert.
QA9.64 .F89 2022
511.3--dc23

Contents

Preface

A form of many-valued logic in which the truth value of variables may be any real number between 0 and 1, including these two is termed as fuzzy logic. The basis of the fuzzy logic is the observation that people make decisions on the basis of imprecise and non-numerical information. Fuzzy logic has applications in many fields, ranging from control theory to artificial intelligence. Fuzzy models are used to mathematically represent vagueness and imprecise information. These models can represent, recognize, interpret and utilize the data and information that are vague. This book is a compilation of chapters that discuss the most vital concepts and emerging trends in the field of fuzzy logic. The various advancements in this field along with its engineering applications are glanced at herein. As this field is emerging at a rapid pace, the contents of this book will help the readers understand the modern concepts and applications of the subject.

Significant researches are present in this book. Intensive efforts have been employed by authors to make this book an outstanding discourse. This book contains the enlightening chapters which have been written on the basis of significant researches done by the experts.

Finally, I would also like to thank all the members involved in this book for being a team and meeting all the deadlines for the submission of their respective works. I would also like to thank my friends and family for being supportive in my efforts.

Editor

1

Implementing Complex Fuzzy Analysis for Business Planning Systems

Danil Dintsis

Abstract

The chapter deals with implementing fuzzy logic for transition of descriptions in natural language to formal fuzzy and stochastic models and their further optimization in terms of effectiveness and efficiency of information modeling and prediction systems. The theoretical methods are implemented in lifelong learning business for development-specific virtual trainings for adult students.

Keywords: fuzzy, fuzzy set, fuzzy risk, lifelong learning, virtual learning, training method prediction, fuzzy analysis, complex definition area

1. Introduction

In the first part of the chapter the author examines challenges in transforming subject description in a natural language to a formal model. Establishing collaboration between specialists in different knowledge areas (technology, information, business, etc.) is usually a very complicated problem. In the process of common work there is a strong need to estimate model clearness, effectiveness, and efficiency for specialists in different knowledge areas. We consider effectiveness as correct interpretation of a subject in a real world by a model. And efficiency is calculated based on the share of the service states of the model.

In the second part, the author shows the implementation of the approach in virtual training design. Developing specific training methods for adult lifelong students is a very complicated task. We implemented fuzzy-based analysis to determine the best learning methods for different student groups and course types.

The special section is devoted to adapting and implementing virtual training for hard of hearing people.

2. Extension for fuzzy model definition area

2.1. Introduction

Information systems are widely spread in our daily life: offices, industry, and home. Each system represents or controls an extra object, such as household appliances or industrial control devices. Efficiency of those information and control systems depends on a wide range of factors. Wide-known methods for control systems' synthesis demand the formal model represented in analytical format [1]. The main problem of the discrete automate models is the strong necessity of formalization at the beginning of the process. It is a rather difficult task for complicated technological and information processes. Moreover, it is more appropriate to set a task of the adaptive control system with parametric adaptation features synthesis.

Let us consider the control system for an informational object as a "black box" with two sets of inputs and outputs [3]. Two main inputs are a math (or analytical) model, and data. One of the important features is a number and percentage of internal states of an information system/control device. Internal states are always necessary to control stability of work, prevent user's mistakes, etc. These internal states and their properties require additional computing resources. The author examines an approach aimed at balancing advantages and resource usage of internal states [2].

Meanwhile these both inputs are (or can be) cross-dependent. Creating an analytical model as the first step of the system synthesis is based on intrinsic and semantic analysis of input data. Establishment of collaboration between specialists in different knowledge areas (technology, information, business, or others) is usually one of the main problems and challenges almost in all practice-based projects [3]. Factor analysis or lingual models may provide partial decision of the problem. Lingual models combine a system description in both formal and descriptive terms. A restriction of linguistic models is in their insufficient formalization and a high level of dependence on subjective expert appraisals.

Fuzzy models implementation ensures an analysis of processes in technical and information-based systems with nonlinear and/or multifactor-based behavior [1, 5]. The author presents the approach that combines model analysis based on natural language with strict formal systems by implementing fuzzy logic approaches.

2.2. General approach based on lingual models

We consider a process of analytical model synthesis as a first phase of a control model synthesis. The first important step at this phase is transition of a description based on natural language to a formal model. We should consider an interaction between specialists in different knowledge areas while creating such models as they may use different terms. Another important task is establishing back coupling between input data and information/control system. It is quite necessary for creating information and control systems with adaptive features. We implement fuzzy logic to solve the task of information system synthesis for complicated technological objects.

Implementing fuzzy logic ensures the opportunity of a semantic analysis of the object description made on natural-based language due to partial entrance of an element in one or several sets. The conceptual structure of the research area is represented as a set of abstract entities relying on concepts and terms of both a natural language and fuzzy sets. Next, we need to extend the existing fuzzy sets' model as an analytical model contains features, appropriate to elements of analyzable object, and own properties of the model, that provide its integrity.

Second step should be to deal with input data analysis to adapt the model and control system to environment changes. We do not need to change our model but make it adaptive. We need to establish clear borders for research object and its analytical model. To resolve this task, we need also to extend current fuzzy sets and models' methods and features. In this work, we present an extension range of definition of fuzzy sets and its elements' logical division to two sets: corresponding to object properties and internal properties of a system itself.

2.3. Model analysis in a partially defined environment based on fuzzy sets

Any analytical model has several internal features that ensure its internal integrity and reliability of a control system to controlled object. One may implement internal model states for internal data integrity control, exchange, additional logic control, etc.

Let's name a set of objects to be synthesized as $S = \{a[i]\}$. Each noun in a lingual model compares to an object $a[i]$ with value (weight) $a(i)$ and functionality $H(a[i])$. Lets' define an expansion of a definition range values for fuzzy attributes to imaginary area:

$$\begin{cases} j*a\,(i), & \text{if an object exists only in a formal model} \\ a\,(i) = a\,(i) & \text{if an object compares to a modelling subject} \end{cases} \tag{1}$$

Based on the above, it is obvious that model S always consists of objects with both rational and imaginary features and functionality weights. $H+$ and $H-$[4, 6, 7]. In this case, total number of object $a[i]$ features is h(n).

1. Number of features compared to lingual model is h+.

2. Total number of object features in fuzzy model– S.

3. Weights of each feature is $s(i)$.

4. A functional as a summary (vector) weight of features divided into rational and imaginary parts $a[i]$ -> H.

A model functional parameter may be represented as the following complex number:

$$H = H + +jH - \tag{2}$$

2.4. Extending fuzzy logic procedures for analysis and synthesis of information systems

Below, we show the extension is correct and does not break the fuzzy logic postulates. The definition area would be the following:

$$H\,(A|B) \in\ [0; \infty[+j([0,\infty[) \tag{3}$$

Lemmas:

If A is the element of a real object and B is the internal element:

$$H\,(A|B) \in\ [0; \infty[\tag{4}$$

If both A, B are internal elements:

$$H\,(A|B) \in j([0; \infty[) \tag{5}$$

$$H(U) = \infty \tag{6}$$

U is a universal set.

We provided a transformation of the traditional fuzzy sets axioms and features to a specific fuzzy model for using complex-based definition area to specify features of models for synthesis of control automation systems.

2.4.1. Fuzzy model synthesis based on lingual model analysis for technological and information objects

First, we need to transform a lingual model based on subject area terms and definitions to a metalanguage-based model. This model still may include some terms from its predecessor— the certain lingual model. Let us mark sets of keywords, and consider them as fuzzy model objects. At the first step, we may consider all nouns as fuzzy model objects [1–3].

Next let's define a transition between fuzzy objects:

$$\begin{cases} \text{fi} \\ a[i] \rightarrow a[i+1], \text{fi is an } a[i] \text{ object's method} \end{cases} \tag{7}$$

If weight $a(i)$ is an imaginary one, then the object $a[i]$ does not match any object in a lingual model, and only meta model contains it.

Then, based on δ-operation, as it is defined in common fuzzy logic, we provide the following transformation between logically tied objects:

$$\begin{cases} a[i] \ \delta i a[i+1] \ \Rightarrow \ a[i+1] \\ \qquad\qquad \text{fi} + 1 \\ a[i] \ \delta i + 1 \ [i+1] \ \Rightarrow \ a[i] \ \rightarrow \ a[i+2] \end{cases} \tag{8}$$

So, we can formalize an object's method based on a 2-step δ-operation.

Let's introduce a weight of a fuzzy object $H\,(M)=A$. We consider $\sum H(a[i]) >= H(P))$, as the model contains both objects and their methods $f(i)$, that define a consequence of transitions between objects in a model. $f(i)$ methods are described by γ and δ operations. δ -operation defines a consequence of operations, events, and nodes of a model, and γ-operation defines weights (for example, possibility, availability, resilience, etc.) for nodes, events, operations. If we take into consideration both types and an optimization factor $H(M)=A\rightarrow\max$, then the following equality is true:

$$H(P) = H(a[1])\gamma H(a[2])\gamma\ \gamma H(a[i])\gamma\ \gamma H(a[n] \tag{9}$$

The following set of conditions provides model and based on it control system integrity:

$$\begin{cases} H(M) \rightarrow \max; \\ H(M) = \Gamma a[i]\ \Delta a[i]; \\ \nabla a[i], H(a[i] \neq 0; \\ \nabla a[i], H(a[i]) \rightarrow \max; \\ \gamma i \in a[i],\ \delta i \in\ a[i]; \\ f(i) = \gamma i \cup \delta i \end{cases} \tag{10}$$

The following operations provide structuration of fuzzy sets in A:

1. Establish relations between sets:

1.1. Relation of entrance Ai ∈ Aj

1.2. Relation of inheritance. Ai inherits Aj if a(i) ∈ Ai has the fixed set of values, and methods no less than a(j) ∈ A(j).

2. Let's introduce meta-set M, which describes a set of sets:

$$Ai:\ M = \cup(n(i), \cup h(i,j)), \tag{11}$$

And a system of their internal relationships, where $n(i)$, Ai's unique identifier (usually string name); $h(i,j)$, a weight of relation between Ai and Aj sets.

An optimization of model parameters provides by consequent iterations. A rate, which weights reliability between fuzzy meta-model and preceding lingual model, is one of the most important optimization criteria. It is based on a feature $\nabla a[i] \in M$, that indicates a belongingness of a set element to a real or imaginary areas.

2.4.2. Fuzzy model synthesis algorithm based on a preceding lingual model

1. Allocate described essences based on the linguistic analysis. Create a set S of subessences.

2. Allocate a set of described attributes of essences. Based on it create a set T of fuzzy model attributes as mentioned in [2, 3].

3. Create a set K of basic knowledge sources, including experts, knowledgebase, and experimental data.

4. Create set C as a united set of weight criteria of each element. Primary weight is proportional to number of its occurrences into subsets $C(i)$.

5.   Create subsets $S(i)$ as based on the S set. $S(i)$ elements are united into a certain subset according to $C(i)$ criteria.

6.   Create sets H(j) containing experts', knowledgebase articles and other data sources' weights: $Ci \rightarrow Hj(Ci)$.

7.   Create sets $A(i)$ including attributes $a(i)$, as Ai ∇ S,t(i)A1, An, where

$$n >= 1, \nabla h(j)(Ai) = f(h(j), A(i), Hj, [Ai] \backslash Ci).$$

8.   Establish fuzzy model M (Ai, H[a(j)].

Synthesis of a control system for technical and/or information object is based on the defined fuzzy set M.

2.5. Scope definition for fuzzy sets usage in control and simulation systems for technical and information systems

While designing formal model (including fuzzy one), it is necessary to estimate the following items:

- Possibility of implementing a certain formalization method to a certain object;

- Degree of model compliance to an object. Consider fuzzy set A, containing $a[i]$ elements. Each a [i] is compliant with an object feature or internal feature of a model. We consider a method of compliance between model and object based on research of mutual consistency of elements. The method is based on a ∪-operation, and indicates subsets, which can describe an object behavior if used in common [2, 3]:

$$M = A \cup B \cup C \cup \, \cup N \tag{12}$$

2.5.1. Internal consistency criteria

1.   Redundancy property:

$$\forall H(a[i]\beta a[j] > 0$$

2.   Compliance property:

$$\forall H(a[i]|a[j] \neq \infty$$

3.   Efficiency and resilience balance:

$$\begin{cases} \sum a[i](h+) > 0 \\ \sum a[i](h-) > 0 \\ \sum a[i](h) > 0 \end{cases} \tag{13}$$

2.5.2. Compliance to modeling object criteria

(1) Compliance between M - model transformations results, and an object fact features: implementing of any possible track of operations of M model cannot lead an object to a prohibited state.

$$\forall H(Xi(Ai)) > 0, \tag{14}$$

or

Implementing of any possible track in M, model can transform the controlled system or object R into a possible state or common null state

$$\forall H(Xi(Ai)) >= 0 \tag{15}$$

Thus, we consider a fuzzy model is applicable in case that its real functional is positive and there is at least one set of allowed methods that transform a control system from its initial to final state.

2.6. Conclusion

Finally, we found that the synthesis of control systems based on descriptive models of natural language may be adequately implemented based on fuzzy sets. Logical separation of elements of fuzzy sets, in which the real domain includes the attributes and functional elements that describe the state of an object, but to the imaginary one—own internal state of the model and the management system that are required to make it operational. Based on this logical separation, we may estimate effectiveness and resilience of control system.

Finally, the authors resume that automated systems' synthesis is appropriately presented and formalized by fuzzy sets' models. Fuzzy logic definition area has been extended to an imaginary area. We established the logical division of model components to real and imaginary areas per their role. Internal objects of a model are presented in the imaginary area, and objects that describe the modeling system to the real area. We introduced necessary functional extensions for fuzzy logic to operate with logical extension.

Transformation algorithm is developed, and we recommend the certain implementation area for it.

3. Defining appropriate training methods for lifelong learning organization

3.1. Introduction

The author has developed a method and algorithms of fuzzy analysis for lingual models with complex digits' implementation. The author used the approach that differentiates native data, attributes of an object and internal model data, and attributes [2, 3]. Dividing these classes into real and imaginary leads to the decrease of dimensions in a model, and in this way to the decrease of computing capacity. This fact allows to decrease the risk of incorrect interpretation of results, and it provides also an opportunity to estimate costs of efficiency.

This article is devoted to implementing fuzzy analysis to define and implement various virtual training methods in a lifelong learning educational organization and reaches the highest possible satisfaction level by different categories of adult students as defined in Ref. [4].

3.2. Big challenges in lifelong learning

The lifelong professional learning training center offers short-term trainings and postdiploma programs to upgrade professional skills or gain a new specialization for adult professionals. A lot of students take multiple courses as bundles or periodically in accordance to new versions of software, technological equipment, or professional standards. It's of great importance for the training organization to analyze big data interdependencies to find out trends, develop new courses, make targeted offers for students, and create specific training methods for certain client groups. Since 2009, the author has been deeply involved into developing and implementing various virtual—online, and blended—training methods. During this work, the author carried out a regular analysis of data from different sources to determine customer requirements, demands for courses, and ways of their representation, technical, and mytho-logical opportunities [4, 5]. The goal of those continual research efforts was the development of strongly targeted training options for certain student groups and courses. The fuzzy-based modeling is considered as the most appropriate approach to the task, because students', customers', trainers', and other staff's feedback, requirements, as well as demand estimations, are mostly represented as a nonformal or mixed way. For example, rating A in a feedback means "more than I can expect." It is obvious that the level of expectations differs among students, and customer representatives.

3.3. Opportunities and threats in lifelong learning

Based on M_o_R™ and Total Risk Management® concepts fundamental characteristics of any risk define organization behavior for it, for example: tolerance level, impact, mitigation and contingency strategies, management level, as well as level of financial reserves. While examin-ing risk nature we often consider that a single risk belongs to different characteristic sets. For example, a risk of incorrect professional behavior can belong to human and organizational, and technical sets simultaneously. Therefore, we can create a fuzzy description of a risk:

$$r(i) \in O, r(i) \in T, \mathrm{r(i)}\, H \tag{16}$$

where O, T, H, fuzzy sets (organizational, technical, human features).

Implementing risk analysis in fuzzy terms ensures complex analysis for risk source, impact, mitigation, and contingency. The author examined complex risk analysis for portfolio (both projects and operational activities) of virtual learning methods in a lifelong adult training center. As a service-based and private user (a student) oriented business, its success depends dramatically on a subjective personalized opinion of students and partially of corporate HR managers. Their feedbacks are represented both in partially formalized manner, and comments in a natural language.

Another challenge concerns representing risk dependencies, or so-called domino effect. As it's a rather complicated task to formalize risks interdependencies, we can implement an approach, starting with an informal description in a natural language with further formalizing it by means of fuzzy-based algorithms.

The fuzzy analysis is the very appropriate tool to transfer statements in a natural language into a formal model, and explore threats and opportunities. The fuzzy analysis is implemented as described by the author in Ref. [5]. Identifying and analyzing risks, and their interdependencies, we include both negative (threat) and positive (opportunity) parts of risk analysis with the primary aim for finding new opportunities for development and quality improvement.

Main threats for an adult professional training organization are in customer dissatisfaction, and on the opposite main opportunities are based on reaching continuous education of students personally, and corporate customers. Let's examine a simple example about modern technology-based virtual learning implementation, and consider online learning process. There are several main opportunities of online learning for an educational organization, which are:

1. Improve organization innovative brand.

2. Attracting more students from distant regions.

3. More students in a class in a certain group.

On the other side, there are threats:

1. Changing in teaching methods.

2. Decrease of teaching quality.

3. Student's and corporate customers' rejection of new training method.

4. Technical issues.

Those risks—both positive and negative—are well-known when we talk about them in a natural language, but training organization's decision-making process requires qualitative and quantitative estimates. As shown in reference [1] we can implement fuzzy analysis to transform natural language to a weak formalized fuzzy model, by placing model-internal risks into an imaginary area, and objective risks into a real area of the model.

3.4. Building current data analysis with fuzzy logic

We investigated our students, trainers, corporate clients, and internal administrative staff feedbacks to discover additional training opportunities.

In 2009 we started online webinar trainings, which are held as simultaneous trainings in groups consisting of online (webinar), and class-based students (named as "webinar-in-class™"). The example of feedbacks is given in a **Table 1**. Total number of feedbacks: 10,000+ student feedbacks, 700+ by trainers, 1000+ by training center administrative staff, and 500+ by corporate customers' representatives.

We compared and analyzed feedbacks of webinars with the excerpt feedbacks of traditional class-based trainings. As the "specialist computer training center (CCT)" has been operated since 1991, we extracted feedbacks for class trainings for previous 5 years, e.g., we included 25,000 students', 5000 trainers', 5000 administrative staff's, and 2000 customer representatives' feedbacks into comparative analysis against "webinar-in-class" feedbacks, which are presented in **Table 2**.

The "trapeze" form of a fuzzy interpretation, as shown at **Figure 1**, is used to represent fuzzy component, because rating values are subjective and personal oriented. For example, we use ratings from "1" or "E" (minimum value, means that a client is completely dissatisfied) to "5" or "A" (maximum value, indicates that a service exceeds customer's expectations). Rate "3" or "C" indicates customer's general satisfaction. These estimations are personally based and depend on a lot of factors, such as professional specialization, job function and rank, individual specialties. Only ratings "E" and "A" strongly indicate satisfactory level. For example, rating "3" or "C" at design or HR trainings is mainly considered as more dissatisfied than satisfied. On the other side a "C" rating at business or project management trainings is mainly considered as satisfied' and rating A" is very rare, because business managers are mostly not as emotional.

Rate	Parameter (%)			
	Trainer	Technical facilities	Course	Willing for further training
A	32	27	45	42
B	48	51	42	47
C	12	14	10	7
D	5	6	2	2
E	3	2	1	1

Table 1. An excerpt from webinar-N-class studies.

Rate	Parameter (%)			
	Trainer	Technical facilities	Course	Willing for further training
A	39	42	41	42
B	46	41	44	47
C	11	13	13	7
D	3	4	2	2
E	1	2	1	1

Table 2. An excerpt from traditional class-based studies.

Satisfaction

Grade

Figure 1. Trapeze interpretation of satisfaction level.

In fact, the total number of analyzed attributes is more than 100, and it changes regularly to follow customer, market demands, technical, and methodological facilities.

Below is a partial list of main attributes in the information system, which contain basic data and we consider them as a real area attributes in an analytical model:

- Student, Client/Customer, Learning format, Country/region, Course, Year/season/month, Vendor, Product Trainer, Trainer rating, Course rating, Training method rating, Number of courses taken by a student afterwards

The total number of real area attributes is more than 50.

Next I show an excerpt from a list of more than 25 additional (information model based) attributes. We consider these attributes in an imaginary area of our fuzzy model:

- Total rating of a training method, comparative rating to class-based training, comparative rating of webinars against class and self-learning combined method, views and filters across client types, regions, time, season, etc.

To build an integral customer satisfaction rating we use multidimensional fuzzy analysis of different partial (single-parameter) rankings as shown at **Figure 2**. Also, different filters and constraints are implemented to localize problems, challenges and find grow-points.

3.5. Investigating students' satisfaction against educational organization efficiency

We can investigate an integral satisfaction/dissatisfaction level of a training group based on the following attributes: trainer ratings, course ratings, willingness to continue training at a next course, and ratings of technical facilities. Each set is fuzzy and contains ranking values (ratings) by each student.

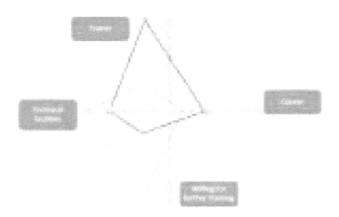

Figure 2. Determining the satisfaction area on an example of four parameter analysis.

In each case (for a student/group/trainer/course, etc.) we form a fuzzy area, in which we may consider that a course/study/trainer/class, etc. are satisfactory. According to company goals and statistical data we can also implement additional weights for attributes. For example, a trainer rank has coefficient "1, 5" and class ranking—"0, 8". Attribute "willing for further training" will have the maximum weight coefficient "2", as it's the most important factor for commercial adult learning company. This model shows a subjective satisfaction level as a set (family) of polygons. Each polygon draws by connecting points, which reflect partial ratings. For example, an area of subjective satisfaction is defined by the following partial ratings:

Trainer rating = 2 AND

Course rating = 4 AND

Technical facilities = 3 AND

Willing to continue education = 5.

In this case, we define that a group is partially satisfied/partially dissatisfied with a trainer, but if most of students of a certain group are ready to continue education at next courses, we can mark this group as "satisfied."

For complex estimation of job effectiveness of an adult life-long training organization we developed more complicated approaches, which include statistical data based on more than 70 attributes (both in real and imaginary areas) and collected them in multidimensional databases—OLAP cubes. This cube has the appropriate number (more than 70) of dimensions, and we need to build a set of fuzzy models, and optimize them for daily calculations and analysis. A real part of a model includes basic facts, and on the other side an imaginary part of a model includes filters, views, and additional states of a model or database. Due to this approach, we decrease number of dimensions to 50 in total, which leads to decrease in computing capacity requirements. Practical result: we have an opportunity to process analytical reports in a real-time mode, and postpone few complicated reports for nonworking hours (night time and Sundays).

Let us examine a comparatively simple set of fuzzy sets, which describes an integral satisfactory factor and training organization efficiency:

- By course, a certain trainer and/or trainer group, a company—customer, learning location, a certain period, a training method, a training branch (e.g., Management, ITSM, software development, HR, etc.).

The developed model contains both real area attributes, which reflect basic states, and imaginary area attributes, which reflect temporary, service states, filter conditions, identifiers, etc.

Below, I show an excerpt from a model. Attributes named in a lingual model terms to simplify understanding

$$\begin{cases} M1 = (CN + St + Tr + TM) + j(V + TP + ST), \\ M2 = (CN + Tr + CCF + TCF + WFT) + j(TP(i) + ACR(i) + ATR(i) + V), \\ M3 = (CN + TL + C + TM) + j(TP(i) + ACR(i) + AMR(i) + V), \end{cases} \qquad (17)$$

where CN, Course name; St, Student identifier; Tr, trainer identifier; V, view name; TP(i), selected time period; St, threshold level of students' satisfaction for the certain model; TM, training method; CCF, course cash flow; TCF, cash flow on courses by a certain trainer; WFT, student's willing for continuous education; ACR, average course ranking for selected period; ATR, average trainer ranking for selected period; TL, training location; C, corporate customer name; and AMR, average ranking of a certain training method for selected period.

Set M1 reflects mean level of students' satisfaction for a certain course and a certain trainer for selected time period.

Set M2 reflects current level of economic efficiency of a certain trainer, based on dynamic trend of students' satisfaction across a number of time periods (for example, month to month or quarter to quarter).

Set M3 reflects dynamics of corporate customers' satisfaction for a certain training location, course, and a training method. This set gives a control how a certain training location provides quality for a certain course and a training method, for example, webinar, or blended, or self-paced, etc.

3.6. Defining training methods and models

Adult learning training organization should offer various training opportunities for its students, such as long- and short-term trainings, class-based, virtual, blended, synchronous, and asynchronous, etc. Based on the analysis model at our Specialist CCT we develop balanced cost-effective vs. "student satisfactory" training methods for precisely defined customer audience and course bundles.

While analyzing results of modeling, we find several maximums. Each of the maximums is characterized by a certain set of parameters, as shown in **Figure 3**.

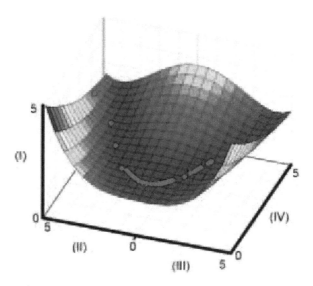

Figure 3. Multidimensional estimation, where I – Individual approach level; II – Trainer level; III – Technical facilities; IV – Training center economical effectiveness.

For example, the maximum satisfaction level which is found in an analytical cube is defined by the following attributes:

- student total expenses (minimal);

- high quality skills received;

- high qualified trainers;

- number of students in a class (maximal);

- collaboration facilities in the group (maximal);

- technical expenses are minimal.

The "webinar-in-class" training option is the best for mentioned attributes, because a webinar-based student has an opportunity to study anywhere, and has no travel or accommodation expenses. Simultaneously, he/she has an access to the best trainers, and can collaborate with classmates in a class and other webinar students, using a very simple software. The webinar students have an access to the same technical facilities such as labs. Thus, the webinar-in-class training method becomes very popular solution for students studying technical (Microsoft, Oracle, CISCO, etc.) courses, as well as project, and IT service management courses.

We worked further to analyze maximums, and another point is based on the following attributes:

- appropriate (frequent) course start date;

- individual approach;

- introvert students;

- students with high level of self-organization capabilities;

- full classes;

- low expenses on training organization by a training center.

In this example, we see more attributes, and it was a bit more difficult to create an appropriate training method. The result was a kind of blended learning, which we named an "open learning."

- blended "open learning" training method is the best solution for very specialized trainings, and self-organized students;

- unlimited webinar subscription is for students, who are unemployed or wish to change profession. Both categories need cheap training at a large number of courses.

To resume I want to stress that the estimating process is everlasting, as well as optimization of the research model. While preparing this article, one more training method was developed, which proves the efficiency of the described approach. The described methods won several professional awards [6, 7].

4. Identifying special tools for virtual training of hard of hearing people

4.1. Introduction

More than 10% of people on the Earth suffers from different hearing impairs as the World Health Organization data shows. Many of them are young people, or employees, which are involved into lifelong learning. They have difficulties with taking both class and virtual trainings, if they do not have or use special hearing aids. Meanwhile, many young people do not use special devices due to medical recommendations or having scruples.

Based on our research of students' with hearing impairs demands our research team deliver a special computer-based technology—named as Petralex©. It is implemented in mobile Apps and Windows driver, which works as a personal hearing assistant [6]. A student passes an "*in cito*" hearing test and the application creates a personal hearing profile for each place or environment (for example, public transport, café, car, room at home, classroom, and work-place). Mobile App acts as a hearing aid in a smartphone, so a student can easily attend classes. The Windows-based driver creates a Virtual audio device (VAD), which adapts streaming audio for both online and asynchronous virtual learning to an appropriate user's hearing profile.

Different virtual training methods—synchronous, asynchronous, blended—which are defined in Ref. [4], include online and/or off-line listening in videos, podcasts, as well as online training delivery, including real-time discussion with a trainer and classmates. So, students with hearing disabilities should have opportunities to be involved into the entire training process.

4.2. Synchronous learning methods

A student with partial hearing losses can feel uncomfortable while studying in class, or at online webinar. If a student studies in a class, he or she can implement the Petralex® mobile app as a hearing assistant, and involve in-depth into a learning process. In a synchronous learning training content is delivered in an online mode as shown in **Figure 4**. A student accesses it using the special audio driver, which ensures audio stream adjustment to personal hearing profile. As a result, a student can attend studies for a long time—up to 8 hours per day—due to improved hearing tolerance, reducing fatigue for long listening sessions, and attenuation of excessive sound pressure [6, 7].

4.2.1. Typical learning cases for online trainings

1. A trainer explains learning materials: a student studies at home. S/he connects to an online tool (for example, Skype®, Citrix GoTo®, WebEx, Adobe® Connect®, or any other), activates "My room" profile. Next, our driver transforms audio stream in a real-time mode with only 10–50 ms delay, so a student can hear a teacher clearly, have concentration on studying, and ask or answer questions; present his/her work, and discuss with other students in a real-time mode.

2. A business game: business games and other forms of group studies are very popular according to our model (Eq. (16)). An online student usually plays a role of a virtual team member or help desk agent. Implementing audio-driver provides both parties an opportunity to collaborate in a clear mode without delays.

4.3. Asynchronous learning methods

In this section let us consider different scenarios for asynchronous learning of students with partial hearing losses. The most popular tools for asynchronous learning are: learning management systems (LMS), stream and offline video, and audio services.

As shown in **Figure 5**, an external audio signal from a learning tool goes through the virtual audio driver, which transforms it according to an activated user hearing profile. Thanks to it, a student can study anywhere. At our training center, and with our partners, the following scenarios, as shown in **Figure 5**, were tested:

In a special class,

At home,

At a workplace, and

On a beach.

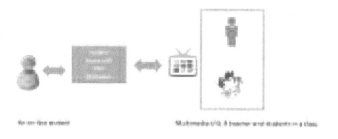

Figure 4. The learning schema for synchronous virtual learning.

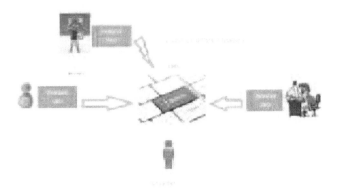

Figure 5. Asynchronous learning scenarios.

One of the most impressive cases in our training practices is short-term learning for adult busy people. We defined lifelong business students as a separate category in our model. Lifelong learners often study during their vacations or weekends. Usually they are strongly motivated, so they can easily combine their rest and studies. As an example, a student creates a "beach" profile and can listen learning records on a comfortable manner for his/her hearing.

5. Resume

Implementing extended definition area for fuzzy set analysis provides vast opportunities for representation of control objects by information systems, their analysis and optimization. Based on implementation of fuzzy analysis the author succeeded in creating and launching various virtual training models for lifelong learning, including people suffering with partial hearing losses.

Author details

Danil Dintsis

Address all correspondence to: consult@dintsis.org

Educational Private organization "Specialist", Moscow, Russian Federation

References

[1] Zadeh L. A. Decision Analysis and Fuzzy logic. In: Conference on Fuzzy Sets and Soft Computing in Economics and International Finance (FSSCEF 2004). Saint-Petersburg, Russia; 2004.

[2] Dintsis D. A modification of discrete-event models algebra for industrial technological systems. Devices and systems. Control, Monitoring, And Diagnostics Journal # 1, 2008.

[3] Dintsis D, Simankov V. The control automation system method based on combined imple-
     mentation of fuzzy logic and discrete automation systems. In: European Modelling Sym-
     posium EMS2013 - 03-C Methodologies, Tools and Operations Research; November 2013;
     Manchester. Print ISBN:978-1-4799-2577-3 INSPEC Accession Number:14199480. DOI:
     10.1109/EMS.2013.15. IEEE. p. 87–90

[4] Ferdinand D.S. Flexible Learning Environments-Theories-Trends-Issues. Monography.
     University of West-Indies. West Indies. St.-Augustine. DOI: 10.13140/RG.2.1.3958.2488.
     2016. 32p

[5] Dintsis D. Implementing Fuzzy Sets For "Big Data" Analysis Based on Large Training
     Centre Feedbacks. In: IEEE AEIT Annual 2015 Conference. Naples, Italy. Publisher: IEEE.
     October, 2015.

[6] Dintsis D, Bredikhin A. Virtual Learning for People with Hearing Impairs. In: IEEE AEIT
     Annual 2015 Conference. Naples, Italy. Publisher: IEEE. October, 2015.

[7] LERN International Award Winners 2016. https://www.flipsnack.com/LearningResour-
     cesNetwork/2016-lern-international-award-winners.html. 2016. LERN. Chicago. [Accessed:
     2017-01-11]

2

Indoor Mobile Positioning Using Neural Networks and Fuzzy Logic Control

Anatoly D. Khomonenko, Sergey E. Adadurov,
Alexandr V. Krasnovidow and Pavel A. Novikov

Abstract

Indoor mobile navigation systems are becoming more prevalent in many areas (transport, public institutions, logistics, etc.). The interior navigation based on the access points, arranged according to the radio fingerprints, is becoming increasingly popular. The model of artificial neural networks (ANN) is often used as a mechanism for storing and processing radio fingerprints. The task of selection of the access point in WLAN network in the case of high user density is quite topical. Such selection must take into account not only the level of the signal received by the mobile device, but also a width in the dedicated channel bandwidth. The main issues related to the creation of program complex for the mobile indoors navigation using neural networks is discussed in the chapter as well as the method of access point selection based on analysis not only the signal level but also the other parameters. To solve this task, fuzzy logic is used.

Keywords: Wi-Fi radio network, neural network, mobile navigation indoor, navigation systems, learning algorithms, mobile devices 802.11k standard, the mobile subscribers, fuzzy logic, MATLAB, frame transmission time

1. Introduction

The modern world cannot exist without precise navigation systems. Satellite navigation systems such as Global Positioning System (GPS) and Global Navigation Satellite System (GLONASS) [1] are widely used in a variety of areas of activity, such as navigation transport, engineering, surveying, and other cellular communication. GPS receivers' consumer level is set in almost all modern phones. In open areas, such receivers allow for positional accuracy in the region of 1–5 m.

At the same time, these receivers do not meet the existing demand to navigate indoors. In such circumstances, GPS does not work or provide location data with a very high error of about 100–150 m.

Navigation systems indoors can be applied in many fields. Including navigation inside large shopping malls, warehouses, or different systems, "smart home," in which different home systems (heating, lighting, air conditioning, and so on) can be centrally managed in automatic mode.

In particular, obvious argument for the need for indoor navigation can serve as tasks of navigation in transportation systems, such as airports and railway stations [2]:

(A) For visitors: positioning; search check-in desks/offices/storage rooms and a cafe, parking, taxi, etc.; installation of the route, taking into account number of storeys of buildings; search colleagues inside the airport/train station, social activity; service based on knowledge of the position of the visitor (location-based service).

(B) For airports, railway stations, and tenants: an additional service to visitors; analyst extensive movements of visitors and staff; advertising opportunities geo contextual advertising (location-based advertising) airlines/shops/cafes, etc., as well as products/services; promotions based on the location of the visitor.

There are now possibilities to improve the methods and the practical use of mobile navigation indoors. Let us briefly consider the modern approaches to the solution of this task and proposals for justifying the choice of learning algorithms and neural networks of the individual parameters of the same interests.

Mobile navigation systems indoors are becoming more widespread in many areas (transport, public institutions, logistics, and others.). It is becoming popular navigation based on fingerprint radio access points Wi-Fi. As a mechanism for storing and processing the radio fingerprint is often considered a model of artificial neural networks (ANN). The chapter examines the main issues related to the creation of complex programs for mobile navigation indoors using neural networks, which are one of the parts of fuzzy logic. We justify the choice of learning algorithms ANN navigation mobile devices indoors.

The data for the neural network training in MATLAB taken from the file "train.txt" is used for functional testing of software navigation. To verify the performance of ANN training, the original file should be divided into two sets (training and testing).

Wireless local area networks 802.11k as precise navigation systems have become very popular for several reasons. They operate in the unlicensed frequency bounds and they need not in large time and cost for deployment. The appearance of vast number of mobile devices supporting Wi-Fi technology gives possibilities of free choice and cost saving for the various kinds of users. WLAN networks have a number of advantages over traditional wired networks.

- Much easier and cheaper to deploy a local wireless network in the new location than a traditional network.

- The subscriber does not have to be next to his desk or local network socket-outlet. He can move freely inside the area coverage.

However, the number of users working in the unlicensed frequency bounds increases day by day. In this context, a very important problem is the way by which the wireless device uses to select an access point to connect to the network. Now, the device selects the access point according to signal power. This way allows determining the nearest access point. In other words, currently used 802.11k standard is aimed at the implementation of load balancing of radio Wi-Fi networks. Nevertheless, the high level of the signal does not always mean high network bandwidth. Suppose, for example, that most of the notebooks operating in the certain conference halls connect to WLAN by using the access point which is above the entrance door. In such a case, the number of subscribers connected to it would be up to tens if not hundreds, while other access points would not be fully loaded. As a result, the network bandwidth per subscriber reduces to a significant degree that leads to network reduction of productivity of the network in whole. Hence, the task of selection of the access point in WLAN network in the case of high user density is quite topical. Such selection must take into account not only the level of the signal received by the mobile device, but also a width in the dedicated channel bandwidth that depends on the number of connected subscribers to the access point. In this chapter, we examined the method based on analysis of not only signal level but also other parameters. To solve this task, fuzzy logic is used in the chapter. Constructed membership functions and linguistic rules are examined. Structure of the developed model and simulation results are presented.

2. Indoor mobile positioning using neural networks

2.1. Characteristics of modern approach to navigation mobile

First, we note that the modern mobile devices contain a variety of different sensors and receivers. The main of them include:

1. GPS.

2. Wi-Fi, a radio signal operates at frequencies of 2.4 and 5 GHz.

3. Bluetooth operates on the same frequencies.

4. The accelerometer and gyroscope—inertial sensors measuring linear and angular acceleration.

5. Magnetometer—a sensor that measures the intensity of magnetic fields.

6. Other sensors—humidity, light, proximity, barometer, etc.

Sensors 1–5 are well represented in many of today's mobile devices that are running operating systems iOS and Android. These systems provide programmatic access to the sensors through its own application program interfaces (API), and any application can receive data from the sensors (with certain insignificant limitations).

Currently, there are several ways to use the mobile navigation device.

1. GPS (Global Positioning System) and GLONASS (Global Navigation Satellite System) [1]: these are navigation using satellites. Well suited for positioning in the open spaces. Because of the need to be in the field of view of at least three satellites, these are poorly suited for closed premises, as they greatly impair the satellite signal. The initial search for satellites might take few minutes.

2. AGPS (Assisted GPS). Navigation using radio signals from cell towers. Typically it used in conjunction with GPS. It accelerates the initial determination of the coordinates by the fact that the use of data on the mobile device serving cell towers.

3. Navigate using radio beacons operating on technology iBeacons (Bluetooth Low Energy) [3]. This is a relatively young technology, the impetus for the development of which will serve standard Bluetooth 4.0 (+) with low power consumption. Tracker is a chip with a radio module, which is a predetermined frequency radio, sends packets with information about themselves. The receiver, knowing the map of the location beacons and signal strength to the nearest of them, calculates their relative location.

4. Navigation on the basis of fingerprints of radio access points Wi-Fi [4]. Such navigation systems are more exploratory in nature. Due to the relative novelty of this approach, ways to implement proven accurate navigation have not yet developed.

5. Inertial navigation system [5]. Navigation is based on data from the inertial sensor device, which is constructed on the basis of the model orientation in space.

Comparative characteristics of the main approaches of navigation using mobile devices [2] are given in **Table 1**.

In addition to these approaches, following approaches are also included. In Ref. [6], the integration of Wi-Fi and an inertial navigation system is considered. In Refs. [7, 8], mobile navigation services and the use of technology OpenCellID to determine the location of mobile devices are studied.

System	Dignity	Disadvantages
GPS	Average precision (5 m) Ease of use Good compatibility	Inability To work Indoor
GSM	Ease of use Good compatibility	Ease of use Good compatibility
Wi-Fi	Average Accuracy (5 m) Work indoors	The need for network deployment Limited compatibility High power consumption
iBeacon	High accuracy (1–2 m) Ease of use Good compatibility Low power consumption	The need to deploy BLE-network

Table 1. Comparative characteristics of approaches.

The article [9] considered a relatively new approach to the positioning of mobile devices in the premises on the basis of two-dimensional barcodes. In Ref. [10], the model of context-aware computing (context-dependent browser) based on network proximity is considered. This mobile phone is considered as a proximity sensor and geo replaced positional information network proximity. An algorithm for calculating the trajectories of mobile networks on the basis of information about network proximity is also considered.

2.2. Rationale for navigation of mobile devices using neural networks

Employment of navigation system via radio fingerprint from the access points of Wi-Fi consists of two parts:

1. Preparation of a database of known fingerprints radio with known coordinates associated with them.

2. Getting new coordinates from the database on the new print of radio signals.

As a mechanism for storing and processing the radio fingerprint has considered a model of artificial neural networks (ANNs).

This approach is interesting for the following reasons:

*   The problem of determining the location based on a previously defined radio fingerprint can be viewed as a problem of classification of multidimensional data.

*   Main computational load of this method accounts for the learning process, which is performed only once and can be executed on an independent computer system.

*   Data on the surrounding Wi-Fi points can be supplemented by the data from other sources, such as Bluetooth LE beacons.

The possibilities of modern ANN are the subject of active research. The approach to the use of ANN to solve the above problem is considered in several publications, for example, Refs. [10–12].

2.3. Characteristics of software navigation

Here examined a complex program [13, 14] to navigate through the Wi-Fi signals using a mobile phone. It consists of two components:

1. Mobile application that

    a. collects data on the surrounding Wi-Fi access points;

    b. uses trained neural network to determine the current location of the mobile device based on the new data on Wi-Fi signals.

2. Desktop application that

    a. prepares data radio prints for further training of the neural network;

    b. training and testing neural network.

As an implementation of a neural network, we used multilayer ANN provided free library FANN (Fast Artificial Neural Network Library). To train the ANN learning algorithm, Resilient Propagation (*RProp*) has been used [15].

Unlike standard algorithm *Backprop*, *RProp* uses only partial signs for adjusting the weighting coefficients. The algorithm uses the so-called "training periods" when the correction occurs after the presentation of the balance of the network of examples from the training set.

To determine the amount of correction using the following rule [15]:

$$\Delta_{ij}^{(t)} = \left\{ \begin{array}{l} \eta^+ \Delta_{ij}^{(t)}, \dfrac{\partial E^{(t)}}{\partial \omega_{ij}} \dfrac{\partial E^{(t-1)}}{\partial \omega_{ij}} > 0 \\[4mm] \eta^- \Delta_{ij}^{(t)}, \dfrac{\partial E^{(t)}}{\partial \omega_{ij}} \dfrac{\partial E^{(t-1)}}{\partial \omega_{ij}} < 0 \end{array} \right\}, \tag{1}$$

$$0 < \eta^- < 1 < \eta^+ \tag{2}$$

If the partial derivative of the corresponding weight $\partial \omega_{ij}$ had changed its sign at the current step, it means that the latest update was great, and the algorithm passed a local minimum and therefore the value of change must be reduced by η and return the previous weight value: in other words, you must make 'roll back'.

$$\partial \omega_{ij}(t) = \partial \omega_{ij}(t) - \Delta_{ij}^{(t-1)}. \tag{3}$$

If the sign of the partial derivative is not changed, it is necessary to increase the amount of compensation η^+ to achieve a more rapid convergence. Fixing factors η^- and η^+ can be dispensed with global settings of the neural network, which can also be seen as an advantage of the algorithm to the standard algorithm *Backprop*.

Recommended values are $\eta^- = 0.5$, $\eta^+ = 1.2$, but there are no restrictions on the use of other values for these parameters.

To prevent too large or small weight values, the correction value limit from above the maximum Δ_{max} and below the minimum Δ_{min} value of the correction value, which default, respectively, shall equal 50 and 1.0E–6.

The initial values for all Δ_{ij} are set to 0.1. Again, this should be seen only as a recommendation, and in the practical implementation it can specify a different value for the initialization.

The current implementation of the navigation software package is a simple one-dimensional classifier, which, by new radio-prints, is able to determine the room in which the mobile device is located.

2.4. Working with software navigation

Working with a program complex navigation is implemented using desktop and mobile software, and includes the following steps:

1. Collection of data on radio-prints in the studied areas. The output of this stage is a set of files, each of which contains a set of vectors (matrix) measuring Wi-Fi signals points (for example, **Table 2**).

    In the first row, there are names of all the access points that were visible in the data collection process. For clarity, we have been selected to work with network names, rather than their mac address. Each line represents the measured signal strength to a point. A value 0 means that the point was not available at this time.

2. Combine all the source files into one.

    The result is a common image with the measurements in all the studied areas which is shown in **Table 3**.

    The first column is stored name space in which the measurement was performed. Null values (0) are replaced by −100 (very weak signal).

    In addition, a file is created "names.txt," which lists the names of all the networks in the same order in which they are placed in the file of training (step 4).

3. Represented by map matching names with their premises of formal numerical representation:

    Cabinet [0] Room [0.5] Kitchen [1]

4. On the basis of the contents of the files of the previous steps 2 and 3, create a file with the data for network training:

    60 15 1

    −86.0 −100.0 −54.0 −69.0 −100.0 −100.0 −88.0 −100.0 −100.0 −100.0 −100.0 −100.0 −100.0 −100.0 −100.0

Grimas	DSL-2640U	NETGEAR	STERH76	InterZet-at-home	InetBezP	ASUS 26
−86	0	−54	−69	0	0	−88
−89	−83	−56	−66	0	0	−91
…	…	…	…	…	…	…

Table 2. Set of vectors (matrix) measuring signals Wi-Fi points.

	Grimas	DSL-2640U	NETGEAR	STERH76	InterZet-at-home	InetBezP	ASUS 26	…
Study	−86	−100	−54	−69	−100	−100	−88	…
Study	−89	−83	−56	−66	−100	−100	−91	…
…	…	…	…	…	…	…	…	…

Table 3. Common image with the measurements in all the studied areas.

0.0

−89.0 −83.0 −56.0 −66.0 −100.0 −100.0 −91.0 −100.0 −100.0 −100.0 −100.0 −100.0 −100.0 −100.0 −100.0

0.0

−90.0 −71.0 −51.0 −67.0 −100.0 −100.0 −88.0 −100.0 −100.0 −100.0 −100.0 −100.0 −100.0 −100.0 −100.0

0.0

The first line shall include: the number of hidden layer neurons, the number of neurons in the input layer and output layer.

The following are a couple of lines:

A. The input vector.

B. The value that the National Assembly should be trained for this vector.

The result of this step is to file "network," which is a trained neural network in the library "FANN." The network name is chosen at random.

The following steps describe the workflow of software application that is running on a mobile device.

5. A mobile application launches library "FANN" and passes the file to the trained neural network.

6. Mobile application starts scanning the surrounding Wi-Fi hotspots. After the completion of the next iteration of the scanning application, an array of the currently available access points is received to which the device may try to connect. Each object of the array, among other things, contains in its structure the following two fields:

A. Title.

B. The strength of the signal to a predetermined point.

With using the array of file names "names.txt" obtained in the second stage and the current array of visible access points built radio fingerprint, which, in essence, is a simple array of numbers. Create a radio footprint that includes the following steps:

A. Create an array of numbers (float []) size which determine the number of elements in the array of names.

B. Go through the array of names in the cycle:

    a. if the array access point is a point with the current name, the add-in radio signals strength to mark this point of the current iteration of the index;

    b. otherwise, add the current iteration index of the default value for the missing point that was made in step 2 (−100).

C. At the output of iteration scanning radio fingerprint is obtained as a vector of values (−100, −50, −75, −100, …).

7. The resulting vector is passed to the neural network, which returns the result vector (float []). Since the ANN has been trained on the basis of dimensional data, we are only interested in the first element of the resulting vector.

8. The resulting value is compared with the data from the map space. In the version of the software complex in the map, closest value to the current value obtained from the network is searched. After finding, it displays the name of the current premises that corresponds to the measured radio-imprint.

2.5. Training a neural network in MATLAB

The data for the neural network training in MATLAB are taken from the file "train.txt" and used for functional testing of software navigation. To verify the performance of ANN training, the original file should be divided into two sets (training and testing).

By analogy with [16], we make a comparative analysis of the main learning algorithms of the neural network used for the navigation of mobile applications for indoors, with position accuracy and complexity ratios depending on the number of neurons in the hidden layer. The corresponding results are shown in **Table 4**.

Table 4 uses the following symbols: *trainlm*—learning algorithm Levenberg-Markarth, *trainscg* —related gradient method scaled association, and *trainbr*—Bayesian regularization method. MSE—mean square error, epochs (s)—the number of training cycles, and in brackets the number of seconds.

Based on the analysis of **Table 1**, we can conclude that the optimal number of hidden layer neurons for a given set of source data is in the range 15–25. It showed the highest accuracy Bayesian regularization algorithm, but it is considerably more time-consuming compared with

Number of neurons	Trainlm		Trainscg		Trainbr	
	MSE	Epochs(s)	MSE	Epochs(s)	MSE	Epochs(s)
5	0.11	12(0.1)	0.08	15(0.1)	0.03	592(25)
10	0.06	16(0.1)	0.09	20(0.2)	0.02	700(20)
15	0.07	9(0.1)	0.05	13(0.2)	0.013	800(23)
20	0.05	11(0.2)	0.13	14(0.2)	0.015	269(48)
30	0.13	6(0.2)	0.19	23(0.3)	0.018	889(120)
50	0.23	13(0.2)	0.21	30(0.5)	0.02	483(187)

Table 4. Characteristics of the complexity and accuracy of learning algorithms NA.

other algorithms. The optimal ratio of accuracy and convergence provides the Levenberg-Marquardt algorithm.

Note that low accuracy is common to all algorithms, which is associated with the original data. Probably, it reduces the dimension of the input vector (data used by Wi-Fi 15 points, most of which are available), and increases the total number of measurements. At the same time in the original data set of vector measurements corresponded to only three different rooms, so get enough accuracy.

3. Using fuzzy logic control for selection of the access point

3.1. Introduction

Wireless local area networks of 802.11k standards become very popular due to some reasons. They operate in the unlicensed frequency bounds and they need not require large time and cost for deployment. The appearance of vast number of mobile devices supporting Wi-Fi technology gives possibilities for free choice and cost saving for the various kinds of users. WLAN networks have a number of advantages over traditional wired networks.

- Much easier and cheaper to deploy a local wireless network in the new location than with a traditional network.

- The subscriber does not need to be next to his desk or local network socket. He can move freely inside the area coverage.

However, number of users working in the unlicensed frequency bounds increases day by day. In this context, a very important problem is the way by which the wireless devices are used to select an access point to connect to the network. Now device selects the access point according with signal power [17]. This way allows determining the nearest access point. In other words, currently used 802.11k standard is aimed at the implementation of load balancing of radio Wi-Fi networks. Nevertheless, the high level of the signal does not always mean high network bandwidth. Suppose, for example, that most notebooks operating in the certain conference hall connects to WLAN using access point which is above the entrance door. In such a case, the amount of subscribers connected to it would be to tens if not hundreds, while other access points would not be fully loaded. As a result the network bandwidth per subscriber reduces to a significant degree that leads to the network reduction of productivity of the network in whole. Hence, the task of selection of the access point in WLAN network in the case of high user density is quite topical. Such selection must take into account not only the level of the signal received by the mobile device, but also a width in the dedicated channel bandwidth that depends on the number of connected subscribers to the access point.

Further, examined the method based on analysis not only signal level but also other parameters. To solve this task, fuzzy logic is used (See Ref. [18, 19]). Constructing membership functions and linguistic rules are examined. Structure of the developed model and simulation results are presented.

3.2. Choice of access points for connecting a mobile device

Signal level and the bandwidth of a system are linked by the well-known Shannon formula, which allows determining the capacity of the data transmission system:

$$C = \Delta F \times \log_2(1 + S/N). \tag{4}$$

The total bandwidth allocated in the range, is divided equally among all active subscribers [17]. If the length of the transmitted packet is L bits, one can determine the time required for transmission of a packet:

$$T(M, S/N) = \frac{L \times M}{F \times \log_2(1 + S/N)}, \tag{5}$$

where $\Delta F = F/M$ is the network bandwidth, and S/N is signal/noise ratio at the receiver input and M is the number of subscribers already connected. Thus, the functional dependence between bandwidth and the number of connected subscribers is linear. Then the task of selecting the best access point to connect can be formulated as follows:

Find the value of function (5), the T_{max} of which does not exceed a predetermined time with the following restrictions: $S/N > P_0$ and $\Delta F \geq \Delta F_{min}$, where P_0 is some ratio threshold signal/noise at which the operation of mobile subscriber receiver is possible and ΔF_{min} is a minimum possible bandwidth width. In other words, the problem is reduced to finding such a pair of values (ΔF, S/N) for which the transmission time has the minimum possible value.

This problem can be solved by various methods:

- Analytical methods that use differential and variational calculus.

- Numerical methods which use prior information in order to find improved solutions using iterative algorithms.

- Mathematical methods (linear and nonlinear programming).

In the case of choice of any method, the finding of a point of extremum of the considered function is usually required. The type of function (5) is shown in **Figure 1**.

Figure 1 shows that the function (5) has minimum values for various combinations of parameters and the number of connected subscribers M. Function (5) has no maximum that determines the above-mentioned formulation of the problem of choosing the access point. **Table 5** shows the values of the function (5) calculated for various combinations of parameters and M.

Analysis of **Table 5** confirms that the high signal level does not always provide an acceptable transmission time. It's known for solve the problem of the selection the access point to connect mobile subscribers on the basis of function (5) using the above methods it is necessary and sufficient that the following conditions are met (as it's shown for instance in Ref. [20, 21]):

1. Function (5) should be continuous and differentiable at the point of extremum.

2. The Hessian matrix of function (5) must be negative definite (for a point of minimum).

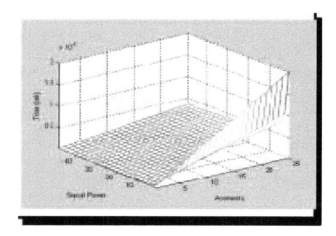

Figure 1. Dependence of the packet transmission time from the signal level and the number of subscribers.

Signal power, db	The bandwidth width, hz	The transmission time, s
30	4E + 6	2.514E − 4
30	8E + 5	1.257E − 3
30	4.444E + 5	2.263E − 3

Table 5. Values of the time of packet transmission for different ratios of parameters.

Clearly, the condition 1 for the function (5) is performed. To simplify the analysis of the condition (2), it is convenient to consider function 1, taking into account that low values of transmission time are achieved with large bandwidth. Then, for the function (4), condition 2 changes to opposite. Condition 2 for the function (5) is not satisfied due to the fact that $\partial^2 C / \partial (\Delta F)^2 = 0$, which implies that:

$$\begin{vmatrix} \dfrac{\partial^2 C}{(\Delta F)^2} & \dfrac{\partial^2 C}{\partial(\Delta F)\partial\left(\dfrac{S}{N}\right)} \\[3em] \dfrac{\partial^2 C}{\partial\left(\dfrac{S}{F}\right)\partial(\Delta F)} & \dfrac{\partial^2 C}{\partial(\frac{S}{N})^2} \end{vmatrix} = \begin{vmatrix} 0 & \dfrac{1}{\log_2 e\left(1+\dfrac{S}{N}\right)} \\[3em] \dfrac{1}{\log_2 e\left(1+\dfrac{S}{N}\right)} & \left(\dfrac{1}{\log_2 e\left(1+\dfrac{S}{N}\right)}\right)^2 \end{vmatrix} \le 0. \qquad (6)$$

It follows that the function in question is not concave. However, the requirement of convexity or concavity of the function is a serious restriction that is far from always performed in practical problems. This is why the concept of such functions is generalized by the introduction of pseudo-convex unimodal functions [21]. The $f: X \to R$ function is called the pseudo-unimodal in the interim $[a, b] \subset X$, if $\exists$ an arbitrary interval $I^* \subset [a, b]$ such that the f function:

- Strictly increasing in the interval $[a, b]$;

- Equals to some constant, $\le \min\{f(c), f(d)\}$ on the some interval I^*;

- Strictly decreasing in the interval $[d, b]$.

The points c and d determined by the following way:

$$c = \inf_{x \subset I^*} x; \quad d = \sup_{x \subset I^*} x. \tag{7}$$

In this case, the interval I^* is the solution of the problem max $\{f(x) : \ x \subset [a, b]\}$. In the particular case if $c = d$, then $I^* = \{x^0\}$ and $x = c = d$, the f function is called unimodal. The example of unimodal function is shown in **Figure 2**.

Then, if we set

$$a = [\Delta F_{min}, P_0]; \quad b = [\Delta F_{min}, P_{max}]. \tag{8}$$

Here P_{max} is some maximum possible value of S/N ratio, then unimodality of the function (4) and, consequently, function (5) derived from their definitions. Consequently, the optimization problem has a solution in the following formulation: find the minimum of function (4) in the interval (8). This solution can be found by any of the methods listed above. However, their use is associated with a large number of calculations (solution of the corresponding equations), or with a large amount of stored data, requiring constant modification (various search methods).

In Ref. [18], to solve above-mentioned problem is proposed to use the apparatus of fuzzy logic, free from above disadvantages. Fuzzy logic operators are very similar to conventional Boolean operators and allow simplified algorithms for solving this problem. Complicated mathematical modeling can be replaced by evaluation of membership functions and rules of fuzzy logic [22]. Various approaches to solving this type of problems are considered in Refs. [23, 24]. In Ref. [25] there is an example of controlling the operation of the charger using intelligent controller which applies various algorithms of fuzzy inference. One of the most powerful tools for solving such problems is the MATLAB system, which provides users a various species of software, including the visual ones. With the help of visual programming, the necessary model can be built, and then can run the simulation in program mode.

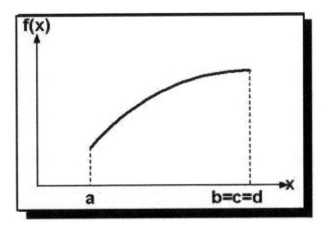

Figure 2. The example of unimodal function.

3.3. Model of algorithm of determination of the best access point

In accordance with the 802.11 standard, the mobile station scans the individual channels for the detection of the best signal from the access point. APs periodically send a Beacon signal in a broadcast mode. Mobile network station accepts these beacon signals and takes note of the relevant signal level. Thus, the received signal level actually characterizes the relative location of the subscriber and the access point. During this process, a mobile subscriber searches such access point. To determine whether channel is free, the well-known algorithm, which is named clear channel assessment (CCA), is used. Its essence lies in the measurement of the signal power at the antenna and determining the received signal strength (RSSI). If the received signal strength is below a certain threshold, then the channel is declared free, and the MAC layer receives the CTS status. If the power is above the threshold, the data transfer is delayed in accordance with the protocol rules. The standard provides another opportunity to determine the idle channel, which can be used either separately or together with the RSSI measurement— method of checking of the carrier. The most appropriate method to use depends on the level of interference in the work area. Various 802.11 standards use one of the five possible CCA modes:

- solution that channel is free and is based on the detection of channel power which exceeds a certain threshold value;

- the decision that the channel is free based on the detection of a carrier signal corresponding to the 802.11 standard;

- carrier signal detection and discovering of power (combination of modes 1 and 2);

- carrier signal detection with message that the ether is free, if neither signal is detected during 3.5 ms timeslot;

- detection of the power corresponding to the increased transmission rate in a physical layer and carrier detection at mode 3, but with reference to the ERP.

802.11 MAC layer is responsible for the way in which the subscriber is connected to the access point. When a subscriber enters into the coverage area of one or more access points, it selects the access point based on signal power values and observed number of errors, selects one of them and connects thereto. Once the subscriber receives confirmation that it is accepted by the access point, it tunes to a radio channel in which it operates. From time to time, it checks all the channels to see if there is another point which provides access services of higher quality. If such an access point is found, then the subscriber connects to it and readjusts to its frequency.

In accordance with this principle, the diagrams of signal levels and levels of channel diagrams of signal levels and levels of channel congestion can be constructed for each access point. These diagrams look like shown in **Figure 3**.

Analysis of these diagrams and subject area makes it possible to apply fuzzy logic to make a decision on selecting the best access point to connect. As shown above, a signal power can be characterized through signal/noise ratio, and a congestion level of AP can be described with the help of number of connected subscribers. Then it becomes obvious that proposed model

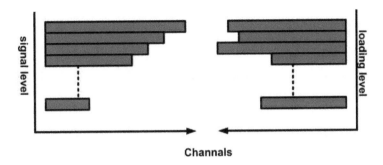

Channals

Figure 3. Diagrams of signal levels and levels of channel congestion.

must have two input linguistic variables (*S/N* ratio and the degree of loading of the access point). As the set of terms of the first linguistic variable "signal/noise" the following set is used:

$$S/N = \{'weak', 'medium', 'high'\}. \tag{9}$$

As the set of terms of the second linguistic variable "degree of loading" the following set is used:

$$\text{NUMUSERS} = \{'few', 'medium', 'many'\}. \tag{10}$$

As the set of terms of the output linguistic variable the following set is used:

$$\text{RESULT} = \{'is\ a\ candidate\ for\ connection', 'is\ not\ a\ candidate\ for\ connection'\} \tag{11}$$

Since the algorithm Mamdami is used for fuzzy inference, the following methods of execution had been chosen for the stages of composition:

1. To perform a logical conjunction in conditions of the fuzzy rules (And method), the minimum value (min) method was chosen;

2. To perform a logical disjunction in conditions of the fuzzy rules (Or method), the maximum value (max) method was chosen;

3. To perform a logical conclusion in the every of fuzzy rules (Implication), the minimum value (min) method was chosen;

4. For aggregation of membership function values of each input variable in conclusions of fuzzy rules (Aggregation), the maximum (max) method was chosen;

5. To perform defuzzification of output variables (Defuzzification), the method of center of gravity for a discrete set of values of the membership functions (centroid) was chosen.

In the process of fuzzy inference, it is necessary to select such an access point for which the convolution of the functions of the accessory of the signal/noise ratio and the degree of congestion of the access point give the best result. To implement the fuzzy inference, the creation of the rule base of fuzzy inference system is required. To implement the fuzzy inference, the creation of the rule base of fuzzy inference system is required. Such base of rules for the solution of discussed task looks like:

- If the *S/N* ratio is weak and access point is lightly loaded (the number of users *M* is few), then the access point is not considered as a candidate for connection.

- If the *S/N* ratio is weak and access point is moderately loaded (the number of users *M* is medium), then the access point is not considered as a candidate for connection.

- If the *S/N* ratio is weak and access point is heavily loaded (the number of users *M* is many), then the access point is not considered as a candidate for connection.

- If the *S/N* ratio is medium and access point is lightly loaded (the number of users *M* is few), then the access point is considered as a candidate for connection.

- If the *S/N* ratio is medium and access point is moderately loaded (the number of users *M* is medium), then the access point is not considered as a candidate for connection.

- If the *S/N* ratio is medium and access point is heavily loaded (the number of users *M* is many), then the access point is not considered as a candidate for connection.

- If the *S/N* ratio is high and access point is lightly loaded (the number of users *M* is few), then the access point is considered as a candidate for connection.

- If the *S/N* ratio is high and access point is moderately loaded (the number of users *M* is medium), then the access point is considered as a candidate for connection.

- If the *S/N* ratio is high and access point is heavily loaded (the number of users *M* is many), then the access point is not considered as a candidate for connection.

The following notations are in use here to simplify the formalization of fuzzy productions:

1. if (*S/N* is A1) and (Numusers is B1) then (Result is E1) (1);

2. if (*S/N* is A1) and (Numusers is B2) then (Result is E1) (1);

3. if (*S/N* is A1) and (Numusers is B3) then (Result is E1) (1);

4. if (*S/N* is A2) and (Numusers is B1) then (Result is E2) (1);

5. if (*S/N* is A2) and (Numusers is B2) then (Result is E1) (1);

6. if (*S/N* is A2) and (Numusers is B3) then (Result is E1) (1);

7. if (*S/N* is A3) and (Numusers is B1) then (Result is E2) (1);

8. if (*S/N* is A3) and (Numusers is B2) then (Result is E2) (1);

9. if (*S/N* is A3) and (Numusers is B3) then (Result is E1) (1).

A1 means the *S/N* ratio is weak, A2 means the *S/N* ratio is medium, A3 means the *S/N* ratio is high, B1 means the number of users is few, B2 means the number of users is medium, B3 means the number of users is many, E1 means that the access point is not a candidate for connection, E2 means that the access point is a candidate for connection. Thus, the connection to the access point occurs only when the access point is not overloaded and has an acceptable signal level. The numbers in round brackets mean the weight of rule (0 or 1). The next step in the construction of the model is to determine the membership functions of input and output variables. Kind of membership functions for the signal/noise ratio, the number of subscribers, and the output variable are shown in **Figure 4**.

For analyzing the adequacy of the developed fuzzy model, the surface fuzzy inference can be quite useful. It allows assessing the impact of changes in the values of the input fuzzy variables on the values of the output fuzzy variables. This surface is shown in **Figure 5**. A comparison of this figure with **Figure 1** allows concluding that the nature of the surface of the fuzzy inference coincides in general with the frame transmission time dependent on the signal level and the number of subscribers. This confirms the adequacy of the proposed model.

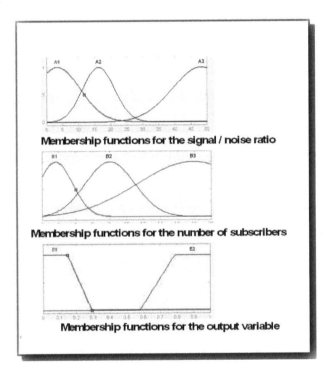

Figure 4. Membership functions for input and output variables.

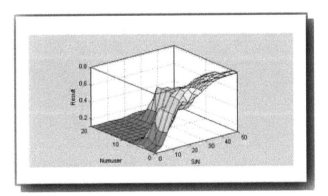

Figure 5. The surface fuzzy inference.

3.4. Simulation of the algorithm for determining the best access point

For checking the correctness and efficiency of the proposed algorithm, its styling is first carried out. MATLAB provides the ability to download a model developed with the help of visual aids into the MATLAB—program and perform simulation in program mode. The data structure of a software model is shown in **Figure 6**.

Each access point is represented by the data structure containing the following data fields:

- Index of the access point (its number in a vector of access points).

- The current value of the signal level at that point.

- The current number of connected subscribers at this point.

- The current time of the frame transmission for this point.

At initialization of this model, these structures combine into a vector. Thus, the sequential number of structure in the vector imitates the Beacon signal. All other fields of structures are set to zero. Also, the vector of signal levels is forming. This vector simulates a signal power at which every access point radiates, and thereby, the location of subscriber is relative to access points in the moment of its connection. The signal levels are forming according with normal distribution and exponential distribution. This adequately reflects the real situation when connecting subscribers grouped in a small area, for example, when entering a room or in some corner of the room, as it is shown in **Figure 7**.

Simulation process starts with the loading of model into the program. Further, the current values of signal level out of the vector of signal levels are moving into the fields of current values of the signal level in every access point. After this, the values of membership functions are calculated for every access point. Further, the values of membership functions are calculated for every access point and their maximum value is looked for. The access point for which this value is maximal, the value of the field current number of connected subscribers to this point is increased by 1. This simulates the RSSI level correction for the next simulation step. Furthermore, the current time of the frame transmission for this point is calculated according with function (5). This process is repeated for all the elements of the vector of

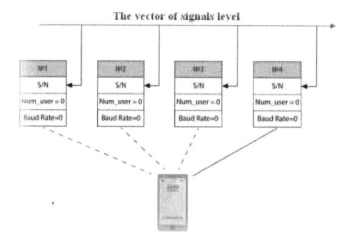

Figure 6. The data structure of model.

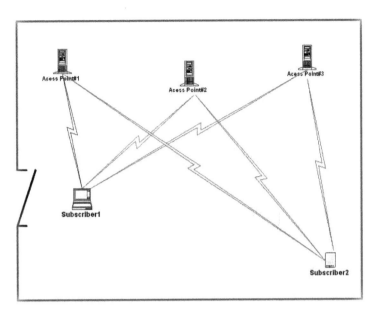

Figure 7. The example of the subscriber's location indoors.

signal levels. Thus, after the completion of simulation process, total loading and the frame transmission time in every point would be determined.

The modeling process is based on a method that was considered in Ref. [26]. In this case the sufficient characteristics are current values of congestion of access point and frame transmission time on every simulation step; the final characteristics are the distributions of load of access points, transmission time, mean value, and dispersion of the transmission time. For the confirmation of efficiency of the proposed algorithm, its result was compared with the result of simulation of classic, which is based on the measuring of maximal signal power. The results of the comparison of the analyzed algorithms are shown in **Figure 8**. In this picture, "Sample Model" means the model is based on the measuring of maximal signal power. This figure shows that the algorithm that uses fuzzy logic (the right-hand side of **Figure 8**), taking into account the current load on each access point, ensures a more even loading of the entire LAN as a whole. The frame transmission time for the second algorithm is approximately same for all access points (the dispersion is equal to 0.0799). For the first algorithm, the transmission time

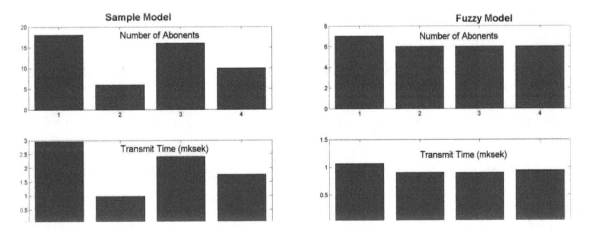

Figure 8. The results of the comparison of the analyzed algorithms.

fluctuates strongly (the dispersion is equal to 0.3129). Hence, it follows that accounting the degree of congestion of access points increases the efficiency of the wireless LAN.

Developed in the framework of this chapter, MATLAB—the program cannot be used directly in some hardware for the following reasons:

- Developed program is a model.

- MATLAB—program runs in interpreted mode and cannot be loaded directly into the controller.

However, there are various possibilities to convert MatLab-program into equivalent program on one of the high-level programming languages. In particular, there is the possibility of constructing an equivalent program on high level language such as C# or C++. Such program can be installed on the controller or other device that will automatically determine the best access point to connect to the local network.

4. Conclusions

We have reviewed the advanced solutions for indoor navigation and briefly reviewed the program complex to navigate through radio fingerprints. Navigation software package uses the model ANN. In addition, by using the MATLAB performed rationale for the selection of ANN learning algorithm and determine the recommended number of neurons of the hidden layer for the considered number of Wi-Fi networks.

As a recommendation, to the use of this software system, one should take into account the importance of using the mac-address of an access point instead of its name because it is not unique. Emerged collision may disrupt the entire complex.

The general advantages of this approach include the fact that the software package can run on the existing infrastructure of Wi-Fi networks that are deployed in a variety of areas, such as residential buildings and shopping malls.

The disadvantages are a feature of this approach lie in the fact that before using it you must manually map the radio fingerprint.

Further studies, in our opinion, are advisable to continue in the following areas.

- The implementation multivariate classifier for converting radio prints multidimensional coordinates (x, y, height).

- Conducting research on the influence of other learning algorithms ANN (Quickprop, Batch, and Incremental) the speed and accuracy of navigation training.

- Development of a method for reducing the dimensionality of the input vector radio finger-print.

- Improving the quality of navigation when combined with inertial navigation system.

- The addition of processing signals from Bluetooth LE beacons to signals from Wi-Fi access points.

The task of selection of the access point in WLAN network in the case of high user density is quite topical. Such selection must take into account not only the level of the signal received by the mobile device, but also a width in the dedicated channel bandwidth that depends on the number of connected subscribers to the access point.

- Uneven loading of access points in a wireless LAN tends to reduce the overall effectiveness of its work. This is manifested in the fact that the frame transmission time for the overloaded access point may increase significantly.

- Connecting the mobile subscriber to the access point in accordance with the maximum received signal level leads to that some access points may be overloaded.

- Accounting of degree of current workload of access points when a subscriber connects to them provides better balancing of total workload in the network.

- To find the best access point for connecting a subscriber with account of its workload is necessary to solve the optimization task.

- The most effective method for solving this task is to use the apparatus of fuzzy logic.

- The developed model can be used in controllers or in embedded devices by converting into an executable program on high-level programming language.

Author details

Anatoly D. Khomonenko, Sergey E. Adadurov, Alexandr V. Krasnovidow*, Pavel A. Novikov

*Address all correspondence to: alexkrasnovidow@mail.ru

Petersburg State Transport University, St. Petersburg, Russia

References

[1] Yuri S. Satellite Navigation Systems. Moscow: ECO Trendz; 2000. p. 267. http://www.indoorsnavi.com/

[2] Hatami A, Pahlavan K. A comparative performance evaluation of RSS-based positioning algorithms used in WLAN networks. In: Proceedings of the IEEE Wireless Communications and Networking Conference (WCNC '05); Vol. 4. March; New Orleans, LA, USA; 2005. pp. 2331-2337

[3] Kukolj D, Vuckovic M, Pletl S. Indoor location fingerprinting based on data reduction. International Conference on Broadband and Wireless Computing, Communication and Applications (BWCCA); 26-28 October; 2011. pp. 327-332

[4] Butakov NA. Applicability inertial navigation in mobile devices. International Journal of Open Information Technologies. 2014;**2**(5):24-32. ISSN: 2307-8162.

[5] Evennou F, Marx F. Advanced integration of wi-fi and inertial navigation systems for indoor mobile positioning. EURASIP Journal on Applied Signal Processing. 2006;**2006**:1-11. Article ID 86706.

[6] Wang S, Min J, Yi BK. Location based services for mobiles: Technologies and standards. LG Electronics Mobile Research, USA. 2008. 122 pp.

[7] Dworkina NB, Namiot DE, Dvorkin BA. Mobile navigation services and the use of technology to determine the location OpenCellID. Geomatics. 2010:**2**;80-87. http://sovzond.ru/upload/iblock/fbf/2010_02_014.pdf.

[8] Abdrakhmanova AM, Namiot DE. Using two-dimensional bar code to create a system of positioning and navigation inside. Applied Informatics. 2013; **1**(43):31-39

[9] Namiot DE, Shneps-Shneppe MA. Analysis of the trajectories in mobile networks on the basis of information about network proximity. Automation and Computer Science. 2013;**3**:S48-S60

[10] Mok E, Cheung Bernard KS. An improved neural network training algorithm for wi-fi fingerprinting positioning. ISPRS International Journal of Geo-Information. 2013;**2**:854-868

[11] Mehmood H, Tripathi NK, Tipdecho T. Indoor positioning system using artificial neural network. Journal of Computer Science. 2010;**6**(10):1219-1225

[12] Fang SH, Lin TN. Indoor location system based on discriminant-adaptive neural network in IEEE 802.11 environments. IEEE Transactions on Neural Networks. 2008;**19**(11):1973-1978

[13] Novikov PA, Khomonenko AD, Yakovlev EL. Justification of the choice of neural networks learning algorithms for indoor mobile positioning. Proceeding CEE-SECR '15 Proceedings of the 11th Central & Eastern European Software Engineering Conference in Russia. Moscow, Russian Federation; 22-24 October 2015; ACM New York, NY, USA©; 2015. Article No. 9. DOI: 10.1145/2855667.2855677

[14] Novikov PA, Khomonenko AD, Yakovlev EL. Software for mobile indoor navigation using neural networks. Informatsionno-Upravliaiushchie Sistemy, [Information and Control Systems]. 2016;**1**:32-39. (In Russian). DOI: 10.15217/issn1684-8853.2016.1.32.

[15] Akobir S. The learning algorithm RProp – mathematical apparatus. http://basegroup.ru/community/articles/rprop.

[16] Khomonenko AD, Yakovlev EL. Neural network approximation of characteristics of multi-channel non-Markovian queuing systems. SPIIRAS Proceedings. 2015;**4**(41):81-93. (In Russian). DOI: http://dx.doi.org/10.15622/sp.41.4.

[17] IEEE. Wireless LAN medium access control (MAC) and physical layer (PHY) specifications. The Institute of Electrical and Electronics Engineers, IEEE 802.11. 2006.

[18] Krasnovidow AV. Model of algorithm to determine a best access point to connect a mobile device to the LAN. Intellectual Technologies on Transport. 2016;2(6):36-42 (In Russian).

[19] Larsson D, Merty R. Adaptivniy Podhod k optimizacii proizvoditelnosty besprovodnyh setey/ Dylan Larsson, Ravi Merty//[Adaptive approach to optimize the performance of wireless networks] Technology@Intel Magazine, - 2004, No 8, pp. 24–27.

[20] Himmelblaw D. Prikladnoe nelineinoe programmirovanie. [Applied Nonlinear Programming]. Moscow: Mir; 1976. p. 448

[21] Elter K-H, Reinhardt R, Schauble M, Donath G. Vvedenie v Nelineinoe Programmirovanie. [Introduction to the Nonlinear Programming]. Moscow: Nauka; 1985. p. 264

[22] Leonenko A. Nechetkoie modelirovanie v srede matlab i fuzzyTECH. [Fuzzy Modelling in MATLAB Environment and FuzzyTECH]. Saint-Petersburg: BHV – Petersburg; 2005. p. 736

[23] Terano T, Asai K, Sugeno M, editors, Prikladnye nechetkie sistemy. [Applied Fuzzy Systems]. Moscow: Mir; 1993. p. 386

[24] Ihmig M. Dynamic channel allocation for self-managing WLAN access points in chaotic wireless networks [Thesis]. Diplomarbeit, Master's Thesis, Technische Universität München, Mar 2006.

[25] Leith DJ, Clifford P. A self-managed distributed channel selection algorithm for WLANs. 4th International Symposium on Modelling and Optimization in Mobile, Ad Hoc and Wireless Networks. 2006; pp. 1-9. DOI: 10.1109/WIOPT.2006.1666484.

[26] Krasnovidow AV. An approach to the construction of algorithms for the statistical analysis of error flows in digital communications channels. Intellectual Technologies on Transport. 2015;2(2):20-25. (In Russian).

3

Design and Stability Analysis of Fuzzy-Based Adaptive Controller for Wastewater Treatment Plant

Mao Li

Abstract

In this chapter, design and stability analyses of direct model reference control system based on wastewater treatment plant are addressed. The purpose of controller design includes input saturation control and two-level control system with fuzzy supervisor control. The wastewater treatment plant is a highly uncertain non-linear system and the plant parameter are unknown, therefore controller design are under those condition.

Keywords: fuzzy control, fuzzy supervisor, wastewater treatment plant, adaptive control, model reference adaptive control, Lyapunov function

1. Introduction

The problem to be solved for this chapter is the dissolved oxygen reference trajectory tracking in an aerobic reactor for nutrient removal using direct model reference adaptive controller at the activated sludge wastewater treatment plant (WWTP). The reference trajectory is provided on-line by upper control layer of the overall control system. The controller design utilizes a different time scale in the internal dissolved oxygen dynamic and in disturbance inputs. In this chapter, we introduce two kinds of adaptive control, one is Direct Model Reference Adaptive Control (DMRAC) and another one is fuzzy logic based on DMRAC with two-level control.

2. Adaptive control

The basic concept of adaptive control is that it comprises of two main types. The first is called model reference adaptive control (MRAC) mode whereas the second is called self-tuning mode. An adaptive control characteristic is that the control parameter are variable, and those parameters are updated online with the signal in the system.

2.1. Model reference adaptive control

A model reference adaptive control can be divided into four parts, such as plant, reference model, control law and controller. A plant includes unknown parameters. The reference model is described as control system output. The closed-loop control law is adjusting mechanism for adjustable control parameters. The controller updates the adjustable parameter with time-varying control system.

The plant is supposed to exist with known system structure, but plant parameters are unknown in the real. The structure of the dynamic equation is known with some unknown parameters in the nonlinear plants. The number of poles/zero are supposed to be known with unknown location poles/zero.

The reference model is used in order to obtain assignation ideal response of adaptive control system to control output. For the adaptive control system, that mean it is supply the ideal response by adjusting ideal plant parameters in the adaptation mechanism. To design the adaptive control system, first step is choice of the reference model. It is needed to meet two following clauses.

- The reference model should satisfy the performance of adaptive control system such as rise time, overshoot and settling time.

- The ideal plant parameter should be implemented by the adaptive control system.

The controllers are composition of several adjustable parameters. This implies that the controllers are distribution signal to each adjustable parameter with online update. The controller needs to have good tracking performance which means it can achieve tracking convergence behaviour. To design controller, two conditions need to be considered.

- If the plant parameters are known, then the plant out should track model reference trajectory by relevant controller parameters.

- If the plant parameters are unknown, then the plant out should track model reference trajectory by adjusting the controller parameters.

The linearly parameterized that mean is the control law with linear term of the adjustable parameters. To guarantee stability and tracking performance, adaptive control design is used by linear parameterization of the controller.

Adjusting parameters in adaptive control law is call adaptation mechanism. In the MRAC systems, the adaptation law is used in order to search the plant parameters, therefore the plant out can track set-point (model reference) with good performance by adaptive controller. The difference between ideal adaptive control parameter and real plant parameter is call tracking error. The tracking error converge to zero that implies that adaptive control system is stable.

2.2. Self-tuning model reference adaptive control

The control parameters estimate plant unknown parameters in control system. If a plant parameter is unknown, then a parameter estimator provides estimation values to those plant unknown parameters. If a plant parameter is known, then control parameters would transmit plant parameters by on-line update on model reference. The estimator provides estimation control parameters with on-line update from model reference, it is called self-tuning controller. The self-tuning controller is estimation unknown parameter in the plant at the same time.

The self-turning MRAC manipulate processes:

- The estimator transfer estimated plant parameters to controller; therefore, it can compute the plant corresponding unknown parameters at the same time. The plant estimation parameters depend on the past plant input and output.

- Computes a control input and rely on control parameters and measured signal, and this control input rely on new plant output.

- The close-loop parameters and plant input are updated on-line with time-varying adaptive control system.

The estimation parameter can be taken from an ideal parameters and real parameters by plant input/plant output data that are updated on-line with time-varying adaptive control system. The error dynamic is described as the difference between ideal plant parameters and real plant parameters; this implies that if tracking errors converge to zero by adjusting parameters adaptation then plant output complete tracking reference model. It is purpose of self-turning adaptive control design.

The self-turning control includes two types of adaptive controllers, one is called Indirect Model Reference Adaptive Control (IMRAC) and the another one is called Direct Model Reference Adaptive Control. The plant unknown parameters are provided by adaptive controller estimation of those plant parameters. If the estimation plant parameters need transfer into controller parameters,furthermore control law parameters can influent plant unknown parameters. This implies that the control parameters can adjust plant unknown parameters with standard estimation approach. It is called IMRAC. On the other hand, if it does not need transfer process, this method is called DMRAC.

2.3. Direct model reference control design

The property of adaptive control is used for plant with unknown parameters; therefore, choosing the adaptive control law is more implicated in controller design. Since we mention before, adaptive control law produce controller parameters. Also the stability analysis for control system need to be considered in controller design. In this chapter, we used Lyapunov theory to analyse control system whether stable or unstable. The process of adaptive control design includes three steps. The first step is choosing control law (include plant variable parameters). The second step is choosing adaptation law. The final step is stability analyses to guarantee convergence of control system.

3. DMRAC with input saturation apply on WWTP

3.1. Introduction

An activated sludge wastewater treatment plant (WWTP) is a complex nonlinear system due to multiple time scale and unmeasurable state variables. In addition, it has time-varying input disturbances and saturation during the WWTP operation; hence, the hierarchical structures which were considered in Refs. [1, 2]. The two-level controller of tracking prescribed a concentration of the dissolved oxygen (*DO*) trajectory, while the reference of concentration dissolved oxygen (*DO*^{ref}) was developed in Refs. [3, 4]. The activated sludge plant contained two main components, such as bioreactor and settler as illustrated in **Figure 1**.

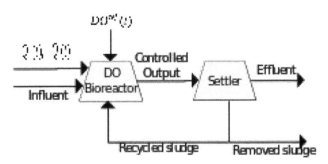

Figure 1. Structure of WWTP for nutrient removal.

The microorganism produced the biomass to nutrient removal in the bioreactor. The concentration of dissolved oxygen control is an important state parameter that feeds the microorganisms. The concentration of *DO* control was considered in Ref. [5]. The upper level controller produced airflow $Q_{\text{air}}^{\text{ref}}(t)$ into the aerobic biological reactor zone. The lower level controller produced the concentration of *DO* to track the $Q_{\text{air}}^{\text{ref}}(t)$ set-point trajectory. The airflow is the control input, and the concentration of *DO* is the control output.

The dissolved oxygen reference trajectory $DO^{\text{ref}}(t)$ set-point was optimized by the upper control layer which was the medium control layer in overall WWTP [1]. The clean water came out from the settler after being separated from the biomass and sludge. The concentration of substrate and biomass were unmeasurable state variables; hence, they were not able to be on-line updated. The upper layer control with input saturation was presented in Ref. [6]. The saturation function was assumed considering that aeration system controller was ideal and thus the airflow was equal to airflow reference. However, the physical modelling of the wastewater treatment plant was used to design the controller. In this chapter, we consider the upper level controller with input saturation by designing the new direct model reference adaptive control (DMRAC).

3.2. Problem statement

A mathematical model of the WWTP is based on the mass balance equations, which are illustrated in **Figure 1**. Hence, they represent the plant variables to produce the model in the state-space format [8]:

$$\frac{dX}{dt} = \mu(t)X(t) - D(t)(1+r)X + rD(t)X_{\text{r}}(t) \tag{1}$$

$$\frac{dS}{dt} = -\frac{\mu(t)X(t)}{Y} - D(t)(1+r)S(t) + D(t)S_{in}(t) \tag{2}$$

$$\frac{dDO}{dt} = -\frac{K_0\mu(t)X(t)}{Y} - D(t)(1+r)DO(t) + k_{La}(Q_{air}(t))(DO_{max} - DO(t)) + D(t)DO_{in}(t) \quad (3)$$

$$\frac{dX_r}{dt} = D(t)(1+r)X(t) - D(t)(\beta+r)X_r(t) \quad (4)$$

$$\mu(t) = \mu_{max} \frac{S(t)}{K_s + S(t)} \times \frac{DO(t)}{K_{DO} + DO(t)} \quad (5)$$

where

$$D(t) = \frac{Q_{in}}{V_a}; \quad r = \frac{Q_r}{Q_{in}}; \quad \beta = \frac{Q_w}{Q_{in}} \quad (6)$$

$X(t)$, $S(t)$, DO_{max}, $X_r(t)$, $D(t)$, $S_{in}(t)$, $DO_{in}(t)$, Y, $\mu(t)$, μ_{max}, K_S, K_{DO}, $Q_{air}(t)$, K_0, r, β, $Q_{in}(t)$, $Q_r(t)$, $Q_w(t)$, V_a are biomass concentration, substrate concentration, maximum dissolved concentration, recycled biomass concentration, dilution rate, substrate concentration in the influent, dissolved oxygen concentration in the influent, biomass yield factor, biomass growth rate, maximum specific growth rate, affinity constant, saturation constant, aeration rate, model constant, recycled sludge rate, removed sludge rate, influent flow rate, effluent flow rate, recycled flow rate, waste flow rate and aerator volume, respectively.

The function $k_{La}(Q_{air}(t))$ is the oxygen transfer, which depends on the aeration actuating system and sludge conditions [4]. In this chapter, it is assumed that

$$k_{La}(t) = \alpha Q_{air}(t) + \delta \quad (7)$$

where α and δ are two known constant values relating to oxygen transfer.

As only the DO output is considered in this chapter, the model is sufficiently accurate. Otherwise, more detailed model, for example, the ASM3, than it should be utilized as it has been done in Ref. [7]. In **Figure 2**, the detailed structure of the activated sludge WWTP for nutrient removal with the airflow actuator is illustrated. The actuator dynamics are described by a complex hybrid model. The output of aeration control system airflow output $Q_{air}(t)$ needs to

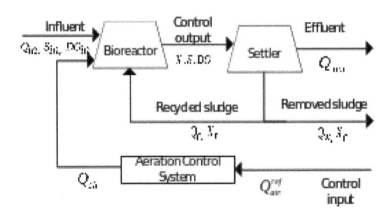

Figure 2. Structure of wastewater treatment plant.

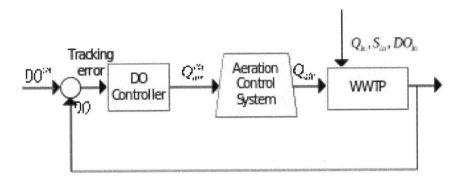

Figure 3. Structure of DO control system with input saturation.

follow the reference airflow input $Q_{air}^{ref}(t)$, which was described in Ref. [8]. The plant input with time-varying disturbances are dissolved oxygen concentration in the fluent $DO_{in}(t)$, the substrate concentration in the influent $S_{in}(t)$ and influent flow rate $Q_{in}(t)$. The controller needs to have high performance to enables the airflow output to track the reference airflow input.

The structure of DO control system for nutrient removal with input saturation at activated sludge WWTP is illustrated in **Figure 3**.

The aeration controller designed in this chapter considers the aeration control system as the input $Q_{air}(t)$ with input saturation to achieve $Q_{air}^{ref}(t) = Q_{air}(t)$. This is the main difference in comparison with Ref. [8]. If the plant dynamics have several serially coupled reactors, the decentralized controller needs to consider the input saturation [6]. Previous papers [1–3] considered the two-level controller to remove the nutrient in the activated sludge WWTP. The upper layer controller generated the expected $Q_{air}^{ref}(t)$ into each of the aerobic biological reactor zones. The input of the lower layer controller was $Q_{air}(t)$, which needs to track prescribed upper layer output $Q_{air}^{ref}(t)$ for each of the reactor zones. If the upper layer controller had an input saturation condition, it influenced global control system stability and performance. As the plant dynamics have very high order and nonlinear dynamics as in Eqs. (1)–(5). The fixed parameter linear controller could not continue to keep the expected performance under full range of operating conditions. This was verified in Ref. [4] by using fixed parameter PI controller in low layer control. The upper layer controller used a fuzzy supervised controller. It obtained the expected performance. In practice, if the disturbance of the input becomes large, fast varying and with saturation input, the PI controller becomes very complex. The DMRAC with input saturation in upper layer control is considered in this chapter, which is not based on previous papers [7]. The $DO(t)$ of the DMRAC input-output model rearranges the state-space model from Eqs. (1)–(4). As the state variable are not measureable, the unknown quantities in this input-output model will integrate into one term known as respiration. The parameter adaptation laws of the adaptive controller enable the respiration to be estimated indirectly and automatically.

3.3. DMRAC design

The direct state-space model of WWTP is represented in Eqs. (1)–(5). The dynamics are uncertain and nonlinear. The state variables $X_r(t)$, $X(t)$, $S(t)$ are unmeasurable. The state variables $Q_{air}(t), Q_{in}(t), Q_w(t), DO(t)$ are measured by on-line updates. To design the direct model reference adaptive controller, we shall derive dissolved oxygen dynamics model in input-output format of first-order and with input disturbance and input saturation. We shall rewrite Eq. (3) by substituting Eqs. (5) and (7). The term $D(t)DO_{in}(t)$ can be neglected in state-space model, since it is very small in comparison with other state variables. The dissolved oxygen input-output model (DOIOM) is derived as follows:

$$\frac{dDO}{dt} = -a_p(t)DO(t) - c_p(t)f(DO(t)) + b_p(t)Q_{air}(t) + d_p \tag{8}$$

where $a_p(t), c_p(t), b_p(t), d_p$ are DOIOM parameters and

$$
\begin{aligned}
a_p(t) &= \frac{Q_{in}(1+r)}{V_a} + \delta \\
c_p(t) &= \frac{K_0 X(t)}{Y} \frac{\mu_{max}S(t)}{(K_S + S(t))} \\
f(DO(t)) &= \frac{DO(t)}{(K_{DO} + DO(t))} \\
b_p(t) &= \alpha(DO_{max} - DO(t)) \\
d_p &= \delta DO_{max}
\end{aligned}
\tag{9}
$$

The parameters $a_p(t)$ and $c_p(t)$ are slowly varying and unknown. The parameters $a_p(t)$ is dependent on upper control layer which operates in the time scale and is slower in comparison with $DO(t)$ control time scale (6) and (9). The parameter $c_p(t)$ is dependent on X and S, and is slower in comparison with $DO(t)$ (1) and (15). The parameter $b_p(t)$ is dependent on the fast internal dynamics of $DO(t)$ time scale (9). Hence, $DO(t)$ is fast varying and known. The parameter d_p is slowly varying and known. The model reference dynamics (MRD) generate achieved $DO(t)$ dynamics.

The $DO(t)$ tracks the prescribed dissolved oxygen trajectory $DO^{ref}(t)$ by the controller. The MRD equation is as follows:

$$\frac{dDO_{m,ref}}{dt} = -a_m DO_{m.ref}(t) + b_m DO^{ref}(t) \tag{10}$$

where $DO_{m.ref}(t)$ is the reference dynamics output and the parameters a_m and b_m are constant.

The $DO(t)$ dynamics SISO input-output model with input saturation yields is as follows:

$$\frac{dDO}{dt} = -a_p(t)DO(t) - c_p(t)f(DO(t)) + b_p(t)W(t) + d_p \tag{11}$$

where $W(t)$ is assumed saturation control input with constraint (SCIC) $W(t) = \text{saturation}(Q_{air}(t))$,

$$
W(t) = \begin{cases} Q^L_{air}(t), & \text{if} \quad Q_{air}(t) > Q^L_{air}(t) \\ Q_{air}(t), & \text{if} \quad Q^L_{air}(t) \le Q_{air}(t) \le Q^U_{air}(t) \\ Q^U_{air}(t), & \text{if} \quad Q_{air}(t) < Q^U_{air}(t) \end{cases}
\tag{12}
$$

where $Q_{\text{air}}^{\text{L}}(t)$ and $Q_{\text{air}}^{\text{U}}(t)$ are actuator lower and upper constant bounds. If under the input saturation condition, the filter tracking error $n(t)$ is increasing, then global stability will be unstable for the control system. The model reference adaptive control law without input saturation was proposed in Ref. [5]. This motivates us to develop a new control law in comparison with Ref. [8] by explicitly considering the influence of the actuator input saturation nonlinearity.

The filter tracking error is applied as follows:

$$n(t) = e(t) - \lambda(t) \tag{13}$$

where $e(t)$ represents the difference between $DO(t)$ and $DO_{\text{m, ref}}(t)$ with on-line update.

$$e(t) = DO(t) - DO_{\text{m, ref}}(t) \tag{14}$$

We define the auxiliary signal as follows:

$$\frac{d\lambda}{dt} = b_p \Delta Q_{\text{air}}(t) - \Phi \lambda(t) \tag{15}$$

where Φ is small position constant parameter. The parameter $\Delta Q_{\text{air}}(t)$ is the difference between SCIC $W(t)$ and control input $Q_{\text{air}}(t)$.

The affine MRAC law is applied as follows:

$$W(t) = \frac{1}{b_p} a_{DO}(t) DO(t) + \frac{1}{b_p} a_f(t) f(DO(t))$$
$$+ \frac{1}{b_p} a_{DO^{\text{ref}}}(t) DO^{\text{ref}}(t) - \frac{1}{b_p} d_p$$
$$- \frac{1}{b_p} \Phi(t)(DO(t) - DO_{\text{m, ref}}(t)) \tag{16}$$

The MRD in Eq. (10) has linear dynamics. The terms $\frac{1}{b_p} a_f(t) f(DO(t))$ and $-\frac{1}{b_p} d_p$ in Eq. (16) can be cancelled by closed-loop with an impact of the nonlinear and additive terms in Eq. (8). The control input saturation is described by the last term in Eq. (16) which is retained in DOIOM. The fifth term in Eq. (16) is updated on-line. The parameters $a_{DO}(t)$, $a_f(t)$ and $a_{DO^{\text{ref}}}(t)$ are updated by adaptive control law. The MRD is achieved in the closed-loop for ideal parameter. Closing the loop by Eq. (16) yields:

$$\frac{dDO}{dt} = -(a_p(t) - a_{DO}(t)) DO(t)$$
$$- (c_p(t) - a_f(t)) f(DO(t))$$
$$+ a_{DO^{\text{ref}}}(t) DO^{\text{ref}}(t) \tag{17}$$
$$- \Phi(DO(t) - DO_{\text{m}}(t))$$

and

$$-(a_{\mathrm{p}}(t) - \hat{a}_{\mathrm{DO}}(t)) = -a_{\mathrm{m}} \tag{18}$$

$$-(c_{\mathrm{p}}(t) - \hat{a}_{\mathrm{f}}(t)) = 0 \tag{19}$$

$$\hat{a}_{\mathrm{DO^{ref}}}(t) = b_{\mathrm{m}} \tag{20}$$

$$-\Phi(DO(t) - DO_{\mathrm{m}}(t)) = -\Phi e(t) \tag{21}$$

where $\hat{a}_{\mathrm{DO}}(t)$, $\hat{a}_f(t)$ and $\hat{a}_{\mathrm{DO^{ref}}}(t)$ are the ideal parameters, which can now be obtained as follows:

$$\hat{a}_{\mathrm{DO}}(t) = -a_m + a_p(t) \tag{22}$$

$$\hat{a}_{\mathrm{f}}(t) = c_{\mathrm{p}}(t) \tag{23}$$

$$\hat{a}_{\mathrm{DO^{ref}}}(t) = b_{\mathrm{m}} \tag{24}$$

The parameter adaption laws which can achieve stability for a DMRAC system with SISO-controlled plant were derived in Ref. [6]. It was a first-order dynamic system composed of the mixed linear uncertainty in constant but not time-varying parameters and additive structured nonlinear. Applying these laws to Eq. (8) yields:

$$\frac{da_{\mathrm{DO}}}{dt} = -\gamma_1 e(t) DO(t) \tag{25}$$

$$\frac{da_f}{dt} = -\gamma_2 e(t) f(DO(t)) \tag{26}$$

$$\frac{da_{\mathrm{DO^{ref}}}}{dt} = -\gamma_3 e(t) DO^{\mathrm{ref}}(t) \tag{27}$$

γ_1, γ_2 and γ_3 are small enough positive constants representing the parameter adaptation gains which are used to control the parameter adaptation rates. In order to guarantee the stability of the closed-loop system, these rates shall be harmonized with the process variable rates. The DMRAC structure is presented in **Figure 4**.

3.4. Stability analysis

The estimated parameters $a_{\mathrm{DO}}(t)$, $a_{\mathrm{f}}(t)$ and $a_{\mathrm{DO^{ref}}}(t)$ are updated on-line by the adaptation laws (25)–(27). The error between estimated parameter and ideal parameters are denoted as $\Delta a_{\mathrm{DO}}(t)$, $\Delta a_{\mathrm{f}}(t)$ and $\Delta a_{\mathrm{DO^{ref}}}(t)$:

$$\Delta a_{\mathrm{DO}}(t) = a_{\mathrm{DO}}(t) - \hat{a}_{\mathrm{DO}}(t) \tag{28}$$

$$\Delta a_{\mathrm{f}}(t) = a_{\mathrm{f}}(t) - \hat{a}_{\mathrm{f}}(t) \tag{29}$$

$$\Delta a_{\mathrm{DO^{ref}}}(t) = a_{\mathrm{DO^{ref}}}(t) - \hat{a}_{\mathrm{DO^{ref}}}(t) \tag{30}$$

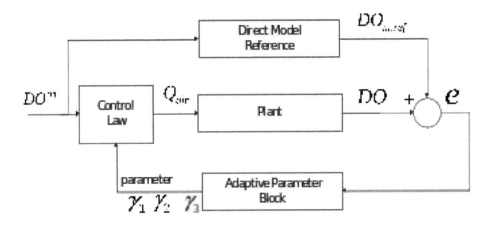

Figure 4. DMRAC structure.

Considering the following Lyapunov function:

$$V(t) = \frac{1}{2}n^2(t) + \frac{1}{2}\Delta a_{DO}{}^2(t) + \frac{1}{2}\Delta a_f{}^2(t) + \frac{1}{2}\Delta a_{DO^{ref}}{}^2(t) \tag{31}$$

Hence,

$$\frac{dV(t)}{dt} = n(t)n(t) + (a_{DO}(t) - \hat{a}_{DO}(t))(a_{DO}(t)) - a_{DO}(t)) = \frac{1}{\gamma 1}$$
$$+ (a_f(t) - a_f(t))(\hat{a}_f(t) - a_f(t))\frac{1}{\gamma_2} \tag{32}$$
$$+ (a_{DO^{ref}}(t)) - \hat{a}_{DO^{ref}}(t))(a_{DO^{ref}}(t) - a_{DO^{ref}}(t))\frac{1}{\gamma_3}$$

It follows from Eqs. (13), (15), (10) and (17) that

$$n(t) = (a_{DO}(t) - \hat{a}_{DO}(t)DO(t))$$
$$+ (a_f(t) - a_f(t))f(DO(t))$$
$$+ (a_{DO^{ref}}(t)) - \hat{a}_{DO^{ref}}(t))DO_{m,ref}(t) \tag{33}$$
$$- \Phi n(t)$$

Applying Eqs. (33), (25) (26) and (27) into (32), yields:

$$\frac{dV(t)}{dt} = -\Phi n^2(t) \tag{34}$$

Summarizing the result of the Lyapunov function (RLF) with input saturation closed-loop $DO(t)$ dynamic system, it can be seen that RLF progressively approaches zero. If the RLF approaches zero, then filter tracking error approaches zero, when time approaches infinity, Φ is small position constant and $n^2(t)$ is positive variable. To find the bounded saturation control input by limiting error between control output and dissolved oxygen trajectory reference with auxiliary signal, yields:

$$\text{limit}\{e(t) - \lambda(t)\} \leq 0 \tag{35}$$

If time approaches infinity, the $e(t)$ approaches zero. To confirm whether the auxiliary signal is negative or positive when time goes to infinity by considering the following Lyapunov function, yields:

$$V_\lambda(t) = \frac{1}{2}\lambda(t) \tag{36}$$

Hence

$$\frac{dV_\lambda(t)}{dt} = \lambda(t)\lambda(t) \tag{37}$$

Applying Eq. (12) into Eq. (37), yields:

$$\frac{dV_\lambda(t)}{dt} = \lambda(t)b_p(t)\Delta Q_{air}(t) - \lambda(t)\lambda(t)\Phi \tag{38}$$

$$\frac{dV_\lambda(t)}{dt} = \lambda(t)$$

Assume term

$$b_p(t)\Delta Q_{air}(t) = \Delta Q_{air}^{plant}(t) \tag{39}$$

It follows Eqs. (38) and (39) so that

$$\frac{dV_\lambda(t)}{dt} = -\lambda^2(t)\Phi + \frac{1}{2}\lambda^2(t) + \frac{1}{2}\Delta Q_{air}^{plant^2}(t) \tag{40}$$

Now we assume

$$\Phi = \frac{1}{2}a_0, \quad a_0 < 0, \tag{41}$$

where a_0 is small positive constant value. Applying Eq. (41) into Eq. (40) yields:

$$\frac{dV_\lambda(t)}{dt} = -2V_\lambda(t)a_0 + \frac{1}{2}\Delta Q_{air}^{plant^2}(t) \tag{42}$$

The second term $\frac{1}{2}\Delta Q_{air}^{plant^2}(t)$ is bounded. To find bound of first term by integral, yields:

$$V_\lambda(t) = \frac{\Delta Q_{air}^{plant^2}(t)}{4a_0} + (V_{\lambda.0}(t) + \frac{\Delta Q_{air}^{plant^2}}{4a_0})e(t)^{-2a_0} \tag{43}$$

where the $V_{\lambda.0}(t)$ is the initial value of the $V_\lambda(t)$. As time approaches infinity and a_0 is large enough for a positive value, then second term is equal to zero in (37).

$$V_\lambda(t) = \frac{\Delta Q_{air}^{plant^2}(t)}{4a_0} \tag{44}$$

It follows from Eqs. (36) and (44) and the limitation $V_\lambda(t)$ as negative or zero by squared.

$$V_\lambda^2(t) = \frac{\Delta Q_{air}^{plant^2}(t)}{4a_0}$$

$$\frac{1}{2}\lambda^2(t) = \frac{\Delta Q_{air}^{plant^2}(t)}{4a_0} \tag{45}$$

$$\lambda(t) = \sqrt{\frac{\Delta Q_{air}^{plant^2}(t)}{2a_0}}$$

It follows from Eqs. (35) and (41) that

$$e(t) \leq \sqrt{\frac{\Delta Q_{air}^{plant^2}(t)}{2a_0}} \tag{46}$$

If the value of a_0 is large enough, then the tracking error $e(t)$ is closer to zero. The control system will be more stable. Finally, the standard application of the Barbalat's lemma allows concluding the adaptive control system that achieves the asymptotic tracking of $DO^{ref}(t)$ under-bounded $a_{DO}(t)$, $\hat{a}_{\hat{D}\hat{O}}(t)$, $a_f(t)$, $a_f(t)$, $a_{DO^{ref}}(t)$, $a_{DO^{ref}}(t)$ if (a) the parameter in adaptive control law are close enough to the set-point in initial condition; (b) the parameter adaptation rates are positive small enough and (c) the saturation input is small enough, the control parameters bounded are stabilized

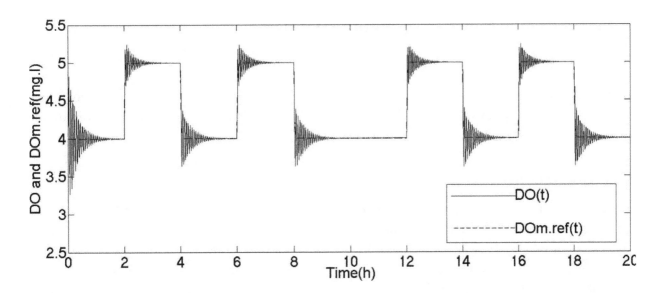

Figure 5. DO and DO^{ref} with input saturation.

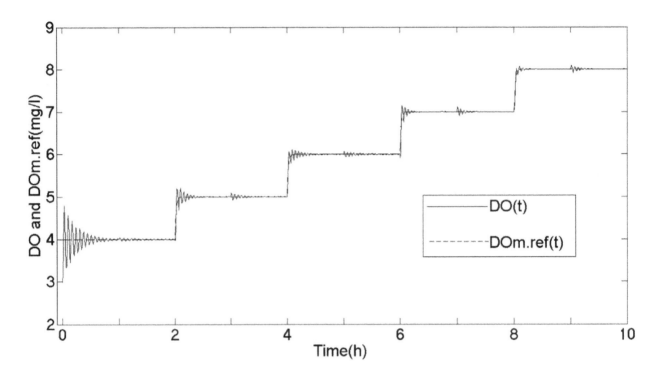

Figure 6. DO and DO^ref^ with input saturation and disturbances.

3.5. Simulation results

The simulation data are based on the real record. We assumed WWTP without disturbance, the very good $DO(t)$ tracking model reference $DO^{ref}(t)$ performance has been shown in **Figure 5**. The real plant contained some disturbances such as effluent flow rate, recycled flow rate and waste flow rate. The controller that we have designed still indicated perfect tracking performance in **Figure 6**.

4. Fuzzy supervisor based on multiple DMRAC

4.1. Introduction

In this section, we consider that fuzzy control are based on multiple DMRAC. The fuzzy control represents upper level control and DMRAC represents lower level control. More detail information are described in the next section.

4.2. Problem statement

In Ref. [4] is descried two-level controller tracking previously set-point of DO trajectory in several serially coupled reactors for the nutrient removal served by one actuator system with several air blower at WWTP. The upper level control delivers airflow into each bioreactors to be bioreactor set-point trajectory close to ideal trajectory. The lower level control is used for the concentration of DO trajectory flowing the set-point. The structure of WWTP with coupled reactors is illustrated in **Figure 7**. The structure of WWTP is different from Section 5 that

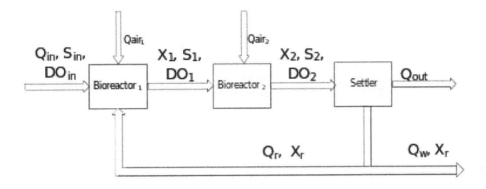

Figure 7. The structure of wastewater treatment plant for nutrient removal with coupled reactors.

contains two bioreactors. The capacity limit is that total airflow $Q_{\text{air}}^{\max}(t)$ should be small or equal to sum of all the adaptive control signals $Q_{\text{air}.k}(t)$.

$$\sum_{k=1}^{q} Q_{\text{air}.k}(t) \le Q_{\text{air}}^{\max}(t) \tag{47}$$

where k is the number of bioreactor.

4.3. Controller design

4.3.1. Lower DMRAC design

As mentioned in Section 3, the process of DMRAC design is explained in detail; therefore, in this section we provide essential equations. The state-space format is same with last section for single reactor as in Eqs. (1)–(6).

- The dissolved oxygen input-output model (DOIOM) with coupled bioreactors is derived as follows:

$$\frac{dDO_i}{dt} = -a_{p.i}(t)DO_i(t) - c_{p.i}(t)f(DO_i(t)) + b_{p.i}(t)Q_{\text{air}.i}(t) + d_{p.i} \tag{48}$$

where $a_{p.i}(t), c_{p.i}(t), b_{p.i}(t), d_{p.i}$ are DOIOM parameters and

$$\begin{aligned}
a_{p.i} &= \frac{Q_{in}(1 + r_1)}{V_{a.i}} + \delta_i \\
c_{p.i} &= \frac{K_{0.i}X_i(t)}{Y_i} \frac{\mu_{\max.i}S_i(t)}{K_{s.i} + S_i(t)} \\
b_{p.i} &= \alpha_i(DO_{\max.i} - DO_i(t)) \\
d_{p.i} &= \delta_i DO_{\max.i}
\end{aligned} \tag{49}$$

where $i = 1, 2$

- The plant parameters status are exactly same with single reactor. The model reference dynamics equation is set as:

$$\frac{dDO_{m.\text{ref}.j}}{dt} = -a_{m.j}DO_{m.\text{ref}.j}(t) + b_{m.j}DO_j^{\text{ref}}(t) \tag{50}$$

where $j = 1, 2$

- The affine model reference adaptive control law is applied as follows:

$$Q_{\text{air}.k}(t) = a_{DO.k}(t)DO_k(t) + a_{f.k}(t)f(DO_k(t)) + a_{DO_k^{\text{ref}}}(t)DO_k^{\text{ref}}(t) - \frac{\delta_k DO_{\text{max}.k}}{b_{p.k}(t)} \tag{51}$$

where $k = 1, 2$

- Model reference adaptive control law is used as:

$$\frac{da_{DO_n}}{dt} = -\gamma_{\text{zone}.z.1}e_l(t)DO_i(t) \tag{52}$$

$$\frac{da_{fn}}{dt} = -\gamma_{\text{zone}.z.2}e_l(t)f(DO_i(t)) \tag{53}$$

where $n = 1, 2; z = 1, 2; l = 1, 2; i = 1, 2.$

4.3.2. Fuzzy supervisor design

The purpose of fuzzy supervisor is to divide total airflow $Q_{air}^{\text{max}}(t)$ into two lower control signal, but those should satisfy capacity limit (47). Each of the bioreactors airflow restrict lower control output by MRAC. This implies that if fuzzy supervisor delivers airflow big enough then bioreactor output is more close to set-point trajectories (model reference). The error dynamic described each bioreactors output approaching uniform level. The fuzzy supervisor is designed as following:

4.3.2.1. Step 1: Fuzzification

Linguistic variable is at lower level for each DMRAC error dynamics. Those error dynamics are divided into three types such as small, medium and big by percentage of lower level error dynamics (54). Membership function used in this chapter are Sigmoidal condition (55) and Gauss condition (56).

$$V(t) = e_i(t)^{-1}g\sum_{i=2}^{q} e_i(t) \tag{54}$$

where $V(t)$ is percentage of lower level error dynamics for each airflow.

$e_i(t)$ is DMRAC error dynamics for each bioreactors.

$$\mu(v(t)) = \frac{1}{1 + \exp\left(-a(v(t)) - c\right)} \tag{55}$$

where a, c are membership function shape parameters.

$$\mu(v(t)) = \begin{cases} \exp\left(-(v(t)) - c_1\right)^2/\sigma_1^2) \\ 1; \\ \exp\left(-(v(t)) - c_2\right)^2/\sigma_2^2) \end{cases} \tag{56}$$

where a, σ are membership function shape parameters.

4.3.2.2. Step 2: Fuzzy rule

4.3.2.2.1. First rule
If error dynamics is small and sum of level airflow is greater than total airflow,

Then bioreactor receives corresponding percentage of total airflow.

If $V(t)$ is small and $\sum\limits_{i=1}^{q} Q_{air.i}(t) \geq Q_{air}^{max}(t)$

Then

$$Q_{air.i.2}^{supervisor}(t) = \frac{Q_{air}^{max}(t)}{\sum\limits_{i=1}^{q} Q_{air.i}(t)} \times Q_{air.i} \, g10\% \tag{57}$$

4.3.2.2.2. Second rule
If error dynamic medium and sum of level airflow is greater than total airflow,

Then bioreactor receives corresponding percentage of total airflow.

If $V(t)$ is medium and $\sum\limits_{i=1}^{q} Q_{air.i}(t) \geq Q_{air}^{max}(t)$

Then

$$Q_{air.1.2}^{supervisor}(t) = \frac{Q_{air}^{max}(t)}{\sum\limits_{i=1}^{q} Q_{air.i}(t)} \times Q_{air.i} \, g30\% \tag{58}$$

4.3.2.2.3. Third rule
If error dynamic is big and sum of level airflow is greater than total airflow,

Then bioreactor receive corresponding percentage of total airflow.

If $V(t)$ is big and $\sum\limits_{i=1}^{q} Q_{air.i}(t) \geq Q_{air}^{max}(t)$

Then

$$Q_{air}^{supervisor}(t) = \frac{Q_{air}^{max}(t)}{\sum\limits_{i=1}^{q} Q_{air.i}(t)} \times Q_{air.i} \, 860\% \tag{59}$$

4.3.2.3. Step 3: Defuzzification

Each of the bioreactors obtain airflow by a fuzzy value.

5. Summary

In this chapter, we considered two different adaptive control. The first adaptive control is applied on WWTP with control input saturation. The second adaptive control descried that how upper level fuzzy control working is based on lower level DMRC applied on the coupling bioreactors of WWTP.

Author details

Mao Li

Address all correspondence to: limaomxl554@gmail.com

The University of Birmingham, Birmingham, UK

References

[1] Brdys MA, Grochowski M, Gminski T, Konarczak K, Drewa M. Hierarchical predictive control of integrated wastewater treatment system. Control Engineering Practice. 2008;**16** (6):751–767.

[2] Piotrowski R, Brdys MA, Konarczak K, Duzinkiewicz K, Chotkowski W. Hierarchical dissolved oxygen control for activated sludge processes. Control Engineering Practice. 2008;**16**:114–131.

[3] Brdys MA, Diaz-Maiquez. Application of fuzzy model predictive control to the dissolved oxygen concentration tracking in an activated sludge process. In: Proceedings of the 15th IFAC World Congress; 21–26 July; Barcelona.

[4] Brdys MA, Chotkowski W, Duzinkiewicz K, Konarczak K, Piotrowski R. Two-level dissolved oxygen control for activated sludge processes. In: Proceedings of the 15th IFAC World Congress; 21–26 July 2002; Barcelona.

[5] Olsson G, Newell R. Wastewater Treatment System. Modelling, Diagnosis and Control. London, UK: IWA Publishing; 1999.

[6] Zubowicz T, Brdys MA, Piotrowski R. Intelligent PI controller and its application to dissolved oxygen tracking problem. Journal of Automation Mobile Robotics & Intelligent Systems. 2010;**4**(3):16–24.

[7] Li M, Brdys MA. Direct model reference adaptive control of nutrient removal at activated sludge wastewater treatment plant. In: The 20th International Conference on Methods and Models in Automation and Robotics; 24–27 August 2015; Miedzyzdroje, Poland.

[8] Duzinkiewicz K, Brdys MA, Kurek W, Piotrowski R. Genetic hybrid predictive controller for optimized dissolved-oxygen tracking at lower control level. IEEE Transaction on Control System Technology. 2009;**17**:1183–1192.

4

Non-Fragile Guaranteed Cost Control of Nonlinear Systems with Different State and Input Delays Based on T-S Fuzzy Local Bilinear Models

Junmin Li, Jinsha Li and Ruirui Duan

Abstract

This paper focuses on the non-fragile guaranteed cost control problem for a class of Takagi-Sugeno (T-S) fuzzy time-varying delay systems with local bilinear models and different state and input delays. A non-fragile guaranteed cost state-feedback controller is designed such that the closed-loop T-S fuzzy local bilinear control system is delay-dependent asymptotically stable, and the closed-loop fuzzy system performance is constrained to a certain upper bound when the additive controller gain perturbations exist. By employing the linear matrix inequality (LMI) technique, sufficient conditions are established for the existence of desired non-fragile guaranteed cost controllers. The simulation examples show that the proposed approach is effective and feasible.

Keywords: fuzzy control, non-fragile guaranteed cost control, delay-dependent, linear matrix inequality (LMI), T-S fuzzy bilinear model

1. Introduction

In recent years, T-S (Takagi-Sugeno) model-based fuzzy control has attracted wide attention, essentially because the fuzzy model is an effective and flexible tool for the control of nonlinear systems [1–8]. Through the application of sector nonlinearity approach, local approximation in fuzzy partition spaces or other different approximation methods, T-S fuzzy models will be used to approximate or exactly represent a nonlinear system in a compact set of state variables. The merit of the model is that the consequent part of a fuzzy rule is a linear dynamic subsystem, which makes it possible to apply the classical and mature linear systems theory to nonlinear systems. Further, by using the fuzzy inference method, the overall fuzzy model will be obtained. A fuzzy controller is designed via the method titled 'parallel distributed compensation (PDC)' [3–6], the main idea of which is that for each linear subsystem, the corresponding linear controller is carried out. Finally, the overall nonlinear controller is obtained via fuzzy blending of each individual linear controller. Based on the above content, T-S fuzzy model has been widely studied, and many results have been obtained [1–8]. In practical applications, time delay often occurs in many dynamic systems such as biological systems, network systems, etc. It is shown that the existence of delays usually becomes the source of instability and deteriorating performance of systems [3–8]. In general, when delay-dependent results were calculated, the emergence of the inner product between two vectors often makes the process of calculation more complicated. In order to avoid it, some model transformations were utilized in many papers, unfortunately, which will arouse the generation of an inequality, resulting in possible conservatism. On the other hand, due to the influence of many factors such as finite word length, truncation errors in numerical computation and electronic component parameter change, the parameters of the controller in a certain degree will change, which lead to imprecision in controller implementation. In this case, some small perturbations of the controllers' coefficients will make the designed controllers sensitive, even worse, destabilize the closed-loop control system [9]. So the problem of non-fragile control has been important issues. Recently, the research of non-fragile control has been paid much attention, and a series of productions have been obtained [10–13].

As we know, bilinear models have been widely used in many physical systems, biotechnology, socioeconomics and dynamical processes in other engineering fields [14, 15]. Bilinear model is a special nonlinear model, the nonlinear part of which consists of the bilinear function of the state and input. Compared with a linear model, the bilinear models have two main advantages. One is that the bilinear model can better approximate a nonlinear system. Another is that because of nonlinearity of it, many real physical processes may be appropriately modeled as bilinear systems. A famous example of a bilinear system is the population of biological species, which can be showed by $\frac{d\theta}{dt} = \theta v$. In this equation, v is the birth rate minus death rate, and θ denotes the population. Obviously, the equation cannot be approximated by a linear model [14].

Most of the existing results focus on the stability analysis and synthesis based on T-S fuzzy model with linear local model. However, when a nonlinear system has of complex nonlinearities, the constructed T-S model will consist of a number of fuzzy local models. This will lead to very heavy computational burden. According to the advantages of bilinear systems and T-S fuzzy control, so many researchers paid their attentions to the T-S fuzzy models with bilinear rule consequence [16–18]. From these papers, it is evident that the T-S fuzzy bilinear model may be suitable for some classes of nonlinear plants. In Ref. [16], a nonlinear system was transformed into a bilinear model via Taylor's series expansion, and the stability of T-S fuzzy bilinear model was studied. Moreover, the result was stretched into the complex fuzzy system with state time delay [17]. Ref. [18] presented robust stabilization for a class of discrete-time fuzzy bilinear system. Very recently, a class of nonlinear systems is described by T-S fuzzy models with nonlinear local models in Ref. [19], and in this paper, the scholars put forward a new fuzzy control scheme with local nonlinear feedbacks, the advantage of which over the existing methods is that a fewer fuzzy rules and less computational burden. The non-fragile guaranteed cost controller was designed for a class of T-S discrete-time fuzzy bilinear systems in Ref. [20]. However, in Refs. [19, 20], the time-delay effects on the system is not considered. Ref. [17] is only considered the fuzzy system with the delay in the state and the derivatives of time-delay, $\dot{d}(t) < 1$ is required. Refs. [21–23] dealt with the uncertain fuzzy systems with time-delay in different ways. It should be pointed out that all the aforementioned works did not take into account the effect of the control input delays on the systems. The results therein are not applicable to systems with input delay. Recently, some controller design approaches have been presented for systems with input delay, see [2, 3, 4, 18, 24–32] for fuzzy T-S systems and [8, 15, 33, 34] for non-fuzzy systems and the references therein. All of these results are required to know the exact delay values in the implementation. T-S fuzzy stochastic systems with state time-vary or distributed delays were studied in Refs. [35–39]. The researches of fractional order T-S fuzzy systems on robust stability, stability analysis about "$0 < \alpha < 1$", and decentralized stabilization in multiple time delays were presented in Refs. [40–42], respectively. For different delay types, the corresponding adaptive fuzzy controls for nonlinear systems were proposed in Refs. [33, 43, 44]. In Refs. [45, 46], to achieve small control amplitude, a new T-S fuzzy hyperbolic model was developed, moreover, Ref. [46] considered the input delay of the novel model. In Ref. [25, 47], the problems of observer-based fuzzy control design for T-S fuzzy systems were concerned.

So far, the problem of non-fragile guaranteed cost control for fuzzy system with local bilinear model with different time-varying state and input delays has not been discussed.

In this paper, the problem of delay-dependent non-fragile guaranteed cost control is studied for the fuzzy time-varying delay systems with local bilinear model and different state and input delays. Based on the PDC scheme, new delay-dependent stabilization conditions for the closed-loop fuzzy systems are derived. No model transformation is involved in the derivation. The merit of the proposed conditions lies in its reduced conservatism, which is achieved by circumventing the utilization of some bounding inequalities for the cross-product between two vectors as in Ref. [17]. The three main contributions of this paper are the following: (1) a non-fragile guaranteed cost controller is presented for the fuzzy system with time-varying delay in both state and input; (2) some free-weighting matrices are introduced in the derivation process, where the constraint of the derivatives of time-delay, $\dot{d}(t) < 1$ and $\dot{h}(t) < 1$, is eliminated; and (3) the delay-dependent stability conditions for the fuzzy system are described by LMIs. Finally, simulation examples are given to illustrate the effectiveness of the obtained results.

The paper is organized as follows. Section 2 introduces the fuzzy delay system with local bilinear model, and non-fragile controller law for such system is designed based on the parallel distributed compensation approach in Section 3. Results of non-fragile guaranteed cost control are given in Section 4. Two simulation examples are used to illustrate the effectiveness of the proposed method in Section 5, which is followed by conclusions in Section 6.

Notation: Throughout this paper, the notation $P > 0(P \geq 0)$ stands for P being real symmetric and positive definite (or positive semi-definite). In symmetric block matrices, the asterisk (*) refers to a term that is induced by symmetry, and diag{....} denotes a block-diagonal matrix.

The superscript T means matrix transposition. The notion $\sum_{i,j=1}^{s}$ is an abbreviation of $\sum_{i=1}^{s}\sum_{j=1}^{s}$. Matrices, if the dimensions are not explicitly stated, are assumed to have compatible dimensions for algebraic operations.

2. System description and assumptions

In this section, we introduce the T-S fuzzy time-delay system with local bilinear model. The ith rule of the fuzzy system is represented by the following form:

Plant Rule i :

IF $\vartheta_1(t)$ is F_{i1} and ... and $\vartheta_v(t)$ is F_{iv}, THEN

$$\dot{x}(t) = A_i x(t) + A_{di}x(t-d(t)) + B_i u(t) + B_{hi}u(t-h(t)) + N_i x(t)u(t) + N_{di}x(t-d(t))u(t-h(t)) \tag{1}$$

$$x(t) = \phi(t), \quad t \in [-\tau_1, 0], \ i = 1, 2, ..., s$$

where F_{ij} is the fuzzy set, s is the number of fuzzy rules, $x(t) \in R^n$ is the state vector, and $u(t) \in R$ is the control input, $\vartheta_1(t)$, $\vartheta_2(t),...,\vartheta_v(t)$ are the premise variables. It is assumed that the premise variables do not depend on the input $u(t)$. $A_i, A_{di}, N_i, N_{di} \in R^{n \times n}$, $B_i, B_{hi} \in R^{n \times 1}$ denote the system matrices with appropriate dimensions. $d(t)$ is a time-varying differentiable function that satisfies $0 \le d(t) \le \tau_1$, $0 \le h(t) \le \tau_2$, where τ_1, τ_2 are real positive constants as the upper bound of the time-varying delay. It is also assumed that $\dot{d}(t) \le \sigma_1$, $\dot{h}(t) \le \sigma_2$, and σ_1, σ_2 are known constants. The initial conditions $\phi(t)$, $\varphi(t)$ are continuous functions of t, $t \in [-\tau, \ 0]$, $\tau = \min(\tau_1, \tau_2)$.

Remark 1: The fuzzy system with time-varying state and input delays will be investigated in this paper, which is different from the system in Ref. [17]. In Ref. [17], only state time-varying delay is considered. And also, here, we assume that the derivative of time-varying delay is less than or equal to a known constant that may be greater than 1; the assumption on time-varying delay in Ref. [17] is relaxed.

By using singleton fuzzifier, product inferred and weighted defuzzifier, the fuzzy system can be expressed by the following globe model:

$$\dot{x}(t) = \sum_{i=1}^{s} h_i(\vartheta(t))[A_i x(t) + A_{di}x(t-d(t)) + B_i u(t) + B_{hi}u(t-h(t)) + N_i x(t)u(t) \tag{2}$$

$$+ N_{di}x(t-d(t))u(t-h(t))]$$

where

$h_i(\vartheta(t)) = \omega_i(\vartheta(t))/\sum_{i=1}^{s}\omega_i(\vartheta(t))$, $\omega_i(\vartheta(t)) = \prod_{j=1}^{v}\mu_{ij}(\vartheta(t))$, $\mu_{ij}(\vartheta(t))$ is the grade of membership of $\vartheta_i(t)$ in F_{ij}. In this paper, it is assumed that $\omega_i(\vartheta(t)) \ge 0$, $\sum_{i=1}^{s}\omega_i(\vartheta(t)) > 0$ for all t. Then, we have the following conditions $h_i(\vartheta(t)) \ge 0$, $\sum_{i=1}^{s}h_i(\vartheta(t)) = 1$ for all t. In the consequent, we use abbreviation $h_i, h_{hi}, x_d(t), u_d(t), x_h(t), u_h(t)$, to replace $h_i(\vartheta(t)), h_i(\vartheta(t-h(t))), x(t-d(t)), u(t-d(t)), x(t-h(t)), u(t-h(t))$, respectively, for convenience.

The objective of this paper is to design a state-feedback non-fragile guaranteed cost control law for the fuzzy system (2).

3. Non-fragile guaranteed cost controller design

Extending the design concept in Ref. [17], we give the following non-fragile fuzzy control law:

$$IF\ \vartheta_1(t)\ is\ F_1^i\ and\ ...\ and\ \vartheta_v(t)\ is\ F_v^i$$

$$THEN\ u(t) = \frac{\rho(K_i + \Delta K_i)x(t)}{\sqrt{1 + x^T(K_i + \Delta K_i)^T(K_i + \Delta K_i)x}} = \rho\sin\theta_i = \rho\cos\theta_i(K_i + \Delta K_i)x(t) \tag{3}$$

where $\rho > 0$ is a scalar to be assigned, and $K_i \in R^{l \times n}$ is a local controller gain to be determined. ΔK_i represents the additive controller gain perturbations of the form $\Delta K_i = H_i F_i(t)E_{ki}$ with H_i and E_{ki} being known constant matrices, and $F_i(t)$ the uncertain parameter matrix satisfying $F_i^T(t)F_i(t) \leq I$. $\sin\theta_i = \frac{\overline{K}_i x(t)}{\sqrt{1 + x^T \overline{K}_i^T \overline{K}_i x}}$, $\cos\theta_i = \frac{1}{\sqrt{1 + x^T \overline{K}_i^T \overline{K}_i x}}$, $\theta_i \in [-\frac{\pi}{2}, \frac{\pi}{2}]$, $\overline{K}_i = K_i + \Delta K_i(t) = K_i + H_i F_i(t)E_{ki}$.

The overall fuzzy control law can be represented by

$$u(t) = \sum_{i=1}^{s} h_i \frac{\rho \overline{K}_i x(t)}{\sqrt{1 + x^T \overline{K}_i^T \overline{K}_i x}} = \sum_{i=1}^{s} h_i \rho \sin\theta_i = \sum_{i=1}^{s} h_i \rho \cos\theta_i \overline{K}_i x(t) \tag{4}$$

When there exists an input delay $h(t)$, we have that

$$u_h(t) = \sum_{l=1}^{s} h_{hl} \rho \sin\varphi_l = \sum_{l=1}^{s} h_{hl} \rho \cos\varphi_l \tilde{K}_l x_h(t) \tag{5}$$

where $\sin\varphi_l = \frac{\tilde{K}_l x_h(t)}{\sqrt{1 + x_h^T \tilde{K}_l^T \tilde{K}_l x_h}}$, $\cos\varphi_l = \frac{1}{\sqrt{1 + x_h^T \tilde{K}_l^T \tilde{K}_l x_h}}$, $\varphi_l \in [-\frac{\pi}{2}, \frac{\pi}{2}]$, $\tilde{K}_l = K_l + \Delta K_l(t - h(t)) = K_l + H_l F_l(t - h(t))E_{kl}$.

So, it is natural and necessary to make an assumption that the functions h_i are well defined all $t \in [-\tau_2, 0]$, and satisfy the following properties:

$h_i(\vartheta(t - h(t))) \geq 0$, for $i = 1, 2, ..., s$, and $\sum_{i=1}^{s} h_i(\vartheta(t - h(t))) = 1$.

By substituting Eq. (5) into Eq. (2), the closed-loop system can be given by

$$\dot{x}(t) = \sum_{i,j,l=1}^{s} h_i h_j h_{hl}(\Lambda_{ij}x(t) + \Lambda_{dij}x_d(t) + \Lambda_{hil}x_h(t)) \tag{6}$$

where

$\Lambda_{ij} = A_i + \rho\sin\theta_j N_i + \rho\cos\theta_j B_i \overline{K}_j$, $\Lambda_{dil} = A_{di} + \rho\sin\varphi_l N_{di}$, $\Lambda_{hil} = \rho\cos\varphi_l B_{hi}\tilde{K}_l$.

Given positive-definite symmetric matrices $S \in R^{n \times n}$ and $W \in R$, we take the cost function

$$J = \int_0^\infty [x^T(t)Sx(t) + u^T(t)Wu(t)]dt \tag{7}$$

Definition 1. The fuzzy non-fragile control law $u(t)$ is said to be non-fragile guaranteed cost if for the system (2), there exist control laws (4) and (5) and a scalar J_0 such that the closed-loop system (6) is asymptotically stable and the closed-loop value of the cost function (7) satisfies $J \leq J_0$.

4. Analysis of stability for the closed-loop system

Firstly, the following lemmas are presented which will be used in the paper.

Lemma 1 [20]: *Given any matrices M and N with appropriate dimensions such that $\varepsilon > 0$, we have $M^T N + N^T M \leq \varepsilon M^T M + \varepsilon^{-1} N^T N$.*

Lemma 2 [21]: *Given constant matrices G, E and a symmetric constant matrix S of appropriate dimensions. The inequality $S + GFE + E^T F^T G^T < 0$ holds, where $F(t)$ satisfies $F^T(t) F(t) \leq I$ if and only if, for some $\varepsilon > 0$, $S + \varepsilon GG^T + \varepsilon^{-1}E^T E < 0$.*

The following theorem gives the sufficient conditions for the existence of the non-fragile guaranteed cost controller for system (6) with additive controller gain perturbations.

Theorem 1. *Consider system (6) associated with cost function (7). For given scalars $\rho > 0$, $\tau_1 > 0$, $\tau_2 > 0$, $\sigma1 > 0$, $\sigma_2 > 0$, if there exist matrices $P > 0$, $Q_1 > 0$, $Q2 > 0$, $R_1 > 0$, $R_2 > 0$, K_i, $i = 1, 2,..., s$, X_1, X_2, X_3, X_4, Y_1, Y_2, Y_3, Y_4, and scalar $\varepsilon > 0$ satisfying the inequalities (8), the system (6) is asymptotically stable and the control law (5) is a fuzzy non-fragile guaranteed cost control law, moreover,*

$$J \leq x^T(0)Px(0) + \int_{-d(0)}^0 x^T(s)Q_1 x(s)ds + \int_{-\tau_1}^0 \int_\theta^0 \dot{x}^T(s)R_1\dot{x}(s)dsd\theta$$

$$+ \int_{-h(0)}^0 x^T(s)Q_2 x(s)ds + \int_{-\tau_2}^0 \int_\theta^0 \dot{x}^T(s)R_2\dot{x}(s)dsd\theta = J_0$$

$$\begin{bmatrix} T_{ijl} & * & * \\ \tau_1 X^T & -\tau_1 R_1 & * \\ \tau_2 Z^T & 0 & -\tau_2 R_2 \end{bmatrix} < 0, \quad i,j,l = 1,2,...,s \tag{8}$$

where $T_{ijl} = \begin{bmatrix} T_{11,ij} & * & * & * \\ T_{21,i} & T_{22,i} & * & * \\ T_{31,i} & T_{32,ij} & T_{33,il} & * \\ T_{41,i} & T_{42,i} & T_{43} & T_{44} \end{bmatrix},$

$T_{11,ij} = Q_1 + Q_2 + X_1 + X_1^T + Y_1A_i + A_i^T Y_1^T + S + 2\varepsilon\rho^2 Y_1 Y_1{}^T + 4\varepsilon^{-1}(N_i^T N_i + (B_i\overline{K}_j)^T(B_i\overline{K}_j))$

$\qquad + Z_1^T + Z_1 + \rho^2\overline{K}_i^T W\overline{K}_i,$

$T_{21,i} = -X_1^T + X_2 + Z_2 + Y_2A_i + A_{di}^T Y_1^T, \qquad T_{31,i} = Z_3 - Z_1 + X_3 + Y_3A_i,$

$T_{22,ij} = -(1-\sigma_1)Q_1 - X_2 - X_2^T + Y_2A_{di} + A_{di}^T Y_2^T + 2\varepsilon\rho^2 Y_2 Y_2{}^T + 4\varepsilon^{-1}N_{di}^T N_{di},$

$T_{32,i} = -X_3 + Y_3A_{di} - Z_2^T, \qquad T_{33,il} = -(1-\sigma_2)Q_2 - Z_3 - Z_3^T + 2\varepsilon\rho^2 Y_3 Y_3{}^T + 4\varepsilon^{-1}(B_{hi}\tilde{K}_l)^T B_{hi}\tilde{K}_l$

$T_{41,i} = P + X_4 + Z_4 + Y_4A_i - Y_1^T, T_{42,i} = -X_4 + Y_4A_i - Y_2^T,$

$T_{43} = -Z_4 - Y_3^T, T_{44} = \tau_1 R_1 + \tau_2 R_2 - Y_4 - Y_4{}^T + 2\varepsilon\rho^2 Y_4 Y_4^T.$

Proof: Take a Lyapunov function candidate as

$$V(x(t), t) = x^T(t)Px(t) + \int_{t-d(t)}^t x^T(s)Q_1x(s)ds + \int_{-\tau_1}^0 \int_{t+\theta}^t \dot{x}^T(s)R_1\dot{x}(s)dsd\theta$$
$$+ \int_{t-h(t)}^t x^T(s)Q_2x(s)ds + \int_{-\tau_2}^0 \int_{t+\theta}^t \dot{x}^T(s)R_2\dot{x}(s)dsd\theta \qquad (9)$$

The time derivatives of $V(x(t),t)$, along the trajectory of the system (6), are given by

$$\dot{V}(x(t), t) = 2x^T(t)P\dot{x}(t) + x^T(t)(Q_1 + Q_2)x(t)$$
$$-(1-\dot{d}(t))x_d^T(t)Q_1x_d(t) + \dot{x}^T(t)(\tau_1R_1 + \tau_2R_2)\dot{x}(t) \qquad (10)$$
$$-\int_{t-\tau_1}^t \dot{x}^T(s)R_1\dot{x}(s)ds - (1-\dot{h}(t))x_h^T(t)Q_2x_h(t) - \int_{t-\tau_2}^t \dot{x}^T(s)R_2\dot{x}(s)ds$$

Define the free-weighting matrices as $X = [X_1^T \ \ X_2^T \ \ X_3^T \ \ X_4^T]^T$, $Y = [Y_1^T \ \ Y_2^T \ \ Y_3^T \ \ Y_4^T]^T$, $Z = [Z_1^T \ \ Z_2^T \ \ Z_3^T \ \ Z_4^T]^T$, where $X_k \in R^{n \times n}$, $Y_k \in R^{n \times n}$, $Z_k \in R^{n \times n}$, k = 1, 2, 3, 4 will be determined later.

Using the Leibniz-Newton formula and system equation (6), we have the following identical equations:

$$[x^T(t)X_1 + x_d^T(t)X_2 + x_h^T(t)X_3 + \dot{x}^T(t)X_4][x(t) - x_d(t) - \int_{t-d(t)}^t \dot{x}(s)ds] \equiv 0,$$

$$[x^T(t)Z_1 + x_d^T(t)Z_2 + x_h^T(t)Z_3 + \dot{x}^T(t)Z_4][x(t) - x_h(t) - \int_{t-h(t)}^t \dot{x}(s)ds] \equiv 0 \qquad (11)$$

$$\sum_{i,j=1}^s h_ih_jh_l[x^T(t)Y_1 + x_d^T(t)Y_2 + x_h^T(t)Y_4 + \dot{x}^T(t)Y_4][\Lambda_{ij}x(t) + \Lambda_{dil}x_d(t) + \Lambda_{hil}x_h(t) - \dot{x}(t)] \equiv 0$$

Then, substituting Eq. (12) into Eq. (11) yields

$$\dot{V}(x(t),t) = 2x^{\mathrm{T}}(t)P\dot{x}(t) + x^{\mathrm{T}}(t)(Q_1 + Q_2)x(t) + \dot{x}^{\mathrm{T}}(t)(\tau_1 R_1 + \tau_2 R_2)\dot{x}(t)$$

$$-(1 - \dot{d}(t))x_d^{\mathrm{T}}(t)Q_1 x_d(t) - (1 - \dot{h}(t))x_h^{\mathrm{T}}(t)Q_2 x_h(t)$$

$$-\int_{t-\tau_1}^t \dot{x}^{\mathrm{T}}(s)R_1\dot{x}(s)ds + 2\eta^{\mathrm{T}}(t)X[x(t) - x_d(t) - \int_{t-d(t)}^t \dot{x}(s)ds]$$

$$-\int_{t-\tau_2}^t \dot{x}^{\mathrm{T}}(s)R_2\dot{x}(s)ds + 2\eta^{\mathrm{T}}(t)Z[x(t) - x_h(t) - \int_{t-h(t)}^t \dot{x}(s)ds]$$

$$+ 2\eta^{\mathrm{T}}(t)Y\sum_{i,j,l=1}^s h_i h_j h_{hl}[\Lambda_{ij}x(t) + \Lambda_{dil}x_d(t) + \Lambda_{hil}x_h(t) - \dot{x}(t)]$$

$$\leq 2x^{\mathrm{T}}(t)P\dot{x}(t) + x^{\mathrm{T}}(t)(Q_1 + Q_2)x(t) + \dot{x}^{\mathrm{T}}(t)(\tau_1 R_1 + \tau_2 R_2)\dot{x}(t)$$

$$-(1 - \sigma_1)x_d^{\mathrm{T}}(t)Q_1 x_d(t) - (1 - \sigma_2)x_h^{\mathrm{T}}(t)Q_2 x_h(t)$$

$$-\int_{t-d(t)}^t \dot{x}^{\mathrm{T}}(s)R_1(s)\dot{x}(s)ds + 2\eta^{\mathrm{T}}(t)X[x(t) - x_d(t) - \int_{t-d(t)}^t \dot{x}(s)ds]$$

$$-\int_{t-h(t)}^t \dot{x}^{\mathrm{T}}(s)R_2(s)\dot{x}(s)ds + 2\eta^{\mathrm{T}}(t)Z[x(t) - x_h(t) - \int_{t-h(t)}^t \dot{x}(s)ds]$$

$$+ 2\eta^{\mathrm{T}}(t)Y\sum_{i,j,l=1}^s h_i h_j h_{hl}[\Lambda_{ij}x(t) + \Lambda_{dil}x_d(t) + \Lambda_{hil}x_h(t) - \dot{x}(t)] + x^{\mathrm{T}}(t)Sx(t)$$

$$+ \sum_{i,j=1}^s h_i h_j \rho^2 x^{\mathrm{T}}(t)\overline{K}_i^{\mathrm{T}}\cos\theta_i W\overline{K}_j\cos\theta_j x(t) - [x^{\mathrm{T}}(t)Sx(t) + u^{\mathrm{T}}(t)Wu(t)]$$

(12)

where $\eta(t) = [x^{\mathrm{T}}(t),\ x_d^{\mathrm{T}}(t),\ x_h^{\mathrm{T}}(t),\ \dot{x}^{\mathrm{T}}(t)]^{\mathrm{T}}$.

Applying Lemma 1, we have the following inequalities:

$$2x^{\mathrm{T}}(t)Y_1\Lambda_{ij}x(t) \leq 2x^{\mathrm{T}}(t)Y_1 A_i x(t) + \varepsilon\rho^2 x^{\mathrm{T}}(t)Y_1 Y_1^{\mathrm{T}}x(t) + \varepsilon^{-1}x^{\mathrm{T}}(t)(N_i^{\mathrm{T}}N_i + (B_i\overline{K}_j)^{\mathrm{T}}(B_i\overline{K}_j))x(t),$$

$$2x^{\mathrm{T}}(t)Y_1\Lambda_{dil}x_d(t) \leq 2x^{\mathrm{T}}(t)Y_1 A_{di}x_d(t) + \varepsilon\rho^2\sin^2\phi_l x^{\mathrm{T}}(t)Y_1 Y_1^{\mathrm{T}}x(t) + \varepsilon^{-1}x_d^{\mathrm{T}}(t)N_{di}^{\mathrm{T}}N_{di}x_d(t),$$

$$2x^{\mathrm{T}}(t)Y_1\Lambda_{hil}x_h(t) \leq \varepsilon\rho^2\cos^2\phi_l x^{\mathrm{T}}(t)Y_1 Y_1^{\mathrm{T}}x(t) + \varepsilon^{-1}x_h^{\mathrm{T}}(t)(B_{hi}\tilde{K}_l)^{\mathrm{T}}(B_{hi}\tilde{K}_l)x_h(t),$$

$$2x_d^{\mathrm{T}}(t)Y_2\Lambda_{ij}x(t) \leq 2x_d^{\mathrm{T}}(t)Y_2 A_i x(t) + \varepsilon\rho^2 x_d^{\mathrm{T}}(t)Y_2 Y_2^{\mathrm{T}}x_d(t) + \varepsilon^{-1}x^{\mathrm{T}}(t)(N_i^{\mathrm{T}}N_i + (B_i\overline{K}_j)^{\mathrm{T}}(B_i\overline{K}_j))x(t),$$

$$2x^{\mathrm{T}}(t)Y_1\Lambda_{hil}x_h(t) \leq \varepsilon\rho^2\cos^2\phi_l x^{\mathrm{T}}(t)Y_1 Y_1^{\mathrm{T}}x(t) + \varepsilon^{-1}x_h^{\mathrm{T}}(t)(B_{hi}\tilde{K}_l)^{\mathrm{T}}(B_{hi}\tilde{K}_l)x_h(t),$$

$$2x_d^{\mathrm{T}}(t)Y_2\Lambda_{ij}x(t) \leq 2x_d^{\mathrm{T}}(t)Y_2 A_i x(t) + \varepsilon\rho^2 x_d^{\mathrm{T}}(t)Y_2 Y_2^{\mathrm{T}}x_d(t) + \varepsilon^{-1}x^{\mathrm{T}}(t)(N_i^{\mathrm{T}}N_i + (B_i\overline{K}_j)^{\mathrm{T}}(B_i\overline{K}_j))x(t),$$

$$2x_d^{\mathrm{T}}(t)Y_2\Lambda_{dil}x_d(t) \leq 2x_d^{\mathrm{T}}(t)Y_2 A_{di}x_d(t) + \varepsilon\rho^2\sin^2\phi_l x_d^{\mathrm{T}}(t)Y_2 Y_2^{\mathrm{T}}x_d(t) + \varepsilon^{-1}x_d^{\mathrm{T}}(t)N_{di}^{\mathrm{T}}N_{di}x_d(t),$$

$$2x_d^{\mathrm{T}}(t)Y_2\Lambda_{hil}x_h(t) \leq \varepsilon\rho^2\cos^2\phi_l x_d^{\mathrm{T}}(t)Y_2 Y_2^{\mathrm{T}}x_d(t) + \varepsilon^{-1}x_h^{\mathrm{T}}(t)(B_{hi}\tilde{K}_l)^{\mathrm{T}}(B_{hi}\tilde{K}_l)x_h(t),$$

$$2x_h^{\mathrm{T}}(t)Y_3\Lambda_{ij}x(t) \leq 2x_h^{\mathrm{T}}(t)Y_3 A_i x(t) + \varepsilon\rho^2 x_h^{\mathrm{T}}(t)Y_3 Y_3^{\mathrm{T}}x_h(t) + \varepsilon^{-1}x^{\mathrm{T}}(t)(N_i^{\mathrm{T}}N_i + (B_i\overline{K}_j)^{\mathrm{T}}(B_i\overline{K}_j))x(t),$$

$$2x_h^{\mathrm{T}}(t)Y_3\Lambda_{dil}x_d(t) \leq 2x_h^{\mathrm{T}}(t)Y_3 A_{di}x_d(t) + \varepsilon\rho^2\sin^2\phi_l x_h^{\mathrm{T}}(t)Y_3 Y_3^{\mathrm{T}}x_h(t) + \varepsilon^{-1}x_d^{\mathrm{T}}(t)N_{di}^{\mathrm{T}}N_{di}x_d(t),$$

$$2x_h^{\mathrm{T}}(t)Y_3\Lambda_{hil}x_h(t) \leq \varepsilon\rho^2\cos^2\phi_l x_h^{\mathrm{T}}(t)Y_3 Y_3^{\mathrm{T}}x_h(t) + \varepsilon^{-1}x_h^{\mathrm{T}}(t)(B_{hi}\tilde{K}_l)^{\mathrm{T}}(B_{hi}\tilde{K}_l)x_h(t),$$

$$2\dot{x}^{\mathrm{T}}(t)Y_4\Lambda_{ij}x(t) \leq 2\dot{x}^{\mathrm{T}}(t)Y_4 A_i x(t) + \varepsilon\rho^2\dot{x}^{\mathrm{T}}(t)Y_4 Y_4^{\mathrm{T}}\dot{x}(t) + \varepsilon^{-1}x^{\mathrm{T}}(t)(N_i^{\mathrm{T}}N_i + (B_i\overline{K}_j)^{\mathrm{T}}(B_i\overline{K}_j))x(t),$$

$$2\dot{x}^{\mathrm{T}}(t)Y_4\Lambda_{dil}x_d(t) \leq 2\dot{x}^{\mathrm{T}}(t)Y_4 A_{di}x_d(t) + \varepsilon\rho^2\dot{x}^{\mathrm{T}}(t)Y_4 Y_4^{\mathrm{T}}\dot{x}(t) + \varepsilon^{-1}x_d^{\mathrm{T}}(t)N_{di}^{\mathrm{T}}N_{di}x_d(t),$$

$$2\dot{x}^{\mathrm{T}}(t)Y_4\Lambda_{hil}x_h(t) \leq \varepsilon\rho^2\cos^2\phi_l \dot{x}^{\mathrm{T}}(t)Y_4 Y_4^{\mathrm{T}}\dot{x}(t) + \varepsilon^{-1}x_h^{\mathrm{T}}(t)(B_{hi}\tilde{K}_l)^{\mathrm{T}}(B_{hi}\tilde{K}_l)x_h(t)$$

(13)

Substituting Eq. (13) into Eq. (12) results in

$$\dot{V}(x(t),t) \le \sum_{i,j,l=1}^{s} h_i h_j h_{hl} \eta^{\mathrm{T}}(t) T_{ij} \eta(t) - \int_{t-d(t)}^{t} \dot{x}^{\mathrm{T}}(s) R_1 \dot{x}(s) ds - \int_{t-h(t)}^{t} \dot{x}^{\mathrm{T}}(s) R_2 \dot{x}(s) ds$$

$$-2\eta^{\mathrm{T}}(t) X \int_{t-d(t)}^{t} \dot{x}(s) ds - 2\eta^{\mathrm{T}}(t) Z \int_{t-h(t)}^{t} \dot{x}(s) ds - [x^{\mathrm{T}}(t) S x(t) + u^{\mathrm{T}}(t) W u(t)]$$

$$\le \sum_{i,j,l=1}^{s} h_i h_j h_{hl} \eta^{\mathrm{T}}(t) (T_{ijl} + \tau_1 X R_1^{-1} X^{\mathrm{T}} + \tau_2 Z R_2^{-1} Z^{\mathrm{T}}) \eta(t)$$

$$-\int_{t-d(t)}^{t} \left(\eta^{\mathrm{T}}(t) X + \dot{x}^{\mathrm{T}}(s) R_1 \right) R_1^{-1} \left(\eta^{\mathrm{T}}(t) X + \dot{x}^{\mathrm{T}}(s) R_1 \right)^{\mathrm{T}} ds$$

$$-\int_{t-h(t)}^{t} \left(\eta^{\mathrm{T}}(t) Z + \dot{x}^{\mathrm{T}}(s) R_2 \right) R_2^{-1} \left(\eta^{\mathrm{T}}(t) X + \dot{x}^{\mathrm{T}}(s) R_2 \right)^{\mathrm{T}} ds - [x^{\mathrm{T}}(t) S x(t) + u^{\mathrm{T}}(t) W u(t)]$$

$$\le \sum_{i,j,l=1}^{s} h_i h_j h_{hl} \eta^{\mathrm{T}}(t) (\tilde{T}_{ijl} + \tau_1 X R_1^{-1} X^{\mathrm{T}} + \tau_2 Z R_2^{-1} Z^{\mathrm{T}}) \eta(t) - [x^{\mathrm{T}}(t) S x(t) + u^{\mathrm{T}}(t) W u(t)]$$

$$(14)$$

where

$$\tilde{T}_{ijl} = \begin{bmatrix} \tilde{T}_{11,ij} & * & * & * \\ T_{21,i} & T_{22,i} & * & * \\ T_{31,i} & T_{32,ij} & T_{33,il} & * \\ T_{41,i} & T_{42,i} & T_{43} & T_{44} \end{bmatrix}, \quad \tilde{T}_{11,ij} = T_{11,ij} + \rho^2 \overline{K}_i^{\mathrm{T}} \cos\theta_i W \overline{K}_j \cos\theta_j - \rho^2 \overline{K}_i^{\mathrm{T}} W \overline{K}_j.$$

In light of the inequality $\overline{K}_i^{\mathrm{T}} W \overline{K}_j + \overline{K}_j^{\mathrm{T}} W \overline{K}_i \le \overline{K}_i^{\mathrm{T}} W \overline{K}_i + \overline{K}_j^{\mathrm{T}} W \overline{K}_j$, we have

$$\dot{V}(x(t),t) \le \sum_{i,j,l=1}^{s} h_i h_j h_{hl} \eta^{\mathrm{T}}(t) (T_{ijl} + \tau_1 X R_1^{-1} X^{\mathrm{T}} + \tau_2 Z R_2^{-1} Z^{\mathrm{T}}) \eta(t) - [x^{\mathrm{T}}(t) S x(t) + u^{\mathrm{T}}(t) W u(t)] \quad (15)$$

Applying the Schur complement to Eq. (8) yields

$$T_{ii} + + \tau_1 X R_1^{-1} X^{\mathrm{T}} + \tau_2 Z R_2^{-1} Z^{\mathrm{T}} < 0, \; T_{ij} + T_{ji} + 2\tau_1 X R_1^{-1} X^{\mathrm{T}} + 2\tau_2 Z R_2^{-1} Z^{\mathrm{T}} < 0.$$

Therefore, it follows from Eq. (15) that

$$\dot{V}(x(t),t) \le -[x^{\mathrm{T}}(t) S x(t) + u^{\mathrm{T}}(t) W u(t)] < 0 \quad (16)$$

which implies that the system (6) is asymptotically stable.

Integrating Eq. (16) from 0 to T produces

$$\int_0^T [x^{\mathrm{T}}(t) S x(t) + u^{\mathrm{T}}(t) W u(t)] dt \le -V(x(T), T) + V(x(0), 0) < V(x(0), 0)$$

Because of $V(x(t),t) \geq 0$ and $\dot{V}(x(t),t) < 0$, thus $\lim_{T \to \infty} V(x(T),T) = c$, where c is a nonnegative constant. Therefore, the following inequality can be obtained:

$$J \leq x^T(0)Px(0) + \int_{-d(0)}^{0} x^T(s)Q_1 x(s)ds + \int_{-\tau_1}^{0}\int_{\theta}^{0} \dot{x}^T(s)R_1\dot{x}(s)dsd\theta + \int_{-h(0)}^{0} x^T(s)Q_2 x(s)ds$$

$$+ \int_{-\tau_2}^{0}\int_{\theta}^{0} \dot{x}^T(s)R_2\dot{x}(s)dsd\theta = J_0 \tag{17}$$

This completes the proof.

Remark 2: In the derivation of Theorem 1, the free-weighting matrices $X_k \in R^{n \times n}$, $Y_k \in R^{n \times n}$, $k = 1, 2, 3, 4$ are introduced, the purpose of which is to reduce conservatism in the existing delay-dependent stabilization conditions, see Ref. [17].

In the following section, we shall turn the conditions given in Theorem 1 into linear matrix inequalities (LMIs). Under the assumptions that Y_1, Y_2, Y_3, Y_4 are non-singular, we can define the matrix $Y_i^{-T} = \lambda Z$, $i = 1, 2, 3, 4$, $Z = P^{-1}, \lambda > 0$.

Pre- and post-multiply (8) and (9) with $\Theta = diag\{Y_1^{-1}, Y_2^{-1}, Y_3^{-1}, Y_4^{-1}, Y_4^{-1}, Y_4^{-1}\}$ and $\Theta^T = diag\{Y_1^{-T}, Y_2^{-T}, Y_3^{-T}, Y_4^{-T}, Y_4^{-T}, Y_4^{-T}\}$, respectively, and letting $\overline{Q}_1 = Y_1^{-1}Q_1Y_1^{-T}$, $\overline{Q}_2 = Y_1^{-1}Q_2Y_1^{-T}$, $\overline{R}_k = Y_4^{-1}R_kY_4^{-T}, k = 1, 2, \overline{X}_i = Y_i^{-1}X_iY_i^{-T}, \overline{Z}_i = Y_i^{-1}Z_iY_i^{-T}$, $i = 1, 2, 3, 4$, we obtain the following inequality (18), which is equivalent to (8):

$$\begin{bmatrix} \overline{T}_{11,ij} & * & * & * & * & * \\ \overline{T}_{21,i} & \overline{T}_{22,i} & * & * & * & * \\ \overline{T}_{31,i} & \overline{T}_{32,i} & \overline{T}_{33,il} & * & * & * \\ \overline{T}_{41,i} & \overline{T}_{42,i} & \overline{T}_{43} & \overline{T}_{44} & * & * \\ \tau_1 X_1 & \tau_1 X_2 & \tau_1 X_3 & \tau_1 X_4 & -\tau_1\overline{R}_1 & * \\ \tau_2\overline{Z}_1 & \tau_2\overline{Z}_2 & \tau_2\overline{Z}_3 & \tau_2\overline{Z}_4 & 0 & -\tau_2\overline{R}_2 \end{bmatrix} < 0, \quad i,j,l = 1,2,...,s \tag{18}$$

where

$$\overline{T}_{11,ij} = \overline{Q}_1 + \overline{Q}_2 + \overline{X}_1 + \overline{X}_1^T + \lambda A_i Z + \lambda ZA_i^T + \lambda^2 ZSZ + 2\varepsilon\rho^2 I + 4\varepsilon^{-1}\lambda^2 ZN_i^T N_i Z$$
$$+ Z_1 + Z_1^T + 4\varepsilon^{-1}\lambda^2(B_i\overline{K}_j Z)^T(B_i\overline{K}_j Z) + \rho^2\lambda^2 Z\overline{K}_i^T W\overline{K}_i Z,$$

$$\overline{T}_{21,i} = -\overline{X}_1^T + \overline{X}_2 + \overline{Z}_2 + \lambda A_i Z + \lambda ZA_{di}^T, \quad \overline{T}_{31,i} = \overline{Z}_3 - \overline{Z}_1 + \overline{X}_3 + \lambda A_i Z,$$

$$\overline{T}_{41,i} = \lambda^2 Z + \lambda A_i Z - \lambda Z + \overline{X}_4 + \overline{Z}_4,$$

$$\overline{T}_{22,i} = -(1-\sigma_1)\overline{Q}_1 - \overline{X}_2 - \overline{X}_2^T + \lambda A_{di} Z + \lambda ZA_{di}^T + 2\varepsilon\rho^2 I + 4\varepsilon^{-1}\lambda^2 ZN_{di}^T N_{di} Z,$$

$$\overline{T}_{32,i} = -\overline{X}_3 - \overline{Z}_2 + \lambda A_{di} Z - \lambda ZA_{di}^T, \quad \overline{T}_{42,i} = -\overline{X}_4 + \lambda A_i Z - \lambda Z,$$

$$\overline{T}_{33,il} = -(1-\sigma_2)\overline{Q}_2 - \overline{Z}_3 - \overline{Z}_3^T + 4\varepsilon^{-1}\lambda^2(B_{hi}\tilde{K}_l Z)^T B_{hi}\tilde{K}_l Z + 2\varepsilon\rho^2 I,$$

$$\overline{T}_{43} = -\overline{Z}_4 - \lambda Z, \quad \overline{T}_{44} = \tau_1 R_1 + \tau_2 R_2 - \lambda Z - \lambda Z^T + 2\varepsilon\rho^2 I.$$

Applying the Schur complement to Eq. (18) results in

$$\Gamma_{ijl} = \begin{bmatrix} \Phi_{11,i} & * & * \\ \Phi_{21,ij} & \Phi_{22} & * \\ \Phi_{31,il} & 0 & \Phi_{33} \end{bmatrix} < 0, \quad i,j,l = 1,2,\ldots,s \tag{19}$$

where

$$\Phi_{11,i} = \begin{bmatrix} \overline{\overline{T}}_{11,i} & * & * & * & * & * \\ \overline{\overline{T}}_{21,i} & \overline{\overline{T}}_{22,i} & * & * & * & * \\ \overline{\overline{T}}_{31,i} & \overline{\overline{T}}_{32,i} & \overline{\overline{T}}_{33,il} & * & * & * \\ \overline{T}_{41,i} & \overline{T}_{42,i} & \overline{T}_{43} & \overline{T}_{44} & * & * \\ \tau_1 X_1 & \tau_1 X_2 & \tau_1 X_3 & \tau_1 X_4 & -\tau_1 \overline{R}_1 & * \\ \tau_2 \overline{Z}_1 & \tau_2 \overline{Z}_2 & \tau_2 \overline{Z}_3 & \tau_2 \overline{Z}_4 & 0 & -\tau_2 \overline{R}_2 \end{bmatrix}$$

With

$$\overline{\overline{T}}_{11,i} = \overline{Q}_1 + \overline{Q}_2 + \overline{X}_1 + \overline{X}_1^T + \lambda A_i Z + \lambda Z A_i^T + Z_1 + Z_1^T + 2\varepsilon\rho^2 I,$$
$$\overline{\overline{T}}_{22,i} = -(1-\sigma_1)\overline{Q}_1 - \overline{X}_2 - \overline{X}_2^T + \lambda A_{di} Z + \lambda Z A_{di}^T + 2\varepsilon\rho^2 I,$$
$$\overline{\overline{T}}_{33} = -(1-\sigma_2)\overline{Q}_2 - \overline{Z}_3 - \overline{Z}_3^T + 2\varepsilon\rho^2 I.$$

$$\Phi_{21,ij} = \begin{bmatrix} \lambda Z & 0 & 0 & 0 \\ \lambda N_i Z & 0 & 0 & 0 \\ \lambda B_i \overline{K}_j Z & 0 & 0 & 0 \\ \rho\lambda \overline{K}_j Z & 0 & 0 & 0 \end{bmatrix}$$

$$\Phi_{31,il} = \begin{bmatrix} 0 & \lambda B_{hi}\tilde{K}_l Z & 0 & 0 \\ 0 & 0 & \lambda N_{di} Z & 0 \end{bmatrix}$$

$$\Phi_{22} = \begin{bmatrix} -S^{-1} & 0 & 0 & 0 \\ 0 & -\dfrac{\varepsilon}{4}I & 0 & 0 \\ 0 & 0 & -\dfrac{\varepsilon}{4}I & 0 \\ 0 & 0 & 0 & -W^{-1} \end{bmatrix}$$

$$\Phi_{33} = \begin{bmatrix} -\dfrac{\varepsilon}{4}I & 0 \\ 0 & -\dfrac{\varepsilon}{4}I \end{bmatrix}$$

Obviously, the closed-loop fuzzy system (6) is asymptotically stable, if for some scalars $\lambda > 0$, there exist matrices $Z > 0, \overline{Q} > 0, \overline{R} > 0$ and $\overline{X}_1, \overline{X}_2, \overline{X}_3, \overline{K}_i, i = 1, 2, \ldots, s$ satisfying the inequality (19).

Theorem 2. *Consider the system (6) associated with cost function (7). For given scalars $\rho > 0$, $\tau_1 > 0$, $\tau_2 > 0$, $\sigma_1 > 0$, $\sigma_2 > 0$ and $\lambda > 0$, $\delta > 0$, if there exist matrices $Z > 0, \overline{Q}_1 > 0, \overline{R}_1 > 0, \overline{Q}_2 > 0, \overline{R}_2 > 0$ and $\overline{X}_1, \overline{X}_2, \overline{X}_3, \overline{X}_4$, M_i, $i = 1,2,\ldots,s$ and scalar $\varepsilon > 0$ satisfying the following LMI (20), the system (6) is asymptotically stable and the control law (5) is a fuzzy non-fragile guaranteed cost control law*

$$\begin{bmatrix} \Theta_{1,ijl} & * \\ \Theta_{2,ijl} & \Theta_3 \end{bmatrix} < 0, \quad i,j,l = 1,2,\ldots,s \tag{20}$$

Moreover, the feedback gains are given by

$$K_i = M_i Z^{-1}, i = 1, 2, \ldots, s$$

and

$$J \leq x^{\mathrm{T}}(0)Px(0) + \int_{-d(0)}^{0} x^{\mathrm{T}}(s)Q_1 x(s)ds + \int_{-\tau_1}^{0}\int_{\theta}^{0} \dot{x}^{\mathrm{T}}(s)R_1 \dot{x}(s)dsd\theta + \int_{-h(0)}^{0} x^{\mathrm{T}}(s)Q_2 x(s)ds$$

$$+ \int_{-\tau_2}^{0}\int_{\theta}^{0} \dot{x}^{\mathrm{T}}(s)R_2 \dot{x}(s)dsd\theta = J_0$$

where

$$\Theta_{2,ijl} = \begin{bmatrix} \lambda E_{kj}Z & 0 & 0 & 0 & 0 & 0 & 0 & 0 & 0 & 0 & 0 & 0 \\ \lambda E_{ki}Z & 0 & 0 & 0 & 0 & 0 & 0 & 0 & 0 & 0 & 0 & 0 \\ 0 & 0 & \lambda E_{kl}Z & 0 & 0 & 0 & 0 & 0 & 0 & 0 & 0 & 0 \\ 0 & 0 & 0 & 0 & 0 & 0 & 0 & 0 & (B_i H_j)^{\mathrm{T}} & 0 & 0 & 0 \\ 0 & 0 & 0 & 0 & 0 & 0 & 0 & 0 & 0 & \rho H_i^{\mathrm{T}} & 0 & 0 \\ 0 & 0 & 0 & 0 & 0 & 0 & 0 & 0 & 0 & 0 & 0 & (B_{hi}H_l)^{\mathrm{T}} \end{bmatrix},$$

$$\Theta_3 = \mathrm{diag}\{-\delta I,\ -\delta I,\ -\delta I,\ -\delta^{-1}I,\ -\delta^{-1}I,\ -\delta^{-1}I\},$$

$$\Theta_{1,ijl} = \begin{bmatrix} \overline{\overline{T}}_{11,i} & * & * & * & * & * & * & * & * & * & * & * \\ \overline{\overline{T}}_{21,i} & \overline{\overline{T}}_{22,i} & * & * & * & * & * & * & * & * & * & * \\ \overline{T}_{31,i} & \overline{T}_{32,i} & \overline{T}_{33} & * & * & * & * & * & * & * & * & * \\ \overline{T}_{41,i} & \overline{T}_{42,i} & \overline{T}_{43,i} & \overline{T}_{44} & * & * & * & * & * & * & * & * \\ \tau_1\overline{X}_1 & \tau_1\overline{X}_2 & \tau_1\overline{X}_3 & \tau_1\overline{X}_4 & -\tau_1\overline{R}_1 & * & * & * & * & * & * & * \\ \tau_2 Z_1 & \tau_2 Z_2 & \tau_2 Z_3 & \tau_2 Z_4 & 0 & -\tau_2\overline{R}_{21} & * & * & * & * & * & * \\ \lambda Z & 0 & 0 & 0 & 0 & 0 & -S^{-1} & * & * & * & * & * \\ \lambda N_i Z & 0 & 0 & 0 & 0 & 0 & 0 & -\frac{\varepsilon}{4}I & * & * & * & * \\ \lambda B_i M_j & 0 & 0 & 0 & 0 & 0 & 0 & 0 & -\frac{\varepsilon}{4}I & * & * & * \\ \rho\lambda M_i & 0 & 0 & 0 & 0 & 0 & 0 & 0 & 0 & -W^{-1} & * & * \\ 0 & \lambda N_{di}Z & 0 & 0 & 0 & 0 & 0 & 0 & 0 & 0 & -\frac{\varepsilon}{4}I & * \\ 0 & 0 & \lambda B_{hi}M_l & 0 & 0 & 0 & 0 & 0 & 0 & 0 & 0 & -\frac{\varepsilon}{4}I \end{bmatrix}$$

Proof: At first, we prove that the inequality (20) implies the inequality (19). Applying the Schur complement to Eq. (20) results in

$$\Phi_{1,ijl} + \delta \begin{bmatrix} 0 & 0 & 0 \\ 0 & 0 & 0 \\ 0 & 0 & 0 \\ 0 & 0 & 0 \\ 0 & 0 & 0 \\ 0 & 0 & 0 \\ 0 & 0 & 0 \\ 0 & 0 & 0 \\ B_i H_j & 0 & 0 \\ 0 & \rho H_i & 0 \\ 0 & 0 & 0 \\ 0 & 0 & B_{hi}H_l \end{bmatrix} \begin{bmatrix} 0 & 0 & 0 & 0 & 0 & 0 & 0 & 0 & (B_i H_j)^{\mathrm{T}} & 0 & 0 & 0 \\ 0 & 0 & 0 & 0 & 0 & 0 & 0 & 0 & 0 & \rho H_i^{\mathrm{T}} & 0 & 0 \\ 0 & 0 & 0 & 0 & 0 & 0 & 0 & 0 & 0 & 0 & 0 & (B_{hi}H_i)^{\mathrm{T}} \end{bmatrix}$$

$$
+\delta^{-1}
\begin{bmatrix}
(\lambda E_{kj}Z)^{\mathrm{T}} & (\lambda E_{ki}Z)^{\mathrm{T}} & 0 \\
0 & 0 & 0 \\
0 & 0 & (\lambda E_{kl}Z)^{\mathrm{T}} \\
0 & 0 & 0 \\
0 & 0 & 0 \\
0 & 0 & 0 \\
0 & 0 & 0 \\
0 & 0 & 0 \\
0 & 0 & 0 \\
0 & 0 & 0 \\
0 & 0 & 0 \\
0 & 0 & 0
\end{bmatrix}
\begin{bmatrix}
\lambda E_{kj}Z & 0 & 0 & 0 & 0 & 0 & 0 & 0 & 0 & 0 & 0 & 0 \\
\lambda E_{ki}Z & 0 & 0 & 0 & 0 & 0 & 0 & 0 & 0 & 0 & 0 & 0 \\
0 & 0 & \lambda E_{kl}Z & 0 & 0 & 0 & 0 & 0 & 0 & 0 & 0 & 0
\end{bmatrix} < 0
$$

$$(21)$$

Using Lemma 2 and noting $M_i = K_i Z$, by the condition (21), the following inequality holds:

$$
\Phi_{1,\,ijl} +
\begin{bmatrix}
0 & * & * & * & * & * & * & * & * & * & * & * \\
0 & 0 & * & * & * & * & * & * & * & * & * & * \\
0 & 0 & 0 & * & * & * & * & * & * & * & * & * \\
0 & 0 & 0 & 0 & * & * & * & * & * & * & * & * \\
0 & 0 & 0 & 0 & 0 & * & * & * & * & * & * & * \\
0 & 0 & 0 & 0 & 0 & 0 & * & * & * & * & * & * \\
0 & 0 & 0 & 0 & 0 & 0 & * & * & * & * & * & * \\
0 & 0 & 0 & 0 & 0 & 0 & 0 & * & * & * & * & * \\
\lambda B_i \Delta\overline{K}_j Z & 0 & 0 & 0 & 0 & 0 & 0 & 0 & * & * & * \\
\rho\lambda \Delta\overline{K}_i Z & 0 & 0 & 0 & 0 & 0 & 0 & 0 & 0 & * & * \\
0 & 0 & 0 & 0 & 0 & 0 & 0 & 0 & 0 & 0 & * \\
0 & 0 & \lambda B_{hi} \Delta\tilde{K}_i Z & 0 & 0 & 0 & 0 & 0 & 0 & 0 & 0
\end{bmatrix} < 0
\qquad (22)
$$

where $\Delta\tilde{K}_i = \Delta K_i(t - d(t))$.

Therefore, it follows from Theorem 1 that the system (6) is asymptotically stable and the control law (5) is a fuzzy non-fragile guaranteed cost control law. Thus, we complete the proof.

Now consider the cost bound of

$$
J \le x^{\mathrm{T}}(0)Px(0) + \int_{-d(0)}^{0} x^{\mathrm{T}}(s)Q_1 x(s)ds + \int_{-\tau_1}^{0}\int_{\theta}^{0} \dot{x}^{\mathrm{T}}(s)R_1\dot{x}(s)dsd\theta + \int_{-h(0)}^{0} x^{\mathrm{T}}(s)Q_2 x(s)ds
$$

$$
+ \int_{-\tau_2}^{0}\int_{\theta}^{0} \dot{x}^{\mathrm{T}}(s)R_2\dot{x}(s)dsd\theta = J_0
$$

Similar to Ref. [23], we supposed that there exist positive scalars $\alpha_1, \alpha_2, \alpha_3, \alpha_4, \alpha_5$, such that $Z^{-1} \le \alpha_1 I, \frac{1}{\lambda^2}P\overline{Q}_1 P \le \alpha_2 I, \frac{1}{\lambda^2}P\overline{Q}_2 P \le \alpha_3 I, \frac{1}{\lambda^2}P\overline{R}_1 P \le \alpha_4 I, \frac{1}{\lambda^2}P\overline{R}_2 P \le \alpha_5 I.$

Then, define $S_{Q1}=\overline{Q}_1^{-1}, S_{Q2}=\overline{Q}_2^{-1}, S_{R1}=\overline{R}_1^{-1}, S_{R2}=\overline{R}_2^{-1}$, by Schur complement lemma, we have the following inequalities:

$$
\begin{bmatrix} -\alpha_1 I & I \\ I & -Z \end{bmatrix} \le 0, \quad \begin{bmatrix} -\alpha_2 I & \frac{1}{\lambda}P \\ \frac{1}{\lambda}P & S_{Q1} \end{bmatrix} \le 0, \quad \begin{bmatrix} -\alpha_3 I & \frac{1}{\lambda}P \\ \frac{1}{\lambda}P & S_{Q2} \end{bmatrix} \le 0, \quad \begin{bmatrix} -\alpha_4 I & \frac{1}{\lambda}P \\ \frac{1}{\lambda}P & S_{R1} \end{bmatrix} \le 0,
$$

$$
\begin{bmatrix} -\alpha_5 I & \frac{1}{\lambda}P \\ \frac{1}{\lambda}P & S_{R2} \end{bmatrix} \le 0, \quad \begin{bmatrix} Z & I \\ I & Z \end{bmatrix} \ge 0, \quad \begin{bmatrix} S_{Q1} & I \\ I & \overline{Q}_1 \end{bmatrix} \ge 0, \quad \begin{bmatrix} S_{Q2} & I \\ I & \overline{Q}_2 \end{bmatrix} \ge 0, \tag{23}
$$

$$
\begin{bmatrix} S_{R1} & I \\ I & \overline{R}_1 \end{bmatrix} \ge 0, \quad \begin{bmatrix} S_{R2} & I \\ I & \overline{R}_2 \end{bmatrix} \ge 0,
$$

Using the idea of the cone complement linear algorithm in Ref. [24], we can obtain the solution of the minimization problem of upper bound of the value of the cost function as follows:

$$
\text{minimize}\{trace(PZ + S_{Q1}\overline{Q}_1 + S_{Q2}\overline{Q}_2 + S_{R1}\overline{R}_1 + S_{R2}\overline{R}_2 + \alpha_1 x^{\mathrm{T}}(0)x(0) + \alpha_2 \int_{-d(0)}^{0} x^{\mathrm{T}}(s)x(s)ds
$$

$$
+ \alpha_4 \int_{-\tau_1}^{0} \int_{\theta}^{0} \dot{x}^{\mathrm{T}}(s)\dot{x}(s)dsd\theta + \alpha_3 \int_{-h(0)}^{0} x^{\mathrm{T}}(s)x(s)ds + \alpha_5 \int_{-\tau_2}^{0} \int_{\theta}^{0} \dot{x}^{\mathrm{T}}(s)\dot{x}(s)dsd\theta\} \tag{24}
$$

subject to (20), (23), $\varepsilon > 0, \overline{Q}_1 > 0, \overline{Q}_2 > 0, \overline{R}_1 > 0, \overline{R}_2 > 0, Z > 0, \alpha_i > 0, i = 1, ..., 5$

Using the following cone complement linearization (CCL) algorithm [24] can iteratively solve the minimization problem (24). □

5. Simulation examples

In this section, the proposed approach is applied to the Van de Vusse system to verify its effectiveness.

Example: Consider the dynamics of an isothermal continuous stirred tank reactor for the Van de Vusse

$$
\begin{aligned}
\dot{x}_1 &= -50x_1 - 10x_1^3 + u(10 - x_1) + u(t - h) + u(t - h)(0.5x_1(t - d) + 0.2x_2(t - d)) + 5x_2(t - d) \\
\dot{x}_2 &= 50x_1 - 100x_2 - u(t - h) + u(t - h)(0.3x_1(t - d) - 0.2x_2(t - d)) + 10x_2(t - d) - 5x_1(t - d)
\end{aligned} \tag{25}
$$

From the system equation (25), some equilibrium points are tabulated in **Table 1**. According to these equilibrium points, $[x_e\ u_e]$, which are also chosen as the desired operating points, $[x'_e\ u'_e]$, we can use the similar modeling method that is described in Ref. [16].

x_e^T	x_{de}^T	u_e	u_{de}
[2.0422 1.2178]	[2.0422 1.2178]	20.3077	20.3077
[3.6626 2.5443]	[3.6626 2.5443]	77.7272	77.7272
[5.9543 5.5403]	[5.9543 5.5403]	296.2414	296.2414

Table 1. Data for equilibrium points.

Thus, the system (25) can be represented by

R^1 : *if* x_1 *is about 2.0422 then*

$$\dot{x}_\delta(t) = A_1 x_\delta(t) + A_{d1} x_{d\delta}(t) + B_1 u_\delta(t) + B_{h1} u_{d\delta}(t) + N_1 x_\delta(t) u_\delta(t) + N_{d1} x_{d\delta}(t) u_{h\delta}(t)$$

R^2 : *if* x_1 *is about 3.6626, then*
$$\dot{x}_\delta(t) = A_2 x_\delta(t) + A_{d2} x_{d\delta}(t) + B_2 u_\delta(t) + B_{d2} u_{h\delta}(t) + N_2 x_\delta(t) u_\delta(t) + N_{d2} x_{d\delta}(t) u_{h\delta}(t)$$
R^3 : *if* x_1 *is about 5.9543, then*
$$\dot{x}_\delta(t) = A_3 x_\delta(t) + A_{d3} x_{d\delta}(t) + B_3 u_\delta(t) + B_{d3} u_{h\delta}(t) + N_3 x_\delta(t) u_\delta(t) + N_{d3} x_{d\delta}(t) u_{h\delta}(t)$$

(26)

where

$$A_1 = \begin{bmatrix} -75.2383 & 7.7946 \\ 50 & -100 \end{bmatrix}, A_2 = \begin{bmatrix} -98.3005 & 11.7315 \\ 50 & -100 \end{bmatrix}, A_3 = \begin{bmatrix} -122.1228 & 8.8577 \\ 50 & -100 \end{bmatrix},$$

$$N_1 = N_2 = N_3 = \begin{bmatrix} -1 & 0 \\ 0 & -1 \end{bmatrix}; B_1 = B_2 = B_3 = \begin{bmatrix} 10 \\ 0 \end{bmatrix}; A_{d1} = A_{d2} = A_{d3} = \begin{bmatrix} 0 & 5 \\ 10 & -5 \end{bmatrix},$$

$$N_{d1} = N_{d2} = N_{d3} = \begin{bmatrix} 0.5 & 0.2 \\ 0.3 & -0.2 \end{bmatrix}, B_{h1} = B_{h2} = B_{h3} = \begin{bmatrix} 1 \\ 0 \end{bmatrix}, x_\delta = x(t) - x_e',$$

$$u_\delta = u(t) - u_e', x_{d\delta} = x(t-d) - x_{de}', u_{h\delta} = u(t-d) - u_{he}'.$$

The cost function associated with this system is given with $S = \begin{bmatrix} 1 & 0 \\ 0 & 1 \end{bmatrix}, W = 1$. The controller gain perturbation ΔK of the additive form is give with $H_1 = H_2 = H_3 = 0.1$, $E_{k1} = [0.05 \quad -0.01]$, $E_{k2} = [0.02 \quad 0.01]$, $E_{k3} = [-0.01 \quad 0]$.

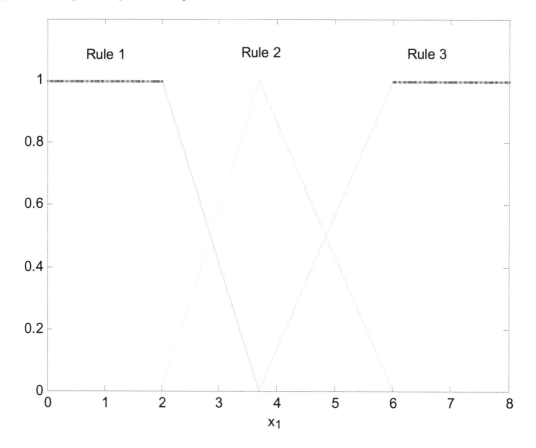

Figure 1. Membership functions.

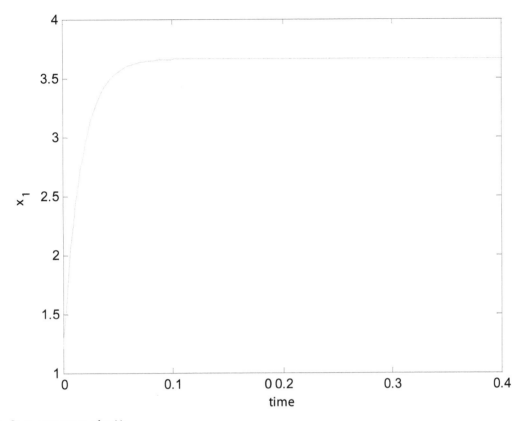

Figure 2. State responses of $x_1(t)$.

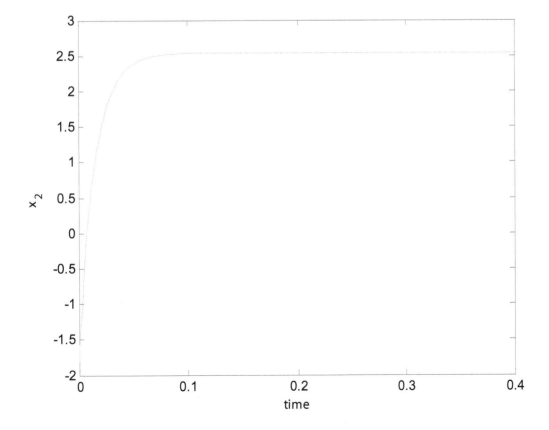

Figure 3. State responses of $x_2(t)$.

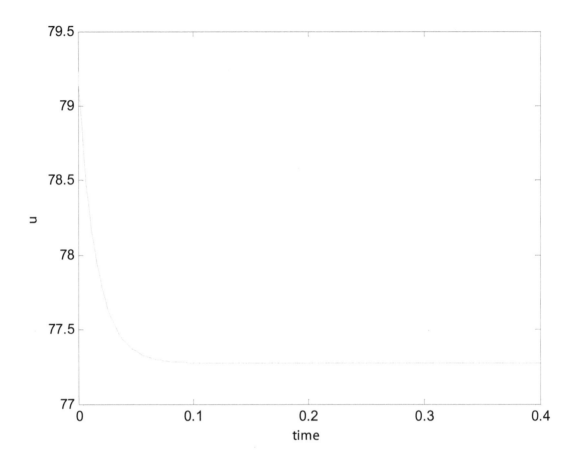

Figure 4. Control trajectory of system.

The membership functions of state x_1 are shown in **Figure 1**.

Then, solving LMIs (23) and (24) for $\rho = 0.45$, $\lambda = 1.02$ and $\delta = 0.11$, $\tau_1 = \tau_2 = 2$, $\sigma_1 = 0$, $\sigma_2 = 0$ gives the following feasible solution:

$$P = \begin{bmatrix} 4.2727 & -1.3007 \\ -1.3007 & 6.4906 \end{bmatrix}, Q_1 = \begin{bmatrix} 14.1872 & -1.9381 \\ -1.9381 & 13.0104 \end{bmatrix}, Q_2 = \begin{bmatrix} 3.1029 & 1.2838 \\ 1.2838 & 2.0181 \end{bmatrix},$$

$$R_1 = \begin{bmatrix} 8.3691 & -1.3053 \\ -1.3053 & 7.0523 \end{bmatrix}, R_1 = \begin{bmatrix} 5.2020 & 2.2730 \\ 2.2730 & 1.0238 \end{bmatrix}, \varepsilon = 1.8043,$$

$$K_1 = [-0.4233 \ -0.5031], K_2 = [-0.5961 \ -0.7049], K_1 = [-0.4593 \ -0.3874].$$

Figures 2–4 illustrate the simulation results of applying the non-fragile fuzzy controller to the system (25) with $x'_e = [3.6626 \ \ 2.5443]^{\mathrm{T}}$ and $u'_e = 77.7272$ under initial condition $\varphi(t) = [1.2 \ -1.8]^{\mathrm{T}}$, $t \in [-2 \ 0]$. It can be seen that with the fuzzy control law, the closed-loop system is asymptotically stable and an upper bound of the guaranteed cost is $J_0 = 292.0399$. The simulation results show that the fuzzy non-fragile guaranteed controller proposed in this paper is effective.

6. Conclusions

In this paper, the problem of non-fragile guaranteed cost control for a class of fuzzy time-varying delay systems with local bilinear models has been explored. By utilizing the Lyapunov stability theory and LMI technique, sufficient conditions for the delay-dependent asymptotically stability of the closed-loop T-S fuzzy local bilinear system have been obtained. Moreover, the designed fuzzy controller has guaranteed the cost function-bound constraint. Finally, the effectiveness of the developed approach has been demonstrated by the simulation example. The robust non-fragile guaranteed cost control and robust non-fragile H-infinite control based on fuzzy bilinear model will be further investigated in the future work.

Acknowledgements

This work is supported by NSFC Nos. 60974139 and 61573013.

Author details

Junmin Li*, Jinsha Li and Ruirui Duan

*Address all correspondence to: jmli@mail.xidian.edu.cn

School of Mathematics and Statistics, Xidian University, Xi'an, PR China

References

[1] Pang CT, Lur YY. On the stability of Takagi-Sugeno fuzzy systems with time-varying uncertainties. IEEE Transactions on Fuzzy Systems. 2008;**16**:162–170

[2] Zhou SS, Lam J, Zheng WX. Control design for fuzzy systems based on relaxed non-quadratic stability and H∞ performance conditions. IEEE Transactions on Fuzzy Systems. 2007;**15**:188–198

[3] Zhou SS, Li T. Robust stabilization for delayed discrete-time fuzzy systems via basis-dependent Lyapunov-Krasovskii function. Fuzzy Sets and Systems. 2005;**151**:139–153

[4] Gao HJ, Liu X, Lam J. Stability analysis and stabilization for discrete-time fuzzy systems with time-varying delay. IEEE Transactions on Systems, Man, Cybernetics, Part B. 2009;**39**:306–316

[5] Wu HN, Li HX. New approach to delay-dependent stability analysis and stabilization for continuous-time fuzzy systems with time-varying delay. IEEE Transactions on Fuzzy Systems. 2007;**15**:482–493

[6] Chen B, Liu XP. Delay-dependent robust H∞ control for T-S fuzzy systems with time delay. IEEE Transactions on Fuzzy Systems. 2005;**13**:238–249

[7] Chen M, Feng G, Ma H, Chen G. Delay-dependent H∞ filter design for discrete-time fuzzy systems with time-varying delays. IEEE Transactions on Fuzzy Systems. 2009;**17**:604–616

[8]   Zhang J, Xia Y, Tao R. New results on H∞ filtering for fuzzy time-delay systems. IEEE Transactions on Fuzzy Systems. 2009;**17**:128–137

[9]   Keel LH, Bhattacharryya SP. Robust, fragile, or optimal?. IEEE Transactions on Automatic Control. 1997;**42**:1098–1105

[10] Yang GH, Wang JL, Lin C. H∞ control for linear systems with additive controller gain variations. International Journal of Control. 2000;**73**:1500–1506

[11] Yang GH, Wang JL. Non-fragile H∞ control for linear systems with multiplicative controller gain variations. Automatica. 2001;**37**:727–737

[12] Zhang BY, Zhou SS, Li T. A new approach to robust and non-fragile H∞ control for uncertain fuzzy systems. Information Sciences. 2007;**177**:5118–5133

[13] Yee JS, Yang GH, Wang JL. Non-fragile guaranteed cost control for discrete-time uncertain linear systems. International Journal of Systems Science. 2001;**32**:845–853

[14] Mohler RR. Bilinear Control Processes. New York, NY: Academic; 1973

[15] Elliott DL. Bilinear Systems in Encyclopedia of Electrical Engineering. New York, NY: Wiley; 1999

[16] Li THS, Tsai SH. T-S fuzzy bilinear model and fuzzy controller design for a class of nonlinear systems. IEEE Transactions on Fuzzy Systems. 2007;**15**:494–505

[17] Tsai SH, Li THS. Robust fuzzy control of a class of fuzzy bilinear systems with time-delay. Chaos, Solitons and Fractals. 2009;**39**:2028–2040

[18] Li THS, Tsai SH, et al. Robust H∞ fuzzy control for a class of uncertain discrete fuzzy bilinear systems. IEEE Transactions on Systems, Man, Cybernetics, Part B. 2008;**38**:510–526

[19] Dong J, Wang Y, Yang G. Control synthesis of continuous-time T-S fuzzy systems with local nonlinear models. IEEE Transactions on Systems, Man, Cybernetics, Part B. 2009;**39**:1245–1258

[20] Zhang G, Li JM. Non-fragile guaranteed cost control of discrete-time fuzzy bilinear system. Journal of Systems Engineering and Electronics. 2010;**21**:629–634

[21] Ho DWC, Niu Y. Robust fuzzy design for nonlinear uncertain stochastic systems via sliding-mode control. IEEE Transactions on Fuzzy Systems. 2007;**15**:350–358

[22] Yang DD, Cai KY. Reliable guaranteed cost sampling control for nonlinear time-delay systems. Mathematics and Computers in Simulation. 2010;**80**:2005–2018

[23] Chen WH, Guan ZH, Lu XM. Delay-dependent output feedback guaranteed cost control for uncertain time-delay systems. Automatica. 2004;**44**:1263–1268

[24] Chen B, Lin C, Liu XP, Tong SC. Guaranteed cost control of T–S fuzzy systems with input delay. International Journal of Robust Nonlinear Control. 2008;**18**:1230–1256

[25] Chen B, Liu XP, Tong SC, Lin C. Observer-based stabilization of T–S fuzzy systems with input delay. IEEE Transactions on Fuzzy Systems. 2008;**16**:652–663

[26] Chen B, Liu X, Tong S, Lin C. guaranteed cost control of T-S fuzzy systems with state and input delay. Fuzzy Sets and Systems. 2007;**158**:2251–2267

[27] Du BZ, Lam J, Shu Z. Stabilization for state/input delay systems via static and integral output feedback. Automatica. 2010;**46**:2000–2007

[28] Kim JH. Delay-dependent robust and non-fragile guaranteed cost control for uncertain singular systems with time-varying state and input delays. International Journal of Control, Automation, and Systems. 2009;**7**:357–364

[29] Li L, Liu XD. New approach on robust stability for uncertain T–S fuzzy systems with state and input delays. Chaos, Solitons and Fractals. *2009*;**40**:2329–2339

[30] Yu KW, Lien CH. Robust H-infinite control for uncertain T–S fuzzy systems with state and input delays. Chaos, Solitons and Fractals. 2008;**37**:150–156

[31] Yue D, Lam J. Non-fragile guaranteed cost control for uncertain descriptor systems with time-varying state and input delays. Optimal Control Applications and Methods. 2005;**26**:85–105

[32] Zhang G, Li JM. Non-fragile guaranteed cost control of discrete-time fuzzy bilinear system with time-delay. Journal of Dynamic Systems, Measurement and Control. 2014;**136**:044502–044504

[33] Yue HY, Li JM. Output-feedback adaptive fuzzy control for a class of nonlinear systems with input delay and unknown control directions. Journal of the Franklin Institute. 2013;**350**:129–154

[34] Yue HY, Li JM. Adaptive fuzzy tracking control for a class of perturbed nonlinear time-varying delays systems with unknown control direction. International Journal of Uncertainty, Fuzziness and Knowledge-based Systems. 2013;**21**:497–531

[35] Wang RJ, Lin WW, Wang WJ. Stabilizability of linear quadratic state feedback for uncertain fuzzy time-delay systems. IEEE Transactions on Systems, Man, Cybernetics, Part B. 2004;**34**:1288–1292

[36] Xia ZL, Li JM, Li JR. Delay-dependent fuzzy static output feedback control for discrete-time fuzzy stochastic systems with distributed time-varying delays. ISA Transaction. 2012;**51**:702–712

[37] Xia ZL, Li JM. Switching fuzzy filtering for nonlinear stochastic delay systems using piecewise Lyapunov-Krasovskii function. International Journal of Fuzzy Systems. 2012;**14**:530–539

[38] Li JR, Li JM, Xia ZL. Delay-dependent generalized H2 fuzzy static-output-feedback control for discrete T-S fuzzy bilinear stochastic systems with mixed delays. Journal of Intelligent and Fuzzy Systems. 2013;**25**:863–880

[39] Xia ZL, Li JM, Li JR. Passivity-based resilient adaptive control for fuzzy stochastic delay systems with Markovian switching. Journal of the Franklin Institute-Engineering and Applied Mathematics. 2014;**351**:3818–3836

[40] Li JM, Li YT. Robust stability and stabilization of fractional order systems based on uncertain T-S fuzzy model with the fractional order. Journal of Computational and Nonlinear Dynamics. 2013;**8**:041005

[41] Li YT, Li JM. Stability analysis of fractional order systems based on T-S fuzzy model with the fractional order α: $0<\alpha<1$. Nonlinear Dynamics. 2014;**78**:2909–2919

[42] Li YT, Li JM. Decentralized stabilization of fractional order T-S fuzzy interconnected systems with multiple time delays. Journal of Intelligent and Fuzzy Systems. 2016;**30**:319–331

[43] Li JM, Yue HY. Adaptive fuzzy tracking control for stochastic nonlinear systems with unknown time-varying delays. Applied Mathematics and Computation. 2015;**256**:514–528

[44] Yue HY, Yu SQ. Adaptive fuzzy tracking control for a class of stochastic nonlinearly parameterized systems with distributed input delay. Journal of the Franklin Institute-Engineering and Applied Mathematics. 2016;**353**:713–734

[45] Duan RR, Li JM, Zhang YN, Yang Y, Chen GP. Stability analysis and H-inf control of discrete T-S fuzzy hyperbolic systems. International Journal of Applied Mathematics and Computer Science. 2016;**26**:133–145

[46] Wang JX, Li JM. Stability analysis and feedback control of T-S fuzzy hyperbolic delay model for a class of nonlinear systems with time-varying delay. Iranian Journal of Fuzzy Systems. 2016;**13**:111–134

[47] Li JR, Li JM, Xia ZL. Observer-based fuzzy control design for discrete time T-S fuzzy bilinear systems. International Journal of Uncertainty, Fuzziness and Knowledge-Based Systems. 2013;**21**:435–454

5

Stabilizing Fuzzy Control via Output Feedback

Dušan Krokavec and Anna Filasová

Abstract

The chapter presents new conditions suitable in design of stabilizing static as well as dynamic output controllers for a class of continuous-time nonlinear systems represented by Takagi-Sugeno models. Taking into account the affine properties of the TS model structure, and applying the fuzzy control scheme relating to the parallel-distributed output compensators, the sufficient design conditions are outlined in the terms of linear matrix inequalities. Depending on the proposed procedures, the Lyapunov matrix can be decoupled from the system parameter matrices using linear matrix inequality techniques or a fuzzy-relaxed approach can be applied to make closed-loop dynamics faster. Numerical examples illustrate the design procedures and demonstrate the performances of the proposed design methods.

Keywords: continuous-time nonlinear systems, Takagi-Sugeno fuzzy systems, linear matrix inequality approach, parallel-distributed compensation, output feedback

1. Introduction

Contrarily to the linear framework, nonlinear systems are too complex to be represented by unified mathematical resources and so, a generic method has not been developed yet to design a controller valid for all types of nonlinear systems. An alternative to nonlinear system models is Takagi-Sugeno (TS) fuzzy approach [1], which benefits from the advantages of suitable linear approximation of sector nonlinearities. Using the TS fuzzy model, each rule utilizes the local system dynamics by a linear model and the nonlinear system is represented by a collection of fuzzy rules. Recently, TS model-based fuzzy control approaches are being fast and successfully used in nonlinear control frameworks. As a result, a range of stability analysis conditions [2–5] as well as control design methods have been developed for TS fuzzy systems [6–9], relying mostly on the feasibility of an associated set of linear matrix inequalities

(LMI) [10]. An important fact is that the design problem is a standard feasibility problem with several LMIs, potentially combined with one matrix equality to overcome the problem of bilinearity. In consequence, the state and output feedback control based on fuzzy TS systems models is mostly realized in such structures, which can be designed using numerical techniques based on LMIs.

The TS fuzzy model-based state control is based on an implicit assumption that all states are available for measurement. If it is impossible, TS fuzzy observers are used to estimate the unmeasurable state variables, and the state controller exploits the system state variable estimate values [11–14]. The nonlinear output feedback design is so formulated as two LMI set problem, and treated by the two-stage procedure using the separation principle, that is, dealing with a set of LMIs for the observer parameters at first and then solving another set of LMIs for the controller parameters [15]. Since, the fuzzy output control does not require the measurement of system state variables and can be formulated as a one LMI set problem, such structure of feedback control is preferred, of course, if the system is stabilizable.

From a relatively wide range of problems associated with the fuzzy output feedback control design for the continuous-time nonlinear MIMO systems approximated by a TS model, the chapter deals with the techniques incorporating the slack matrix application and fuzzy membership-relaxed approaches. The central idea of the TS fuzzy model-based control design, that is, to derive control rules so as to compensate each rule of a fuzzy system and construct the control strategy based on the parallel-distributed compensators (PDC), is reflected in the approach of output control. Motivated by the above mentioned observations, the proposed design method respects the results presented in Refs. [16, 17], and is constructed on an enhanced form of quadratic Lyapunov function. Comparing with the approaches based only on quadratic Lyapunov matrix [18], which are particular in the case of large number of rules, that are very conservative as a common symmetric positive definite matrix, is used to verify all Lyapunov inequalities, presented principle naturally extends the affine TS model properties using slack matrix variables to decouple Lyapunov matrix and the system matrices in LMIs, and gives substantial reducing of conservativeness. Moreover, extra quadratic constraints are included to incorporate fuzzy membership functions relaxes [19, 20] and applied for static as well as dynamic TS fuzzy output controllers design. Note, other constraints with respect to, for example, to decay rate and closed-loop pole clustering can be utilized to extend the proposed design procedures.

The remainder of this chapter is organized as follows. In Section 2, the structure of TS model for considered class of nonlinear systems is briefly described, and some of its properties are outlined. The output feedback control design problem for systems with measurable promise variables is given in Section 3, where the design conditions that guarantees global quadratic stability are formulated and proven. To complete the solutions, Section 4 formulate the static decoupling principle in static TS fuzzy output control, and the method is reformulated in Section 5 in defined criteria for TS fuzzy dynamic output feedback control design. Section 6 gives the numerical examples to illustrate the effectiveness of the proposed approach, and to confirm the validity of the control scheme. The last section, Section 7, draws conclusions and some future directions.

Throughout the chapter, the following notations are used: x^T, X^T denotes the transpose of the vector x and matrix X, respectively, for a square matrix $X = X^T > 0$ (respectively, $X = X^T < 0$)

means that X is a symmetric positive definite matrix (respectively, negative definite matrix), the symbol I_n represents the n-th order unit matrix, $\mathbb{R}$ denotes the set of real numbers, and $\mathbb{R}^{n \times r}$ denotes the set of all $n \times r$ real matrices.

2. Takagi-Sugeno fuzzy models

The systems under consideration are from one class of multi-input and multi-output (MIMO) dynamic systems, which are nonlinear in sectors and represented by TS fuzzy model. Constructing the set of membership functions $h_i(\theta(t))$, $i = 1, 2, ..., s$, where

$$\theta(t) = \begin{bmatrix} \theta_1(t) & \theta_2(t) & \cdots & \theta_q(t) \end{bmatrix}, \tag{1}$$

is the vector of premise variables, the final states of the systems are inferred in the TS fuzzy system model as follows

$$\dot{q}(t) = \sum_{i=1}^{s} h_i(\theta(t))(A_i q(t) + B_i u(t)), \tag{2}$$

with the output given by the relation

$$y(t) = Cq(t), \tag{3}$$

where $q(t) \in \mathbb{R}^n$, $u(t) \in \mathbb{R}^r$, $y(t) \in \mathbb{R}^m$ are vectors of the state, input, and output variables, $A_i \in \mathbb{R}^{n \times n}$, $B_i \in \mathbb{R}^{n \times r}$, $C \in \mathbb{R}^{m \times n}$ are real finite values matrix, and where $h_i(\theta(t))$ is the averaging weight for the i-th rule, representing the normalized grade of membership (membership function).

By definition, the membership functions satisfy the following convex sum properties.

$$0 \le h_i(\theta(t)) \le 1, \quad \sum_{i=1}^{s} h_i(\theta(t)) = 1 \quad \forall i \in \langle 1, ..., s \rangle. \tag{4}$$

It is assumed that the premise variable is a system state variable or a measurable external variable, and none of the premise variables depends on the inputs $u(t)$.

It is evident that a general fuzzy model is achieved by fuzzy amalgamation of the linear system models. Using a TS model, the conclusion part of a single rule consists no longer of a fuzzy set [21], but determines a function with state variables as arguments, and the corresponding function is a local function for the fuzzy region that is described by the premise part of the rule. Thus, using linear functions, a system state is described locally (in fuzzy regions) by linear models, and at the boundaries between regions an interpolation is used between the corresponding local models.

Note, the models, Eqs. (2) and (3), are mostly considered for analysis, control, and state estimation of nonlinear systems.

Assumption 1 *Each triplet* (A_i, B_i, C) *is locally controllable and observable, the matrix* C *is the same for all local models.*

It is supposed in the next that the aforementioned model does not include parameter uncertainties or external disturbances, and the premise variables are measured.

3. Static fuzzy output controller

In the next, the fuzzy output controller is designed using the concept of parallel-distributed compensation, in which the fuzzy controller shares the same sets of normalized membership functions like the TS fuzzy system model.

Definition 1 *Considering Eqs. (2) and (3), and using the same set of normalized membership function Eq. (4), the fuzzy static output controller is defined as*

$$u(t) = \sum_{j=1}^{s} h_j(\theta(t)) K_j y(t) = \sum_{j=1}^{s} h_j(\theta(t)) K_j C q(t). \tag{5}$$

Note that the fuzzy controller Eq. (5) is in general nonlinear.

Considering the system, Eqs. (2) and (3), and the control law, Eq. (5), yields

$$\dot{q}(t) = \sum_{i=1}^{s}\sum_{j=1}^{s} h_i(\theta(t)) h_j(\theta(t)) (A_i + B_i K_j C) q(t) = \sum_{i=1}^{s}\sum_{j=1}^{s} h_i(\theta(t)) h_j(\theta(t)) A_{cij} q(t), \tag{6}$$

$$A_{cij} = A_i + B_i K_j C, \quad A_{cji} = A_j + B_j K_i C. \tag{7}$$

Proposition 1 (*standard design conditions*). *The equilibrium of the fuzzy system Eqs. (2) and (3), controlled by the fuzzy controller Eq. (5), is global asymptotically stable if there exist a positive definite symmetric matrix* $W \in \mathbb{R}^{n \times n}$ *and matrices* $Y_j \in \mathbb{R}^{r \times m}$, $H \in \mathbb{R}^{m \times m}$ *such that*

$$W = W^T > 0, \tag{8}$$

$$A_i W + W A_i^T + B_i Y_i C + C^T Y_i^T B_i^T < 0, \tag{9}$$

$$\frac{A_i W + W A_i^T}{2} + \frac{A_j W + W A_j^T}{2} + \frac{B_i Y_j C + C^T Y_j^T B_i^T}{2} + \frac{B_j Y_i C + C^T Y_i^T B_j^T}{2} < 0, \tag{10}$$

$$CW = HC \tag{11}$$

for $i = 1, 2, \ldots, s$ as well as $i = 1, 2, \ldots, s-1$, $j = i+1, i+2, \ldots, s$, and $h_i(\theta(t)) h_j(\theta(t)) \neq 0$.

When the above conditions hold, the control law gain matrices are given as

$$K_i = Y_i H^{-1}. \tag{12}$$

Proof. (compare, for example, Ref. [16]) Prescribing the Lyapunov function candidate of the form

$$v(q(t)) = q^T(t) P q(t) > 0, \tag{13}$$

where $P \in \mathbb{R}^{n \times n}$ is a symmetric positive definite matrix, the time derivative of Eq. (13) along the system trajectory is

$$\dot{v}(q(t)) = \dot{q}^T(t) P q(t) + q^T(t) P \dot{q}(t) < 0. \tag{14}$$

Inserting Eq. (6) into Eq. (14), it has to be satisfied

$$\dot{v}(q(t)) = \sum_{i=1}^{s} \sum_{j=1}^{s} h_i(\theta(t)) h_j(\theta(t)) q^T(t) P_{cij} q(t) < 0, \tag{15}$$

$$P_{cij} = P A_{cij} + A_{cij}^T P. \tag{16}$$

Since P is positive definite, the state coordinate transform can be defined as

$$q(t) = W p(t), \quad W = P^{-1}, \tag{17}$$

and subsequently, Eqs. (15) and (16) can be rewritten as

$$\dot{v}(p(t)) = \sum_{i=1}^{s} \sum_{j=1}^{s} h_i(\theta(t)) h_j(\theta(t)) p^T(t) W_{cij} p(t) < 0, \tag{18}$$

$$W_{cij} = A_{cij} W + W A_{cij}^T. \tag{19}$$

Permuting the subscripts i and j in Eq. (18), also it can write

$$\dot{v}(q(t)) = \sum_{i=1}^{s} \sum_{j=1}^{s} h_i(\theta(t)) h_j(\theta(t)) p^T(t) W_{cji} p(t) < 0, \tag{20}$$

$$W_{cji} = A_{cji} W + W A_{cji}^T. \tag{21}$$

Thus, adding Eqs. (17) and (19), it yields

$$2\dot{v}(p(t)) = \sum_{i=1}^{s} \sum_{j=1}^{s} h_i(\theta(t)) h_j(\theta(t)) p^T(t) \left(W_{cij} + W_{cji} \right) p(t) < 0 \tag{22}$$

and subsequently,

$$\dot{v}(\boldsymbol{p}(t)) = \sum_{i=1}^{s} h_i^2(\boldsymbol{\theta}(t))\boldsymbol{p}^T(t)\boldsymbol{W}_{cii}\boldsymbol{p}(t) + 2\sum_{i=1}^{s-1}\sum_{j=i+1}^{s} h_i(\boldsymbol{\theta}(t))h_j(\boldsymbol{\theta}(t))\boldsymbol{p}^T(t)\frac{\boldsymbol{W}_{cij}+\boldsymbol{W}_{cji}}{2}\boldsymbol{p}(t) < 0, \quad (23)$$

which leads to the set of inequalities.

$$(A_i + B_iK_iC)W + W(A_i + B_iK_iC)^T < 0, \quad (24)$$

$$\frac{(A_i + B_iK_jC)W}{2} + \frac{(A_j + B_jK_iC)W}{2} + \frac{W(A_i + B_iK_jC)^T}{2} + \frac{W(A_j + B_jK_iC)^T}{2} < 0 \quad (25)$$

for i = 1, 2, ..., s as well as i = 1, 2, ..., s − 1, j = 1 + 1, i + 2, ..., s and $h_i(\boldsymbol{\theta}(t))h_j(\boldsymbol{\theta}(t)) \neq 0$.

Thus, setting here

$$K_jCW = K_jHH^{-1}CW, \quad (26)$$

where H is a regular square matrix of appropriate dimension and defining

$$H^{-1}C = CW^{-1}, \quad Y_j = K_jH, \quad (27)$$

the LMI forms of Eqs. (9) and (10) are obtained from Eqs. (24) and (25), respectively, and Eq. (27) implies Eq. (11). This concludes the proof.

Trying to minimize the number of LMIs owing to the limitation of solvers, Proposition 1 is presented in the structure, in which the number of stabilization conditions, used in fuzzy controller design, is equal to $N = (s^2 + s)/2 + 1$. Evidently, the number of stabilization conditions is substantially reduced if s is large.

Proposition 2 (*enhanced design conditions*). *The equilibrium of the fuzzy system Eqs. (2) and (3), controlled by the fuzzy controller Eq. (5), is global asymptotically stable if for given a positive $\delta \in \mathbb{R}$, there exist positive definite symmetric matrices $V, S \in \mathbb{R}^{n \times n}$, and matrices $Y_j \in \mathbb{R}^{r \times m}$, $H \in \mathbb{R}^{m \times m}$ such that*

$$S = S^T > 0, \quad V = V^T > 0, \quad (28)$$

$$\begin{bmatrix} A_iS + SA_i^T + B_iY_iC + C^TY_i^TB_i^T & * \\ V - S + \delta A_iS + \delta B_iY_iC & -2\delta S \end{bmatrix} < 0, \quad (29)$$

$$\begin{bmatrix} \boldsymbol{\Phi}_{ij} & * \\ V - S + \delta\frac{A_iS + A_jS}{2} + \delta\frac{B_iY_j + B_jY_i}{2}C & -2\delta S \end{bmatrix} < 0, \quad (30)$$

$$CS = HC, \quad (31)$$

for i = 1, 2, ..., s, as well as i = 1, 2, ..., s − 1, j = 1 + 1, i + 2, ..., s, $h_i(\boldsymbol{\theta}(t))h_j(\boldsymbol{\theta}(t)) \neq 0$, and

$$\Phi_{ij} = \frac{A_iS + SA_i^T}{2} + \frac{A_jS + SA_j^T}{2} + \frac{B_iY_jC + C^TY_j^TB_i^T}{2} + \frac{B_jY_iC + C^TY_i^TB_j^T}{2}. \tag{32}$$

When the above conditions hold, the control law gain matrices are given as

$$K_i = Y_iH^{-1}. \tag{33}$$

Here and hereafter, $*$ denotes the symmetric item in a symmetric matrix.

Proof. Writing Eq. (6) in the form

$$\sum_{i=1}^{s}\sum_{j=1}^{s}h_i(\boldsymbol{\theta}(t))h_j(\boldsymbol{\theta}(t))\left(A_{cij}\boldsymbol{q}(t) - \dot{\boldsymbol{q}}(t)\right) = 0, \tag{34}$$

then with an arbitrary symmetric positive definite matrix $S \in \mathbb{R}^{n \times n}$ and a positive scalar $\delta \in \mathbb{R}$, it yields

$$\sum_{i=1}^{s}\sum_{j=1}^{s}h_i(\boldsymbol{\theta}(t))h_j(\boldsymbol{\theta}(t))\left(\boldsymbol{q}^T(t)S + \delta\dot{\boldsymbol{q}}^T(t)S\right)\left(A_{cij}\boldsymbol{q}(t) - \dot{\boldsymbol{q}}(t)\right) = 0. \tag{35}$$

Since S is positive definite, the new state variable coordinate system can be introduced so that

$$\boldsymbol{p}(t) = S\boldsymbol{q}(t), \quad \dot{\boldsymbol{p}}(t) = S\dot{\boldsymbol{q}}(t), \quad V = S^{-1}PS^{-1}. \tag{36}$$

Therefore, Eq. (14) can be rewritten as

$$\dot{v}(\boldsymbol{p}(t)) = \dot{\boldsymbol{p}}^T(t)V\boldsymbol{p}(t) + \boldsymbol{p}^T(t)V\dot{\boldsymbol{p}}(t) < 0 \tag{37}$$

and Eq. (35) takes the form

$$\sum_{i=1}^{s}\sum_{j=1}^{s}h_i(\boldsymbol{\theta}(t))h_j(\boldsymbol{\theta}(t))\left(\boldsymbol{p}^T(t) + \delta\dot{\boldsymbol{p}}^T(t)\right)\left(A_{cij}S\boldsymbol{p}(t) - S\dot{\boldsymbol{p}}(t)\right) = 0. \tag{38}$$

Thus, adding Eq. (38) as well as the transposition of Eq. (38) to Eq. (37), it yields

$$\begin{aligned}
\dot{v}(\boldsymbol{p}(i)) = {}& \dot{\boldsymbol{p}}^T(t)V\boldsymbol{p}(t) + \boldsymbol{p}^T(t)V\dot{\boldsymbol{p}}(t) \\
& + \sum_{i=1}^{s}\sum_{j=1}^{s}h_i(\boldsymbol{\theta}(t))h_j(\boldsymbol{\theta}(t))\left(\boldsymbol{p}^T(t) + \delta\dot{\boldsymbol{p}}^T(t)\right)\left(A_{cij}S\boldsymbol{p}(t) - S\dot{\boldsymbol{p}}(t)\right) \\
& + \sum_{i=1}^{s}\sum_{j=1}^{s}h_i(\boldsymbol{\theta}(t))h_j(\boldsymbol{\theta}(t))\left(A_{cij}S\boldsymbol{p}(t) - S\dot{\boldsymbol{p}}(t)\right)^T\left(\boldsymbol{p}(t) + \delta\dot{\boldsymbol{p}}(t)\right) < 0.
\end{aligned} \tag{39}$$

Using the notation

$$p_c^T(t) = \begin{bmatrix} p^T(t) & \dot{p}^T(t) \end{bmatrix}, \tag{40}$$

the inequality Eq. (39) can be written as

$$\dot{v}(p_c(t)) = \sum_{i=1}^{s}\sum_{j=1}^{s} h_i(\theta(t)) h_j(\theta(t)) p_c^T(t) S_{cij} p_c(t) < 0, \tag{41}$$

$$S_{cij} = \begin{bmatrix} (A_i + B_i K_j C)S + S(A_i + B_i K_j C)^T & * \\ V - S + \delta(A_i + B_i K_j C)S & -2\delta S \end{bmatrix} < 0. \tag{42}$$

Permuting the subscripts i and j in Eq. (41), and following the way used above, analogously it can obtain

$$\dot{v}(p_c(t)) = \sum_{i=1}^{s} h_i^2(\theta(t)) p_c^T(t) S_{cii} p_c(t) + 2\sum_{i=1}^{s-1}\sum_{j=i+1}^{s} h_i(\theta(t)) h_j(\theta(t)) p_c^T(t) \frac{S_{cij} + S_{cji}}{2} p_c(t) < 0. \tag{43}$$

Since $r = m$, it is now possible to set

$$K_j C S = K_j H H^{-1} C S, \tag{44}$$

where H is a regular square matrix of appropriate dimension and introducing

$$H^{-1}C = CS^{-1}, \quad Y_j = K_j H \tag{45}$$

then Eqs. (42) and (45) imply Eqs. (29)–(31). This concludes the proof.

Note, Eq. (42) leads to the set of LMIs only if δ is a prescribed constant. (δ can be considered as a tuning parameter). Considering δ as a LMI variable, Eq. (42) represents the set of bilinear matrix inequalities (BMI).

Theorem 1 (*enhanced relaxed design conditions*). *The equilibrium of the fuzzy system Eqs. (2) and (3), controlled by the fuzzy controller Eq. (5), is global asymptotically stable if for given a positive $\delta \in \mathbb{R}$ there exist positive definite symmetric matrices $V, S \in \mathbb{R}^{n \times n}$, the matrices $X_{ij} = X_{ji}^T \in \mathbb{R}^{r \times n}$, and $Y_j \in \mathbb{R}^{r \times m}, H \in \mathbb{R}^{m \times m}$ such that*

$$S = S^T > 0, \quad V = V^T > 0, \quad \begin{bmatrix} X_{11} & X_{12} & \cdots & X_{1s} \\ X_{21} & X_{22} & \cdots & X_{2s} \\ \vdots & \vdots & \ddots & \vdots \\ X_{s1} & X_{s2} & \cdots & X_{ss} \end{bmatrix} > 0, \tag{46}$$

$$\begin{bmatrix} A_i S + SA_i^T + B_i Y_i C + C^T Y_i^T B_i^T + X_{ii} & * \\ V - S + \delta A_i S + \delta B_i Y_i C & -2\delta S \end{bmatrix} < 0, \tag{47}$$

$$\begin{bmatrix} \Phi_{ij} & * \\ V - S + \delta\frac{A_i S + A_j S}{2} + \delta\frac{B_i Y_j + B_j Y_i}{2}C & -2\delta S \end{bmatrix} < 0, \tag{48}$$

$$CS = HC, \tag{49}$$

for $i = 1, 2, \ldots, s$, as well as $i = 1, 2, \ldots, s - 1$, $j = 1 + 1$, $i + 2, \ldots, s$, $h_i(\boldsymbol{\theta}(t))h_j(\boldsymbol{\theta}(t)) \neq 0$ and

$$\boldsymbol{\Phi}_{ij} = \frac{A_i S + S A_i^T}{2} + \frac{A_j S + S A_j^T}{2} + \frac{B_i Y_j C + C^T Y_j^T B_i^T}{2} + \frac{B_j Y_i C + C^T Y_i^T B_j^T}{2} + \frac{X_{ij} + X_{ji}}{2}. \tag{50}$$

When the above conditions hold, the control law gain matrices are given as

$$K_i = Y_i H^{-1}. \tag{51}$$

Proof. Introducing the positive real term

$$v_v(\boldsymbol{\theta}(t)) = \boldsymbol{q}^T(t) Z(\boldsymbol{\theta}(t)) \boldsymbol{q}(t) > 0, \tag{52}$$

$$Z(\boldsymbol{\theta}(t)) = Z^T(\boldsymbol{\theta}(t)) = \sum_{i=1}^{s} \sum_{j=1}^{s} h_i(\boldsymbol{\theta}(t)) h_j(\boldsymbol{\theta}(t)) Z_{ij} > 0, \tag{53}$$

where $Z_{ij} = Z_{ji}^T \in \mathbb{R}^{n \times n}$, $i, j = 1, 2, \ldots, s$ is the set of associated matrices and using the state coordinate transform Eq. (36), then Eq. (53) can be rewritten as

$$v_v(\boldsymbol{p}(t)) = \sum_{i=1}^{s} \sum_{j=1}^{s} h_i(\boldsymbol{\theta}(t)) h_j(\boldsymbol{\theta}(t)) \boldsymbol{p}^T(t) X_{ij} \boldsymbol{p}(t) > 0, \quad X_{ij} = S^{-1} Z_{ij} S^{-1} = X_{ji}^T, \tag{54}$$

where

$$Z(\boldsymbol{\theta}(t)) = \begin{bmatrix} h_1(\boldsymbol{\theta}(t)\boldsymbol{p}(t) & h_2(\boldsymbol{\theta}(t)\boldsymbol{p}(t) & \cdots & h_s(\boldsymbol{\theta}(t)\boldsymbol{p}(t) \end{bmatrix} \begin{bmatrix} X_{11} & X_{12} & \cdots & X_{1s} \\ X_{21} & X_{22} & \cdots & X_{2s} \\ \vdots & \vdots & \ddots & \vdots \\ X_{s1} & X_{s2} & \cdots & X_{ss} \end{bmatrix} \begin{bmatrix} h_1(\boldsymbol{\theta}(t)\boldsymbol{p}(t) \\ h_2(\boldsymbol{\theta}(t)\boldsymbol{p}(t) \\ \vdots \\ h_s(\boldsymbol{\theta}(t)\boldsymbol{p}(t) \end{bmatrix} \tag{55}$$

is symmetric, an positive definite if Eq. (46) is satisfied. Then, in the sense of the Krasovskii theorem (see, for example, Ref. [22]), it can be set up in Eq. (39)

$$\begin{aligned} \dot{v}(\boldsymbol{p}(i)) = {}& \dot{\boldsymbol{p}}^T(t) V \boldsymbol{p}(t) + \boldsymbol{p}^T(t) V \dot{\boldsymbol{p}}(t) \\ & + \sum_{i=1}^{s} \sum_{j=1}^{s} h_i(\boldsymbol{\theta}(t)) h_j(\boldsymbol{\theta}(t)) \left(\boldsymbol{p}^T(t) + \delta \dot{\boldsymbol{p}}^T(t) \right) \left(A_{cij} S \boldsymbol{p}(t) - S \dot{\boldsymbol{p}}(t) \right) \\ & + \sum_{i=1}^{s} \sum_{j=1}^{s} h_i(\boldsymbol{\theta}(t)) h_j(\boldsymbol{\theta}(t)) \left(A_{cij} S \boldsymbol{p}(t) - S \dot{\boldsymbol{p}}(t) \right)^T \left(\boldsymbol{p}(t) + \delta \dot{\boldsymbol{p}}(t) \right) \\ & < - \sum_{i=1}^{s} \sum_{j=1}^{s} h_i(\boldsymbol{\theta}(t)) h_j(\boldsymbol{\theta}(t)) \boldsymbol{p}^T(t) X_{ij} \boldsymbol{p}(t) \\ & < 0, \end{aligned} \tag{56}$$

which in the consequence, modifies Eq. (42) as follows

$$S_{cij} = \begin{bmatrix} (A_i + B_i K_j C)S + S(A_i + B_i K_j C)^T + X_{ij} & * \\ V - S + \delta(A_i + B_i K_j C)S & -2\delta S \end{bmatrix} < 0. \tag{57}$$

Following the same way as in the proof of Proposition 2, then Eqs. (47) and (48) can be derived from Eq. (57), while Eq. (55) implies Eq. (46). This concludes the proof.

This principle naturally exploits the affine TS model properties. Introducing the slack matrix variable S into the LMIs, the system matrices are decoupled from the equivalent Lyapunov matrix V. Note, to respect the conditions $X_{1j} = X_{ji}^T$, the set of inequalities Eqs. (47) and (48) have to be constructed. In the opposite case, constructing a set on s^2 LMIs, the constraint conditions have to be set as $X_{1j} = X_{ij}^T > 0$, that is, the weighting matrices have to be symmetric positive definite.

Corollary 1 *Prescribing S = V and using the Schur complement property, then Eq. (57) implies*

$$A_{cij}S + SA_{cij}^T + X_{ij} + 0.5\delta SA_{cij}^T \delta^{-1} S^{-1} \delta A_{cij} S < 0 \tag{58}$$

and for $\delta = 0$ evidently, it has to be

$$A_{cij}S + SA_{cij}^T + X_{ij} < 0. \tag{59}$$

Evidently, then Eqs. (47) and (48) imply

$$S(A_i + B_i K_i C)^T + (A_i + B_i K_i C)S + X_{ii} < 0, \tag{60}$$

$$\frac{(A_i + B_i K_j C)S}{2} + \frac{(A_j + B_j K_i C)S}{2} + \frac{S(A_i + B_i K_j C)^T}{2} + \frac{S(A_j + B_j K_i C)^T}{2} + \frac{X_{ij} + X_{ji}}{2} < 0. \tag{61}$$

Considering $S = W$ and comparing with Eqs. (23) and (24), then Eqs. (60) and (61) are the extended set of inequalities Eqs. (23) and (24). The result is that the equilibrium of the fuzzy system Eqs. (2) and (3), controlled by the fuzzy controller Eq. (5), is global asymptotically stable if there exist a positive definite symmetric matrices $S \in \mathbb{R}^{n \times n}$, the matrices $X_{1j} = X_{ji}^T \in \mathbb{R}^{r \times n}$, and $Y_j \in \mathbb{R}^{r \times n}$, $H \in \mathbb{R}^{m \times m}$ such that

$$S = S^T > 0, \quad \begin{bmatrix} X_{11} & X_{12} & \cdots & X_{1s} \\ X_{21} & X_{22} & \cdots & X_{2s} \\ \vdots & \vdots & \ddots & \vdots \\ X_{s1} & X_{s2} & \cdots & X_{ss} \end{bmatrix} > 0, \tag{62}$$

$$A_i S + SA_i^T + B_i Y_i C + C^T Y_i^T B_i^T + X_{ii} < 0, \tag{63}$$

$$\frac{A_i S + SA_i^T}{2} + \frac{A_j S + SA_j^T}{2} + \frac{B_i Y_j C + C^T Y_j^T B_i^T}{2} + \frac{B_j Y_i C + C^T Y_i^T B_j^T}{2} \frac{X_{ij} + X_{ji}}{2} < 0, \tag{64}$$

$$CS = HC, \tag{65}$$

for $i = 1, 2, ..., s$, as well as $i = 1, 2, ..., s - 1$, $j = 1 + 1, i + 2, ..., s$, and $h_i(\theta(t))h_j(\theta(t)) \neq 0$. Subsequently, if this set of LMIs is satisfied, the set of control law gain matrices is given as

$$K_i = Y_i H^{-1}. \tag{66}$$

These LMIs form relaxed design conditions.

Note the derived results are linked to some existing finding when the design problem involves additive performance requirements and the relaxed quadratic stability conditions of fuzzy control systems (see, e.g., Refs. [11, 19]) are equivalently steered.

4. Forced mode in static output control

In practice, the plant with $r = m$ (square plants) is often encountered, since in this case, it is possible to associate with each output signal as a reference signal, which is expected to influence this wanted output. Such mode, reflecting nonzero set working points, is called the forced regime.

Definition 2 *A forced regime for the TS fuzzy system Eqs. (2) and (3) with the TS fuzzy static output controller Eq. (5) is foisted by the control policy*

$$u(t) = \sum_{j=1}^{s} h_j(\theta(t))K_j y(t) + \sum_{i=1}^{s}\sum_{j=1}^{s} h_i(\theta(t))h_j(\theta(t))W_{ij}w(t), \tag{67}$$

where $r = m$, $w(i) \in \mathbb{R}^m$ is desired output signal vector, and $W_{ij} \in \mathbb{R}^{m \times m}$, $i, j = 1, 2, ... s$ is the set of the signal gain matrices.

Lemma 1. *The static decoupling challenge is solvable if (A_i, B_i) is stabilizable and*

$$rank\begin{bmatrix} A_i & B_i \\ C & 0 \end{bmatrix} = n + m. \tag{68}$$

Proof. If (A_i, B_i) is stabilizable, it is possible to find K_j such that matrices $A_{cij} = A_i + B_i K_j C$ are Hurwitz. Assuming that for such K_j, it yields

$$rank\begin{bmatrix} A_i & B_i \\ C & 0 \end{bmatrix} = rank\begin{bmatrix} A_i & B_i \\ C & 0 \end{bmatrix}\begin{bmatrix} I_n & 0 \\ K_j C & I_m \end{bmatrix} = rank\begin{bmatrix} A_i + B_i K_j C & B_i \\ C & 0 \end{bmatrix}, \tag{69}$$

$$rank\begin{bmatrix} A_i + B_i K_j C & B_i \\ C & 0 \end{bmatrix} = rank\begin{bmatrix} I_n & 0 \\ -C(A_i + B_i K_j C)^{-1} & I_m \end{bmatrix}\begin{bmatrix} A_i + B_i K_j C & B_i \\ C & 0 \end{bmatrix}, \tag{70}$$

respectively, then

$$rank\begin{bmatrix} A_i & B_i \\ C & 0 \end{bmatrix} = rank\begin{bmatrix} A_i + B_i K_j C & B_i \\ 0 & -C(A_i + B_i K_j C)^{-1}B_i \end{bmatrix} = n + m, \tag{71}$$

since $rank(A_i + B_i K_j C) = n$, and $rankB_i = m$.

Thus, evidently, it has to be satisfied

$$\text{rank}\left(C(A_i + B_iK_jC)^{-1}B_i\right) = m. \tag{72}$$

This concludes the proof.

Theorem 2. *To reach a forced regime for the TS fuzzy system Eqs. (2) and (3) with the TS fuzzy control policy Eq. (67), the signal gain matrices have to take the forms*

$$W_{ij} = \left(C(A_i + B_iK_jC)^{-1}B_i\right)^{-1}, \tag{73}$$

where $W_{ij} \in \mathbb{R}^{m \times m}$, $i, j = 1, 2, \ldots s$.

Proof. In a steady state, which corresponds to $\dot{q}(t) = 0$, the equality $y_o = w_o$ must hold, where $q_o \in \mathbb{R}^n$, $\theta_o \in \mathbb{R}^q$, y_o, $w_o \in \mathbb{R}^m$ are the vectors of steady state values of $q(t)$, $\theta(t)$, $y(t)$, $w(t)$, respectively.

Substituting Eq. (67) in Eq. (2) yields the expression

$$\sum_{i=1}^{s}\sum_{j=1}^{s}h_i(\theta_o)h_j(\theta_o)\left((A_i + B_iK_jC)q_o + B_iW_{ij}w_o\right) = 0, \tag{74}$$

$$-\sum_{i=1}^{s}\sum_{j=1}^{s}h_i(\theta_o)h_j(\theta_o)q_o = -q_o = \sum_{i=1}^{s}\sum_{j=1}^{s}h_i(\theta_o)h_j(\theta_o)(A_i + B_iK_jC)^{-1}B_iW_{ij}w_o, \tag{75}$$

respectively, and it can be set

$$y_o = Cq_o = -\sum_{i=1}^{s}\sum_{j=1}^{s}h_i(\theta_o)h_j(\theta_o)C(A_i + B_iK_jC)^{-1}B_iW_{ij}w_o = I_mw_o. \tag{76}$$

Thus, Eq. (76) gives the solution

$$W_{ij}^{-1} = -C(A_i + B_iK_jC)^{-1}B_i, \tag{77}$$

which implies Eq. (68). Hence, declaredly,

$$\text{rank}W_j = \text{rank}\left(C(A_i + B_iK_jC)^{-1}B_i\right) = m. \tag{78}$$

This concludes the proof.

The forced regime is basically designed for constant references and is very closely related to shift of origin. If the command value $w(t)$ is changed "slowly enough," the above scheme can do a reasonable job of tracking, that is, making $y(t)$ follow $w(t)$ [23].

5. Bi-proper dynamic output controller

The full order biproper dynamic output controller is defined by the equation

$$\dot{p}(t) = \sum_{j=1}^{s} \text{h}_j(\theta(t))\left(J_j p(t) + L_j y(t)\right), \tag{79}$$

$$u(t) = \sum_{j=1}^{s} \text{h}_j(\theta(t))\left(M_j p(t) + N_j y(t)\right), \tag{80}$$

where $p(t) \in \mathbb{R}^h$ is the vector of the controller state variables and the parameter matrix

$$K_j^{\circ} = \begin{bmatrix} J_j & L_j \\ M_j & N_j \end{bmatrix}, \tag{81}$$

$K_j^{\circ} \in \mathbb{R}^{(n+r)\times(h+m)}$, is considered in this block matrix structure with respect to the matrices $J_j \in \mathbb{R}^{h \times h}$, $L_j \in \mathbb{R}^{h \times m}$, $M_j \in \mathbb{R}^{r \times h}$, and $N_j \in \mathbb{R}^{r \times m}$. For simplicity, the full order $p = n$ controller is considered in the following.

To analyze the stability of the closed-loop system structure with the dynamic output controller, the closed-loop system description implies the following form

$$\dot{q}^{\circ}(t) = \sum_{i=1}^{s}\sum_{j=1}^{s} h_i(\theta(t)) h_j(\theta(t)) A_{cij}^{\circ} q^{\circ}(t), \tag{82}$$

$$y^{\circ}(t) = I^{\circ} C^{\circ} q^{\circ}(t), \tag{83}$$

where

$$q^{\circ T}(t) = \begin{bmatrix} q^T(t) & p^T(t) \end{bmatrix}, \tag{84}$$

$$A_{cij}^{\circ} = \begin{bmatrix} A_i + B_i N_j C & B_i M_j \\ L_j C & N_j \end{bmatrix}, \quad I^{\circ} = \begin{bmatrix} 0 & I_m \end{bmatrix}, \quad C^{\circ} = \begin{bmatrix} 0 & I_n \\ C & 0 \end{bmatrix} \tag{85}$$

and $A_{cij}^{\circ} \in \mathbb{R}^{2n\times 2n}$, $I^{\circ} \in \mathbb{R}^{m \times (n + m)}$, $C^{\circ} \in \mathbb{R}^{(n + m) \times 2n}$.

Introducing the notations

$$A_i^{\circ} = \begin{bmatrix} A_i & 0 \\ 0 & 0 \end{bmatrix}, \quad B_i^{\circ} = \begin{bmatrix} 0 & B_i \\ I_n & 0 \end{bmatrix}, \tag{86}$$

where $A_i^{\circ} \in \mathbb{R}^{2n\times 2n}$, $B_i^{\circ} \in \mathbb{R}^{2n\times(n+r)}$, the closed-loop system matrices take the equivalent forms

$$A_{cij}^{\circ} = A_i^{\circ} + B_i^{\circ} K_j^{\circ} C^{\circ}. \tag{87}$$

In the sequel, it is supposed that $(A_i^{\circ}, B_i^{\circ})$ is stabilizable, $(A_i^{\circ}, C_i^{\circ})$ is detectable [24].

Note this kind of controllers can be preferred in fault tolerant control (FTC) structures with virtual actuators [25].

Theorem 3 (*relaxed design conditions*). *The equilibrium of the fuzzy system Eqs. (2) and (3) controlled by the fuzzy dynamic output controller Eqs. (79) and (80) is global asymptotically stable if there exist a positive definite symmetric matrix $S^{\circ} \in \mathbb{R}^{2n \times 2n}$, symmetric matrices $X_{ij}^{\circ} = X_{ji}^{\circ} \in \mathbb{R}^{2n \times 2n}$, a regular matrix $H^{\circ} \in \mathbb{R}^{(n+m) \times (n+m)}$ and matrices $Y_j^{\circ} \in \mathbb{R}^{(n+r) \times (n+m)}$ such that*

$$S^{\circ} = S^{\circ T} > 0, \quad \begin{bmatrix} X_{11}^{\circ} & X_{12}^{\circ} & \cdots & X_{1s}^{\circ} \\ X_{21}^{\circ} & X_{22}^{\circ} & \cdots & X_{2s}^{\circ} \\ \vdots & \vdots & \ddots & \vdots \\ X_{s1}^{\circ} & X_{s2}^{\circ} & \cdots & X_{ss}^{\circ} \end{bmatrix} > 0, \tag{88}$$

$$A_i^{\circ} S^{\circ} + S^{\circ} A_i^{\circ T} + B_i^{\circ} Y_i^{\circ} C^{\circ} + C^{\circ T} Y_i^{\circ T} B_i^{\circ T} + X_{ii}^{\circ} < 0, \tag{89}$$

$$\frac{A_i^{\circ} + A_j^{\circ}}{2} S^{\circ} + S^{\circ} \frac{A_i^{\circ T} + A_j^{\circ T}}{2} + \frac{B_i^{\circ} Y_j^{\circ} + B_j^{\circ} Y_i^{\circ}}{2} C^{\circ} + C^{\circ T} \frac{Y_j^{\circ T} B_i^{\circ T} + Y_i^{\circ T} B_j^{\circ T}}{2} + \frac{X_{ij}^{\circ} + X_{ji}^{\circ}}{2} < 0, \tag{90}$$

$$C^{\circ} S^{\circ} = H^{\circ} C^{\circ}, \tag{91}$$

for all $i \in \langle 1, 2, \ldots s \rangle$, $i < j \le s$, $i, j \in \langle 1, 2, \ldots s \rangle$, respectively, and $h_i(\theta(t)) h_j(\theta(t)) \ne 0$.

When the above conditions hold, the set of control law gain matrices are given as

$$K_j^{\circ} = Y_j^{\circ} (H^{\circ})^{-1}, \quad j = 1, 2, \ldots, s \tag{92}$$

Proof. Defining the Lyapunov function as follows

$$v(q^{\circ}(t)) = q^{\circ T}(t) P^{\circ} q^{\circ}(t) > 0, \tag{93}$$

where $P^{\circ} \in \mathbb{R}^{2n \times 2n}$ is a positive definite matrix, then the time derivative of $v(q(t))$ along a closed-loop system trajectory is

$$\dot{v}(q^{\circ}(t)) = \dot{q}^{\circ T}(t) P^{\circ} q^{\circ}(t) + q^{\circ T}(t) P^{\circ} \dot{q}^{\circ}(t) < 0. \tag{94}$$

Substituting Eq. (87), then Eq. (94) implies

$$\dot{v}(q^{\circ}(t)) = \sum_{i=1}^{s} \sum_{j=1}^{s} h_i(\theta(t)) h_j(\theta(t)) q^{\circ T}(t) P_{cij}^{\circ} q^{\circ}(t) < 0, \tag{95}$$

$$P_{cij}^{\circ} = P^{\circ} A_{cij}^{\circ} + A_{cij}^{\circ T} P^{\circ}. \tag{96}$$

Since P° is positive definite, the state coordinate transform can now be defined as

$$q^{\circ}(t) = S^{\circ}p^{\circ}(t), \quad S^{\circ} = (P^{\circ})^{-1}, \tag{97}$$

and subsequently Eqs. (95) and (96) can be rewritten as

$$\dot{v}(p^{\circ}(t)) = \sum_{i=1}^{s}\sum_{j=1}^{s} h_i(\theta(t))h_j(\theta(t))p^{\circ T}(t)S_{cij}^{\circ}p^{\circ}(t) < 0, \tag{98}$$

$$S_{cij}^{\circ} = A_{cij}^{\circ}S^{\circ} + S^{\circ}A_{cij}^{\circ T}. \tag{99}$$

Introducing, analogously to Eqs. (54) and (55), the positive term

$$v_v(p^{\circ}(t)) = p^{\circ T}(t)Z^{\circ}(\theta(t))p^{\circ}(t) > 0, \tag{100}$$

defined by the set of matrices $\left\{ X_{ij}^{\circ} = X_{ji}^{\circ T} \in \mathbb{R}^{n \times n}, \ i,j = 1, 2, ..., s \right\}$ in the structure Eq. (88) such that

$$Z^{\circ}(\theta(t)) = Z^{\circ T}(\theta(t)) = \sum_{i=1}^{s}\sum_{j=1}^{s} h_i(\theta(t))h_j(\theta(t))X_{ij}^{\circ} > 0, \tag{101}$$

then, in the sense of Krasovskii theorem, it can be set up

$$\dot{v}(p^{\circ}(t)) = \sum_{i=1}^{s}\sum_{j=1}^{s} h_i(\theta(t))h_j(\theta(t))p^{\circ T}(t)S_{cij}^{\circ}p^{\circ}(t) < 0, \tag{102}$$

where

$$S_{cij}^{\circ} = A_{cij}^{\circ}S^{\circ} + S^{\circ}A_{cij}^{\circ T} + X_{ij}^{\circ}. \tag{103}$$

Therefore, Eq. (102) can be factorized as follows

$$\dot{v}(p^{\circ}(t)) = \sum_{i=1}^{s} h_i^2(\theta(t))p^{\circ T}(t)S_{cii}^{\circ}p^{\circ}(t) + 2\sum_{i=1}^{s-1}\sum_{j=i+1}^{s} h_i(\theta(t))h_j(\theta(t))p^{\circ T}(t)\frac{S_{cij}^{\circ} + S_{cji}^{\circ}}{2}p^{\circ}(t) < 0, \tag{104}$$

which, using Eq. (87), leads to the following sets of inequalities

$$A_i^{\circ}S^{\circ} + S^{\circ}A_i^{\circ T} + B_i^{\circ}K_i^{\circ}C^{\circ}S^{\circ} + S^{\circ}C^{\circ T}K_i^{\circ T}B_i^{\circ T} + X_{ij}^{\circ} < 0, \tag{105}$$

$$\frac{\left(A_i^{\circ} + B_i^{\circ}K_j^{\circ}C^{\circ}\right)S^{\circ}}{2} + \frac{\left(A_j^{\circ} + B_j^{\circ}K_i^{\circ}C^{\circ}\right)S^{\circ}}{2} + \frac{S^{\circ}\left(A_i^{\circ} + B_i^{\circ}K_j^{\circ}C^{\circ}\right)^T}{2}$$
$$+ \frac{S^{\circ}\left(A_j^{\circ} + B_j^{\circ}K_i^{\circ}C^{\circ}\right)^T}{2} + \frac{X_{ij}^{\circ} + X_{ji}^{\circ}}{2} < 0, \tag{106}$$

for $i = 1, 2, ..., s$, as well as $i = 1, 2, ..., s - 1$, $j = 1 + 1, i + 2, ..., s$, and $h_i(\theta(t))h_j(\theta(t)) \neq 0$.

Analyzing the product $B_i^{\circ} K_j^{\circ} C^{\circ} S^{\circ}$, it can set

$$B_i^{\circ} K_j^{\circ} C^{\circ} S^{\circ} = B_i^{\circ} K_j^{\circ} H^{\circ} (H^{\circ})^{-1} C^{\circ} S^{\circ} = B_i^{\circ} Y_j^{\circ} C^{\circ}, \tag{107}$$

where

$$K_j^{\circ} H^{\circ} = Y_j^{\circ}, \quad (H^{\circ})^{-1} C^{\circ} = C^{\circ} (S^{\circ})^{-1} \tag{108}$$

and $H^{\circ} \in \mathbb{R}^{(m+n) \times (m+n)}$ is a regular square matrix. Thus, with Eq. (108), then Eqs. (105) and (106) implies Eqs. (89) and (90) and Eq. (108) gives Eq. (91). This concludes the proof.

This theorem provides the sufficient condition under LMIs and LME formulations for the synthesis of the dynamic output controller reflecting the membership function properties.

For the same reasons as in Theorem 1, the following theorem is proven.

Theorem 4 (*enhanced relaxed design conditions*). *The equilibrium of the fuzzy system Eqs. (2) and (3) controlled by the fuzzy dynamic output controller Eqs. (79) and (80) is global asymptotically stable if for given a positive $\delta \in \mathbb{R}$ there exist positive definite symmetric matrices V°, $S^{\circ} \in \mathbb{R}^{n \times n}$, and matrices $Y_j^{\circ} \in \mathbb{R}^{r \times n}$, $H^{\circ} \in \mathbb{R}^{m \times m}$ such that*

$$S^{\circ} = S^{\circ T} > 0, \quad V^{\circ} = V^{\circ T} > 0, \quad \begin{bmatrix} X_{11}^{\circ} & X_{12}^{\circ} & \cdots & X_{1s}^{\circ} \\ X_{21}^{\circ} & X_{22}^{\circ} & \cdots & X_{2s}^{\circ} \\ \vdots & \vdots & \ddots & \vdots \\ X_{s1}^{\circ} & X_{s2}^{\circ} & \cdots & X_{ss}^{\circ} \end{bmatrix} > 0, \tag{109}$$

$$\begin{bmatrix} A_i^{\circ} S^{\circ} + S^{\circ} A_i^{\circ T} + B_i^{\circ} Y_i^{\circ} C^{\circ} + C^{\circ T} Y_i^{\circ T} B_i^{\circ T} & * \\ V^{\circ} - S^{\circ} + \delta A_i^{\circ} S^{\circ} + \delta B_i^{\circ} Y_i^{\circ} C^{\circ} & -2\delta S^{\circ} \end{bmatrix} < 0, \tag{110}$$

$$\begin{bmatrix} \boldsymbol{\Phi}_{ij}^{\circ} & * \\ V^{\circ} - S^{\circ} + \delta \dfrac{A_i^{\circ} S^{\circ} + A_j^{\circ} S^{\circ}}{2} + \delta \dfrac{B_i^{\circ} Y_j^{\circ} + B_j^{\circ} Y_i^{\circ}}{2} C^{\circ} & -2\delta S^{\circ} \end{bmatrix} < 0, \tag{111}$$

$$C^{\circ} S^{\circ} = H^{\circ} C^{\circ}, \tag{112}$$

for $i = 1, 2, \ldots, s$, as well as $i = 1, 2, \ldots, s-1$, $j = 1+1, i+2, \ldots, s$, $h_i(\theta(t)) h_j(\theta(t)) \neq 0$, and

$$\boldsymbol{\Phi}_{ij}^{\circ} = \frac{A_i^{\circ} S^{\circ} + S^{\circ} A_i^{\circ T}}{2} + \frac{A_j^{\circ} S^{\circ} + S^{\circ} A_j^{\circ T}}{2} + \frac{B_i^{\circ} Y_j^{\circ} C^{\circ} + C^{\circ T} Y_j^{\circ T} B_i^{\circ T}}{2} + \frac{B_j^{\circ} Y_i^{\circ} C^{\circ} + C^{\circ T} Y_i^{\circ T} B_j^{\circ T}}{2}. \tag{113}$$

When the above conditions hold, the control law gain matrices are given as

$$K_i^{\circ} = Y_i^{\circ} (H^{\circ})^{-1}. \tag{114}$$

Proof. Since Eq. (82), Eq. (87) takes formally the same structure as Eqs. (6) and (7), following the same way as in the proof of Theorem 1, the conditions given in Theorem 4 can be obtained. From this reason, the proof is omitted. Compare, for example, Ref. [17].

Following the presented results, it is evident that the standard as well as the enhanced conditions for biproper dynamic output controller design can be derived from Theorem 3 and Theorem 4 in a simple way.

6. Illustrative example

The nonlinear dynamics of the system is represented by TS model with s = 3 and the system model parameters [20]

$$A_1 = \begin{bmatrix} -1.0522 & -1.8666 & 0.5102 \\ -0.4380 & -5.4335 & 0.9205 \\ -0.5522 & 0.1334 & -0.4898 \end{bmatrix}, A_2 = \begin{bmatrix} -1.0565 & -1.8661 & 0.5116 \\ -0.4380 & -5.4359 & 0.9214 \\ -0.5565 & 0.1339 & -0.4884 \end{bmatrix},$$

$$A_3 = \begin{bmatrix} -1.0602 & -1.8657 & 0.5133 \\ -0.4381 & -5.4353 & 0.9216 \\ -0.5602 & 0.1343 & -0.4867 \end{bmatrix}, B = \begin{bmatrix} -0.1765 & 0.0000 \\ 0.0000 & 0.0000 \\ 0.1176 & 0.4721 \end{bmatrix}, C = \begin{bmatrix} 1 & 0 & 0 \\ 0 & 1 & 0 \end{bmatrix}.$$

To the state vector $q(t)$ are associated the premise variables and the membership functions as follows

$$\theta(t) = \begin{bmatrix} \theta_1(t) \\ \theta_2(t) \\ \theta_3(t) \end{bmatrix}, \theta_i(t) = \begin{cases} \theta_1(t) \text{ if } q_1(t) \text{ is about } 2.5, \\ \theta_2(t) \text{ if } q_1(t) \text{ is about } 0, \\ \theta_3(t) \text{ if } q_1(t) \text{ is about } -2.5, \end{cases}$$

$$h_1(\theta_2(t)) = 1 - \frac{1}{2.5}|\theta_2(t) - 2.5|$$
$$h_2(\theta_1(t)) = 1 - \frac{1}{2.5}|\theta_1(t)|$$
$$h_3(\theta_3(t)) = 1 - \frac{1}{2.5}|\theta_3(t) + 2.5|$$

while the generalized premise variable is $\theta(t) = q_1(t)$.

Thus, solving Eqs. (46)–(49) for prescribed $\delta = 1.2$ with respect to the LMI matrix variables S, V H, Y_i, j = 1, 2, 3, and X_{ij}, i, j = 1, 2, 3 using Self–Dual–Minimization (SeDuMi) package for Matlab [26], then the feedback gain matrix design problem was feasible with the results

$$S = \begin{bmatrix} 0.3899 & -0.0102 & -0.0000 \\ -0.0102 & 0.1596 & -0.0000 \\ -0.0000 & -0.0000 & 0.4099 \end{bmatrix}, V = \begin{bmatrix} 0.9280 & 0.1235 & -0.1525 \\ 0.1235 & 1.1533 & -0.3979 \\ -0.1525 & -0.3979 & 0.7574 \end{bmatrix},$$

$$H = \begin{bmatrix} 0.3899 & -0.0102 \\ -0.0102 & 0.1596 \end{bmatrix},$$

$$X = \begin{bmatrix} 0.4567 & 0.0983 & -0.0517 & 0.0694 & 0.0463 & -0.0174 & 0.0694 & 0.0463 & -0.0174 \\ 0.0983 & 0.7153 & -0.1118 & 0.0463 & 0.1906 & -0.0441 & 0.0463 & 0.1905 & -0.0440 \\ -0.0517 & -0.1118 & 0.1883 & -0.0175 & -0.0442 & 0.0143 & -0.0175 & -0.0442 & 0.0142 \\ 0.0694 & 0.0463 & -0.0175 & 0.4573 & 0.0981 & -0.0515 & 0.0695 & 0.0463 & -0.0174 \\ 0.0463 & 0.1906 & -0.0442 & 0.0981 & 0.7154 & -0.1115 & 0.0463 & 0.1905 & -0.0440 \\ -0.0174 & -0.0441 & 0.0143 & -0.0515 & -0.1115 & 0.1876 & -0.0175 & -0.0441 & 0.0142 \\ 0.0694 & 0.0463 & -0.0175 & 0.0695 & 0.0463 & -0.0175 & 0.4578 & 0.0978 & -0.0514 \\ 0.0463 & 0.1905 & -0.0442 & 0.0463 & 0.1905 & -0.0441 & 0.0978 & 0.7152 & -0.1111 \\ -0.0174 & -0.0440 & 0.0142 & -0.0174 & -0.0440 & 0.0142 & -0.0514 & -0.1111 & 0.1868 \end{bmatrix},$$

$$Y_1 = \begin{bmatrix} 0.5607 & -0.4590 \\ 0.1544 & -0.1191 \end{bmatrix}, Y_2 = \begin{bmatrix} 0.5558 & -0.4577 \\ 0.1579 & -0.1207 \end{bmatrix}, Y_3 = \begin{bmatrix} 0.5518 & -0.4566 \\ 0.1606 & -0.1222 \end{bmatrix},$$

Substituting the above parameters into Eq. (51) to solve the controller parameters, the following gain matrices are obtained

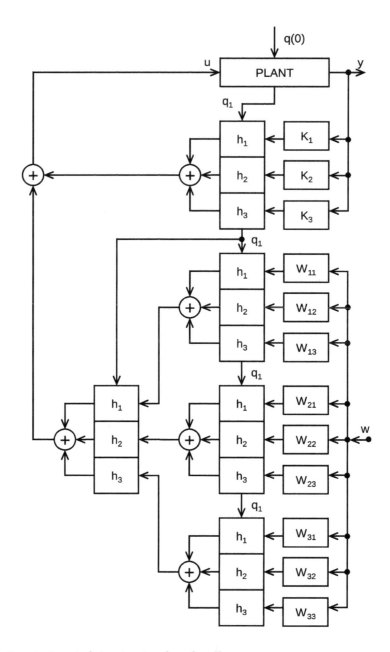

Figure 1. TS fuzzy static output control structure in a forced mode.

$$K_1 = \begin{bmatrix} 1.3653 & -2.7895 \\ 0.3772 & -0.7224 \end{bmatrix}, K_2 = \begin{bmatrix} 1.3530 & -2.7823 \\ 0.3860 & -0.7318 \end{bmatrix}, K_3 = \begin{bmatrix} 1.3428 & -2.7761 \\ 0.3925 & -0.7406 \end{bmatrix},$$

$$A_{c22} = \begin{bmatrix} -1.2953 & -1.3750 & 0.5116 \\ -0.4380 & -5.4359 & 0.9214 \\ -0.2152 & -0.5388 & -0.4884 \end{bmatrix}, A_{c31} = \begin{bmatrix} -1.3012 & -1.3734 & 0.5133 \\ -0.4381 & -5.4353 & 0.9216 \\ -0.2216 & -0.5348 & -0.4867 \end{bmatrix},$$

For simplicity, other closed-loop matrices of subsystem dynamics are not listed here.

Since the diagonal elements of A_{cij}, $i, j = 1, 2, 3$, are dominant, in terms of Gerschgorin theorem [27, 28], all eigenvalues of A_{cij} are real, resulting in the aperiodic dynamics, that is,

$$\tilde{n}(\mathbf{A}_{c11}) = \{-0.6751, \quad -1.0816, \quad -5.4598\}, \quad \tilde{n}(\mathbf{A}_{c21}) = \{-0.6756, \quad -1.0842, \quad -5.4620\},$$
$$\tilde{n}(\mathbf{A}_{c31}) = \{-0.6757, \quad -1.0861, \quad -5.4613\}, \quad \tilde{n}(\mathbf{A}_{c12}) = \{-0.6745, \quad -1.0805, \quad -5.4593\},$$
$$\tilde{n}(\mathbf{A}_{c22}) = \{-0.6750, \quad -1.0831, \quad -5.4615\}, \quad \tilde{n}(\mathbf{A}_{c32}) = \{-0.6751, \quad -1.0851, \quad -5.4609\},$$
$$\tilde{n}(\mathbf{A}_{c13}) = \{-0.6742, \quad -1.0795, \quad -5.4588\}, \quad \tilde{n}(\mathbf{A}_{c23}) = \{-0.6748, \quad -1.0820, \quad -5.4610\},$$
$$\tilde{n}(\mathbf{A}_{c33}) = \{-0.6748, \quad -1.0840, \quad -5.4604\}.$$

Figure 1 gives the associated TS fuzzy static output control structure in a forced mode.

For Eqs. (88)–(91), it can find the following feasible solutions by using the given design procedure

$$S^\circ = \begin{bmatrix} 0.6194 & -0.0614 & 0.0000 & 0.0000 & 0.0000 & 0.0000 \\ -0.0614 & 0.1305 & 0.0000 & 0.0000 & 0.0000 & 0.0000 \\ 0.0000 & 0.0000 & 0.8724 & 0.0000 & 0.0000 & 0.0000 \\ 0.0000 & 0.0000 & 0.0000 & 0.7066 & 0.0000 & 0.0000 \\ 0.0000 & 0.0000 & 0.0000 & 0.0000 & 0.7066 & 0.0000 \\ 0.0000 & 0.0000 & 0.0000 & 0.0000 & 0.0000 & 0.7066 \end{bmatrix},$$

$$H^\circ = \begin{bmatrix} 0.7066 & 0.0000 & 0.0000 & 0.0000 & 0.0000 \\ 0.0000 & 0.7066 & 0.0000 & 0.0000 & 0.0000 \\ 0.0000 & 0.0000 & 0.7066 & 0.0000 & 0.0000 \\ 0.0000 & 0.0000 & 0.0000 & 0.6808 & -0.0614 \\ 0.0000 & 0.0000 & 0.0000 & 0.4889 & 0.0691 \end{bmatrix},$$

$$Y_1 = \begin{bmatrix} -0.5668 & 0.0000 & 0.0000 & 0.0000 & 0.0000 \\ 0.0000 & -0.5668 & 0.0000 & -0.0001 & 0.0000 \\ 0.0000 & 0.0000 & -0.5667 & 0.0000 & 0.0000 \\ 0.0000 & 0.0000 & 0.0000 & 0.3612 & -0.2783 \\ 0.0000 & 0.0000 & 0.0000 & 0.7396 & -1.1397 \end{bmatrix},$$

$$Y_2 = \begin{bmatrix} -0.5668 & 0.0000 & 0.0000 & 0.0000 & 0.0000 \\ 0.0000 & -0.5668 & 0.0000 & -0.0001 & 0.0000 \\ 0.0000 & 0.0000 & -0.5667 & 0.0000 & 0.0000 \\ 0.0000 & 0.0000 & 0.0000 & 0.3615 & -0.2784 \\ 0.0000 & 0.0000 & 0.0000 & 0.7397 & -1.1397 \end{bmatrix},$$

$$Y_3 = \begin{bmatrix} -0.5667 & -0.0001 & 0.0000 & 0.0000 & 0.0000 \\ -0.0001 & -0.5667 & 0.0000 & -0.0001 & 0.0000 \\ 0.0000 & 0.0000 & -0.5668 & 0.0000 & 0.0000 \\ 0.0000 & 0.0000 & 0.0000 & 0.3519 & -0.2859 \\ -0.0001 & 0.0000 & -0.0001 & 0.7486 & -1.1421 \end{bmatrix}$$

and, computing the biproper dynamic output controller parameters, then

$$J_1 = \begin{bmatrix} -0.8022 & 0.0000 & 0.0000 \\ 0.0000 & -0.8021 & 0.0000 \\ 0.0000 & 0.0000 & -0.8021 \end{bmatrix}, \quad L_1 = 10^{-3} \begin{bmatrix} 0.0394 & 0.0048 \\ -0.3143 & 0.3318 \\ 0.0221 & -0.0508 \end{bmatrix},$$

$$M_1 = 10^{-4} \begin{bmatrix} -0.2041 & 0.1504 & -0.0600 \\ -0.5318 & 0.0915 & -0.3275 \end{bmatrix}, \quad N_1 = \begin{bmatrix} 2.0889 & -2.1701 \\ 7.8914 & -9.4765 \end{bmatrix},$$

$$J_2 = \begin{bmatrix} -0.8022 & 0.0001 & 0.0000 \\ 0.0001 & -0.8022 & 0.0000 \\ 0.0000 & 0.0000 & -0.8021 \end{bmatrix}, \quad L_2 = 10^{-3} \begin{bmatrix} -0.2009 & 0.3531 \\ 0.0453 & -0.2017 \\ -0.1903 & 0.1765 \end{bmatrix},$$

$$M_2 = 10^{-4} \begin{bmatrix} -0.2022 & 0.1779 & 0.1796 \\ -0.4575 & 0.0413 & 0.2985 \end{bmatrix}, \quad N_2 = \begin{bmatrix} 2.0897 & -2.1707 \\ 7.8915 & -9.4766 \end{bmatrix},$$

$$J_3 = \begin{bmatrix} -0.8020 & -0.0001 & 0.0000 \\ -0.0001 & -0.8021 & 0.0000 \\ 0.0000 & 0.0000 & -0.8022 \end{bmatrix}, \quad L_3 = 10^{-3} \begin{bmatrix} -0.0641 & 0.0139 \\ -0.1516 & 0.2382 \\ -0.2116 & 0.2630 \end{bmatrix},$$

$$M_3 = 10^{-4} \begin{bmatrix} -0.0135 & 0.0020 & -0.0238 \\ -0.0917 & 0.0218 & -0.1102 \end{bmatrix}, \quad N_3 = \begin{bmatrix} 2.1286 & -2.2445 \\ 7.9148 & -9.4907 \end{bmatrix}.$$

It is evident that all matrices J_i, $i = 1.2.3$ are Hurwitz, which rise up a TS fuzzy stable dynamic output controller, and based on the solutions obtained, the TS fuzzy dynamic controller can be designed via the concept of PDC.

Verifying the closed-loop stability, it can compute the eigenvalue spectra as follows

$$\tilde{n}(A_{c11}) = \{-0.8022, \quad -0.8021, \quad -0.8021, \quad -4.3774, \quad -1.2919 \pm 0.2804i\},$$

$$\tilde{n}(A_{c21}) = \{-0.8022, \quad -0.8021, \quad -0.8021, \quad -4.3774, \quad -1.2919 \pm 0.2804i\},$$

$$\tilde{n}(A_{c21}) = \{-0.8022, \quad -0.8021, \quad -0.8021, \quad -4.3774, \quad -1.2919 \pm 0.2804i\},$$

$$\tilde{n}(A_{c12}) = \{-0.8022, \quad -0.8021, \quad -0.8021, \quad -4.3774, \quad -1.2919 \pm 0.2805i\},$$

$$\tilde{n}(A_{c22}) = \{-0.8022, \quad -0.8021, \quad -0.8021, \quad -4.3774, \quad -1.2919 \pm 0.2805i\},$$

$$\tilde{n}(A_{c32}) = \{-0.8022, \quad -0.8021, \quad -0.8021, \quad -4.3788, \quad -1.2946 \pm 0.2963i\},$$

$$\tilde{n}(A_{c13}) = \{-0.8020, \quad -0.8023, \quad -0.8023, \quad -4.3713, \quad -1.2919 \pm 0.2797i\},$$

$$\tilde{n}(A_{c23}) = \{-0.8020, \quad -0.8023, \quad -0.8023, \quad -4.3713, \quad -1.2919 \pm 0.2797i\},$$

$$\tilde{n}(A_{c33}) = \{-0.8020, \quad -0.8023, \quad -0.8023, \quad -4.3728, \quad -1.2945 \pm 0.2958i\}.$$

7. Concluding remarks

New approach for static and dynamic output feedback control design, taking into account the affine properties of the TS fuzzy model structure, is presented in the chapter. Applying the fuzzy output control schemes relating to the parallel-distributed output compensators, the method presented methods that significantly reduces the conservativeness in the control design conditions. Sufficient existence conditions of the both output controller realization, manipulating the global stability of the system, implies the parallel decentralized control framework which stabilizes the nonlinear system in the sense of Lyapunov, and the design of controller parameters, resulting directly from these conditions, is a feasible numerical problem. An additional benefit of the method is that controllers use minimum feedback information with respect to desired system output and the approach is flexible enough to allow the inclusion of additional design conditions. The validity and applicability of the approach is demonstrated through numerical design examples.

Acknowledgement

The work presented in this chapter was supported by VEGA, the Grant Agency of Ministry of Education and Academy of Science of Slovak Republic, under Grant No. 1/0608/17. This support is very gratefully acknowledged.

Author details

Dušan Krokavec* and Anna Filasová

*Address all correspondence to: dusan.krokavec@tuke.sk

Department of Cybernetics, Artificial Intelligence, Faculty of Electrical Engineering, Informatics, Technical University of Košice, Košice, Slovakia

References

[1] Takagi T, Sugeno M. Fuzzy identification of systems and its applications to modeling and control. IEEE Transactions on Systems, Man, and Cybernetics. 1985;**15**(1):116–132. DOI: 10.1109/TSMC.1985.6313399.

[2] Wang HO, Tanaka K, Griffin MF. An approach to fuzzy control of nonlinear systems: Stability and design issues. IEEE Transactions on Fuzzy Systems. 1996;**4**(1):14–23. DOI: 10.1109/91.481841.

[3] Johansson M, Rantzer A, Arzen KE. Piecewise quadratic stability of fuzzy systems. Transactions on Fuzzy Systems. 1999;**7**(6):713–722. DOI: 10.1109/91.811241

[4] Tanaka K, Wang HO. Fuzzy Control Systems Design and Analysis. A Linear Matrix Inequality Approach. New York: John Wiley & Sons; 2001:309 p.

[5] Lam HK. Polynomial Fuzzy Model-Based Control Systems. Stability Analysis and Control Synthesis Using Membership Function-Dependent Techniques. Cham: Springer-Verlag; 2016:307 p.

[6] Michels K, Klawonn F, Kruse R, Nürnberger N. Fuzzy Control. Fundamentals, Stability and Design of Fuzzy Controllers. Berlin: Springer-Verlag; 2006:416 p.

[7] Abdelmalek I, Golea N, Hadjili ML. A new fuzzy Lyapunov approach to non-quadratic stabilization of Takagi-Sugeno fuzzy models. International Journal of Applied Mathematics and Computer Science. 2007;**17**(1):39–51. DOI: 10.2478/v10006-007-0005-4.

[8] Krokavec D, Filasová A. Optimal fuzzy control for a class of nonlinear systems. Mathematical Problems in Engineering. 2012;**2012**. 29 p. DOI: 10.1155/2012/481942.

[9] Pan J, Fei S, Ni Y, Xue M. New approaches to relaxed stabilization conditions and H-infinity control designs for T-S fuzzy systems. Journal of Control Theory and Applications. 2012;**10**(1):82–91. DOI: 10.1007/s11768-012-0088-9.

[10] Boyd B, El Ghaoui L, Peron E, Balakrishnan V. Linear Matrix Inequalities in System and Control Theory. Philadelphia: SIAM;1994:205 p. DOI: http://dx.doi.org/10.1137/1.9781611970777.

[11] Liu X, Zhang Q. New approaches to H_∞ controller designs based on fuzzy observers for T-S fuzzy systems via LMI. Automatica. 2003;**39**(9):1571-1582. http://dx.doi.org/10.1016/S0005-1098(03)00172-9.

[12] Nguang SK, Shi P. H_∞ fuzzy output feedback control design for nonlinear systems: An LMI approach. IEEE Transactions on Fuzzy Systems. 2003;**11**(3):331–340. DOI: 10.1109/TFUZZ.2003.812691.

[13] Kau SW, Lee HJ, Yang CM, Lee CH, Hong L, Fang CH. Robust H_∞ fuzzy static output feedback control of T-S fuzzy systems with parametric uncertainties. Fuzzy Sets and Systems. 2007;**158**(2):135–146. DOI: 10.1016/j.fss.2006.09.010.

[14] Tognetti ES, Oliveira RCLF, Peres PLD. Improved stabilization conditions for Takagi-Sugeno fuzzy systems via fuzzy integral Lyapunov functions. In Proceedings of the 2011 American Control Conference; 29 Jun–01 Jul 2011; San Francisco, USA, pp. 4970–4975.

[15] Chen BS, Tseng CS, Uang HJ. Mixed H_2/H_∞ fuzzy output feedback control design for nonlinear dynamic systems: An LMI approach. IEEE Transactions on Fuzzy Systems. 2000;**8**(3):249–265. DOI: 10.1109/91.855915.

[16] Krokavec D, Filasová A. Stabilizing fuzzy output control for a class of nonlinear systems. Advances in Fuzzy Systems. 2013;**2013**:9 p. DOI:10.1155/2013/294971.

[17] Krokavec D, Filasová A, Liščinský P. Dynamic output control of nonlinear systems described by Takagi-Sugeno models. In: Proceedings of the 2014 IEEE Multi-conference on Systems and Control MSC 2014; 8-10 October 2014; Antibes, France, pp. 959–964. DOI: 10.1109/CCA.2014.6981460.

[18] Huang D, Nguang SK. Static output feedback controller design for fuzzy systems: An ILMI approach. Information Sciences. 2007;**177**(14):3005–3015. DOI: 10.1016/j.ins.2007.02.014.

[19] Kim E, Lee H. New approaches to relaxed quadratic stability condition of fuzzy control systems. IEEE Transactions on Fuzzy Systems. 2000;**8**(5):523–534. DOI: 10.1109/91.873576.

[20] Krokavec D, Filasová A. Relaxed design conditions for Takagi-Sugeno unknown input observers. In: Proceedings of the 15th IEEE International Symposium on Applied Machine Intelligence and Informatics SAMI 2017; 26-28 January 2017; Herlany, Slovakia: pp. 61–66.

[21] Passino KM, Yurkovich S. Fuzzy Control. Berkeley: Addison-Wesley Longman; 1998:522 p.

[22] Haddad WM, Chellaboina V. Nonlinear Dynamical Systems and Control. A Lyapunov-Based Approach. Princeton: Princeton University Press; 2008:976 p.

[23] Kailath T. Linear Systems. Englewood Cliffs: Prentice-Hall; 1980:704 p.

[24] Doyle JC, Glover K, Khargonekar PP, Francis BA. State-space solutions to standard H_2 and H_∞ control problems. IEEE Transactions on Automatic Control. 1989;**34**(8):831–847. DOI: 10.1109/9.29425.

[25] Krokavec D, Filasová A, Serbák V FTC structures with virtual actuators and dynamic output controllers. IFAC-PapersOnLine. 2015;**48**(21):511–516. DOI: 10.1016/j.ifacol.2015.09.577.

[26] Peaucelle D, Henrion D, Labit Y, Taitz K. User's Guide for SeDuMi Interface 1.04. Toulouse: LAAS-CNRS; 2002:36 p.

[27] Gerschgorin S. On the limitation of the eigenvalues of a matrix. Bulletin of the Academy of Sciences of the USSR, Section of Mathematical and Natural Sciences. 1931;**1931**(6):749–754. (in German).

[28] Feingold DG, Varga RS. Block diagonally dominant matrices and generalizations of the Gerschgorin circle theorem. Pacific Journal of Mathematics. 1962;**12**(4):1241–1250. DOI: 10.2140/pjm.1962.12.1241.

6

A Fuzzy Logic Approach for Separation Assurance and Collision Avoidance for Unmanned Aerial Systems

Brandon Cook, Tim Arnett and Kelly Cohen

Abstract

In the coming years, operations in low altitude airspace will vastly increase as the capabilities and applications of small unmanned aerial systems (sUAS) continue to multiply. Therefore, finding solutions to managing sUAS in highly congested airspace will facilitate sUAS operations. In this study, a fuzzy logic-based approach was used to help mitigate the risk of collisions between aircraft using separation assurance and collision avoidance techniques. The system was evaluated for its effectiveness at mitigating the risk of mid-air collisions between aircraft. This system utilizes only current state information and can resolve potential conflicts without knowledge of intruder intent. The avoidance logic was verified using formal methods and shown to select the correct action in all instances. Additionally, the fuzzy logic controllers were shown to always turn the vehicles in the correct direction. Numerical testing demonstrated that the avoidance system was able to prevent a mid-air collision between two sUAS in all tested cases. Simulations were also performed in a three-dimensional environment with a heterogeneous fleet of sUAS performing a variety of realistic missions. Simulations showed that the system was 99.98% effective at preventing mid-air collisions when separation assurance was disabled (unmitigated case) and 100% effective when enabled (mitigated case).

Keywords: fuzzy logic, UAS, collision avoidance, separation assurance, formal methods, satisfiability modulo theories

1. Introduction

In recent times, there have been substantial advances in the capability of mobile robots in several aerospace applications. These advances include autonomous intelligence, surveillance, and reconnaissance (ISR) efforts [1], aerial firefighting [2], and aerial delivery services [3]. However, despite the potential benefits, these advancements are currently being under-utilized due to several unresolved safety issues with integrating these platforms into the National Airspace System (NAS). As a result of these shortcomings, there is a need to develop algorithms that allow a heterogeneous team of small unmanned aerial systems (sUAS) to interact autonomously and perform time-critical tasks in complex environments. As the applications and capabilities of sUAS continue to proliferate, it is imperative to address the safe integration of these vehicles into the NAS.

Most of the work in this area deals with separation assurance, as it typically takes priority in NAS conflict resolution scenarios [4, 5]. However, most methods necessitate the communication of state information between the vehicles in order to properly select resolution actions [6]. For collision avoidance, several intelligent systems have been developed with promising results [7–12], but few have also shown behavioral verification using formal methods [13, 14].

To facilitate real-time control of a large number of sUAS, a fuzzy logic approach was implemented. This approach was utilized to mitigate the risk of losses of separation and ultimately collisions, between the sUAS. In order to generate scenarios to test the sUAS's ability to avoid collisions, a realistic simulation environment was created. This simulation environment was developed in a modular fashion, such that various algorithms could be implemented to coordinate sUAS maneuvers. This enables various vehicle platforms, sensor models, software packages, and traffic management methodologies to be tested and evaluated.

The main goal of this research is to develop a high-level concept of operations for a UAS traffic management (UTM) system. This system must address the challenges of collision avoidance and separation assurance. Each of these platforms will utilize fuzzy logic controllers (FLCs) to enable real-time decision-making and dynamic control. Additionally, the confidence in correct decision-making and avoidance control outputs needs to be extremely high. Therefore, formal methods were employed for behavioral verification.

The remainder of the paper is as follows. In Section 2, background material on some of the methods and tools used in this work is described. Section 3 details the proposed solution, which includes the separation assurance and collision avoidance methods. This includes detailed development procedures for the decision-making and fuzzy avoidance controllers. Section 4 presents the methodology for implementing and evaluating the decision-making and fuzzy avoidance controllers using formal methods. Section 5 then explains the test cases, their implementations, and an overview of the simulation environment and constraints. Section 6 presents results from the formal methods evaluations and simulation runs, and finally, Section 7 discusses conclusions and opportunities for future work.

2. Background

2.1. Hybrid fuzzy systems

Most fuzzy inference systems (FISs) involve multiple operations that associate inputs to outputs based on multiple if-then rules that are resolved to a singleton. The output space is typically nonlinear and difficult to describe as a function of the input variables. However, by constraining the FIS to have particular properties and association methods, an explicit expression can be more easily found.

Hybrid systems are systems that have regions of continuous behavior separated by discrete transitions [15]. This is analogous to a subset of FISs that contain membership functions that are constrained to a finite domain. Such FISs can be represented as hybrid systems after an explicit expression is found. This expression maps an input set to an output set using a set of mathematical functions. This is useful due to the number of low-level tools that have been developed for analyzing hybrid systems. Among these are formal methods tools [16], which are described in the following section.

2.2. Formal methods

In systems such as UTM collision avoidance algorithms, the level of confidence that they will always behave as intended needs to be extremely high. Typical methods for evaluating these algorithms usually involve simulation, but simulation and other numerical methods can miss critical cases that result in undesired behavior. To increase the confidence that the avoidance algorithms presented work as intended, formal methods were employed. Formal methods are defined by NASA as "mathematically rigorous techniques and tools for the specification, design, and verification of software and hardware systems." [17] There are numerous types of tools that fall under this definition, but in this work, satisfiability modulo theories (SMT) solvers and model checkers were used.

SMT solvers are tools that extend the Boolean Satisfiability (SAT) problem to first order logic (FOL) sentences and incorporate other theories for evaluating the truth assignments of variables (real values, bitvectors, etc.). If a behavior can be described in FOL, it can be encoded and evaluated by an SMT solver to find truth assignments that violate this behavior. If a behavior is found, it is returned as satisfying the behavioral specification. If there are no possible assignments to the variables that render the specification true, it is then said to be unsatisfiable. Therefore, "safety" properties, properties which should always hold true, can be evaluated by negating a specification that encapsulates the respective behavior. If a satisfying case is found for the negated specification, this means that there are conditions that violate the original specification. If no satisfying cases are found, then the original specification will hold for all possible conditions.

Model checkers are tools that exhaustively check the states of a system to search for combinations of variable assignments that violate behavioral specifications. In finite state systems, they use deductive proofs, and in infinite state systems, they can use inductive methods. These tools can also use SAT or SMT solvers in conjunction with their own search methods for finding counterexample cases. Encoding safety properties in model checkers is slightly different, however, as model checkers typically use some type of temporal operator in conjunction with logical sentences. However, there are methods for relating quantified FOL sentences for safety properties to temporal representations for use in model checkers [18].

In this work, an infinite-state model checker named JKind [19, 20] was used. JKind is a Java implementation of the Kind model checker which uses k-induction. To evaluate the truth

A Fuzzy Logic Approach for Separation Assurance and Collision Avoidance for Unmanned Aerial...

107

assignments for variables within each state, JKind employs SMT solvers. The SMT solver used for this work is Z3 [21], a state-of-the-art SMT solver developed by Microsoft.

3. Proposed solution

To ensure that two or more sUAS do not collide with one another, an intruder avoidance system was developed. This avoidance problem is broken down into two sub-systems: strategic (separation assurance) and tactical (collision avoidance). The strategic separation assurance platform uses a centralized approach to coordinate trajectory modifications for sUAS to ensure that vehicles do not get too close to one another. This separation assurance technique is employed when two or more vehicles come within 0.4 nmi laterally of one another (separation alert threshold), 100 ft. vertically, and are predicted to have a loss of separation (LOS), defined by when vehicles come within 0.1 nmi laterally and 100 ft. vertically of one another. This LOS threshold was determined based on the characteristics of the vehicle platforms and feasible sensing abilities of sUAS. Based on the system constraints, the avoidance platform would have roughly 2 sec to resolve maximum closure rate encounters. If the separation assurance system fails to prevent an LOS, the vehicles will employ their onboard sense and avoid systems to prevent a mid-air collision. A mid-air collision occurs when two vehicles come within 60 m of one another. This collision threshold is intentionally conservative to introduce a notion of spatial uncertainty. Since the sensor models provide perfect state information, as described in Section 5, all vehicle locations are precisely known. For this study, the collision avoidance platform uses a de-centralized approach, that is, all vehicles attempt to avoid intruding vehicles independently. Thus, no communication between aircraft is available (i.e., uncoordinated maneuvers). In **Table 1**, the various distance thresholds used to describe the separation boundaries are shown.

Prior to presenting the details of each avoidance sub-system, Section 3.1 provides an overview of the avoidance system architecture. This overarching logic is used to determine when a vehicle should perform an avoidance maneuver. When deemed necessary, the system will activate the appropriate avoidance platform. In each avoidance platform, a set of heuristics are used to determine the appropriate action to resolve a conflict. These details are presented in Sections 3.2 and 3.3. Once the appropriate action has been decided, an FLC is used to control the vehicle's turn rate in the desired direction. The details of each FLC are shown in Section 3.4.

Finally, it is important to note that these two sub-systems use different approaches when trying to resolve conflicts between aircraft. This is primarily due to the overall purpose each

Threshold label	Lateral distance	Vertical distance
Separation alert	0.4 nmi	100 ft.
LOS	0.1 nmi	100 ft.
Collision	60 m	50 ft.

Table 1. Separation threshold values.

sub-system serves, and the information that is available to each. If vehicles are reporting their state information to a ground-based station, a centralized separation assurance platform could be used to coordinate a trajectory modification to one or more of the vehicles. Thus, coordinated maneuvers are possible. However, when two vehicles are within seconds away from a collision, minimizing the time between sensing the vehicle and performing an action is critical. Therefore, when the collision avoidance system is activated, the vehicles must independently choose the appropriate action using onboard processors. In these collision avoidance scenarios, there is no communication between aircraft. Thus, each sub-system requires a different set of rules to determine the appropriate action.

3.1. Overarching control logic

The overarching control logic determines whether to perform a separation assurance maneuver, activate the collision avoidance system, or allow vehicles to continue along their desired trajectories. This logic is shown in flow chart form in **Figure 1**. First, the system will find the distance separating all aircraft pairs. With this information, a calculation is made to see how much time can pass prior to two vehicles coming within 0.4 nmi. To calculate this value, the current separation, minus the 0.4 nmi threshold, is divided by the maximum closure rate of the aircraft pair. Therefore, if both vehicles moved directly toward one another at their maximum allowable speeds, this is the time it would take them to reach the 0.4 nmi separation threshold. This future time is known as the "time threshold", as shown in **Figure 1**. Using this time threshold, if two vehicles cannot possibly be within 0.4 nmi of one another, the system will not unnecessarily check if the two aircraft are in conflict. Rather, it remains idle between checks to improve the performance of the system.

Once enough time has passed and an aircraft pair reaches their assigned time threshold, the system will again check their separation. If the two aircraft are still more than 0.4 nmi apart, a new time threshold is calculated and set. However, if the aircraft pair has reached the 0.4 nmi threshold, it will next check to see if an LOS has occurred. If the vehicles have violated the 0.1 nmi LOS threshold, the collision avoidance system is enabled. Otherwise, the separation assurance system may be needed to ensure that two vehicles do not have an LOS. This decision is based on two criteria: if the predicted closest point of approach (pCPA) creates an LOS and if the time to LOS (tLOS) is within 2 min.

If both criteria are met, a final check is used to see if the aircraft pair has already been assigned a separation assurance maneuver. If neither vehicle has been assigned a maneuver to avoid an impending LOS, a resolution advisory is sent from the centralized system to one of the sUAS. However, if the sUAS was already assigned a maneuver and is currently in the middle of its resolution, a check is used to see if turning back toward its preferred heading will cause another predicted LOS. If resuming its originally intended mission will not cause an LOS, it will do so, otherwise, the sUAS will continue on its current bearing.

If neither criterion (pCPA and tLOS) is met, then no separation assurance command is given and the aircraft will continue toward its respective target using its navigation controller. After determining the appropriate separation assurance action, or deciding that no action is needed, the algorithm calculates another time threshold for each aircraft pair.

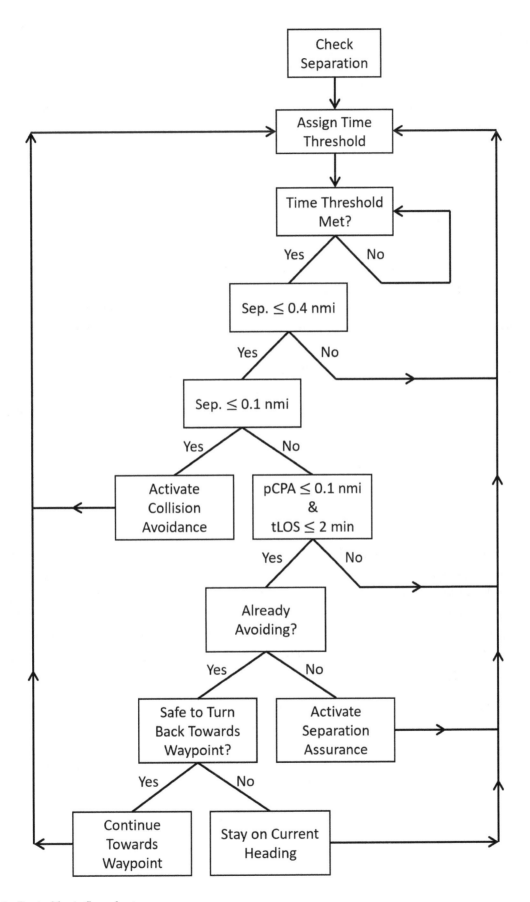

Figure 1. Control logic flow chart.

3.2. Separation assurance logic

The centralized separation assurance system observes only the current position, heading, and velocity of each vehicle. With this limited information, vehicle intent is unknown. Therefore, the system must be robust to dynamic scenarios and resolve conflicts without the knowledge of other vehicles' goals.

The separation assurance platform will be enabled if three criteria are met: separation less than 0.4 nmi, the pCPA is less than 0.1 nmi, and the tLOS is within 2 min. If two aircraft meet all three of these criteria, the separation assurance platform will activate and assign one of the vehicles a new trajectory in an effort to avoid the predicted LOS.

To determine what action the separation assurance platform should use to avoid a potential LOS, a series of conflict classification techniques are used. For this study, three pieces of information are used to classify all conflict scenarios: relative heading, relative angle, and crossing time. These parameters can be described using the more common parameters: location, speed, and heading. In **Figure 2**, a sample conflict scenario is shown. Here, the triangular objects each represent an sUAS, the arrows represent the velocities of each aircraft (both magnitude and direction), and the "x" represents the heading intersection point location. The heading intersection point is not to be confused with the pCPA. It is simply the point where the projected headings intersect with one another. For this example, the vehicle with the small circle represents aircraft 1, and the other represents aircraft 2.

The relationship used to describe the heading of vehicle 2 relative to vehicle 1's perspective is shown in Eq. (1).

$$R_{H_1} = H_2 - H_1 \tag{1}$$

where H_1 is the heading of vehicle 1, H_2 is the heading of vehicle 2, and R_{H_1} is the relative heading from vehicle 1's perspective. In this study, $0° \leq R_{h_i} < 360°$ for all vehicles, where i represents the index for each vehicle. Therefore, if $H_1 > H_2$, a 360° phase shift must be added to R_{H_1} to remain within the constrained range. Computing the relative heading for the example shown in **Figure 2**, R_{H_1} would be 140° (i.e., moving to the left with respect to vehicle 1), whereas, from vehicle 2's perspective, R_{H_2} would be roughly 220° after applying the 360° phase shift (i.e., moving to the right with respect to vehicle 2).

Similarly, the relative angle between two vehicles describes the relative position of one vehicle with respect to the other. This relationship has been shown in Eq. (2).

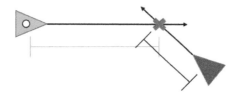

Figure 2. Conflict scenario classification information.

$$R_{A_1} = \tan^{-1}\left(\frac{y_2 - y_1}{x_2 - x_1}\right) - H_1 \tag{2}$$

where x_2 and y_2 are the two-dimensional coordinates of vehicle 2 in the global frame, x_1 and y_1 are the two-dimensional coordinates of vehicle 1 in the global frame, H_1 is the heading of vehicle 1, and R_{A_1} is the relative angle of vehicle 2 from vehicle 1's perspective. Like the relative heading, the relative angle is constrained. Here, we constrain the relative angle by the following relationship: $-180° \leq R_{A_1} \leq 180°$. Therefore, if the relative angle is less than $-180°$, a $360°$ phase shift is added to meet this constraint, or if the angle is greater than $180°$, a $360°$ phase shift is subtracted. Again, using **Figure 2** as an example, R_{A_1} would be roughly $-15°$ after subtracting a $360°$ phase shift (i.e., vehicle 2 is to the right of vehicle 1 from vehicle 1's perspective), and R_{A_2} would be roughly $25°$ (i.e., vehicle 1 is on the left of vehicle 2 from vehicle 2's perspective).

Lastly, the crossing time, t_1, can be defined by the relationship shown in Eq. (3). This relationship defines how long it would take for vehicle 1 to reach the heading intersection point, as shown in **Figure 2**, if they remained on their current trajectory.

$$t_1 = sign\left(\vec{V_1} \cdot \vec{C_1}\right) \frac{c_1}{v_1} \tag{3}$$

where $sign$ is a function used to determine the sign (positive or negative) of an expression, $\vec{V_1}$ is the velocity of vehicle 1, $\vec{C_1}$ is the vector used to describe the location of the heading intersection point relative to the vehicle's current position, v_1 is the speed of vehicle 1, and c_1 is the magnitude of the vector $\vec{C_1}$.

With these relationships, all possible encounter scenarios can be described. To aid in understanding what each of these parameters represent, **Table 2** describes, in linguistic terms, what each range of values represents in the physical conflict scenarios. Here, the term crossing point

Parameter	Range	Meaning
Relative heading	$0° < R_{H_1} < 180°$	Moving from right to left
	$180° < R_{H_1} < 360°$	Moving from left to right
	$R_{H_1} = 0°$	Same direction
	$R_{H_1} = 180°$	Head-on
Relative angle	$R_{A_1} > 0°$	On left
	$R_{A_1} < 0°$	On right
	$R_{A_1} = 0°$	Straight ahead
Time to crossing point	$t_1 > 0$	Crossing point in front
	$t_1 < 0$	Crossing point behind
	$t_1 > t_2$	Farther from crossing point
	$t_1 < t_2$	Closer to crossing point

Table 2. Linguistic descriptions of encounter scenarios.

is synonymous to the heading intersection point. Each of these descriptions has been listed to describe the motion, location, or crossing time of vehicle 2 from vehicle 1's perspective.

Although the primary goal of this system is to ensure safe separation of vehicles, it is also important to try and limit the number of unnecessary flight adjustments. This is particularly important when operating sUAS due to their typical limitations in power and endurance. Because vehicle intent is unknown in this study, a predicted LOS does not guarantee an LOS is imminent. Therefore, there is a tradeoff between using strict and relaxed criteria when determining if a trajectory modification is necessary. The criteria should be relaxed to ensure sUAS do not repetitively perform unnecessary adjustments but strict enough to ensure safe operation.

Aside from optimizing this time to predicted LOS threshold, a second way to limit the number of vehicles that divert from their desired flight paths is to assign vehicles priority. This priority assignment ranks all vehicles in conflict from highest priority to lowest priority. Therefore, the vehicle with the highest priority will continue on its preferred trajectory without modification. However, all vehicles with a lower priority must avoid all other vehicles with a higher priority.

To determine which aircraft has a lower priority, a series of evaluations are made. First, the system will be checked to see if the two aircraft are moving in a similar direction. If two vehicles have a heading within 5° of one another, that is, $355° \leq R_{H_1} < 360°$ or $0° \leq R_{H_1} \leq 5°$, the trailing aircraft will have lower priority. This encounter scenario can be seen in **Figure 3**. If several aircraft have similar headings, the aircraft furthest behind will be assigned the lowest priority so must avoid all other aircraft. However, the vehicle in the front of the group will have the highest priority and will disregard all other aircraft.

If the vehicles in conflict do not have similar headings (i.e., more than a 5° difference), the vehicle closest to its next waypoint is given priority. Since the separation assurance system logic does not use the location of a vehicle's next waypoint (i.e., intent is unknown), this priority assignment was simply a means to an end. In practice, the priority of each vehicle in these scenarios would be randomly assigned.

To predict whether an LOS will occur, the separation assurance algorithm uses the current location and velocity of each aircraft to calculate a projected flight path for each. Using these projected trajectories, the pCPA between the aircraft is found. If the pCPA will result in an LOS within the next 2 min, a resolution is calculated and employed to prevent the predicted LOS.

Recalling the sample encounter scenario shown in **Figure 2**, the definitions described by Eqs. (1) through (3), and the constraints shown in **Table 2**, all encounter scenarios can be described. **Figure 4** depicts all the possible conflict scenarios when vehicle 2 is located to the right of vehicle

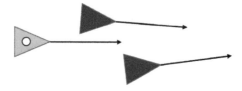

Figure 3. Encounter example with relative heading within 5°.

1. In each diagram, the aircraft with the small circle represents vehicle 1 and the other is vehicle 2. Thus, all parameters used to describe a particular conflict scenario are from the perspective of vehicle 1. Within the scope of the separation assurance system, vehicle 2 is classified as the vehicle that has been assigned the higher priority. Thus, vehicle 1 (lower priority) must perform a maneuver to prevent an LOS.

In **Figure 4(a)**, vehicle 2 is moving to the left, vehicle 1 is approaching from behind, and vehicle 1 is more than 45 sec closer to the heading intersection point. In this case, vehicle 1 would decide to go in front of vehicle 2. However, if vehicle 1 is not at least 45 sec closer, it will go behind.

In **Figure 4(b)**, vehicle 2 is still going to the left, but in this case, it is coming toward vehicle 1. In these scenarios, vehicle 1 must be more than 30 sec closer to the intersection point to go in front. In **Figure 4(c)**, vehicle 2 is to the right of vehicle 1 but is also going to the right. In these instances, the logic will determine vehicle 1 should turn left to avoid a potential LOS. This also holds for when vehicle 2 is located directly in front of vehicle 1. If, however, vehicle 2 is located on the left of vehicle 1 and going left, it will be instructed to turn right. (NOTE: The 30 and 45 sec buffers were selected after testing a handful of design iterations. Optimizing these buffer thresholds is left to future work.)

In **Figure 4(d)**, vehicle 2's heading is parallel and coming toward vehicle 1. If vehicle 2 is directly in front of, or to the left of, vehicle 1, the logic will instruct vehicle 1 to turn right. However, if vehicle 2 is located to the right of vehicle 1, it will be instructed to turn left.

To prevent an aircraft from prematurely exiting an avoidance maneuver, the system checks if reverting to the navigation controller generates another predicted LOS. Since the avoidance controller has only local sensor knowledge (i.e., $-90° \le R_{A_1} \le 90°$), switching back to the navigation controller can result in a turning action that generates another predicted LOS. If turning back to its desired target would create another predicted LOS, the avoiding aircraft will continue with its trajectory until authorized to resume its desired mission.

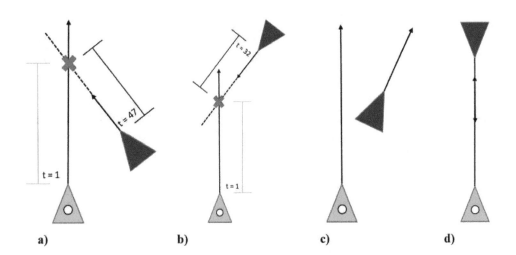

Figure 4. Separation assurance conflict scenario classifications: (a) from behind, (b) coming toward, (c) diverging, and (d) head-on.

Condition	Relative angle or time to cross	Connector	Relative heading	Action
IF	Any angle within sensor range $(-90° \leq R_{A_1} \leq 90°)$	AND	Similar direction $(R_{H_1} < 5°$ OR $R_{H_1} > 355°)$	Go behind
ElseIF	On right OR straight ahead $(R_{A_1} \leq 0°)$	AND	Going right $(180° < R_{H_1} < 360°)$	Go behind
ElseIF	On left $(R_{A_1} > 0°)$	AND	Going left $(0° < R_{H_1} < 180°)$	Go behind
ElseIF	On right $(R_{A_1} < 0°)$	AND	Head-on $(R_{H_1} = 180°)$	Turn left
ElseIF	On left OR straight ahead $(R_{A_1} \geq 0°)$	AND	Head-on $(R_{H_1} = 180°)$	Turn right
ElseIF	I'm more than 45+ seconds closer $(t_1 < (t_2 - 45))$	AND	Approaching from behind $(R_{H_1} < 90°$ OR $R_{H_1} > 270°)$	Go in front
ElseIF	I'm NOT 45+ seconds closer $(t_1 \geq (t_2 - 45))$	AND	Approaching from behind $(R_{H_1} < 90°$ OR $R_{H_1} > 270°)$	Go behind
ElseIF	I'm more than 30+ seconds closer $(t_1 < (t_2 - 30))$	AND	Coming towards $(90° \leq R_{H_1} \leq 270°)$	Go in front
ElseIF	I'm NOT 30+ seconds closer $(t_1 \geq (t_2 - 30))$	AND	Coming towards $(90° \leq R_{H_1} \leq 270°)$	Go behind

Table 3. Summary of separation assurance logic.

A summary of the separation assurance logic can be found in **Table 3**. For all cases, the crossing time is strictly positive. That is, the absolute value of the true crossing time found using Eq. (3) is used for all separation assurance logic.

3.3. Collision avoidance logic

When two vehicles have an LOS, are converging, and are within one another's sensor ranges, the collision avoidance system will be activated. In this study, each sUAS will attempt to avoid all intruders within its sensor range; therefore, no vehicle priority will be assigned. Like the approach used for the separation assurance platform to classify conflict scenarios, the collision avoidance system will use the same inputs to decide the appropriate action (i.e., relative angle, relative heading, and time to crossing point). Here, it is important to note that no two vehicles can communicate with one another. Therefore, the same logic is used onboard each system independently. This means that from each vehicle's perspective, we need to ensure that both vehicles will choose complementary actions, that is, the action will not force the vehicles to turn toward one another.

In **Figure 5**, all possible encounter scenarios are shown. Here, the black triangle and arrow represent the "ownship" (vehicle 1) location and heading respectively, the filled circle represents the "intruder" (vehicle 2) location, the dashed line connecting the two vehicles represents the relative position, and the other two dashed lines represent intruder headings that are either parallel or perpendicular to the ownship's heading. In this figure, the intruder can have any heading between 0° and 360°.

Using these dashed lines to divide the possible intruder heading into cases, the geometry of each encounter scenario can be broken down into twelve cases, provided that two of the three dashed lines do not coincide with one another. In **Figure 5(a)**, the twelve cases are depicted: two cases where the intruder has a parallel relative heading (vertical line), two cases where the headings are perpendicular (horizontal line), two cases where the intruder heading is directly toward or away from the ownship position (line connecting the two vehicles), and all headings that lie in between these angles each count as one case (i.e., six angle ranges in between the lines). If two of the three dashed lines coincide, this possible geometric space reduces to eight possible cases, as shown in **Figure 5(b)** and **c)**.

Now that the geometric configurations have been defined, let us now introduce the third characteristic, time to heading intersection point. Unlike the separation assurance platform, the time to the heading intersection point, or "crossing time," can be either positive or negative. Therefore, if the crossing point lies behind the vehicle, the crossing time becomes negative. Using

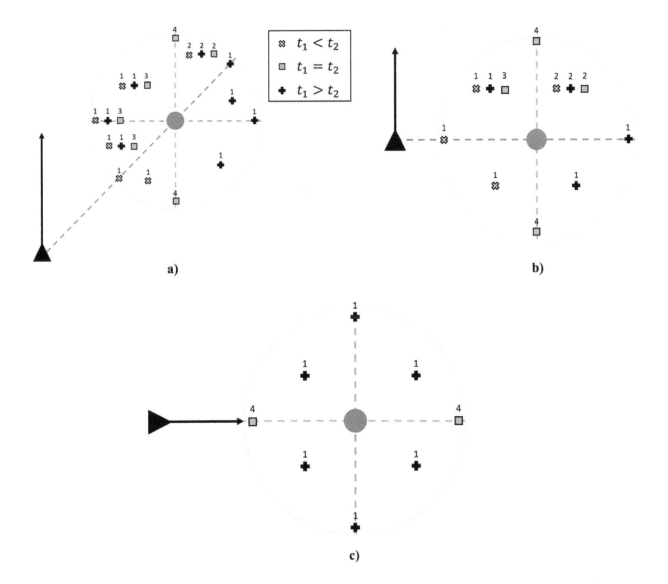

Figure 5. Classification of all possible encounter scenarios: (a) intruder not straight ahead or on side, (b) intruder on side, (c) intruder straight ahead.

the crossing time, there are up to three possible new situations for each of the twelve cases (or eight cases): the times are equal, the ownship crossing time is greater than that of the intruder, or the intruder crossing time is greater than that of the ownship. All possible crossing time scenarios based on the relative heading and angle have been shown. All instances where the ownship can have a crossing time less than the intruder crossing time have been marked by an "x." The black cross represents scenarios where the intruder crossing time can be less than the ownship crossing time. Finally, the square represents the situations where the two vehicles can have equal crossing times.

Using these three designations, all pairwise encounters where an intruder is not directly in front of or beside the ownship can be described by 20 possible cases, as shown in **Figure 5(a)**. In **Figure 5(b)**, cases where the intruder is directly beside the ownship are shown, resulting in 12 possible cases. Lastly, if the intruder is directly in front of the ownship, 8 additional cases can be attained, as shown in **Figure 5(c)**. Thus, a total of 40 cases can be attained using these three parameters to describe the pairwise encounter space.

Knowing that 40 possible cases have been shown, a total of four conflict classifications can be used to solve all possible encounter scenarios. In **Figure 5**, the number above each icon represents which of the four conflict classifications the scenario belongs. In **Figures 6** and **7**, the four conflict scenarios have been shown. In each figure, the ownship (vehicle 1) location is marked by a black triangle and its heading is designated by the black arrow. The small circle represents the location of the intruder (vehicle 2). This intruder can have any heading, but the

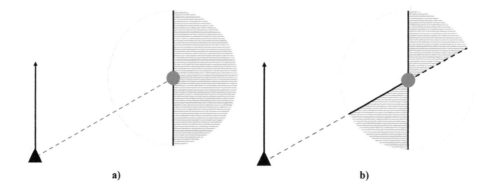

Figure 6. Conflict classification #1 where $(t_1 > 0) \vee (t_2 > 0)$ and: (a) $t_1 < t_2$, (b) $t_1 > t_2$.

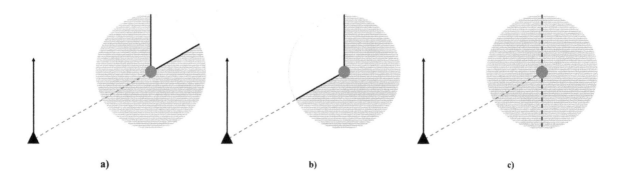

Figure 7. Conflict classifications #2, #3, and #4: (a) $(t_1 < 0) \wedge (t_2 < 0)$, (b) $(t_1 = t_2) \wedge (t_1 \neq \infty) \wedge (t_1 > 0)$, (c) $(t_1 = t_2) \wedge (t_1 = \infty)$.

different headings have been separated into different sections, as designated by the shaded regions. In each figure, the shaded regions represent the intruder headings that are excluded by that particular encounter scenario, whereas, the unshaded regions are the possible intruder headings allowed by that encounter scenario. In addition, like **Figure 5**, there is a dashed line connecting the two vehicles to represent the relative position. Lastly, if a dashed black line is on the boundary of the included and excluded regions, this represents an inclusive boundary (i.e., that heading is included in the possible headings allowed), whereas, the solid black line between the regions represents an exclusive boundary.

Figure 6 shows the first conflict classification scenario. Here, at least one of the vehicles must have a positive crossing time (t_i), and they are not equal to one another. As shown in **Figure 6(a)**, the ownship crossing time must be strictly less than that of the intruder. Thus, the intruder crossing time can be negative, or equal to zero (i.e., pointed directly at the ownship). If the intruder heading passes into the excluded region, either both values are negative, or the ownship value must be greater than the intruder value. For all the cases that satisfy this relationship, the ownship would determine to go in front of the intruder. Including the instances where the intruder is to the left of the ownship.

In **Figure 6(b)**, the ownship crossing time must be strictly greater than that of the intruder crossing time. As seen in the figure, the boundary along the relative position line is excluded when the intruder is pointing toward the ownship (i.e., the ownship crossing time is zero, but the intruder crossing time is positive), violating the relationship. However, when the intruder is pointed directly away from the ownship, the boundary is inclusive. In all possible instances, the ownship will determine to go behind the intruder. This includes the cases when the intruder is located to the left of the ownship or is directly in front of the ownship (i.e., $t_2 = 0$). For all cases represented by conflict classification #1, if one vehicle decides to go in front, the other will decide to go behind, given that they are both within one another's sensor field of view.

In the second conflict classification, as shown in **Figure 7(a)**, both the intruder and the ownship have crossing times less than zero. These negative crossing times, and the fact that the vehicles cannot have the same heading, result in the intruder never sensing the ownship. In these scenarios, if the intruder is on the left, the ownship will turn right. But, if the intruder is on the right, the ownship will turn left.

In **Figure 7(b)**, the scenarios where both the ownship and the intruder have the same time to the crossing point are shown. In this classification case, the intruder cannot have the same heading as the ownship, thus it must be crossing the ownship's path. In addition, this case is restricted to instances where both vehicles have strictly positive crossing times. For these instances, regardless of whether the vehicle is on the left, or on the right, both vehicles will decide to turn right. Since the crossing times are equivalent, and there is no coordination of intent with the other vehicle, both vehicles must choose the same action.

There is one remaining aircraft orientation in the encounter space. This occurs when an intruder is parallel to the ownship, either traveling in the same or opposite direction. This scenario has been shown in **Figure 7(c)**. As seen from this figure, only intruder headings that lie on the dashed line are included. If the intruder is to the right of the ownship, each vehicle will turn to the left (given that the intruder can see the ownship as well). However, if the intruder is directly in front of, or to the left of the ownship, both vehicles will be instructed to turn right.

Although the above classifications describe all possible encounters between moving aircraft, the quad-rotor vehicles can stop and hover. Therefore, a final classification must be described. If an intruder is stationary, the intruder crossing time is set to negative infinity. When this is the case, if the intruder is to the left or directly in front of the ownship, the controller will instruct the vehicle to turn right. However, if the intruder is to the right of the ownship, the logic will instruct the vehicle to turn left.

Table 4 describes the different encounter scenarios using both linguistic and mathematical descriptions, as well as the decided actions. Each of the above conflict classification numbers numerically matches the respective cases in this table. However, the encounter scenario where the intruder vehicle is stationary is referred to as case 0. Like **Table 3**, the linguistic descriptions in **Table 4** represent how the ownship perceives the intruder. Furthermore, all values with the subscript 1 represent the ownship, whereas, all values with the subscript 2 represent the intruder. (NOTE: the * designation indicates that the crossing time is negative infinity for that vehicle.)

3.4. Fuzzy inference systems

Using the methodology described in Sections 3.2 and 3.3, four possible actions can be used to avoid an intruding sUAS: go behind, go in front, turn right, and turn left. When the command

Case	Position	Direction	Time to cross	Crossing point location	Action
0	On left or straight $(0° \leq R_{A_1} \leq 90°)$	N/A	More $(t_1 > t_2{}^*)$	N/A	Turn right
	On right $(-90° \leq R_{A_1} < 0°)$	N/A	More $(t_1 > t_2{}^*)$	N/A	Turn left
1	Any $(-90° \leq R_{A_1} \leq 90°)$	Not parallel $(R_{H_1} \neq \{180, 0\})$	Less $(t_1 < t_2)$	Not behind both $(t_1 \geq 0 \text{ OR } t_2 \geq 0)$	Go in front
	Any $(-90° \leq R_{A_1} \leq 90°)$	Not parallel $(R_{H_1} \neq \{180, 0\})$	More $(t_1 > t_2)$	Not behind both $(t_1 \geq 0 \text{ OR } t_2 \geq 0)$	Go behind
2	On left $(R_{A_1} > 0°)$	Going left away $(R_{H_1} < 90°)$	Any	Behind both $(t_1 < 0 \text{ AND } t_2 < 0)$	Turn right
	On right $(R_{A_1} < 0°)$	Going right away $(R_{H_1} > 270°)$	Any	Behind both $(t_1 < 0 \text{ AND } t_2 < 0)$	Turn left
3	On left $(R_{A_1} > 0°)$	Going right $(180° < R_{H1} < 360°)$	Equal $(t_1 = t_2)$	In front of both $(t_1 > 0 \text{ AND } t_2 > 0)$	Turn right
	On right $(R_{A_1} < 0°)$	Going left $(0° < R_{H_1} < 180°)$	Equal $(t_1 = t_2)$	In front of both $(t_1 > 0 \text{ AND } t_2 > 0)$	Turn right
4	On left or straight $(R_{A_1} \geq 0°)$	Head-on or same $(R_{H_1} = \{180, 0\})$	Equal $(t_1 = t_2)$	N/A	Turn right
	On right $(R_{A_1} < 0°)$	Head-on or same $(R_{H_1} = \{180, 0\})$	Equal $(t_1 = t_2)$	N/A	Turn left

Table 4. Summary of collision avoidance logic.

action is either go in front or go behind, the corresponding FIS is activated to execute the maneuver. Therefore, two FISs were developed for this study: go in front and go behind. If a turn left or turn right command is selected, the turn rate of the vehicle will always be a constant value, either positive or negative, depending on which way it should turn. This constant value is one half of the maximum turn rate for collision avoidance maneuvers and one eighth of the maximum turn rate for separation assurance maneuvers.

Both the go in front and go behind fuzzy systems are of Mamdani-type and were constructed in such a way that the input-output relationship can be described using a simple mathematical representation. By using a hybrid representation, as described in Section 2.1, the fuzzy system can easily be expressed mathematically. In this study, the fuzzy systems have a common architecture: triangular membership functions, normalized inputs and outputs, membership function partitioning, product "and" method, minimum implication method, sum aggregation, and mean of maximum defuzzification. If more than one membership function exists for a particular input or output, membership functions are partitioned such that the endpoints of one membership function coincides with the center points of the neighboring membership functions.

Each FIS was developed using a three-input one-output structure. Each FIS uses the distance separating the two aircraft, their relative heading, and their closure rate as inputs to determine the appropriate turn rate output. Since a heterogeneous system is used in this study, the FIS must provide a sufficient turn rate output to avoid a collision for all vehicle type combinations. By considering the separation and closure rate, the conflict can be solved without expelling more energy than required.

In order to use the FISs for both the separation assurance and the collision avoidance platforms, all inputs and outputs must be normalized. Regardless of the avoidance platform being used, the relative heading and closure rate inputs are always normalized by the same values. The relative heading which falls between 0° and 360° is divided by 360°. Thus, a normalized relative heading of 0.5 would represent a head-on encounter. The closure rate is normalized by dividing the true closure rate by the maximum possible closure rate between two vehicles (i.e., 61.762 m/sec in this study). This maximum closure rate would be a result of two fixed wing vehicles approaching one another in a head-on scenario.

The third input, distance, is normalized by 0.4 nmi for separation assurance cases and 0.1 nmi for collision avoidance cases. Lastly, the turn rate output is always between −1 and 1. This output is then scaled by the respective vehicle platform's maximum turn rate. In the case of the collision avoidance system, the output is also multiplied by 1.58. This is to compensate for the fuzzy output not providing a sufficient turn rate command to avoid a collision, especially in head-on scenarios.

Figure 8 shows the structure of each avoidance FIS. Here, the number of membership functions and the corresponding classification can be seen for each input and output. Both the relative heading and the turn rate are partitioned such that the endpoints of the center membership functions coincide with the center points of the adjacent membership functions. As a result of this, and using a product "and" connector, for all possible inputs, at most two of the

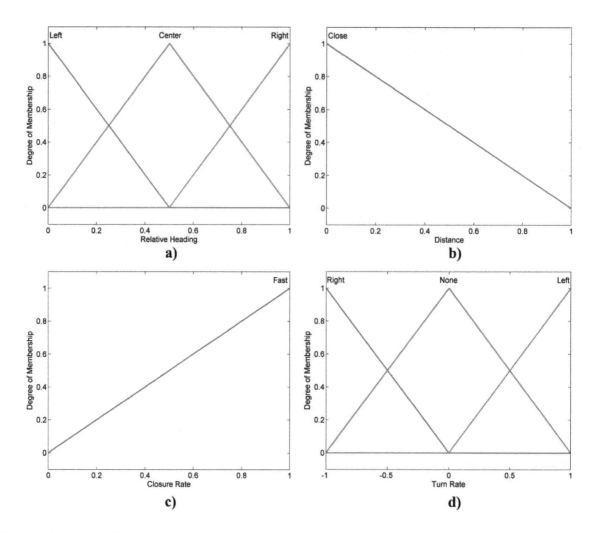

Figure 8. Avoidance FIS structure: (a) Input 1, (b) Input 2, (c) Input 3, (d) Output.

three rules will be active at one time. This drastically reduces the possible solution space, making it much easier to represent the system mathematically.

The input and output membership function sets for both the go behind and go in front FISs are identical. However, the rule bases associating the inputs and outputs are opposite, therefore, when one FIS outputs "turn right" (i.e., negative turn rate), the other FIS would output "turn left" (i.e., positive turn rate), and vice versa. In **Table 5**, the respective rule bases can be seen. Because the other two inputs only have one membership function, they have been excluded from the table.

Rule #	Input 1: relative heading	Go in front output	Go behind output
1	Left	Left	Right
2	Center	Center	Center
3	Right	Right	Left

Table 5. FIS logic.

Mode #	$\mathcal{D}_1$	$\mathcal{D}_2$	$\mathcal{D}_3$
1	[0,0.5)	[0,1]	[0,1]
2	[0.5]	[0,1]	[0,1]
3	(0.5,1]	[0,1]	[0,1]

Table 6. Input domains.

To map the fuzzy system to a set of nonlinear expressions, the following process was used. First, the system was discretized into three possible modes based on the domain of the ith input, D_i. These modes are described in **Table 6**. Here, let a square bracket represent an inclusive bound and a round bracket represent an exclusive bound. Based on the structure of the FIS, if input 1 is exactly 0.5 (Mode 2 in **Table 6**), the output will yield a turn rate of 0. It remains to find the explicit input-to-output mappings for modes 1 and 3.

When the FIS is in mode 1, only the "Left" and "Center" membership functions are active. Thus, the output will be independent of rule 3. Therefore, given that a product "and" method and a mean of maximum aggregation technique is used, the following relationship describes how the output is calculated.

$$\dot{\Psi} = \left[\left(\prod_{i=1}^{3} h_{i_1} \right) + \left(1 - \prod_{i=1}^{3} h_{i_2} \right) \right] / 2 \tag{4}$$

where, $\dot{\Psi}$, is the turn rate, h_{i_1} is the degree of membership for the ith input membership function when using rule 1 (i.e., left, close, fast membership functions), and h_{i_2} is the degree of membership for each input when using rule 2. When substituting the equation of each membership function into Eq. (4), the expression shown in Eq. (5) is found, which can be reduced to the polynomial shown in Eq. (6).

$$\dot{\Psi} = \left\{ \left[(-2\mu_1 + 1)(-\mu_2 + 1)(\mu_3) \right] + \left[1 - (2\mu_1)(-\mu_2 + 1)(\mu_3) \right] \right\} / 2 \tag{5}$$

$$\dot{\Psi} = \left(4\mu_1\mu_2\mu_3 - 4\mu_1\mu_3 - \mu_2\mu_3 + \mu_3 + 1 \right) / 2 \tag{6}$$

where μ_1, μ_2, and μ_3 are inputs 1, 2, and 3, respectively. The polynomial shown in Eq. (6) can be used to map any combination of inputs that belong to D_1 to an output for the go in front FIS.

Using the same methodology for mode 3, Eqs. (7) through (9) can be found.

$$\dot{\Psi} = \left[\left(-\prod_{i=1}^{3} h_{i_3} \right) + \left(\prod_{i=1}^{3} h_{i_2} - 1 \right) \right] / 2 \tag{7}$$

$$\dot{\Psi} = \left\{ \left[-(2\mu_1 + 1)(-\mu_2 + 1)(\mu_3) \right] + \left[(-2\mu_1 + 2)(-\mu_2 + 1)(\mu_3) - 1 \right] \right\} / 2 \tag{8}$$

$$\dot{\Psi} = \left(4\mu_1\mu_2\mu_3 - 4\mu_1\mu_3 - 3\mu_2\mu_3 + 3\mu_3 - 1 \right) / 2 \tag{9}$$

The polynomial shown in Eq. (9) will map any combination of inputs belonging to D_3 to an output for the go in front FIS.

This same approach was used to map any combination of inputs for the go behind FIS to an output using a polynomial function. Since the rule bases are exactly opposite to one another, the output is the negation of Eqs. (6) and (9). Eqs. (10) and (11) describe the input-output relationships for modes 1 and 3, respectively, for the go behind FIS.

$$\dot{\Psi} = \left(-4\mu_1\mu_2\mu_3 + 4\mu_1\mu_3 + \mu_2\mu_3 - \mu_3 - 1\right)/2 \tag{10}$$

$$\dot{\Psi} = \left(-4\mu_1\mu_2\mu_3 + 4\mu_1\mu_3 + 3\mu_2\mu_3 - 3\mu_3 + 1\right)/2 \tag{11}$$

It is important to note that if three or more vehicles are in conflict, each pair of vehicles will be evaluated separately. Thus, for a single ownship, several turn rate outputs will be obtained. Once all respective turn rates are calculated for each intruder, the values are averaged into a single value. This mean turn rate serves as the final vehicle turn rate command.

4. Avoidance algorithm verification

To verify that the avoidance algorithm performed as intended, two levels of avoidance control were evaluated. The first was the high-level, decision-making logic that determined which action a vehicle would take during potential collision scenarios as shown in **Table 4**. The second that was evaluated was the low-level logic in the avoidance FLCs. These FLCs determine the actual vehicle turn rate output after being selected by the decision-making heuristics. For each of these levels, specifications about their behavior were developed and then translated into FOL sentences that could be evaluated by an SMT solver. For the first cases that deal with the avoidance decision-making logic, the specifications and system model were implemented in JKind, with Z3 being used as the SMT solver. The evaluation of the avoidance FISs was performed directly in Z3. The difference was purely a practical one, as the language JKind uses, Lustre [22], is more conducive to easily create a more detailed environment model.

4.1. Collision avoidance decision-making logic

As shown in **Table 4**, there are several conditions for which there are different output actions for avoidance. The specifications were first translated into FOL sentences. The sentences are shown in the following equations. Note that *RAL* is a predicate that acts on the relative angle limit to represent the vehicle's sensors detecting an intruder. Since they can only sense intruders between ±90°, the relative angle values were limited in the specifications such that being in that range implied that the output action would be the correct one. If the intruder is outside of this range, the specifications do not say what the output action should be. Note that the variables *out1* and *out2* are the output actions for the two vehicles. Since both vehicles pick actions based on the states and have no knowledge of the other vehicle's selected action, the specifications need to go both ways. Also, the actions are represented by integer values 1–4 such that {1,2,3,4} = {go behind, go in front, turn left, turn right}, respectively.

Although several avoidance actions could be taken by each vehicle, only cases 1, 3, and 4 required formal verification. In these cases, both vehicles can sense one another and will perform some type of avoidance maneuver. Thus, their actions must be such that they do not move closer to one another. In cases 0 and 2, however, there was no need to write requirements because only one vehicle performs an avoidance action. In case 0, vehicle 2 is stationary, so it does not try to avoid vehicle 1. In case 2, vehicle 2 cannot sense vehicle 1, thus, there is no need to check that the two vehicles' actions produce a converging result.

Eqs. (12) through (15) are the specifications for case 1 in **Table 4** and are intended to ensure that the vehicles do not both choose to go in front, or go behind.

$$S_{1_1} = \forall R_{A_1} \forall R_{A_2} \forall R_{H_1} \forall R_{H_2} (RAL \rightarrow (out1 = 1 \rightarrow out2 = 2)) \tag{12}$$

$$S_{1_2} = \forall R_{A_1} \forall R_{A_2} \forall R_{H_1} \forall R_{H_2} (RAL \rightarrow (out1 = 2 \rightarrow out2 = 1)) \tag{13}$$

$$S_{1_3} = \forall R_{A_1} \forall R_{A_2} \forall R_{H_1} \forall R_{H_2} (RAL \rightarrow (out2 = 1 \rightarrow out1 = 2)) \tag{14}$$

$$S_{1_4} = \forall R_{A_1} \forall R_{A_2} \forall R_{H_1} \forall R_{H_2} (RAL \rightarrow (out2 = 2 \rightarrow out1 = 1)) \tag{15}$$

Eqs. (16) and (17) are the specifications for case 3 and ensure that the vehicles turn the same way when resolving these particular conflicts. Recall that in this case, both vehicles are at the same time from the crossing point. This specification ensures that they will then be forced into new positions such that the crossing times are not equal and the FISs are then selected.

$$S_{3_1} = \forall R_{A_1} \forall R_{A_2} \forall R_{H_1} \forall R_{H_2} (RAL \rightarrow ((t_1 = t_2 \wedge t_1 > 0 \wedge t_2 > 0 \wedge ((R_{H_1} \geq 0 \wedge R_{H_1}$$
$$< 180) \vee (R_{H_1} > 180 \wedge R_{H_1} < 360))) \rightarrow (out1 = 4 \wedge out2 = 4))) \tag{16}$$

$$S_{3_2} = \forall R_{A_1} \forall R_{A_2} \forall R_{H_1} \forall R_{H_2} (RAL \rightarrow ((t_1 = t_2 \wedge t_1 > 0 \wedge t_2 > 0 \wedge ((R_{H_2} \geq 0 \wedge R_{H_2}$$
$$< 180) \vee (R_{H_2} > 180 \wedge R_{H_2} < 360))) \rightarrow (out2 = 4 \wedge out1 = 4))) \tag{17}$$

Finally, Eqs. (18) and (19) are for case 4. These two specifications are for cases where the vehicles are head-on, or traveling next to each other in the same direction, respectively. The first specification ensures that while in a head-on encounter, both vehicles turn the same direction (i.e., both left, or both right, forcing them to diverge). The second specification ensures that while traveling in the same direction, the vehicles turn in opposite directions.

$$S_{4_1} = \forall R_{A_1} \forall R_{A_2} \forall R_{H_1} \forall R_{H_2} (RAL \rightarrow ((t_1 = t_2 \wedge (R_{H_1} = 180 \wedge R_{H_2}$$
$$= 180)) \rightarrow ((out1 = 3 \wedge out2 = 3) \vee (out1 = 4 \wedge out2 = 4)))) \tag{18}$$

$$S_{4_2} = \forall R_{A_1} \forall R_{A_2} \forall R_{H_1} \forall R_{H_2} (RAL \rightarrow ((t_1 = t_2 \wedge (R_{H_1} = 0 \wedge R_{H_2}$$
$$= 0)) \rightarrow ((out1 = 3 \wedge out2 = 4) \vee (out1 = 4 \wedge out2 = 3)))) \tag{19}$$

where t_1 is the time until the crossing point, R_{H_1} is the relative heading from vehicle 1 to vehicle 2, and R_{A_1} is the relative angle from vehicle 1 to vehicle 2. Similarly, t_2, R_{H_2}, and R_{A_2} are for vehicle 2. In addition to these specifications, another specification was created to ensure that the vehicles always chose one of the valid actions. This specification is not shown but is similar to Eqs. (12) through (19) such that the output actions are one of the possible outcomes (1–4). These specifications were then translated to a temporal representation for evaluation in JKind using previously developed methods [18].

4.2. Avoidance fuzzy inference systems

The method for verifying the avoidance FISs is similar, but the specifications were left in FOL and then implemented directly into Z3. The main reason for this was that less of the system model was needed to check these outputs. The behavior that the specifications needed to encapsulate was that the turn rate output for each FIS needs to always be in the correct direction. The correct direction for each of these cases is shown in **Table 7**.

These can then be encoded in FOL sentences using the polynomial representation of the FISs shown in Section 3.4. These sentences are then negated to show that there are no possible variable values that make the negated sentences true. The negated FOL sentences are shown in Eqs. (20) through (23). Note that μ_1, μ_2, μ_3, $\dot{\Psi}$, and modes 1 and 3 are the same as detailed in Section 3.4.

$$S_{behind_1} = \exists \mu_1 \exists \mu_2 \exists \mu_3 \left(\dot{\Psi} \left(\mu_1, \mu_2, \mu_3 \right) \geq 0 \right) \tag{20}$$

$$S_{behind_3} = \exists \mu_1 \exists \mu_2 \exists \mu_3 \left(\dot{\Psi} \left(\mu_1, \mu_2, \mu_3 \right) \leq 0 \right) \tag{21}$$

$$S_{front_1} = \exists \mu_1 \exists \mu_2 \exists \mu_3 \left(\dot{\Psi} \left(\mu_1, \mu_2, \mu_3 \right) \leq 0 \right) \tag{22}$$

$$S_{front_3} = \exists \mu_1 \exists \mu_2 \exists \mu_3 \left(\dot{\Psi} \left(\mu_1, \mu_2, \mu_3 \right) \geq 0 \right) \tag{23}$$

These negated sentences were then implemented in Z3. If Z3 finds that these sentences were all unsatisfiable, there are no possible real-valued assignments to μ_1, μ_2, or μ_3 that allow the FISs to turn the vehicles in an undesired direction.

Mode	Action	Intruder position	Intruder direction	Turn direction
1	Go behind	On right	Going left	Right (negative)
3	Go behind	On left	Going right	Left (positive)
1	Go in front	On right	Going left	Left (positive)
3	Go in front	On left	Going right	Right (negative)

Table 7. Avoidance FIS outputs.

5. Simulation environment descriptions

5.1. Testing environment

Prior to integrating the controllers presented in Section 3 into the full simulation environment, each avoidance platform was tested using pairwise encounter scenarios. This component testing was used to ensure that each was operating as desired. In this section, the methods used to test each controller are described.

5.1.1. Separation assurance

A testing environment was created to evaluate a considerable amount of pairwise encounters between aircraft. This testing environment was used to identify potential controller failures. To accomplish this, various initial relative headings and relative angles were tested. In all cases, the initial location and heading of one aircraft was held constant. Then, by placing the intruding vehicle at a relative angle of $-90°$ and just outside the vehicle's sensing radius, as shown in **Figure 9**, we evaluated the interactions for 720 initial intruder heading values. This was then repeated four more times by changing the initial relative angle between $-90°$ (to the right) and $0°$ (straight ahead). A visualization of these scenarios is shown in **Figure 9**. Note that the radius of the sensing semi-circle for the separation assurance tests was set at 0.4 nmi.

Although intruders can approach a vehicle from the left, that is, a relative angle between $0°$ and $90°$, symmetry allows us to limit the initial relative angles to lie between -90 and $0°$. To verify, a sample scenario was tested for the full field of view. In all cases, the trajectories of the vehicles were symmetric to one another (i.e., when reflected across the vehicle's initial heading).

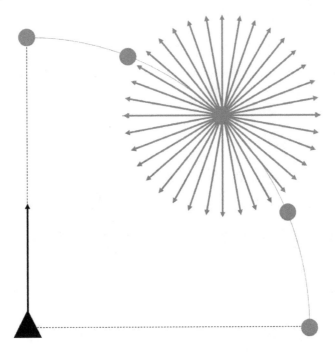

Figure 9. Separation and avoidance testing scenarios between ownship (triangle) and intruder UAS for multiple different initial positions (circles).

5.1.2. Collision avoidance

The collision avoidance platform was tested in the same manner as the separation assurance. The difference being that the sensing radius for the interaction tests as shown in **Figure 9** is 0.1 nmi. Thus, the initial position of each intruder scenario was just outside of this sensing radius.

5.2. Full simulation environment

5.2.1. Airspace description

The simulation environment created for this study models a portion of the US airspace over central Ohio. A depiction of the selected airspace can be seen in **Figure 10**. This airspace covers approximately 2500 square miles where sUAS can operate at a maximum altitude of 400 ft.

5.2.2. Mission types and objectives

Many sUAS will be active throughout this airspace, each with individual missions, such as, precision agriculture, forest monitoring, roadway surveillance, disaster management, and package delivery. During simulation runs, the UAS will travel to various waypoints to fulfill their assigned missions. After visiting all waypoints for a given mission, the aircraft will return to their respective starting locations. For more on the mission types, please refer to Refs. [11, 12].

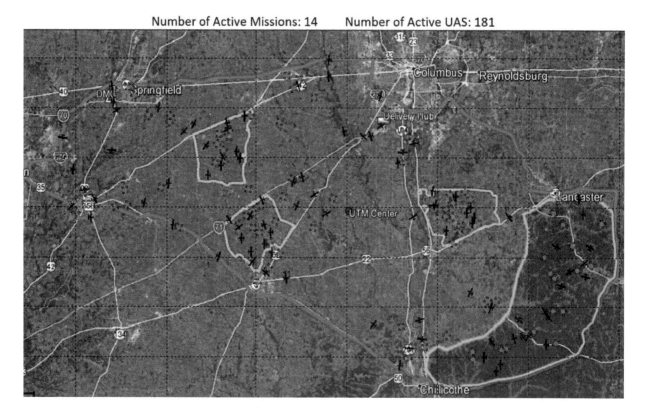

Figure 10. Simulation platform example.

5.2.3. Scalability and operations

The full simulation environment can accommodate any number of sUAS and missions. However, these numbers were constant throughout testing. A maximum of 184 sUAS can be airborne at any given time. This is a result of having centralized control of the aircraft. In a realistic environment, some of the computationally heavy components can be handled in parallel onboard each individual sUAS.

5.2.4. Aircraft models

Two vehicle platforms were used in all simulations: fixed wing and quad-rotor. Kinematic models were developed for each within the constraints of the environment. These constraints include maximum turn rate, maximum climb/decent rate, minimum/maximum speed, and maximum altitude.

For this study, each aircraft is assumed to climb at 4 ft./sec upon takeoff. The vehicles will continue to climb at this rate until an altitude of 400 ft. is reached. When vehicles are in conflict and are required to make trajectory modifications, all adjustments are constrained to lateral deviations in flight path (i.e., speed and altitude modifications are not used). Therefore, UAS are limited to level, two-dimensional flight during conflict resolution scenarios. Using this assumption, the maximum turn rate for each fixed wing vehicle is described in Eq. (24).

$$\dot{\Psi}_{max} = \frac{g\sqrt{n^2 - 1}}{V} \tag{24}$$

All fixed wing vehicles travel at 60 knots and have a maximum load factor of 3.5. Therefore, they are constrained to a maximum turn rate of 61.06 deg/sec. The multi-rotor systems, however, can travel at a maximum airspeed of 38 knots. Due to the nature of the quad-rotor sUAS, Eq. (24) does not accurately model the maximum turn rate for this vehicle type and it is assumed that the aircraft can yaw at a maximum rate of 45 deg/sec. Also, each aircraft is assumed to have the capability to detect an intruding aircraft at a distance of 0.1 nmi if within a 180° field of view in front of the aircraft (i.e., $-90° \leq R_{A_1} \leq 90°$).

As previously described in **Table 1**, the collision threshold is defined by aircraft coming within 60 m laterally and 50 ft. vertically of one other. To track the vehicles, ground-based sensors for detecting aircraft have been dispersed in the airspace. These sensors, along with telemetry data, provide continuous and reliable vehicle state information (i.e., position and velocity). This capability allows the implementation of global separation assurance practices. More details about the simulation environment and its properties can be found in Refs. [11, 12]. (NOTE: The collision buffer value was used to accommodate for position uncertainties while tracking the sUAS. In this study, the avoidance system has perfect knowledge of all vehicle state information acquired from ground based and onboard sensors.)

6. Results

6.1. Avoidance systems testing

For each pairwise encounter shown in **Figure 9**, the closest point of approach (CPA) was found. The CPA is defined as the minimum recorded distance between the two vehicles throughout the entire encounter. For both the collision avoidance and separation assurance platforms, a total of four different vehicle platform trials were conducted: fixed vs. fixed, quad vs. quad, quad vs. fixed, and fixed vs. quad. The first vehicle type designation represents the ownship vehicle's type in **Figure 9** (i.e., has the same starting position and heading for all tested cases), whereas, the second vehicle platform designation represents the intruder vehicle's type (i.e., initial conditions change for each tested scenario).

To measure the effectiveness of the avoidance logic, the minimum CPA was recorded for all initial relative angles tested. In addition, the total number of collisions for each case were tallied, and for the separation assurance case, the total number of LOSs. As a reminder, a collision is deemed by two vehicles coming within 60 m of one another, and an LOS is when two vehicles come with 0.1 nmi of one another.

The results for the separation assurance testing have been shown in **Table 8**. Here, the "angle case" refers to the various initial relative angles, from −90 to 0°, respectively. Thus, case 1 represents an intruder directly to the right, and case 5 represents an intruder directly in front of the ownship.

Although all vehicle platform combinations had more than one LOS, no LOS resulted in two vehicles colliding (i.e., a CPA less than 60 m). To try and understand where the separation assurance platform was breaking down to allow an LOS to occur, the CPA results were plotted for each initial intruder heading. When evaluating the results of each vehicle case, it was found that although several LOSs occurred, the failures tended to lie in groups near the same intruder angle depending on the initial position of the intruder. For example, in the fixed vs. quad case, it can be seen that no LOSs occurred in the first three trials. However, once the intruder was positioned such that it was nearly in front of or directly in front of the ownship,

Angle case	Fixed vs. Fixed		Quad vs. Quad		Fixed vs. Quad		Quad vs. Fixed	
	Min CPA (m)	LOS	Min CPA (m)	LOS	Min CPA (m)	LOS	Min CPA (m)	LOS
1	185.3	0	185.1	0	574.3	0	185.8	0
2	185.6	0	185.5	0	351.4	0	158.6	12
3	185.3	0	185.4	0	185.6	0	133.2	24
4	186.1	0	131.2	9	175.1	24	137.3	31
5	98.4	116	137.0	8	128.1	161	132.0	28

Table 8. Separation assurance testing results.

the separation assurance platform began to fail. This was caused by the fixed wing vehicle traveling at higher speeds than the quad-rotor vehicle. Therefore, when the intruder heading was away from the ownship, the ownship tended to approach the intruder from behind and begin to pass the vehicle. When approaching the vehicle from behind, it proved difficult for the avoidance platform to solve the conflict prior to an LOS in all vehicle configurations, as shown by angle case 5.

Table 9 shows the results of the collision avoidance testing. Each case had a minimum CPA greater than 60 m, implying no collisions were found throughout testing. Although not all possible encounter scenarios have been tested, this shows that the avoidance system logic is quite robust. As seen from the results, the homogeneous quad-rotor and the fixed vs. quad cases showed promising results. They consistently had a higher minimum CPA than the other two cases. The closure rates in the fixed vs. fixed cases were higher than cases involving quad-rotors. This resulted in consistently lower minimum CPA values. A noteworthy result is in the fixed vs. fixed scenario for angle case 5. The intruder being head-on and directly in front of the ownship resulted in a CPA of 60.8 m. Although this is close to the collision boundary, this shows that even in the highest closure rate scenario, the collision avoidance system was able to resolve the conflict.

6.2. Formal verification

6.2.1. Avoidance logic

After evaluating all the specifications outlined in Eqs. (12) through (19), JKind returned that they always held. This means that for all possible real-valued assignments to the variables (within the sensor domain limitations), the vehicles will always select the desired output action.

Although the final version of the avoidance logic adhered to all of the specifications, during development there were several cases where JKind found values that violated one or more of the specifications. These counterexamples are invaluable as they identify exact cases that result in undesired behavior. This gives way to corrections based on the counterexample conditions.

	Fixed vs. Fixed	Quad vs. Quad	Fixed vs. Quad	Quad vs. Fixed
Angle Case	Min CPA (m)	Min CPA (m)	Min CPA (m)	Min CPA (m)
1	132.1	138.9	154.7	125.3
2	111.9	125.2	133.3	121.0
3	101.9	113.5	122.9	111.1
4	82.9	104.4	103.5	97.8
5	60.8	96.7	98.9	99.0

Table 9. Collision avoidance testing results.

Specification	R_{H_1}	R_{A_1}	out1	R_{H_2}	R_{A_2}	out2
S_{3_2}	180	$-5 \cdot 10^{-15}$	3	180	$-5 \cdot 10^{-15}$	4

Table 10. Avoidance logic counter-example values.

As an example of this, one of the conditions that violated a specification found during development is shown in **Table 10**.

These conditions mean that one vehicle is heading in the exact opposite direction of the other and there is a slight position offset between them as shown in **Figure 11**. One vehicle selects the turn left action (3) while the other selects the turn right action (4). This implies they are not turning away from each other. The reason for this was that the range of angles that would force vehicle 1 into the correct action was not inclusive on one of its boundaries. This then meant that the conditions forced vehicle 1 into a different action and generated this counterexample.

6.2.2. Avoidance FISs

Similarly, after evaluating the specifications in Eqs. (20) through (23), Z3 showed that they were all unsatisfiable. This shows that the FLCs will always make the ownship turn away from an intruder.

6.3. Full simulation results

To test the algorithms in a dynamic environment, simulations were run both with the separation assurance mitigations and then without. The number of LOSs and number of collisions were recorded in order to directly compare the mitigated and unmitigated cases.

6.3.1. Unmitigated study

For this unmitigated study, the separation assurance system was disabled. The results of this study are shown in **Table 11**.

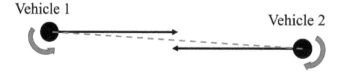

Figure 11. Counterexample showing head-on vehicles turning into each other.

Separation less than 0.4 nmi	LOSs	Collision avoidance maneuvers	Collisions	Collision avoidance success rate	Number of flight hours	LOSs per flight hour	Collisions per flight hour
26,576	8263	8252	2	99.98%	25,116	0.33	$7.96 \cdot 10^{-15}$

Table 11. Results for simulation without separation assurance.

Over the span of 25,116 flight hours, there were 26,576 recorded violations of the 0.4 nmi separation threshold. These resulted in 8263 LOSs. The collision avoidance algorithm was employed for all except for 11 LOS occurrences. In those cases, the vehicles were outside of one another's field of view, thus the collision avoidance system was not used. The collision avoidance system was 99.98% successful at resolving conflicts.

The only collisions that occurred throughout simulation can be attributed to the restriction on the detection sensor field of view and having no memory of state time histories. Therefore, if two vehicles were nearly parallel and directly beside one another, they would turn to resolve the conflict (i.e., turn away from one another). However, this turning again puts each intruder outside of the other vehicle's field of view. The lack of state memory combined with no sensor input caused a switch back to their navigation controllers. The navigation controller caused them to go back toward one another. Since the navigation controller had a higher turn rate output than the avoidance output, this cycle would continue (each vehicle turning away then toward) until they converged and were within 60 m of one another.

6.3.2. Mitigated study

For this study, the separation assurance features were enabled to help mitigate the risk of having an LOS. Although fewer LOSs were expected with the mitigations enabled, some LOSs were expected due to sub-optimal performance in head-on and trailing situations. The results of this mitigated study are shown in **Tables 12** and **13**.

Table 12 presents the results of the separation assurance platform. In this mitigated study, only 9277 flight hours were recorded. Thus, sUAS were able to complete their respective missions in a shorter period of time. Throughout the simulation aircraft came within 0.4 nmi on 33,550 occasions. However, of those instances, the separation assurance system predicted an LOS to occur within 2 min only 14,750 times. Of these resolution advisories, only 75.74% were successful, resulting in 3579 LOSs and 0.39 LOSs per flight hour. Although this number is slightly larger than the number of LOSs per flight hour in the unmitigated study, this additional layer of avoidance kept vehicles from entering any scenarios that resulted in collision. Thus, the overall safety of the UTM system has been improved.

Separation less than 0.4 nmi	Separation assurance maneuvers	LOSs	Separation assurance success rate	Number of flight hours	LOSs per flight hour
33,550	14,750	3579	75.74%	9277	0.39

Table 12. Separation assurance results.

Collision avoidance maneuvers	Collisions	Collision avoidance success rate	Number of flight hours	Collisions per flight hour
3568	0	100.00%	9277	0

Table 13. Collision avoidance results.

If an LOS occurred and the vehicles were within one another's sensor ranges, the sense and avoid software would activate. The results of the collision avoidance software can be seen in **Table 13**. Of the 3568 encounters, the collision avoidance software was 100.00% successful at resolving conflicts.

7. Conclusion

In this work, multiple fuzzy logic controllers and decision-making systems were used in conjunction to prevent potential losses of separation in a congested, three-dimensional airspace. This simulation environment allowed for extensive encounter scenarios between heterogeneous vehicles to test the two conflict resolution systems. First, a sense and avoid system was developed to prevent potential collisions using only current state information and without communication between vehicles. Next, a separation assurance platform was developed to further mitigate the risk of a potential collision. This platform uses global aircraft state information to predict if two aircraft will have an LOS within a given look-ahead time. If an LOS was predicted, the system would issue necessary resolution advisories to the proper aircraft to prevent an LOS.

Once the controllers were developed, numerical simulations and formal methods were used to verify the controllers performed as expected. Using a formal methods approach, we could show that the controller output was always in the correct direction (i.e., always performed as expected). In addition, we were able to verify that in all pairwise encounter scenarios between sUAS, the actions of each vehicle were such that they would never turn toward one another when avoiding a collision.

After a formal methods approach verified the control logic behavior and fuzzy logic controller outputs, numerical simulations were conducted. In all simulations, the avoidance system had perfect knowledge of all vehicle state information (i.e., speed, heading, and location). For the collision avoidance scenarios tested, the fuzzy system was successful at resolving all potential conflicts for both the homogeneous and heterogeneous cases. However, the separation assurance platform had trouble resolving certain types of encounter scenarios. Thus, it sometimes would not prevent an LOS between vehicles. However, when an LOS occurred, the collision avoidance system again prevented any mid-air collisions from occurring.

Several full simulation environment missions were also run to evaluate the effectiveness of the avoidance algorithms. These missions included cases where the separation assurance mitigations were both enabled and disabled. Overall, the results of this experiment were as expected. In the mitigated study, no collisions between aircraft occurred. However, when the mitigations were removed, vehicles encountered scenarios where the collision avoidance system could not prevent a collision. These collisions were not due to the collision avoidance logic or the fuzzy logic controllers, but were attributed to the limited vehicle sensor performance and lack of memory.

For future work, we aim to improve upon the separation assurance techniques to prevent an LOS in all encounter scenarios. Also, representing the system with a higher fidelity model of the environment in the formal methods tools would allow for more complete specifications (i.e., vehicles never lose separation) and then identify cases that violate them. In addition, since the avoidance system had perfect vehicle state information, we would like to introduce a level of uncertainty to the sensor models. Finally, we wish to implement the proposed avoidance software into hardware testing environments.

Appendix: Nomenclature

CPA	Closest Point of Approach
FIS	Fuzzy Inference System
FLC	Fuzzy Logic Controller
FOL	First Order Logic
LOS	Loss of Separation
NAS	National Airspace System
pCPA	Predicted Closest Point of Approach
SAT	Satisfiability (Boolean)
SMT	Satisfiability Modulo Theories
sUAS	Small Unmanned Aerial System
tLOS	Time to Loss of Separation
UAS	Unmanned Aerial System
UTM	UAS Traffic Management

Author details

Brandon Cook[1,2*], Tim Arnett[2] and Kelly Cohen[2]

*Address all correspondence to: cookb9@mail.uc.edu

1 NASA Ames Research Center, Moffett Field, CA, USA

2 Department of Aerospace Engineering and Engineering Mechanics, University of Cincinnati, Cincinnati, OH, USA

References

[1] Cook K. The silent force multiplier: The history and role of UAVs in warfare. Proceedings of the IEEE Aerospace Conference; 3–10 March 2007; Big Sky, MT, USA. IEEE. 2007:1-7. DOI: 10.1109/AERO.2007.352737

[2] Ollero A, Merino L. Unmanned aerial vehicles as tools for forest-fire fighting. Forest Ecology and Management. 2006;**234**(1):S263

[3]   Bamburry D. Drones: Designed for product delivery. Design Management Review. 2015;**26**(1):40-48. DOI: 10.1111/drev.10313

[4]   Prevot T, Homola J, Mercer J. Human-in-the-loop evaluation of ground-based automated separation assurance for NEXTGEN. In: The 26th Congress of ICAS and 8th AIAA ATIO. 2008 Sep. 8885

[5]   Erzberger H, Heere K. Algorithm and operational concept for resolving short-range conflicts. Proceedings of the Institution of Mechanical Engineers, Part G: Journal of Aerospace Engineering. 2010 Feb 1;**224**(2):225-243

[6]   Lauderdale TA, Erzberger H. Automated separation assurance with weather and uncertainty. Air Traffic Management and Systems. 2014:35-47. Springer, Japan

[7]   Temizer S, Kochenderfer M, Kaelbling L, Lozano-Pérez T, Kuchar J. Collision avoidance for unmanned aircraft using Markov decision processes. In: AIAA Guidance, Navigation, and Control Conference. 2010 Aug 2. 8040

[8]   Durand N, Alliot JM, Noailles J. Collision avoidance using neural networks learned by genetic algorithms. In: IEA-AEI 1996, 9th International Conference on Industrial and Engineering Applications of Artificial Intelligence and Expert systems. 1996 Jun 1

[9]   Hromatka M. A fuzzy logic approach to collision avoidance in smart UAVs. Honors Thesis. Collegeville, MN: College of Saint Benedict and Saint John's University; 2013

[10] Kuchar JE, Drumm AC. The traffic alert and collision avoidance system. Lincoln Laboratory Journal. 2007 Nov 2;**16**(2):277

[11] Cook B, Cohen K, Kivelevitch EH. A fuzzy logic approach for low altitude uas traffic management (UTM). In: AIAA Infotech@ Aerospace. 2016:1905. DOI: 10.2514/6.2016-1905

[12] Cook BM. Multi-Agent Control Using Fuzzy Logic. Electronic Thesis or Dissertation. University of Cincinnati. 2015. OhioLINK Electronic Theses and Dissertations Center. pp. 90-166

[13] Peled D. Software Reliability Methods. New York, NY: Springer Science & Business Media; 2013. 332

[14] Baier C, Katoen J, Larsen K. Principles of Model Checking. Cambridge, MA: MIT press; 2008. 984

[15] Clark M, Rattan K. Piecewise affine hybrid automata representation of a multistage fuzzy pid controller. In: Proceedings of the 2014 AAAI Spring Symposium Series: Formal Verification and Modeling in Human-Machine Systems; 24–26 March 2014

[16] Ross T. Fuzzy Logic with Engineering Applications. 3rd ed. Hoboken, NJ: John Wiley & Sons; 2009. 606

[17] Butler RW. "What is Formal Methods?" NASA LaRC Formal Methods Program [Internet]. 2001. Available from: https://shemesh.larc.nasa.gov/fm/fm-what.html. [Accessed: 03-02-2017]

[18] Wagner L, Fifarek A, DaCosta D, Gross K. SpeAR: Specification and Analysis of Requirements. InS5 Symposium. 2014

[19] Hagen GE. Verifying safety properties of Lustre programs: An SMT-based approach. Ann Arbor, MI: ProQuest; 2008

[20] Ghassabani E, Gacek A, Whalen MW. Efficient generation of inductive validity cores for safety properties. In: Proceedings of the 2016 24th ACM SIGSOFT International Symposium on Foundations of Software Engineering. 2016 Nov 1:314-325. ACM

[21] De Moura L, Bjørner N. Z3: An efficient SMT solver. In: International Conference on Tools and Algorithms for the Construction and Analysis of Systems. 2008 Mar 29. 337-340. Berlin Heidelberg: Springer

[22] Halbwachs N, Caspi P, Raymond P, Pilaud D. The synchronous data flow programming language LUSTRE. Proceedings of the IEEE. 1991 Sep;79(9):1305-1320

7

A New Methodology for Tuning PID-Type Fuzzy Logic Controllers Scaling Factors Using Genetic Algorithm of a Discrete-Time System

Wafa Gritli, Hajer Gharsallaoui and
Mohamed Benrejeb

Abstract

In this chapter, a proportional-integral derivative (PID)-type fuzzy logic controller (FLC) is proposed for a discrete-time system in order to track a desired trajectory generated using the flatness property. In order to improve the performance of the proposed controller, genetic algorithm (GA) based on minimizing the integral of the squared error (ISE) is used for tuning the input and output PID-type FLC scaling factors online. The considered controller is applied to an electronic throttle valve (ETV). GA tuning shows a better and robust performance compared to Simulink design optimization (SDO) algorithm in terms of tracking a desired trajectory with disturbances rejection.

Keywords: PID-type FLC, scaling factors, genetic algorithm, integral of the squared error, Simulink design optimization technique, flatness, electronic throttle valve

1. Introduction

Fuzzy logic control (FLC) has been widely used in many successful industrial applications. The first FLC algorithm was implemented by Mamdani in 1974. Unlike conventional control, which is based on mathematical model of a plant, an FLC usually embeds the intuition and experience of a human operator and may provide a nonlinear relationship induced by membership functions, rules and defuzzification. In that respect, FLC has been reported to be successfully used for a number of complex and nonlinear systems and are proved to be more robust and their performances are less sensitive to parametric variations than conventional controllers.

In the literature, various types such as proportional integral (PI), proportional derivative (PD) and proportional-integral derivative (PID) of FLCs have been proposed. For example, PI-type FLCs have been successfully implemented in many physical applications such the control of the temperature and pressure of a steam engine and control the steering and speed of an automobile. However, performance of PI-type FLCs for higher order systems and nonlinear systems may be poor due to the large overshoot and the excessive oscillation. PD-type FLCs are suitable for a limited class of systems and they are not recommendable in the presence of measurement noise and sudden load disturbances. Theoretically, PID-type FLCs provide a good performance. However, there are difficulties associated with the generation of an efficient rule base and the tuning of parameters.

In the proposed PID-type FLC, the design of parameters within two groups: structural parameters and tuning parameters. Basically, structural parameters include input/output (I/O) variables to fuzzy inference, fuzzy linguistic sets, membership functions, fuzzy rules, inference mechanism and defuzzification mechanism, which are usually determined during offline design. Tuning parameters include I/O scaling factors (SF) and parameters of membership functions (MF), which can be calculated during online adjustments of the controller in order to enhance the process performance [1].

The appropriate selection of input and output scaling factors is very important because they have significant effects on the dynamic of fuzzy controller. This leads researchers to explore the best method in searching optimum PID-type FLC parameters. Various strategies or methods have been used up to now. In Ref. [2], Qiao and Mizumoto proposed a peak observer mechanism-based method to adjust the PID-type FLC parameters. This self-tuning mechanism decreases the equivalent integral control component of the fuzzy controller gradually with the system response process time. Furthermore, Woo et al. [3] developed a method based on two empirical functions evolved with the system's error information. In Ref. [1], Guzelkaya et al. proposed a technique that adjusts the scaling factors, corresponding to the derivative and integral components, using a fuzzy inference mechanism. However, the major disadvantages of all these PID-type FLC tuning method are the difficult choice of their relative parameters and mechanisms. To overcome these difficulties, differential search algorithm (DSA) meta-heuristic technique is proposed for systematically tuning the scaling factors of the PID-type FLC in Ref. [4]. The fuzzy control design is formulated as a constrained optimization problem, which is efficiently solved based on an improved DSA. In this proposed technique, different optimization criteria such as integral square error (ISE) and maximum overshoot are considered in order to guarantee more robustness and performance control objectives.

In this chapter, a genetic algorithm (GA)-based heuristic optimization technique has been implemented to obtain better performance compared to the Simulink design optimization (SDO) technique. GA is based upon minimizing the error between the output system and the desired trajectory starting from a flat output variable generated using the flatness property. Various performance indices can be used. In this study, the integral of squared error (ISE) index has been used in order to minimize the error between the output and the desired flat trajectory. The methods are applied in a discrete-time framework to an electronic throttle valve as a case of study.

2. PID-type fuzzy logic controller description

In this study, we will deal with fuzzy PID-type controllers formed using one PD-type FLC with an integrator at the output.

The PID-type fuzzy logic controller structure is shown in **Figure 1** [5], where K_e and K_d ($K_e, K_d \in \mathbb{R}^+$) are the input scaling factors are α and β ($\alpha, \beta \in \mathbb{R}^+$) the output scaling factors.

The inputs variables, well known as the error e_k between the desired trajectory y_k^d and the measure y_k, as well as the error variation Δe_k given by Eqs. (1) and (2) where T_e is the sampling period.

$$e_k = y_k^d - y_k \tag{1}$$

$$\Delta e_k = \frac{e_k - e_{k-1}}{T_e} \tag{2}$$

The output variable Δu_k of such a controller is the variation of the control signal u_k which can be defined as Eq. (3).

$$\Delta u_k = \frac{u_k - u_{k-1}}{T_e} \tag{3}$$

The output of the PID-type fuzzy is given by Eq. (4) [5]

$$
\begin{aligned}
u_k &= \alpha \Delta u_k + \beta \int \Delta u_k dt \\
&= \alpha(A + PK_e e_k + DK_d \Delta e_k) \\
&\quad + \beta \int (A + PK_e e_k + DK_d \Delta e_k) dt \\
&= \alpha A + \beta A t + (\alpha K_e P + \beta K_d D) e_k \\
&\quad + \beta K_e P \int e_k dt + \alpha K_d D \Delta e_k
\end{aligned} \tag{4}
$$

Thus, the equivalent control components of the PID-type FLC are such that

Proportional gain: $\alpha K_e P + \beta K_d D$

Integral gain: $\beta K_e P$

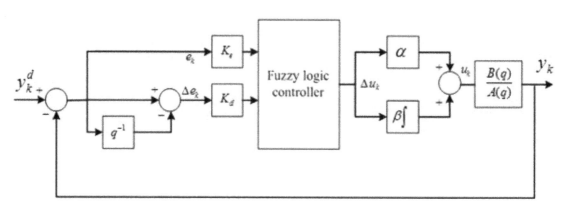

Figure 1. PID-type FLC.

$e_k \backslash \Delta e_k$	N	ZR	P
N	NL	N	ZR
ZR	N	ZR	P
P	ZR	P	PL

Table 1. Fuzzy rules-base.

Derivative gain: $\alpha K_d D$

where the terms P and D are given by Eqs. (5) and (6) [2].

$$P = \frac{\Delta u_{(i+1)j} - \Delta u_{ij}}{e_{i+1} - e_i} \tag{5}$$

$$D = \frac{\Delta u_{i(j+1)} - \Delta u_{ij}}{\Delta e_{j+1} - \Delta e_j} \tag{6}$$

The fuzzy controllers with a product-sum inference method, centroid defuzzification method and triangular uniformly distributed membership functions for the inputs and a crisp output proposed in Refs. [2, 6] are used in our case of study.

Table 1 gives the linguistic levels, assigned to the variables e_k, Δe_k and Δu_k, as follows: *NL*: negative large; *N*: negative; *ZR*: zero; *P*: positive; *PL*: positive large.

3. Scaling factors tuning using genetic algorithm

In this work, a new method is proposed for tuning the coefficients of PID-type FLCs. This method adjusts the input scaling factor corresponding to the derivative coefficient and the output scaling factor corresponding to the integral coefficient of the PID-type FLC using genetic algorithm, as shown in **Figure 2**. The integral of squared error (ISE) index has been used in order to minimize the error between the output and the desired flat trajectory.

3.1. Genetic algorithm

Genetic algorithm was first proposed by Holland [7]. It is a heuristic optimization technique inspired by the mechanism of natural selection. It is used in order to solve highly complex problems. GA starts with an initial population containing a number of parameters, where each one is regarded as the genes of a chromosome and can be structured by a string of concatenated values. Each chromosome represents a solution of the problem and its performance is evaluated based on fitness function.

In the beginning, an initial chromosome population is randomly generated. The chromosomes are candidate solutions to the problem. Then, the fitness values of all chromosomes are evaluated by calculating the objective function. So, a group of the best chromosomes is selected based on the fitness of each individual. In this 'surviving' population, the genetic operators of

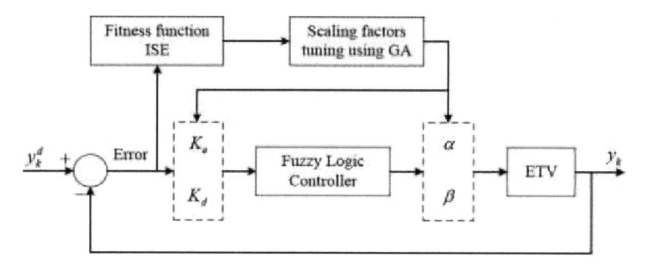

Figure 2. PID-type FLC scaling factors tuning.

crossover and mutation are applied in order to create the next population solution. The above steps are repeated until a specific termination criterion is found.

- **Reproduction**: Create a part of the new population by simply copying without changing the selected individuals from the present population. Also, new population has the possibility of selection by already developed solutions [8].

- **Crossover**: Create new individuals as offspring of two parents. It is a recombination operator that combines selected subparts called crossover points of two parent chromosomes. The individuals resulting in this way are the offspring [8].

- **Mutation**: Create a new individual for the new population by randomly mutating a selected individual. The modifications can consist of changing one or more values in the representation or adding/deleting parts of the representation [8].

To compute the fitness of each chromosome, the objective functions are used. Many authors use integral of time multiplied by absolute error (ITAE), mean of the squared error (MSE), integral of absolute error (IAE) and integral of the squared error (ISE) as performance index [9, 10].

In this chapter, the method of tuning PID-type FLC parameters using GA consists in finding the optimal I/O scaling factors, which minimize the defined objective function, chosen as the ISE in order to specify more performance in terms of tracking a desired trajectory.

If $y^d(t)$ is the desired trajectory and y is the output trajectory, then error $e(t)$ is

$$e(t) = y^d(t) - y(t) \qquad (7)$$

and the ISE can be defined by

$$ISE = \int_0^\tau e(t)^2 \, dt \qquad (8)$$

Fitness function is taken as inverse of error, i.e., performance index.

$$Fitness\ value = \frac{1}{Performance\ index} \tag{9}$$

3.2. Tuning procedure

The overall flowchart for optimization using GA is shown in **Figure 3**. Initially, a number of populations N have been generated for the scaling factors K_e, K_d, α and β. Each individual of these N sets in the current population is evaluated using the objective function ISE. Based on the values of the objective function, out of these N possible solutions, the good solutions are retained and the others are eliminated. A new population is formed by applying the genetic operators (reproduction, crossover and mutation) to these selected individuals. This process of

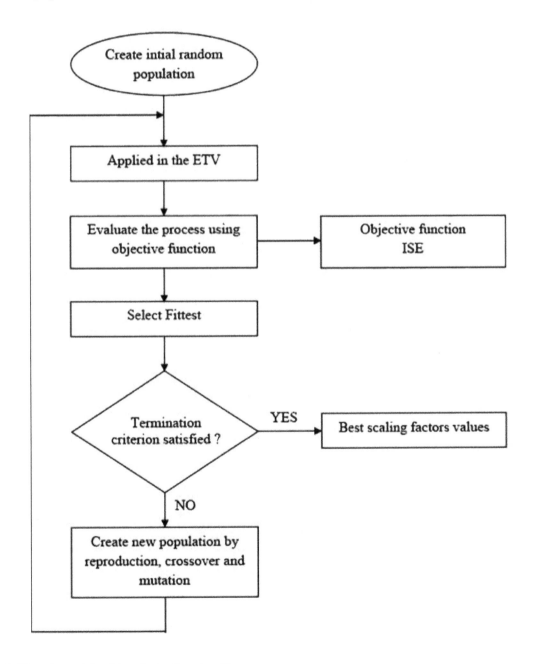

Figure 3. Flowchart of the GA optimization algorithm.

production of a new generation and its evaluation is performed repetitively. The algorithm continues until the population converges to the stop criterion.

4. Flatness and trajectory planning

The flat property has been introduced in Ref. [11] for continuous-time nonlinear systems. It can be stated in a discrete-time version which leads for the design of a control which ensures a tracking of a desired trajectory. One major property of differential flatness is that the state and the input variables can be directly expressed, without integrating any differential equation, in terms of the flat output and a finite number of its derivatives. The flatness approach will be used in this chapter in a discrete-time framework.

The studied dynamic linear discrete system is described by Eq. (10).

$$A(q)y_k = B(q)u_k \tag{10}$$

where q is the forward operator, u_k and y_k are the input and the output, respectively, and $A(q)$ and $B(q)$ are polynomials defined by

$$A(q) = q^n + a_{n-1}q^{n-1} + \ldots + a_1 q + a_0 \tag{11}$$

$$B(q) = b_{n-1}q^{n-1} + \ldots + b_1 q + b_0 \tag{12}$$

where the parameters a_i and b_i are constants, $i=0,1,\ldots,n-1$. The partial state of such a dynamic system can be considered as a discrete flat output z_k which can be expressed as a function of input and output signals as following

$$A(q)z_k = u_k \tag{13}$$

$$B(q)z_k = y_k \tag{14}$$

Often, the real output signal y_k to be controlled is not a flat output. Then, it is necessary to plan a desired trajectory for the flat output [11] and to consider thereafter the relation (14).

The open loop control law can be determined by the following relations [12].

$$u^d(t) = f(z^d(t),\ldots,z^{d^{(r+1)}}(t)) \tag{15}$$

$$y^d(t) = g(z^d(t),\ldots,z^{d^{(r)}}(t)) \tag{16}$$

where f and g are the vectorial functions. Then, it is sufficient to find a desired continuous flat trajectory $t \mapsto z^d(t)$ that must to be differentiable at the $(r+1)$ order.

The polynomial interpolation technique is used in order to plan the desired flat trajectory $z^d(t)$. Let consider the state vector $Z^d(t) = (z^d(t) \quad \dot{z}^d(t) \quad \ldots \quad z^{d^{(r+1)}}(t))^T$ containing the desired continuous flat output and its successive derivatives. The expression of $Z^d(t)$ can be given in Eq. (17); t_0 and t_f are the two moments known in advance.

$$Z^d(t) = M_1(t - t_0)c_1(t_0) + M_2(t - t_0)c_2(t_0, t_f) \qquad (17)$$

where M_1 and M_2 are such as [12]

$$M_1 = \begin{pmatrix} 1 & t & \cdots & \dfrac{t^{n-1}}{(n-1)!} \\ 0 & 1 & \cdots & \dfrac{t^{n-2}}{(n-2)!} \\ \vdots & \ddots & \ddots & \vdots \\ 0 & \cdots & 0 & 1 \end{pmatrix} \qquad (18)$$

$$M_2 = \begin{pmatrix} \dfrac{t^n}{n!} & \dfrac{t^{n+1}}{(n+1)!} & \cdots & \dfrac{t^{2n-1}}{(2n-1)!} \\ \dfrac{t^{n-1}}{(n-1)!} & \dfrac{t^n}{n!} & \cdots & \dfrac{t^{(n-2)}}{(n-2)!} \\ \vdots & \ddots & \ddots & \vdots \\ t & \cdots & \dfrac{t^{n-1}}{(n-1)!} & \dfrac{t^n}{n!} \end{pmatrix} \qquad (19)$$

and the vectors c_1 and c_2 defined by

$$c_1 = Z^d(t_0) \qquad (20)$$

$$c_2 = M_2^{-1}(t_f - t_0)(Z^d(t_f) - M_1(t_f - t_0)Z^d(t_0)) \qquad (21)$$

Then, the output desired trajectory y_k^d is defined. In the discrete-time framework, the real output y_k has asymptotically to track this such as Eq. (22).

$$y_k^d = B(q)z_k^d \qquad (22)$$

In the following section of this chapter, the efficiency of the proposed methodology for tuning PID-type FLC scaling factors has been validated on a discrete-time system: an electronic throttle valve for a defined desired trajectory generated using the flatness property and compared to the Simulink design optimization (SDO) technique.

5. Case of study: electronic throttle valve (ETV)

Throttle valve is one of the most important devices in the engine management system. In conventional engine, the amount of airflow into the combustion system has been adjusted by the throttle valve, which is connected mechanically to an accelerator pedal [13]. The electronic throttle body (ETB) regulates air inflow into the car engine. Compared to the mechanical throttle, a well-controlled ETB can reduce fuel consumption.

5.1. System modelling

The case of the ETV is described in **Figure 4**.

The electrical part is modelled by Eq. (23)

$$u(t) = L\frac{d}{dt}i(t) + Ri(t) + k_v\omega_m(t) \tag{23}$$

where L is the inductance R is the resistance $u(t)$ and $i(t)$ are the voltage and the armature current, respectively, k_v is an electromotive force constant and $\omega_m(t)$ is the motor rotational speed.

The mechanical part of the throttle is modelled by a gear reducer characterized by its reduction ratio γ such as Eq. (24)

$$\gamma = \frac{C_g}{C_L} \tag{24}$$

where C_L is the load torque and C_g is the gear torque. The mechanical part is modelled according to Eq. (25), such that [14, 15].

$$J\frac{d}{dt}\omega_m(t) = C_e - C_f - C_r - C_a \tag{25}$$

and

$$\frac{d}{dt}\theta(t) = (180/\pi/\gamma)\omega_m(t) \tag{26}$$

where $\theta(t)$ is the throttle plate angle, J is the overall moment of inertia, $C_e = k_e i(t)$ is the electrical torque where K_e is a constant, C_f is the torque caused by mechanical friction, C_r is the spring resistive torque and C_a is the torque generated by the airflow. The electronic throttle valve involves two complex nonlinearities due to the nonlinear spring torque Cr and the friction

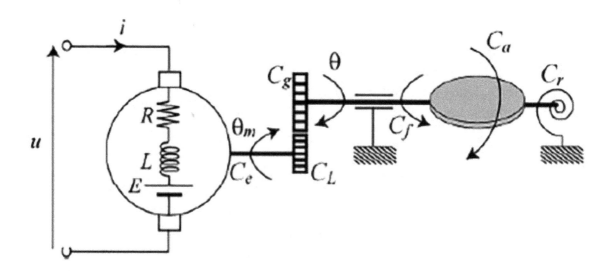

Figure 4. Electronic throttle valve system.

torque C_f. They are given by their static characteristics [16]. The static characteristic of the nonlinear spring torque C_r is defined by

$$C_r = \frac{k_r}{\gamma}(\theta - \theta_0) + D\,\text{sgn}(\theta - \theta_0) \tag{27}$$

For $\theta_{min} \leq \theta \leq \theta_{max}$, k_r is the spring constant, D is a constant, θ_0 is the default position and sgn(.) is the following signum function

$$\text{sgn}(\theta - \theta_0) = \begin{cases} 1, & \text{if } \theta \geq \theta_0 \\ -1, & \text{else} \end{cases} \tag{28}$$

The friction torque function C_f of the angular velocity of the throttle plate can be expressed as

$$C_f = f_v \omega + f_c \,\text{sgn}(\omega) \tag{29}$$

where f_v and f_c are two constants. By substituting in Eq. (25) the expressions of C_g, C_f and C_r and by neglecting the torque generated by the airflow C_a, the two nonlinearities sgn($\theta - \theta_0$) and sgn(ω) and the two constants $\frac{k_r}{\gamma}\theta_0$ and f_v the transfer function of the linear model becomes (30) [15].

$$H(q) = \frac{(180/\pi/\gamma)k_e}{JLq^3 + JRq^2 + (k_e k_v + Lk_s)q + Rk_s} \tag{30}$$

with $k_s = (180/\pi/\gamma^2)k_r$ and q as the Laplace operators.

5.2. Simulation results

The identified parameters of $H(q)$ are given in **Table 2** at 25°C temperature [15].

The corresponding discrete-time transfer function is given by Eq. (31) for the sample time $T_e = 0.002$s.

$$H(q^{-1}) = \frac{0.007833q^{-1} + 0.01396q^{-2} + 0.0007724q^{-3}}{1 - 1.948q^{-1} + 0.954q^{-2} - 0.006152q^{-3}} \tag{31}$$

Parameters	Values
R(Ω)	2.8
L(H)	0.0011
ke (N.m/A)	0.0183
kv (v/rad/s)	0.0183
J (kg.m^2)	4×10^{-6}
γ	16.95

Table 2. Model's parameters.

The desired continuous time flat trajectory $z^d(t)$ can be computed according to the following polynomial form

$$z^d(k) = \begin{cases} \dfrac{cst1}{B(1)}, & \text{if } 0 \le k \le k_0 \\[2mm] Poly_1(k), & \text{if } k_0 \le k \le k_1 \\[2mm] \dfrac{cst2}{B(1)}, & \text{if } k_1 \le k \le k_2 \\[2mm] Poly_2(k), & \text{if } k_2 \le k \le k_3 \\[2mm] \dfrac{cst1}{B(1)}, & \text{if } k \ge k_3 \end{cases} \tag{32}$$

where $cst1$ and $cst2$ are constants, $k_0 = 3s$, $k_1 = 6s$, $k_2 = 10s$ and $k_3 = 15s$ are the instants of transitions, $B(1)$ is the static gain between the flat output z_k and the output signal y_k for each operating mode and $Poly_1(k)$ and $Poly_2(k)$ are polynomials calculated using the technique of polynomial interpolation.

The desired trajectory is then given in **Figure 5**.

The obtained optimal I/O scaling factors (*Ke, Kd, α, β*) for Simulink design optimization technique and GA are summarized in **Table 3**.

The obtained results are given in **Figures 6–9**.

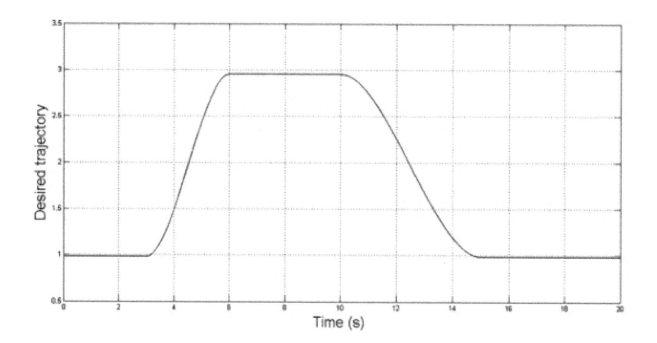

Figure 5. Desired trajectory.

SF\Method	SDO	GA
Ke	0.1144	0.0086
Kd	1.5997	0.4612
α	2.6239	0.1108
β	0.0001	0.1934

Table 3. PID-type fuzzy scaling factors values.

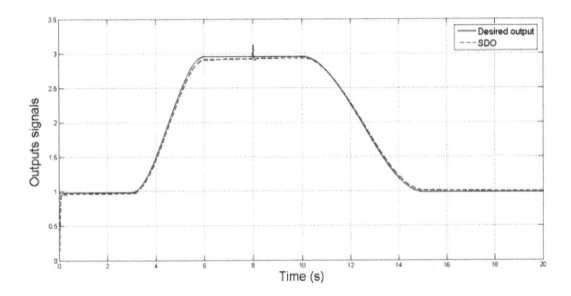

Figure 6. System outputs using Simulink design optimization.

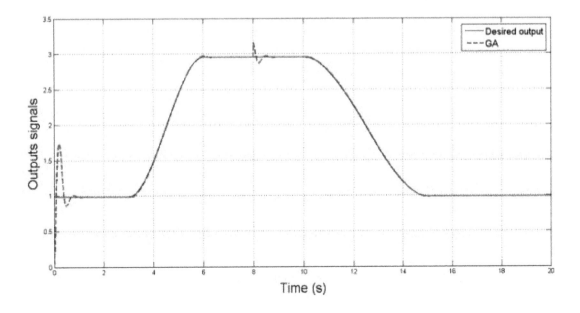

Figure 7. System outputs using genetic algorithm.

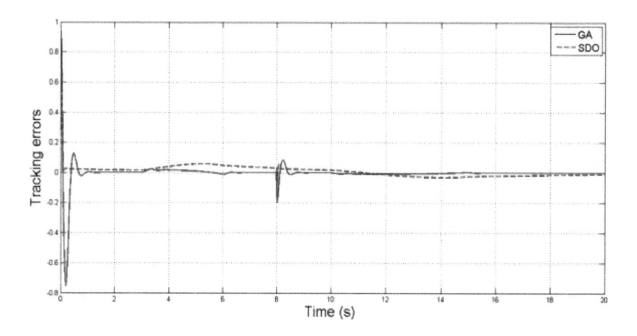

Figure 8. Tracking errors.

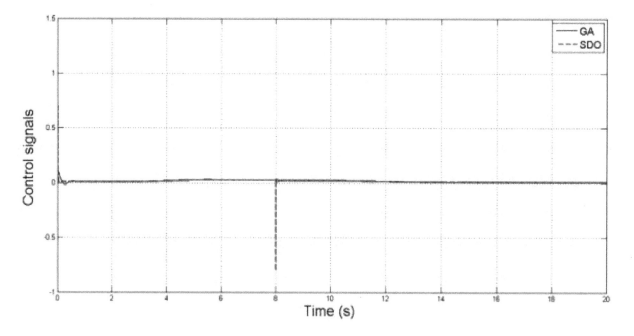

Figure 9. Control signals.

Figures 8 and **9** show the responses with Simulink design optimization technique and GA tuning using ISE criterion. Based on a comparative analysis, better results were there obtained with the GA tuning method.

All results, for obtained scaling factors values, are acceptable and show the effectiveness of the proposed GA tuning method in terms of the tracking desired trajectory with disturbances rejection in comparison with the SDO technique.

6. Conclusion

In this chapter, an optimization technique was introduced to tune the parameters of PID-type fuzzy logic controller (FLC). The idea is to use the genetic algorithm (GA)-based heuristic optimization technique in order to solve highly complex problems. In order to specify more robustness and performance of the proposed GA-tuned PID-type FLC, optimization criteria such as integral square error (ISE) is considered.

The proposed controller is applied to an electronic throttle valve (ETV) in the discrete-time framework in order to track a desired trajectory starting from a flat output generated using flatness property. The performance comparison with the Simulink design optimization (SDO) technique shows the efficiency of the proposed GA-tuned approach in terms of tracking a desired trajectory with disturbances rejection.

Author details

Wafa Gritli*, Hajer Gharsallaoui and Mohamed Benrejeb

*Address all correspondence to: wafa_gritli@yahoo.fr

National Engineering School of Tunis, Tunis, Tunisia

References

[1] Guzelkaya M, Eksin I, Yesil E. Self-tuning of PID-type fuzzy logic controller coefficients via relative rate observer. Engineering Applications of Artificial Intelligence. 2003;**16** (3):227–236

[2] Qiao WZ, Mizumoto M. PID type fuzzy controller and parameters adaptive method. Fuzzy Sets and Systems. 1996;**78**:23–35

[3] Woo ZW, Chung HY, Lin JJ. A PID type fuzzy controller with self-tuning scaling factors. Fuzzy Sets and Systems. 2000;**115**:321–326

[4] Toumi F, Bouallègue S, Haggège J, Siarry P. Differential search algorithm-based approach for PID-type fuzzy controller tuning. In: International Conference on Control, Engineering & Information Technology (CEIT'14); 2014. pp. 329–334

[5] Gritli W, Gharsallaoui H, Benrejeb M. PID-type fuzzy scaling factors tuning using genetic algorithm and Simulink design optimization for electronic throttle valve. In: International Conference on Control, Decision and Information Technologies (CoDIT'16); 6-8 April; Malta. 2016. pp. 216–221

[6] Galichet S, Foulloy L. Fuzzy controllers: Synthesis and equivalences. IEEE Transactions on Fuzzy Systems. 1995;**3**:140–148

[7]   Holland JJ. Adaptation in Natural and Artificial Systems, University of Michigan Press; 1975

[8]   Kim JS, Kim JH, Park JM, Park SM, Choe WY, Heo H. Auto tuning PID controller based on improved genetic algorithm for reverse osmosis plant. International Journal of Computer, Electrical, Automation, Control and Information Engineering. 2008;**2**(11):3707–3712

[9]   Gaing ZL. Particle swarm optimization approach for optimum design of PID controller in AVR system. IEEE Transactions on Energy Conversion. 2004;**19**:384–391

[10] Mahony TO, Downing CJ, Fatla K. Genetic algorithm for PID parameter optimization: minimizing error criteria. In: Process Control and Instrumentation; 26–28 July; 2000. pp. 148–153

[11] Fliess M, Levine J, Martin P, Rouchon P. On differentially flat non linear systems. In: Proc IFAC Symposium on Nonlinear Control Systems Design (NOLCOS), IFAC, Laxenburg, Austria; 1992, pp. 408–412

[12] Gharsallaoui H, Ayadi M, Benrejeb M, Borne P. Robust flatness-based multi-controllers approach. Studies in Informatics and Control. 2010;**19**(4):357–368

[13] Costin M, Schaller R, Maiorana M, Purcell J. An architecture for electronic throttle control systems. In SAE Technical Paper, SAE International; 2003.

[14] Lebbal Ml, Chafouk H, Hoblos G, Lefebvre D. Modelling and identification of non-linear systems by a multimodel approach: Application to a throttle valve. International Journal Information and Systems Science. 2007;**3**:67–87

[15] Yang C. Model-based analysis and tuning of electronic throttle controllers. In: Visteon Corporation, SAE Paper; March 8-11; Detroit, Michigan. 2004.

[16] Aidi I, Ayadi M, Benrejeb M, Borne P. Flatness-based control of throttle valve using neural observer. International Journal of Research and Surveys. 2012;**12**:333–344

8

Fuzzy Interpolation Systems and Applications

Longzhi Yang, Zheming Zuo, Fei Chao and
Yanpeng Qu

Abstract

Fuzzy inference systems provide a simple yet effective solution to complex non-linear problems, which have been applied to numerous real-world applications with great success. However, conventional fuzzy inference systems may suffer from either too sparse, too complex or imbalanced rule bases, given that the data may be unevenly distributed in the problem space regardless of its volume. Fuzzy interpolation addresses this. It enables fuzzy inferences with sparse rule bases when the sparse rule base does not cover a given input, and it simplifies very dense rule bases by approximating certain rules with their neighbouring ones. This chapter systematically reviews different types of fuzzy interpolation approaches and their variations, in terms of both the interpolation mechanism (inference engine) and sparse rule base generation. Representative applications of fuzzy interpolation in the field of control are also revisited in this chapter, which not only validate fuzzy interpolation approaches but also demonstrate its efficacy and potential for wider applications.

Keywords: fuzzy inference systems, fuzzy interpolation, adaptive fuzzy interpolation, sparse rule bases, fuzzy control

1. Introduction

Fuzzy logic and fuzzy sets have been used successfully as tools to manage the uncertainty of fuzziness since their introduction in the 1960s, which have been applied to many fields, including [1–6]. The most widely used fuzzy systems are fuzzy rule-based inference systems, each comprising of a rule base and an inference engine. Different inference engines were invented to support different situations, such as the Mamdani inference engine [7] and the TSK inference engine [8]. The rule bases are usually extracted from expert knowledge or learned from data. The TSK model produces crisp outputs due to its polynomial rule consequences in TSK-style rule bases, while the Mamdani model is more appealing in handling inferences based on human natural language due to its fuzzy rule consequences. Despite of the wide applications, these conventional fuzzy inference mechanisms are only workable with dense rule bases which fully cover the entire input domain.

Fuzzy interpolation systems (FISs) were proposed to address the above issue [9], and they also help in complexity reduction for fuzzy models with too complex (dense) rule bases. If there is only a spare rule base available and a given input does not overlap with any rule antecedent, conventional fuzzy inference systems will not be applicable. However, FISs are still able to generate a conclusion by means of fuzzy interpolation in such situations, thus enhancing the applicability of conventional fuzzy inference systems. FISs can also improve the efficiency of complex fuzzy inference systems by excluding those rules that can be accurately interpolated or extrapolated using other rules in a complex rule base. Various fuzzy interpolation methods based on Mamdani-style rule bases have been proposed in the literature such as Refs. [9–20], with successful applications in the fields of decision-making support, prediction and control, amongst others.

FISs have also been developed to support TSK-style sparse fuzzy rule bases by extending the traditional TSK fuzzy inference system [21]. This approach was developed based on a modified similarity degree measure that enables the effective utilisation of all rules during inference process to generate a global result. In particular, the modified similarity measure guarantees that the similarity degree between any given input and any rule antecedent is greater than 0 even when they do not overlap at all. Therefore, all the rules in the rule base can be fired to certain degrees such that they all contribute to the final result to some extents and consequently a conclusion still can be generated even when no rule antecedent is overlapped with the given observation. The extended TSK fuzzy model enjoys the advantages of both TSK model and fuzzy interpolation, which is able to obtain crisp inference results from either sparse, dense or unevenly distributed (including dense parts and spare parts) TSK-style fuzzy rule bases.

FISs have been successfully applied to real-world problems. In some real world scenarios, neither complete expert knowledge nor complete data set is available or readily obtainable to generate evenly distributed dense rule bases. FISs therefore have been applied in such situations. For instance, a FIS has been applied to building evaluation in the work of Molnárka et al. [22] in an effort to help estate agencies making decisions for residential building maintenance, when some necessary relevant data have been lost. In Ref. [23], a FIS system was applied successfully to reduce the complexity and improve the efficiency of a fuzzy home heating control system. The work of Bai et al. [24] applied a FIS to calibrate parallel machine tools for industry use. A behaviour-based fuzzy control system is introduced in Ref. [25], which applied a FIS to make decisions when only incomplete knowledge base has been provided or available. Most recently, FISs have also been used to support network quality of service [26] and network intrusion detection [27].

The remainder of this chapter is organised as follows. Section 2 reviews the theoretical underpinnings of conventional fuzzy inference systems, that is, the Mamdani inference system and the TSK inference system. Section 3 discusses different fuzzy interpolation approaches to support sparse Mamdani-style rule bases. Section 4 presents the extension of the conventional TSK inference system in supporting sparse TSK-style rule bases. Section 5 reports two representative examples of fuzzy interpolation systems in the field of system control. Section 6 concludes the chapter and points out the directions for future work.

2. Fuzzy inference systems

The process of fuzzy inference is basically an iteration of computer paradigm based on fuzzy set theory, fuzzy-if-then-rules and fuzzy reasoning. Each iteration takes an input which can be an observation or a previously inferred result, crisp or fuzzy. Then, these inputs are used to fire the rules in a given rule base, and the output is the aggregation of the inferred results from all the fired rules. There are generally two primary ways to construct a rule base for a given problem. The first way is directly translating expert knowledge to rules, and the fuzzy inference systems with such rule bases are usually called fuzzy expert systems or fuzzy controllers [28]. In this case, rules are fuzzy representations of expert knowledge, and the resultant rule base offers a high semantic level and a good generalisation capability. The difficulty of building rule bases for complex problems has resulted in the development of another approach of rule base construction, which is driven by data, that is, fuzzy rules are obtained from data by employing machine learning techniques rather than expert knowledge [29, 30]. In contrast, the rule bases built in this way lack comprehensibility and transparency. There are two types of rule bases depending on the expression of the consequences of the fuzzy rules composing the rule base. Mamdani-style fuzzy rules consider fuzzy terms or linguistic values in the consequence, while TSK-style fuzzy rules represent the consequences as polynomial functions of crisp inputs.

2.1. Inference with Mamdani-style rule bases

There are a number of fuzzy inference mechanisms that can be utilised to derive a consequence from a given observation using a Mamdani rule base. The two most significant modes are the compositional rule of inference (CRI) [31] and analogy-based reasoning [24, 33], which are introduced below.

2.1.1. Compositional rule of inference

The introduction of CRI marks the era of fuzzy inference [31]. Given a rule 'IF x is A, THEN y is B'' and an observation 'x is A^*', the conclusion B^* can be generated through CRI as:

$$\mu_{B^*}(v) = sup_{u \in U_x} T\Big(\mu_{A^*}(u), \mu_R(u, v)\Big), \tag{1}$$

where T is a triangular norm, sup represents supremum, and R is the relationship between variables x and y. Essentially, CRI is a fuzzy extension of classical modus ponens which can be viewed from two perspectives. Firstly, classical modus ponens only supports predicates concerning singleton elements, but CRI is able to deal with predicates which concern a set of elements in the variable domain. This is achieved by representing a fuzzy rule as a fuzzy relation over the Cartesian product of the domains of the antecedent and consequent variables. Various fuzzy implication relations have been proposed [7, 32–34], each of which may have its own properties and therefore is suitable for a certain group of applications. Secondly, classical modus ponens only supports Boolean logic, but CRI supports multi-value logic. That is, CRI is able to deal with predicates with partial truth values, which are implemented by a compositional operator sup T, where T represents a t-norm [35].

A number of existing fuzzy reasoning methods based on CRI have been developed [36, 37], including the first successful practical approach, that is, the Mamdani inference [28]. This approach is also the most commonly seen fuzzy methodology in physical control systems thus far. It was originally proposed as an attempt to control a steam engine and boiler combination by synthesising a set of linguistic control rules obtained from experienced human operators. Mamdani inference implements CRI using *minimum* as the t-norm operator due to its simplicity. In particular, the inferred result from each fired rule is a fuzzy set which is transformed from the rule consequence by restricting the membership of those elements whose memberships are greater than the firing strength. The firing strength is also sometimes termed the satisfaction degree, which is the supremum within the variable domain of the minimum of the rule antecedent and the given observation. A defuzzification process is needed when crisp outputs are required.

2.1.2. Analogy-based fuzzy inference

Despite the success of CRI in various fuzzy system applications, it suffers various criticisms including its complexity and vague underlying semantics [34, 38]. This has led to another group of fuzzy reasoning approaches which are based on similarity degree, usually called analogy-based fuzzy reasoning [38–41]. Similarity considerations play a major role in human cognitive processes [42], so do they in approximate reasoning. It is intuitive that if a given observation is similar to the antecedent of a rule, the conclusion from the observation should also be similar to the consequence of the rule. Different to CRI-based fuzzy reasoning, analogy-based fuzzy reasoning does not require the construction of a fuzzy relation. Instead, it is based on the degree of similarity (given a certain similarity metric) between the given observation and the antecedent of a rule. Utilising the computed similarity degree, the consequence of the fired rule can be modified to the consequence of the given observation.

Approximate analogical reasoning schema is a typical analogy-based fuzzy inference approach [34, 38]. In this method, rules are fired according to the similarity degrees between a given observation and the antecedents of rules. If the degree of similarity between the given observation and the antecedent of a rule is greater than a predefined threshold value, the rule will be fired and the consequence of the observation is deduced from the rule consequence by a given modification procedure. Another analogy-based fuzzy inference approach was proposed in Refs. [39, 40], which particularly targets medical diagnostic problems. This approach is based on the cosine angle between the two vectors that represent the actual and the user's specified values of the antecedent variable. Several modification procedures can be found in Refs. [43, 44]. Particularly, a fuzzy reasoning method which employs similarity measures based on the degree of subsethood between the propositions in the antecedent and a given observation is proposed in Ref. [45]. This method has also been extended to consider the weights of the propositions in the antecedent [46]. Analogy-based fuzzy inference approaches usually arrive at solutions with more natural appeal than those introduced in the last section.

2.2. Inference with TSK-style rule bases

The TSK fuzzy inference system was proposed for the direct generation of crisp outputs [8]. In difference with the Mamdani-style fuzzy rule bases, TSK-style rule bases are usually generated from data using a clustering algorithm such as K-Means and an algorithm to determine the number of clusters such as Ref. [47]. Also, the consequence of a TSK fuzzy rule is a polynomial function rather than a fuzzy set. A typical TSK fuzzy rule can be defined as:

$$\text{IF } x_1 \text{ is } A_1 \wedge \dots \wedge x_m \text{ is } A_m \text{ THEN } z = f(x_1, \dots, x_m), \tag{2}$$

where $A_1, \dots A_m$ are fuzzy values with regard to antecedent variables $x_1, \dots, x_m$ respectively, and $f(x_1, \dots, x_m)$ is a crisp polynomial function of crisp inputs determining the crisp output value. The rule consequent polynomial functions $f(x_1, \dots, x_m)$ are usually zero order or first order. For simplicity, suppose that a TSK-style rule base is formed by two-antecedent rules as follows:

$$\begin{aligned} R_i : \text{IF } x \text{ is } A_i \wedge y \text{ is } B_i \text{ THEN } z = f_i(x, y) \\ R_j : \text{IF } x \text{ is } A_j \wedge y \text{ is } B_j \text{ THEN } z = f_j(x, y). \end{aligned} \tag{3}$$

Suppose that (x_0, y_0) is the crisp input pair, then the inference process can be shown in **Figure 1**. As the input values overlap with both rule antecedents, both rules are fired. Using rules R_i and R_j, the given input then leads to system outputs $f_i(x_0, x_0)$ and $f_j(x_0, x_0)$, respectively. The consequences from both rules are then integrated using weighted average function, where

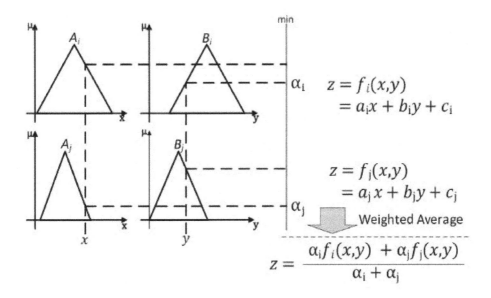

Figure 1. TSK fuzzy inference [21].

the values of weights represent the matching degrees between the given input and the rule antecedents (often referred to as firing strengths). Assume that $\mu_{A_i}(x_0)$ and $\mu_{B_i}(y_0)$ are the matching degree between inputs (x_0 and y_0) and rule antecedents (A_i and B_i), respectively. The firing strength of rule R_i, denoted as α_i, is calculated as:

$$\alpha_i = \mu_{A_i}(x_0) \wedge \mu_{B_i}(y_0), \tag{4}$$

where $\wedge$ stands for a t-norm operator. Different implementations can be used for the t-norm operator, with the minimum operator being used most widely. Of course, if another system input (x_1, y_1) is presented and it is not covered by the rule base, the matching degrees between this new input and rule antecedents of R_i and R_j are equal to 0. In this case, no rule will be fired, and thus traditional TSK is not applicable. In this case, fuzzy interpolation is required, which is introduced in Section 4.

3. Fuzzy interpolation with sparse Mamdani-style rule bases

FISs based on Mamdani-style rule bases can be categorised into two classes. One group of approaches were developed based on the decomposition and resolution principle, termed as 'resolution principle-base interpolation'. In particular, the approach represents each fuzzy set as a series of α-cuts ($\alpha \in (0,1]$), and the α-cut of the conclusion is computed from the α-cuts of the observation and the α-cuts of rules. The final fuzzy set is assembled from all the α-cut consequences using the resolution principle [48–50]. The other group of fuzzy interpolation approaches were developed using the analogy reasoning system, thus termed as 'analogy-based fuzzy interpolation'. This group of approaches firstly generates an intermediate rule whose antecedent maximally overlaps with the given observation, then the system output is produced from the observation using the intermediate rule. Two representative approaches of the two classes, the KH approach [10] and the scale and move transformation-based approach [9, 51, 52], are discussed in this section based on simple rule bases with two antecedent rules. Despite of the simple examples used herein, both of these approaches have been extended to work with multiple multi-antecedent rules.

3.1. Resolution principle-based interpolation

Single step interpolation approaches are computationally efficient, such as the KH approach proposed in Refs. [9, 10, 53]. Following these approaches, all variables involved in the reasoning process must satisfy a partial ordering, denoted as $\prec$ [31]. According to the decomposition principle, a normal and convex fuzzy set A can be represented by a series of α-cut intervals, each denoted as A_α, $\alpha \in (0,1)$. Given fuzzy sets A_i and A_j which are associated with the same variable, the partial ordering $A_i \prec A_j$ is defined as:

$$\inf\{A_{i\alpha}\} < \inf\{A_{j\alpha}\} \text{ and } \sup\{A_{i\alpha}\} < \sup\{A_{j\alpha}\}, \quad \forall \alpha \in (0,1], \tag{5}$$

where $\inf\{A_{i\alpha}\}$ and $\sup\{A_{i\alpha}\}$ denote the infimum and supremum of $A_{i\alpha}$, respectively.

Take the KH approach as an example here. For simplicity, suppose there are two fuzzy rules: If x is A_i, then y is B_i, and If x is A_j then y is B_j, shorten as $A_i \Rightarrow B_i$ and $A_j \Rightarrow B_j$, respectively. Also, suppose that these two rules are adjacent, in other words, there is no rule $A \Rightarrow B$ existing such that $A_i \prec A \prec A_j$ or $A_j \prec A \prec A_i$. Given an observation A^* which satisfies $A_i \prec A^* \prec A_j$ or $A_j \prec A^* \prec A_i$, a conclusion B^* can be computed as:

$$\frac{D(A_{i\alpha}, A_{\alpha}^*)}{D(A_{\alpha}^*, A_{j\alpha})} = \frac{D(B_{i\alpha}, B_{\alpha}^*)}{D(B_{\alpha}^*, B_{j\alpha})}, \tag{6}$$

where given any $0 < \alpha \le 1$, the distance $D(A_{i\alpha}, A_{j\alpha})$ between the α-cuts $A_{i\alpha}$ and $A_{j\alpha}$ is defined by the interval $[D^L(A_{i\alpha}, A_{j\alpha}), D^U(A_{i\alpha}, A_{j\alpha})]$ with:

$$D^L(A_{i\alpha}, A_{j\alpha}) = \inf\{A_{j\alpha}\} - \inf\{A_{i\alpha}\}, D^U(A_{i\alpha}, A_{j\alpha}) = \sup\{A_{j\alpha}\} - \sup\{A_{i\alpha}\}. \tag{7}$$

Following Eqs. (4) and (5), the following is resulted:

$$\begin{cases} \min\{B_{\alpha}^*\} = \dfrac{\dfrac{\inf(B_{i\alpha})}{D^L(A_{i\alpha}, A_{\alpha}^*)} + \dfrac{\inf(B_{j\alpha})}{D^L(A_{\alpha}^*, A_{j\alpha})}}{\dfrac{1}{D^L(A_{i\alpha}, A_{\alpha}^*)} + \dfrac{1}{D^L(A_{\alpha}^*, A_{j\alpha})}} \\[3em] \max\{B_{\alpha}^*\} = \dfrac{\dfrac{\sup(B_{i\alpha})}{D^U(A_{i\alpha}, A_{\alpha}^*)} + \dfrac{\sup(B_{j\alpha})}{D^U(A_{\alpha}^*, A_{j\alpha})}}{\dfrac{1}{D^U(A_{i\alpha}, A_{\alpha}^*)} + \dfrac{1}{D^U(A_{\alpha}^*, A_{j\alpha})}} \end{cases} \tag{8}$$

For simplicity, let

$$\begin{cases} \Lambda_{\alpha}^L = \dfrac{\inf\{A_{\alpha}^*\} - \inf\{A_{i\alpha}\}}{\inf\{A_{j\alpha}\} - \inf\{A_{i\alpha}\}} \\[1.5em] \Lambda_{\alpha}^U = \dfrac{\sup\{A_{\alpha}^*\} - \sup\{A_{i\alpha}\}}{\sup\{A_{j\alpha}\} - \sup\{A_{i\alpha}\}} \end{cases} \tag{9}$$

Also, denote $\Lambda = [\Lambda_{\alpha}^L, \Lambda_{\alpha}^U]$ hereafter. From this, Eq. (8) can be re-written as:

$$\begin{cases} \min\{B_{\alpha}^*\} = (1 - \Lambda_{\alpha}^L)\inf\{B_{i\alpha}\} + \Lambda_{\alpha}^L\inf\{B_{j\alpha}\} \\ \max\{B_{\alpha}^*\} = (1 - \Lambda_{\alpha}^U)\sup\{B_{i\alpha}\} + \Lambda_{\alpha}^U\sup\{B_{j\alpha}\} \end{cases} \tag{10}$$

This means $B_{\alpha}^* = [\min\{B_{\alpha}^*\}, \max\{B_{\alpha}^*\}]$ is generated. The final consequence B^* is then reassembled as:

$$B^* = U_{\alpha \in (0,1]}\alpha B_{\alpha}^*. \tag{11}$$

The KH approach may generate invalid interpolated results [54], which is usually called 'the abnormal problem'. To eliminate this deficiency, a number of modifications or improvements have been proposed, including Refs. [9, 10, 13, 14, 18, 53, 55–60]. Approaches such as Refs. [15, 16, 61–63] also belong to this group.

3.2. Analogy-based interpolation

The scale and move transformation-based fuzzy interpolation [51, 52, 64] is a representative approach in the analogy-based interpolation group. For simplicity, following the same assumption of a simple rule base containing two rules with two antecedents, the transformation-based approach is shown in **Figure 2** and outlined as follows.

Given neighbouring rules If x is A_i, then y is B_i, and If x is A_j then y is B_j and observation A^*, this method first maps fuzzy sets A_i, A_j and A^* to real numbers a_i, a_j and a^* (named as *representative values*) respectively, using real function f_1. Then, the location relationship between A^* and rule antecedents (A_i and A_j) is computed. This is achieved by another mapping function f_2, which results in the *relative placement factor* λ. In contrast to the resolution-based interpolation approaches, the generated *relative placement factor* in analogy-based fuzzy interpolation approach is a crisp real number. Finally, linear interpolation is implemented using mapping function f_3 of λ, which leads to the intermediate rule $A^{*'} \Rightarrow B^{*'}$.

Note that the *representative value* of intermediate rule antecedent $A^{*'}$ equals to that of A^* (the given observation), although $A^{*'}$ and A^* are not identical for most of the situations. In the scale and move transformation-based fuzzy interpolation approach, the similarity degree between two fuzzy sets A^* and $A^{*'}$ with the same representative value is expressed as the scale rate s, scale ratio $\mathbb{S}$ and move rate $\mathbb{M}$, which is obtained by real function f_4. From this, the consequence B^* is calculated from $B^{*'}$ using a transformation function f_5 which imposes the similarity degree between A^* and $A^{*'}$. Different approaches have been developed for intermediate rule generation and final conclusion production from the intermediate rule [17, 55, 63, 65].

3.3. Adaptive fuzzy interpolation

Fuzzy interpolation strengthens the power of fuzzy inference by enhancing the robustness of fuzzy systems and reducing the systems' complexity. Common to both classes of fuzzy

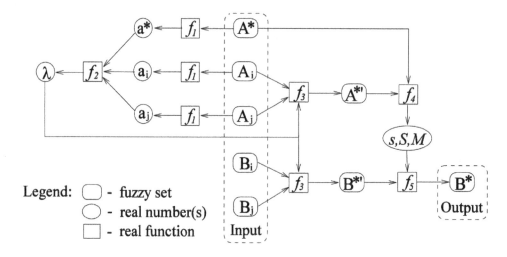

Figure 2. Transformation-based fuzzy interpolation [12].

interpolation approaches discussed above is the fact that interpolation is carried out in a linear manner. This may conflict with the nature of some realistic problems and consequently this may lead to inconsistencies during rule interpolation processes. Adaptive fuzzy interpolation was proposed to address this [12, 66–68]. It was developed upon FIS approaches, which detects inconsistencies, locates possible fault candidates and modifies the candidates in order to remove all the inconsistencies.

Each pair of neighbouring rules is defined as a *fuzzy reasoning component* in adaptive fuzzy interpolation. Each fuzzy reasoning component takes a fuzzy value as input and produces another as output. The process of adaptive interpolation is summarised in **Figure 3**. Firstly, the interpolator carries out interpolation and passes the interpolated results to the truth maintenance system (ATMS) [69, 70], which records the dependencies between an interpolated value (including any contradiction) and its proceeding interpolation components. Then, the ATMS relays any β_0-contradictions (i.e. inconsistency between two different values for a common variable at least to the degree of a given threshold β_0 $(0 \leq \beta_0 \leq 1)$) as well as their dependent fuzzy reasoning components to the general diagnostic engine (GDE) [71] which diagnoses the problem and generates all possible component candidates. After that, a modification process takes place to correct a certain candidate to restore consistency by modifying the original linear interpolation to become first-order piecewise linear.

The adaptive approach has been further generalised [11, 72, 73], which allows the identification and modification of observations and rules, in addition to that of interpolation procedures that were addressed in Ref. [12]. This is supported by introducing extra information of certainty degrees associated with such basic elements of FIS. The work also allows for all candidates for modification to be prioritised, based on the extent to which a candidate is likely to lead to all the detected contradictions, by extending the classic ATMS and GDE. This study has significantly improved the efficiency of the work in Ref. [12] by exploiting more information during both the diagnosis and modification processes. Another alternative implementation of the adaptive approach has also been reported in Ref. [74].

3.4. Sparse rule base generation

A Mamdani-style fuzzy rule base is usually implemented through either a data-driven approach [75] or a knowledge-driven approach [76]. The data-driven approach using artificial intelligence approach extracts rules from data sets, while the knowledge-driven approach generates rules by human expert. Due to the limited availability of expert knowledge, data-driven approaches have been increasingly widely applied. However, the application of such

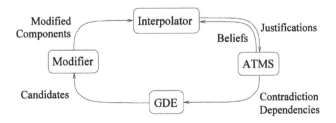

Figure 3. Adaptive fuzzy interpolation [12].

approaches usually requires a large amount of training data, and it often leads to dense rule bases to support conventional fuzzy inference systems, despite of the availability of rule simplification approaches such as Refs. [77, 78].

A recent development or rule base generation has been reported with compact sparse rule bases targeted [79]. This approach firstly partitions the problem domain into a number of sub-regions and each sub-region is expressed as a fuzzy rule. Then, the importance of each sub-region is analysed using curvature value by artificially treating the problem space as a geography object (and high-dimensional problem space is represented as a collection of sub-three-dimensional spaces). Briefly, the profile curvature of a surface expresses the extent to which the geometric object deviates from being 'flat' or 'straight', the curvature values of the sub-regions are then calculated to represent how important they are in terms of linear interpolation. Given a predefined threshold, important sub-regions can be identified, and their corresponding rules are selected to generate a raw sparse rule base. The generated raw rule base can then be optimised by fine-tuning the membership functions using an optimisation algorithm. Generic algorithm has been widely used for various optimisation problems, such as Ref. [80], which has also been used in the work of Ref. [79].

Compared to most of the existing rule base generation approaches, the above approach differs in its utilisation of the curvature value in rule selection. Mathematically, curvature is the second derivate of a surface or the slope of slope. The profile curvature [81] is traditionally used in geography to represent the rate at which a surface slope changes whilst moving in the direction, which represents the steepest downward gradient for the given direction. Given a sub-region $f(x, y)$ and a certain direction, the curvature value is calculated as the directional derivative which refers to the rate at which any given scalar field is changing. The overall linearity of a sub-region can thus be accurately represented as the maximum profile curvature value on all directions. From this, those rules corresponding to sub-regions with higher profile curvature values (with respect to a given threshold) are selected, which jointly form the sparse rule base to support fuzzy rule interpolation.

FISs relax the requirement of complete expert knowledge or large data sets covering the entire input domain from the conventional fuzzy inference systems. However, it is still difficult for some real-world applications to obtain sufficient data or expert knowledge for rule base generation to support FISs. In addition, the generated rule resulted from most of the existing rule base generation approaches are fixed and cannot support changing situations. An experience-based rule base generation and adaptation approach for FISs has therefore been proposed for control problems [82]. Briefly, the approach initialises the rule base with very limited rules first. Then, the initialised rule base is revised by adding accurate interpolated rules and removing out-of-date rules guided by the performance index from a feedback mechanism and the performance experiences of rules.

4. Fuzzy interpolation with sparse TSK-style rule base

The traditional TSK inference system has been extended to work with sparse TSK fuzzy rule base [21]. This approach, in the same time, also enjoys the benefit from its original version, which directly generates crisp outputs. The extended TSK inference approach is built upon a modified similarity measure which always generates greater than zero similarity degrees between observations and rule antecedents even when they do not overlap at all. Thanks to this property, a global consequence can always be generated by integrating the results from all rules in the rule base.

4.1. Rule firing strength

The modified similarity measure is developed from the work described in Ref. [83]. Suppose there are two fuzzy sets A and A' in a normalised variable domain. Without loss generality, a fuzzy set with any membership can be approximated by a polygonal fuzzy membership function with n odd points. Therefore, A and A' can be represented as $A = (a_1, a_2, \ldots a_n)$ and $A' = (a'_1, a'_2, \ldots a'_{n'})$, as shown in **Figure 4**. The similarity degree $S(A,A')$ between A and A' is computed as:

$$S(A, A') = \left(1 - \frac{\sum_{i=1}^{n}|a_i - a'_i|}{n}\right)(DF)^{\tilde{B}(supp_A, supp_{A'})} \frac{\min\left(\mu(C_A), \mu(C_{A'})\right)}{\max\left(\mu(C_A), \mu(C_{A'})\right)}, \tag{12}$$

where c_A is the centre of gravity of fuzzy sets A, and $\mu(c_A)$ is the membership of the centre of gravity of fuzzy set A; DF represents a distance factor which is a function of the distance between two concerned fuzzy sets, and $B(supp_A, supp_{A'})$ is defined as follows:

$$B(supp_A, supp_{A'}) = \begin{cases} 1, & if\, supp_A + supp_{A'} \neq 0, \\ 0, & if\, supp_A + supp_{A'} = 0, \end{cases} \tag{13}$$

where $supp_A$ and $supp_{A'}$ are the supports of A and A', respectively.

In Eq. (13), $B(supp_A, supp_{A'})$ is used to determine whether distance factor is considered. That is, if both A and A' are of crisp values, the distance factor DF will not take into consideration during the calculation of the similarity degree; otherwise, DF will be considered. The centre of gravity of a fuzzy set is commonly approximated as the average of its odd points. That is:

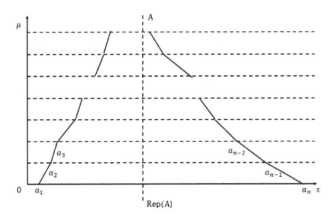

Figure 4. An arbitrary fuzzy set with n odd points.

$$c_A = \frac{a_1 + a_2 + \ldots + a_n}{n}, \tag{14}$$

$$\mu(c_A) = \frac{\mu(a_1) + \mu(a_2) + \ldots + \mu(a_n)}{n}. \tag{15}$$

The distance factor DF is represented as:

$$DF = 1 - \frac{1}{1 + e^{-hd+5}} \tag{16}$$

where d is the distance between the two fuzzy sets, and $h(h > 0)$ is a sensitivity factor. The smaller the value of h is, the more sensitive the similarity degree to their distance is. The value of h is usually within the range of (20, 60), but the exact value is problem specific.

4.2. Fuzzy interpolation

Using the modified similarity measure as traduced above, the similarity between any given observation and a rule antecedent is always greater than zero. This means that all the rules in the rule base are fired for inference. Therefore, if only a sparse rule base is available and a given observation is not covered by the sparse rule base, a consequence still can be generated by firing all the rules in the rule base. The inference process is summarised as below:

1. Calculate the matching degree $S(A^*, A_i)$ and $S(B^*, B_i)$ between each pair of rule antecedent (A_i, B_i) and the input values (A^*, B^*) based on Eq. (12).

2. Determine the firing strength of each rule by integrating the matching degrees between the input items and rule antecedents as calculated in Step 1:

$$\alpha_i = S(A^*, A_i) \wedge S(B^*, B_i). \tag{17}$$

3. Compute the consequence of each rule in line with the given input and the polynomial function in rule consequent:

$$f_i(A^*, A_i) = \alpha_i \cdot c_{A^*} + b_i \cdot c_{B^*} + c_i. \tag{18}$$

4. Obtain the final result z by integrating the sub-consequences from all m rules in the rule base:

$$z = \frac{\sum_{i=1}^{n} \alpha_i f_i(A^*, B^*)}{\sum_{i=1}^{n} \alpha_i}. \tag{19}$$

5. Applications of fuzzy interpolation

Fuzzy interpolation systems have been successfully applied to a number of real-world problems including Refs. [23, 22, 25, 52, 57], two of which are reviewed in the section below.

5.1. Truck backer-upper control

Backing a trailer truck to a loading dock is a challenging task for all yet the most skilled truck drivers. Due to the difficulties, this challenge has been used as a control benchmark problem with various solutions proposed [75, 84, 85]. For instance, an artificial neural network has been applied to this problem, but a large amount of training data is required [84]. An adaptive fuzzy control system was also proposed for this problem, but the generation of the rule base is computationally expensive. Another solution combines empirical knowledge and data [85]. That is, a combined fuzzy rule base is generated by joining the previously generated rules (data-driven) and linguistic rules (expert knowledge-driven). More recently, a supervisory control system was proposed with fewer number of state variables required due to its capability to the decomposition of the control task, thus relieving the curse of dimensionality [86].

Fuzzy interpolation system has also been applied to the trailer truck backer-upper problem [52] to further reduce the system complexity. The problem can be formally formulated as $\theta = f(x, y, \varnothing)$. Variables x and y represent the coordinate values corresponding to horizontal and vertical axes; $\varnothing$ refers to the azimuth angle between the truck's onward direction and the horizontal axis; and θ is the steering angle of the truck. Given that enough clearance is present between the truck and loading lock in most cases, variable y can be safely omitted and hence results in a simplified formula to $\theta = f(x, \varnothing)$. By evenly partitioning each variable domain into three fuzzy sets, nine (i.e. 3*3) fuzzy rules were generated using FISMAT [87] and each of which is denoted as IF x is A AND $\varnothing$ is B THEN θ is C, where A, B and C are three linguistic values. Noting that domain partitions appear to be symmetrical in some sense, the three rules which are flanked by other rule pairs were removed from the rule base resulting a more compact rule base with only six fuzzy rules.

If the traditional fuzzy inference system were applied, the sparse rule base would cause a sudden break of the truck for some situations as no rule would be fired when the truck is in the position that can be represented by the omitted rules. In this case, fuzzy interpolation is naturally applied and the sudden break problem can be avoided. In addition, thanks to the great generalisation ability of the fuzzy interpolation systems, smooth performance is also demonstrated compared to the conventional fuzzy inference approaches. This study clearly demonstrates that fuzzy interpolation systems are able to simplify rule bases and support inferences with sparse rule bases.

5.2. Heating system control

The demotic energy waste contributes a large part of CO^2 emissions in the UK, and about 60% of the household energy has been used for space heating. Various heating controllers have been developed to reduce the waste of energy on heating unoccupied properties, which are usually programmable and developed using a number of sensors. These systems are able to successfully switch off heating systems when a property is unoccupied [88–92], but they cannot intelligently preheat the properties by warming the property before users return home without manual inputs or leaving the heating systems on unnecessarily for longer time. A smart home heating controller has been developed using a FIS, which allows efficient home heating by accurately predicting the users' home time using users' historic and current location data obtained from portable devices [23].

The overall flow chart of the smart home heating system is shown in **Figure 5**. The controller first extracts the resident's location and moving information. There are four types of residents' location and moving information that need to be considered: At Home, Way Back Home, Leaving Home and Static (i.e. at Special Location). The user's current location and moving states are obtained effectively using the GPS information provided by user's portable devices. From this, if the resident's current state is At Home, the algorithm terminates; and if the residents' current state is Leaving Home, that is the residents are moving away from home,

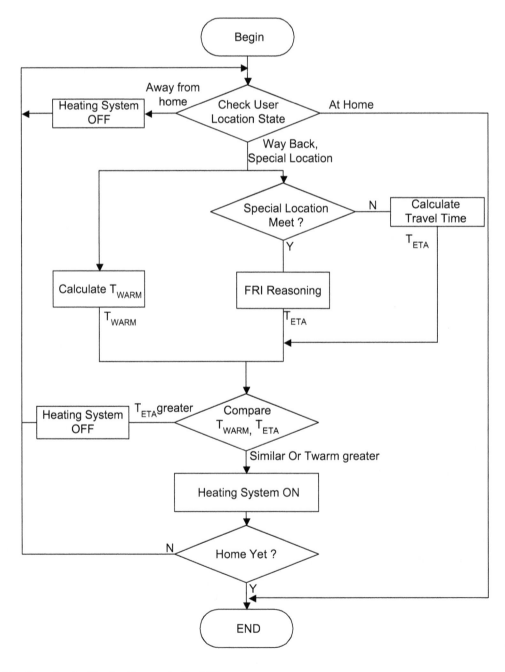

Figure 5. The flow chart of the heating controller [23].

the boiler is off and the system will check the resident's location and moving information again in a certain period of time. Otherwise, the time to arriving home (denoted as TAH) is predicted and the time to preheat the home to a comfortable temperature (denoted as TPH) is also calculated, based on the resident's current situation and the current environment around home.

The user's current travel modes (i.e. driving, walking or bicycling) can be detected by employing a naïve Bayes classifier [93] using the GPS information. Then the travel distance and time between the current location and home can be estimated using Google Distance Matrix API. Note that the time spent on different locations may vary significantly, and also different residents usually spend different amount of times at the same special location as people have their own living styles. The time that the residents spent at the current location is therefore estimated using fuzzy interpolation systems, thanks to the complexity of the problem. In particular, the fuzzy interpolation engine takes five fuzzy inputs and produces one fuzzy output which is the estimate of the time to getting home. The five inputs are the current location, the day of the week, the time of the day, the time already spent at the current location and the estimated travel between the current location and home.

If each input domain is fuzzy partitioned by 5 to 13 fuzzy, tens of thousands of rules will be resulted which requires significant resources during inferences. The proposed system, however, has selected the most important 72 rules forming a sparse rule base to support fuzzy rule interpolation, which significantly improve the system performance. Once the home time is calculated, the home can then be accurately preheated based on a heating gain table developed based on the particular situation and environment of a concerned property [91]. This work has been applied to a four-bedroom detached house with a total hearing space of 100 m²(*floor area*) × 2.4 m(*hight*). The house is heated by a 15 kW heating boiler. The study has shown that the controller developed using fuzzy inference has successfully reduced the burning time of the boiler for heating and more accurately preheat the home.

Despite of the success of the applications introduced above, there is a potential for FISs to be applied to more and larger scales real-world problems, especially in the field of system control. Note that robotics has taken the centre in the control field to perform tasks from basic robot calligraphy system [94] to complex tasks which require hand-eye (camera) coordination [95]. FISs can also be applied to such advanced areas in the field of robotics, which require further investigation.

6. Conclusions

This chapter reviewed fuzzy interpolation systems and their applications in the field of control. There are basically two groups of fuzzy interpolation approaches using the two most common types of fuzzy rule bases (i.e. Mamdani-style rule bases and TSK-style rule bases) to supplement the two groups of widely used fuzzy inference approaches (i.e. the Mamdani inference and the TSK inference). The applications of fuzzy interpolation systems have also been discussed in the chapter which demonstrate the power of the approaches. FISs can be further improved despite of its promising performance. Firstly, type-2 FISs have already been proposed in the literature, but how type-2 FISs can be applied in real-world applications requires further investigation. Also, more theoretical analysis for FISs is needed to mathematically prove the convergence property of the approaches. In addition, most of the existing fuzzy interpolation approaches are proposed as a supplementary of the existing fuzzy inference models. It is interesting to investigate the development of a united platform which integrates both the existing fuzzy models and fuzzy inference systems such that the new system can benefit from both approaches.

Acknowledgements

This work was jointly supported by the National Natural Science Foundation of China (No. 61502068) and the China Postdoctoral Science Foundation (Nos. 2013M541213 and 2015T80239).

Author details

Longzhi Yang[1]*, Zheming Zuo[1], Fei Chao[2] and Yanpeng Qu[3]

*Address all correspondence to: longzhi.yang@northumbria.ac.uk

1 Department of Computer and Information Sciences, Northumbria University, Newcastle, UK

2 School of Information Science and Engineering, Xiamen University, Xiamen, PR China

3 Information Science and Technology College, Dalian Maritime University, Dalian, PR China

References

[1] Fu X, Zeng XJ, Wang D, Xu D, Yang L. Fuzzy system approaches to negotiation pricing decision support. Journal of Intelligent & Fuzzy Systems. 2015;29(2):685–699

[2] Yang L, Neagu D. Integration strategies for toxicity data from an empirical perspective. In: 2014 14th UK Workshop on Computational Intelligence (UKCI). 2014. pp. 1–8

[3] Yang L, Neagu D. Toxicity risk assessment from heterogeneous uncertain data with possibility-probability distribution. In: 2013 IEEE International Conference on Fuzzy Systems (FUZZ-IEEE). 2013. pp. 1–8

[4] Yang, Neagu D, Cronin MTD, Hewitt M, Enoch SJ, Madden JC, Przybylak K. Towards a fuzzy expert system on toxicological data quality assessment. Molecular Informatics. 2012;32(1):65–78

[5] Yang L, Neagu D. Towards the integration of heterogeneous uncertain data. In: 2012 IEEE 13th International Conference on Information Reuse & Integration (IRI). 2012. pp. 295–302

[6] Guo Q, Qu Y, Deng A, Yang L. A new fuzzy-rough feature selection algorithm for mammographic risk analysis. In: 2016 12th International Conference on Natural Computation, Fuzzy Systems and Knowledge Discovery (ICNC-FSKD). 2016. pp. 934–939

[7] Mamdani EH. Application of fuzzy logic to approximate reasoning using linguistic synthesis. IEEE Transactions on Computers. 1976;**26**(12):1182–1191

[8] Takagi T, Sugeno M. Fuzzy identification of systems and its applications to modeling and control. IEEE Transactions on Systems, Man, and Cybernetics. 1985;**1**:116–132

[9] Kóczy L, Hirota K. Approximate reasoning by linear rule interpolation and general approximation. International Journal of Approximate Reasoning. 1993;**9**(3): 197–225

[10] Kóczy L, Hirota K. Interpolative reasoning with insufficient evidence in sparse fuzzy rule bases. Information Sciences. 1993;**71**(1–2):169–201

[11] Yang L, Chao F, Shen Q. Generalised adaptive fuzzy rule interpolation. IEEE Transactions on Fuzzy Systems. 2016. DOI: 10.1109/TFUZZ.2016.2582526

[12] Yang L, Shen Q. Adaptive Fuzzy Interpolation. IEEE Transactions on Fuzzy Systems. 2011;**19**(6):1107–1126

[13] Yang L, Shen Q. Closed form fuzzy interpolation. Fuzzy Sets and Systems. 2013;**225**:1–22

[14] Tikk D, Baranyi P. Comprehensive analysis of a new fuzzy rule interpolation method. IEEE Transactions on Fuzzy Systems. 2000;**8**(3):281–296

[15] Kovács S. Extending the fuzzy rule interpolation "FIVE" by fuzzy observation. In: Computational Intelligence, Theory and Applications. Springer; 2006. pp. 485–497

[16] Johanyák ZC, Kovács S. Fuzzy rule interpolation based on polar cuts. In: Computational Intelligence, Theory and Applications. Springer; 2006. pp. 499–511

[17] Baranyi P, Kóczy LT, Gedeon TD. A generalized concept for fuzzy rule interpolation. IEEE Transactions on Fuzzy Systems. 2004;**12**(6):820–837

[18] Dubois D, Prade H. On fuzzy interpolation. International Journal of General System. 1999;**28**(2–3):103–114

[19] Jin S, Diao R, Quek C, Shen Q. Backward fuzzy rule interpolation. IEEE Transactions on Fuzzy Systems. 2014;**22**(6):1682–1698

[20] Chen C, Parthaláin NM, Li Y, Price C, Quek C, Shen Q. Rough-fuzzy rule interpolation. Information Sciences. 2016;**351**:1–17

[21] Li J, Qu Y, Shum HP, Yang L. TSK inference with sparse rule bases. In: Advances in Computational Intelligence Systems. 2017. pp. 107–123

[22] Molnárka GI, Kovács S, Kóczy LT. Fuzzy rule interpolation based fuzzy signature structure in building condition evaluation. In: 2014 IEEE International Conference on Fuzzy Systems (FUZZ-IEEE). 2014. pp. 2214–2221

[23] Li J, Yang L, Shum HP, Sexton G, Tan Y. Intelligent home heating controller using fuzzy rule interpolation. In: 2015 15th UK Workshop on Computational Intelligence (UKCI). 2015

[24] Bai Y, Zhuang H, Wang D. Apply fuzzy interpolation method to calibrate parallel machine tools. The International Journal of Advanced Manufacturing Technology. 2012;**60**(5–8):553–560

[25] Kovács S, Koczy LT. Application of interpolation-based fuzzy logic reasoning in behaviour-based control structures. In: 2004 IEEE International Conference on Fuzzy Systems. 2004

[26] Li J, Yang L, Fu X, Chao F, Qu Y. Dynamic QoS solution for enterprise networks using TSK fuzzy interpolation. In: 2017 IEEE International Conference on Fuzzy Systems (FUZZ-IEEE). 2017

[27] Yang L, Li J, Fehringer G, Barraclough P, Sexton G, Cao Y. Intrusion detection system by fuzzy interpolation. In: 2017 IEEE International Conference on Fuzzy Systems (FUZZ-IEEE). 2017

[28] Mamdani EH, Assilian S. An experiment in linguistic synthesis with a fuzzy logic controller. International Journal of Man-Machine Studies. 1975;**7**(1):1–13

[29] Castro JL, Zurita JM. An inductive learning algorithm in fuzzy systems. Fuzzy Sets and Systems. 1997;**89**(2):193–203

[30] Chen SM, Lee SH, and Lee CH. A new method for generating fuzzy rules from numerical data for handling classification problems. Applied Artificial Intelligence. 2001;**15**(7):645–664

[31] Zedeh LA. Outline of a new approach to the analysis of complex systems and decision processes. IEEE Transactions on Systems, Man, and Cybernetic. 1973;**3**:28–44

[32] Bandler W, Kohout L. Fuzzy power sets and fuzzy implication operators. Fuzzy Sets and Systems. 1980;**4**(1):13–30

[33] Turksen IB. Four methods of approximate reasoning with interval-valued fuzzy sets. International Journal of Approximate Reasoning. 1989;**3**(2):121–142

[34] Turksen IB, Zhong Z. An approximate analogical reasoning approach based on similarity measures. IEEE Transactions on Systems, Man, and Cybernetics. 1988;**18**(6):1049–1056

[35] Klement EP, Mesiar R, Pap E. Triangular norms. Position paper I: Basic analytical and algebraic properties. Fuzzy Sets and Systems. 2004;**143**(1):5–26

[36] Mizumoto M, Zimmermann HJ. Comparison of fuzzy reasoning methods. Fuzzy Sets and Systems. 1982;**8**(3):253–283

[37] Nakanishi H, Turksen IB, Sugeno M. A review and comparison of six reasoning methods. Fuzzy Sets and Systems. 1993;57(3):257–294

[38] Turksen IB, Zhong Z. An approximate analogical reasoning schema based on similarity measures and interval-valued fuzzy sets. Fuzzy Sets and Systems. 1990;34(3): 323–346

[39] Chen SM. A new approach to handling fuzzy decision-making problems. IEEE Transactions on Systems, Man, and Cybernetics. 1988;18(6):1012–1016

[40] Chen SM. A Weighted fuzzy reasoning algorithm for medical diagnosis. Decision Support Systems. 1994;11(1):37–43

[41] Yeung DS, Tsang ECC. A comparative study on similarity-based fuzzy reasoning methods. IEEE Transactions on Systems, Man, and Cybernetics, Part B (Cybernetics). 1997;27(2):216–227

[42] Tversky A. Features of similarity. Psychological Review. 1977;84(4):327

[43] Yeung DS, Tsang ECC. Fuzzy knowledge representation and reasoning using petri nets. Expert Systems with Applications. 1994;7(2):281–289

[44] Yeung DS, Tsang ECC. Improved Fuzzy Knowledge Representation and Rule Evaluation Using Fuzzy Petri Nets and Degree of Subsethood. International Journal of Intelligent Systems. 1994;9(12):1083–1100

[45] Kosko B. Neural Networks and Fuzzy Systems: A Dynamical Systems Approach to Machine Intelligence. New Jersey: Prentice-Hall; 1992

[46] Yeung DS, Ysang ECC. A multilevel weighted fuzzy reasoning algorithm for expert systems. IEEE Transactions on Systems, Man, and Cybernetics-Part A: Systems and Humans. 1998;28(2):149–158

[47] Thorndike RL. Who belongs in the family? Psychometrika. 1953;18(4):267–276

[48] Klir GJ, Yuan B. Fuzzy Sets and Fuzzy Logic: Theory and Applications. Prentice Hall PTR; 1995

[49] Robinson JA. A machine-oriented logic based on the resolution principle. Journal of the ACM (JACM). 1965;12(1):23–41

[50] Zadeh LA. Quantitative fuzzy semantics. Information Sciences. 1971;3(2):159–176

[51] Huang Z, Shen Q. Fuzzy interpolative reasoning via scale and move transformations. IEEE Transactions on Fuzzy Systems. 2006;14(2):340–359

[52] Huang Z, Shen Q. Fuzzy interpolation and extrapolation: A practical approach. IEEE Transactions on Fuzzy Systems. 2008;16(1):13–28

[53] Kóczy LT, Hirota K. Size reduction by interpolation in fuzzy rule bases. IEEE Transactions on Systems, Man, and Cybernetics, Part B (Cybernetics). 1997;27(1):14–25

[54] Yan S, Mizumoto M, Qiao WZ. Reasoning conditions on Koczy's interpolative reasoning method in sparse fuzzy rule bases. Fuzzy Sets and Systems. 1995;**75**(1):63–71

[55] Chen SM, Ko YK. Fuzzy interpolative reasoning for sparse fuzzy rule-based systems based on ?-cuts and transformations techniques. IEEE Transactions on Fuzzy Systems. 2008;**16**(6):1626–1648

[56] Hsiao WH, Chen SM, Lee CH. A new interpolative reasoning method in sparse rule-based systems. Fuzzy Sets and Systems. 1998;**93**(1):17–22

[57] Wong KW, Tikk D, Dedeon TD, Kóczy LT. Fuzzy rule interpolation for multidimensional input spaces with applications: A case study. IEEE Transactions on Fuzzy Systems. 2005;**13**(6):809–819

[58] Yam Y, Kóczy LT. Representing membership functions as points in high-dimensional spaces for fuzzy interpolation and extrapolation. IEEE Transactions on Fuzzy Systems. 2000;**8**(6):761–772

[59] Yeung Y, Wong ML, Baranyi P. Interpolation with function space representation of membership functions. IEEE Transactions on Fuzzy Systems. 2006;**14**(3):398–411

[60] Yang L, Chen C, Jin N, Fu X, Shen Q. Closed form fuzzy interpolation with interval type-2 fuzzy sets. In: 2014 IEEE International Conference on Fuzzy Systems (FUZZ-IEEE). 2014. pp. 2184–2191

[61] Chang YC, Chen SM, Liau CJ. Fuzzy interpolative reasoning for sparse fuzzy-rule-based systems based on the areas of fuzzy sets. IEEE Transactions on Fuzzy Systems. 2008;**16** (5):1285–1301

[62] Tikk D, Joó I, Kóczy L, Várlaki P, Moser B, Gedeon TD. Stability of interpolative fuzzy KH controllers. Fuzzy Sets and Systems. 2002;**125**(1):105–119

[63] Ughetto L, Dubois D, Prade H. Fuzzy interpolation by convex completion of sparse rule bases. In: 2000 IEEE International Conference on Fuzzy Systems (FUZZ-IEEE). 2000. pp. 465–470

[64] Shen Q, Yang L. Generalisation of scale and move transformation-based fuzzy interpolation. Journal of Advanced Computational Intelligence and Intelligent Informatics. 2011;**15**(3):288–298

[65] Jenei S, Klement EP, Konzel R. Interpolation and extrapolation of fuzzy quantities-The multiple-dimensional case. Soft Computing. 2002;**6**(3–4):258–270

[66] Yang L, Shen Q. Towards adaptive interpolative reasoning. In: 2009 IEEE International Conference on Fuzzy Systems (FUZZ-IEEE). 2009. pp. 542–549

[67] Yang L, Shen Q. Extending adaptive interpolation: From triangular to trapezoidal. In: 2009 9th UK Workshop on Computational Intelligence (UKCI). 2009. pp. 25–30

[68] Yang L, Shen Q. Adaptive fuzzy interpolation and extrapolation with multiple-antecedent rules. In: 2010 IEEE International Conference on Fuzzy Systems (FUZZ-IEEE). 2010. pp. 1–8

[69] Kleer JD. An assumption-based TMS. Artificial Intelligence. 1986;**28**(2):127–162

[70] Kleer JD. Extending the ATMS. Artificial Intelligence. 1986;**28**(2):163–196

[71] Kleer JD, Williams BC. Diagnosing multiple faults. Artificial Intelligence. 1987;**32**(1):97–130

[72] Yang L, Shen Q. Adaptive fuzzy interpolation with prioritized component candidates. In: 2011 IEEE International Conference on Fuzzy Systems (FUZZ-IEEE). 2011. pp. 428–435

[73] Yang L, Shen Q. Adaptive fuzzy interpolation with uncertain observations and rule base. In 2011 IEEE International Conference on Fuzzy Systems (FUZZ-IEEE). 2011. pp. 471–478

[74] Cheng SH, Chen SM, Chen CL. Adaptive fuzzy interpolation based on ranking values of polygonal fuzzy sets and similarity measures between polygonal fuzzy sets. Information Sciences. 2016;**342**:176–190

[75] Wang LX, Mendel JM. Generating fuzzy rules by learning from examples. IEEE Transactions on Systems, Man, and Cybernetics. 1992;**22**(6):1414–1427

[76] Johanyák ZC, Kovács S. Sparse fuzzy system generation by rule base extension. In: 2007 11th IEEE International Conference on Intelligent Engineering Systems. 2007. pp. 99–104

[77] Bellaaj H, Ketata R, Chtourou M. A new method for fuzzy rule base reduction. Journal of Intelligent & Fuzzy Systems. 2013;**25**(3):605–613

[78] Tao CW. A reduction approach for fuzzy rule bases of fuzzy controllers. IEEE Transactions on Systems, Man, and Cybernetics, Part B (Cybernetics). 2002;**32**(5):668–675

[79] Tan Y, Li J, Wonders M, Chao F, Shum HP, Yang L. Towards sparse rule base generation for fuzzy rule interpolation. In: 2016 IEEE International Conference on Fuzzy Systems (FUZZ-IEEE). 2016. pp. 110–117

[80] Cowton J, Yang L. A smart calendar system using multiple search techniques. In: 2015 15th UK Workshop on Computational Intelligence (UKCI). 2015

[81] Peckham SD. Profile, plan and streamline curvature: A simple derivation and applications. In: Proceedings of Geomorphometry. 2011. pp. 27–30

[82] Li J, Shum PH, Fu X, Sexton G, Yang L. Experience-based rule base generation and adaptation for fuzzy interpolation. In: 2016 IEEE International Conference on Fuzzy Systems (FUZZ-IEEE). 2016. pp. 102–109

[83] Chen SJ, Chen SM. Fuzzy risk analysis based on similarity measures of generalized fuzzy numbers. IEEE Transactions on Fuzzy Systems. 2003;**11**(1):45–56

[84] Nguyen D, Widrow B. The truck backer-upper: An example of self-learning in neural networks. In: Proceedings of the International Joint Conference on Neural Networks (IJCNN). 1989;**2**:357–363

[85] Kong SG, Kosko B. Adaptive fuzzy systems for backing up a truck-and-trailer. IEEE Transactions on Neural Networks. 1992;**3**(2):211–223

[86] Riid A, Rustern E. Fuzzy logic in control: Truck backer-upper problem revisited. In: 2001 IEEE International Conference on Fuzzy Systems (FUZZ-IEEE). 2001;**1**:513–516

[87] Lotfi A. Fuzzy Inference Systems Toolbox for Matlab (FISMAT). 2000

[88] Haissig C. Adaptive fuzzy temperature control for hydronic heating systems. IEEE Control Systems. 2000;**20**(2):39–48

[89] Lu J, Sookoor T, Srinivasan V, Gao G, Holben B, Stankovic J, Field E, Whitehouse K. The Smart Thermostat: Using Occupancy Sensors to Save Energy in Homes. In: Proceedings of the 8th ACM Conference on Embedded Networked Sensor Systems. 2010. pp. 211–224

[90] Nevius M, Pigg S. Programmable thermostats that go berserk: Taking a social perspective on space heating in Wisconsin. In: Proceedings of the 2000 ACEEE Summer Study on Energy Efficiency in Buildings. 2000;8:e44

[91] Scott, J, Bernheim Brush AJ, Krumm J, Meyers B, Hazas M, Hodges S, Villar N. PreHeat: Controlling home heating using occupancy prediction. In: Proceedings of the 13th International conference on Ubiquitous Computing. 2011 pp. 281–290

[92] Von Altrock, C, Arend HO, Krausse B, Steffens C. Customer-adaptive fuzzy logic control of home heating system. In: 1994 IEEE International Conference on Fuzzy Systems (FUZZ-IEEE). 1994;**3**:1713–1718

[93] Friedman N, Geiger D, Goldszmidt M. Bayesian network classifiers. Machine Learning. 1997;**29**(2–3):131–163

[94] Chao F, Huang Y, Zhang X, Shang C, Yang L, Zhou C, Hu H, Lin CM. A robot calligraphy system: From simple to complex writing by human gestures. Engineering Applications of Artificial Intelligence. 2017;**59**:1–14

[95] Chao F, Zhu Z, Lin CM, Hu H, Yang L, Shang C, Zhou C. Enhanced robotic hand-eye coordination inspired from human-like behavioral patterns. IEEE Transactions on Cognitive and Developmental Systems. 2017. DOI: 10.1109/TCDS.2016.2620156

9

EMG-Controlled Prosthetic Hand with Fuzzy Logic Classification Algorithm

Beyda Taşar and Arif Gülten

Abstract

In recent years, researchers have conducted many studies on the design and control of prosthesis devices that take the place of a missing limb. Functional ability of prosthesis hands that mimic biological hand functions increases depending on the number of independent finger movements possible. From this perspective, in this study, six different finger movements were given to a prosthesis hand via bioelectrical signals, and the functionality of the prosthesis hand was increased. Bioelectrical signals were recorded by surface electromyography for four muscles with the help of surface electrodes. The recorded bioelectrical signals were subjected to a series of preprocessing and feature extraction processes. In order to create meaningful patterns of motion and an effective cognitive interaction network between the human and the prosthetic hand, fuzzy logic classification algorithms were developed. A five-fingered and 15-jointed prosthetic hand was designed via SolidWorks, and a prosthetic prototype was produced by a 3D printer. In addition, prosthetic hand simulator was designed in Matlab/SimMechanics. Pattern control of both the simulator and the prototype hand in real time was achieved. Position control of motors connected to each joint of the prosthetic hand was provided by a PID controller. Thus, an effective cognitive communication network established between the user, and the real-time pattern control of the prosthesis was provided by bioelectrical signals.

Keywords: EMG, fuzzy logic classification, multifunctional prosthesis hand, pattern recognition

1. Introduction

People lose limbs due to accidents and medical conditions. Robotic devices, which imitate the shape and function of a missing limb, are manufactured for use by people who lose their limb in such situations. In recent years, researchers have studied to design and control multifunctional prosthetics hand [1–7]. The complexity of the movement, that is, the number of independent movements, increases in proportion to the number of joints. There are 206 bones in the adult skeletal system. The 90 bones of the skull and face are connected to each other by non-immobilized joints, and the 33 bones of the spine are connected to each other by semi-movable joints. Movable joints are only present between the bones (except the metacarpals bones) of the arm (25) and leg (25). In light of this information, aside from the wrist joints, the human hand has 15 independent joints with three on each finger. Therefore, the biological hand movement involves the control of these joints independently. Thus, control of the hand is quite complex. Thus, of all the human parts, the hand is the most complicated in terms of kinetic analysis [8].

Two main factors enable the functional and visual prosthesis to be used like a biological hand:

- Prosthetic hand mechanical design and modeling [9, 10] and

- Perform the position and speed controls of each joint efficiently and precisely [11–19].

However, no matter how perfect the design and manufacture of the prosthetic hand may be, the utility depends on the cognitive interaction, i.e., the control algorithm, being designed properly, e.g., the type of movement and coordination between fingers. If information is not transferred to the prosthetic hand rapidly enough, then the prosthesis will not assume the desired position. Cognitive interaction is the most important factor for user to use effectively. There are many studies about cognitive interaction between human and robotic devices [20–25].

All voluntary muscle movements in humans occur as a result of bioelectrical signals transmitted from the brain through the muscle nerves. Bioelectrical electromyogram (EMG) signals transmitted to the muscles carry information about the type of movement, speed, and degree of muscle contraction or relaxation. The biological hand performs the basic tasks of holding and gripping, which involve various finger movements. The wrist movements essentially constitute the axis and assist in these gripping and holding movements. The main factor that increases the functionality of the prosthetic hand is the movement of the fingers. As the number of independent movements made by the prosthetic hand increases, it can mimic the biological hand more successfully. This study realizes the design of the bioelectrical signal control algorithm and the extension of the bioelectrical signal database with the purpose of increasing the finger motion function of bioelectrical signal-controlled prosthesis hands.

Figure 1 shows bioelectrical signals in the context of the activity of the muscle movements (e.g., flexion, relaxation force), as seen from the block flow diagram. EMG can be used to detect signals from the flexor pollicis longus, flexor carpi radialis, brachioradialis, extensor carpi radialis, extensor digiti minimi, and extensor carpi ulnaris. Bioelectrical signals were recorded with the help of four surface electrodes and subjected to a series of preprocessing and classification operations to understand the relationships between EMG signals and hand and finger movements. These signals were then applied to the prosthetic hand (space and simulator) as a reference motion signal. With the designed controllers, the position of the prosthetic hand finger joints can be controlled. Thus, a cognitive interface and communication network are established between the user and the prosthetic hand. Briefly summarized, the study creates a bioelectrical database of the activities of the hand muscles and the interaction network between the human and prosthetic hand using this database and interface to design a simulator and develop a control algorithm.

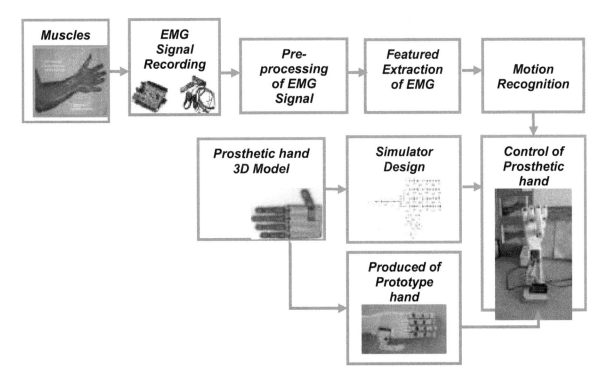

Figure 1. Control of multifunctional prosthetic hand simulator and prototype with EMG signals.

2. Recording, preprocessing, and featured extractions of EMG signal

2.1. Recording of EMG signals

EMG signals were recorded from the forearm muscles (the flexor pollicis longus, flexor carpi radialis, brachioradialis, extensor carpi radialis, extensor digiti minimi, and extensor carpi ulnaris) with the help of four surface electrodes. Electrode placements are shown in **Figure 2**. Electrode layout was chosen according to the protocol [26–28].

The signals, which support movements of the thumb, middle, ring, index, and pinkie fingers, were recorded separately for each of the respective muscles. Channels and finger relations are shown in **Table 1**.

2.2. Preprocessing of EMG signals

The recorded EMG signals also include various noise signals. It is necessary to separate the noise signals from the EMG signals, so that the characteristics of the signal can be accurately

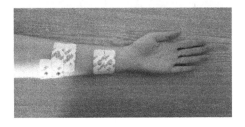
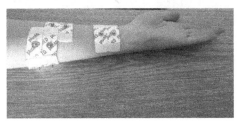

Figure 2. Placement of surface electrodes.

Channel 1	Channel 2	Channel 3	Channel 4
Pinkie finger muscle	Ring finger muscle	Middle finger muscle	İndex finger muscle

Table 1. Channel finger relations.

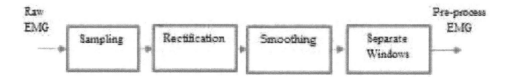

Figure 3. Preprocessing steps.

determined. For this reason, the raw EMG signal is first preprocessed. The block diagram of the preliminary preparation stage, including the separation, rectification, and sampling of the recorded EMG signals from noise, is shown in **Figure 3**.

2.2.1. Numerical sampling

EMG signals are analog voltage signals. Their amplitudes change constantly over the voltage range. Analog-to-digital conversion is the process by which the amplitude of the analog signal voltage is represented by a number sequence at specific time points [29–31]. The EMG voltage signals used in this study are converted into a number sequence by sampling with a period of 0.001 s.

2.2.2. Rectification process

Rectification is the evaluation of only the positive parts of the signal. This is done either by half-wave or full-wave rectification of the signal. A full-wave rectification method was applied to preserve the energy of the signal [25, 29–34], and the expression for the method is given in Eq. (1).

$$X\_training = |x\,(t)| \tag{1}$$

2.2.3. Smoothing of signal

A bandpass filter (50–500 Hz) was designed to soften the signal by eliminating high-frequency components.

2.2.4. Separate the signal into windows

Before the attributes of the obtained EMG signals are calculated, the frame is processed by the method adjacent to the signal. Experiments in the study of Englehart [18, 19] for framing and optimal framing values ($R = 256$, $r = 32$ ms) reached with calculations were used.

2.3. Featured extractions of EMG signal

The EMG signal is a non-stationary, time-varying signal that varies in amplitude by random negative and positive values [25, 31, 32]. Bioelectrical signals have certain characteristic values, i.e., information. Features in time domain have been widely used in medical and engineering practices and researches. Time domain features are used in signal classification due to its easy and quick implementation. Furthermore, they do not need any transformation, and the features are calculated based on raw EMG time series. Moreover, much interference that is acquired through the recording because of their calculations is based on the EMG signal amplitude. However, compared to frequency domain and time-frequency domain, time domain features have been widely used because of their performances of signal classification in low noise environments and their lower computational complexity [29]. In this study, five time domain features methods widely used in the literature have been utilized to obtain the features of the EMG signal.

2.3.1. Signal energy

Mathematically, the energy of the signal m (t) is calculated as in Eq. (2), where t_j and t_i denote the lower and upper bounds of the part of the signal to be integrated, respectively. The above expression represents the area below the absolute value of the signal curve at time $T = t_i - t_j$ [30–35].

$$E = \int_{t_i}^{t_j} |m(t)| dt \tag{2}$$

2.3.2. Maximum value of signal

The maximum value of the signal represents the largest of the sampled signal values in each packet divided by windows [29].

2.3.3. Signal average value

Mathematically, the average of the signal m (t) is calculated as Eq. (3) [30, 31], where t_i and t_j denote the upper and lower bounds of the part of the signal to be integrated, respectively. The above expression represents the overall average of the signal at time interval $T = t_i - t_j$.

$$AVR = \frac{1}{t_j - t_i} \int_{t_i}^{t_j} |m(t)| dt \tag{3}$$

2.3.4. Effective value of the signal

Effective value is a commonly used signal analysis method in the time domain, such as average rectification [29–32]. The effective value of the $m(t)$ signal is calculated as Eq. (4).

$$RMS = \left(\frac{1}{T} \int_0^t m^2(t) dt \right)^{\frac{1}{2}} \tag{4}$$

2.3.5. Variance of signal

The variance value of the signal represents the amount of deviation from the mean of the sampled signal values in each packet divided by windows [30]. $p(t)$ is the variance of the signal to represent the probability density function of t:

$$VAR = \left(\frac{1}{T} \int_0^t (x - ORT)^2 p(t) dt \right) \tag{5}$$

3. Pattern recognition with fuzzy logic algorithm

A classifier's function should be able to map different patterns, match them appropriately, and, in this case, select different hand grip postures. The extracted features were then fed into the fuzzy logic (FL) classifier for the developed control system. FL developed by Lofty Zadeh [35–41] provides a simple way to arrive at a definite conclusion based solely on imprecise input information. A summary of the feature extraction process from the forearm muscles is shown in **Table 2** according to motion.

In total, there are 20 features of EMG signal for four channels. In order to make relations easier, a featured function, which occurs at RMS, AVR, MAX, VAR, and E values, is defined for each channel. Finally, the number of inputs is reduced by four. The featured function is calculated as follows in Eq. (6).

$$F_i = E_i + AVR_i + MAX_i + VAR_i + RMS_i \tag{6}$$

For the FL classification analysis, the triangular shape of the membership function (MF) for the inputs (F_i) and output and the centroid method for defuzzification are used. The rules are created

	Signal	Hand closure	Hand opening	Index-thumb touch	Middle-thumb touch	Ring-thumb touch	Pinky-thumb touch
Energy	Channel 1	16,41091	9,949203	5,853087	5,405963	5,354211	**12,84222**
	Channel 2	12,48169	10,92331	7,334108	6,46115	**13,25441**	5,029002
	Channel 3	12,02946	9,254157	8,313991	**12,82708**	7,183281	4,252198
	Channel 4	14,59524	7,548085	**11,22431**	6,920272	9,376161	4,381767
Maximum value	Channel 1	2,378095	1,398911	0,822295	0,61429	0,725287	**2,255524**
	Channel 2	1,674114	1,183987	1,126519	0,961061	**1,90971**	0,609637
	Channel 3	1,606747	1,351835	1,163335	**1,60762**	1,147475	0,666139
	Channel 4	1,990469	0,844166	**1,437937**	0,906574	1,485923	0,532234
Average value	Variance	0,656436	0,397968	0,234123	0,216239	0,214168	**0,513689**
	Channel 1	0,499268	0,436932	0,293364	0,258446	**0,530176**	0,20116
	Channel 2	0,481178	0,370166	0,33256	**0,513083**	0,287331	0,170088
	Channel 3	0,58381	0,301923	**0,448973**	0,276811	0,375046	0,175271
RMS value	Channel 4	0,474695	0,273057	0,163739	0,134428	0,148438	**0,387735**
	Channel 1	0,325763	0,25909	0,207215	0,173207	**0,370618**	0,124443
	Channel 2	0,316673	0,25826	0,223731	**0,339657**	0,213173	0,122159
	Channel 3	0,383453	0,188114	**0,295885**	0,180392	0,269928	0,10675
Variance	Channel 4	0,72476	0,223357	0,08254	0,045411	0,066981	**0,508143**
	Channel 1	0,293061	0,15076	0,133987	0,086676	**0,422607**	0,038505
	Channel 2	0,281122	0,204654	0,145503	**0,326644**	0,150682	0,047588
	Channel 3	0,410777	0,089351	**0,246002**	0,089669	0,232966	0,027352

Table 2. Summary of the feature extraction process from the forearm muscles.

based on information from the states of contraction. FLC rules are shown in **Table 3**. Recorded SEMG signals have been used to initial testing. Then real time data implemented to Prosthetic hand model.

Fi Featured functions were inputs to the FL. The limits of F were set to [0, 20]. The three linguistic variables used were Small (S), Medium (M), and Big (B). The outputs of FL were Hand closure, Hand opening, Index-thumb contact, Middle-thumb contact, Ring-thumb contact, and Pinky-thumb contact. **Figure 4** shows the flow diagram of FL classification process from four SEMG signals for six hand patterns [35].

Rules	F1	F2	F3	F4	Result
1	BIG	BIG	BIG	BIG	Hand closure
2	MEDIUM	MEDIUM	MEDIUM	MEDIUM	Hand opening
3	MEDIUM	MEDIUM	MEDIUM	BIG	Index-thumb touch
4	MEDIUM	MEDIUM	BIG	MEDIUM	Middle-thumb touch
5	MEDIUM	BIG	MEDIUM	MEDIUM	Ring-thumb touch
6	BIG	MEDIUM	MEDIUM	MEDIUM	Pinky-thumb touch
7	SMALL	SMALL	SMALL	SMALL	Relax-no motion

Table 3. FL rules.

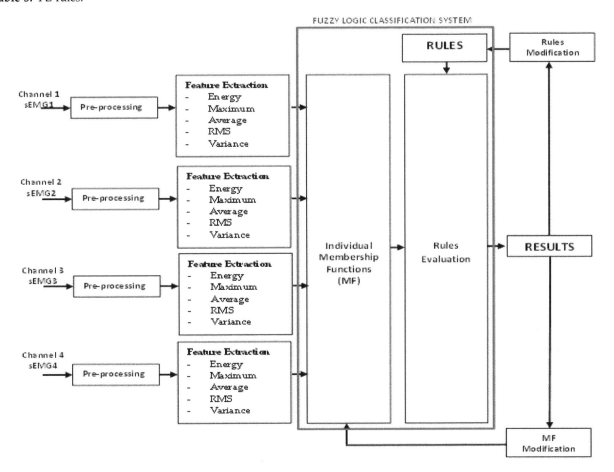

Figure 4. The flow diagram of the control system with FL classification components.

Performance of FL tested 200 hand motions. Classification performance value for the six motions is shown in **Table 4**.

In the medical decision-making process, ROC analysis method is used to determine the discrimination of the test or classification algorithm. In this study, performance of FLC algorithm for six motion class are demonstrated in **Table 5** via ROC analysis.

Performance values calculated as Eqs. (7)–(10) for each hand motion

$$Accuracy(ACC) = \Sigma True\ positive + \Sigma True\ negative/\Sigma Total\ population \tag{7}$$

$$Positive\ predictive\ value(PPV), Precision = \Sigma True\ positive/\Sigma Test\ out\ comepositive \tag{8}$$

$$True\ positive\ rate(TPR), Sensitivity = \Sigma True\ positive/\Sigma Condition\ positive \tag{9}$$

$$False\ positive\ rate(FPR) = \Sigma False\ positive/\Sigma Condition\ negative \tag{10}$$

Hand pattern	Pattern number	Tested total number of motion (A + B)	Number of true classified motion (A)	Number of wrong classified motion (B)	Average percentage of success (%)
Hand closure	MOTION 1	84	84	0	100
Hand opening	MOTION 2	84	84	0	100
Index-thumb touch	MOTION 3	84	76	8	90.476
Middle-thumb touch	MOTION 4	84	66	18	78.57
Ring-thumb touch	MOTION 5	84	72	12	85.714
Pinky-thumb touch	MOTION 6	84	76	8	90.476

Table 4. Classification achievement percentages.

ROC analysis	Motions					
Classification algorithm result	Hand closure	Hand opening	Index-thumb touch	Middle-thumb touch	Ring-thumb touch	Pinky-thumb touch
Hand closure	84	0	0	0	0	0
Hand opening	0	84	0	0	0	0
Index-thumb touch	0	0	76	6	6	4
Middle-thumb touch	0	0	1	66	2	0
Ring-thumb touch	0	0	4	10	72	3
Pinky-thumb touch	0	0	2	0	1	76
No motion	0	0	1	2	1	1

Table 5. ROC analysis.

Hand closure			Hand opening			Index -thumb touch		
TP=84	FN=0	84	TP=84	FN=0	84	TP=76	FN=16	92
FP=0	TN=420	420	FP=0	TN=420	420	FP=8	TN=404	412
84	420	504	84	420	504	84	420	504
TPR= 1.00			TPR= 1.00			TPR= 0.826		
FPR= 0.00			FPR= 0.00			FPR= 0.0194		
PPV=1.00			PPV=1.00			PPV=0.904		
ACC=1.00			ACC=1.00			ACC=0.952		
Middle -thumb touch			Ring -thumb touch			Pinky -thumb touch		
TP=66	FN=4	70	TP=72	FN=17	89	TP=76	FN=4	80
FP=18	TN=416	434	FP=12	TN=403	415	FP=8	TN=416	424
84	420	504	84	420	504	84	420	504
TPR= 0.942			TPR= 0.808			TPR= 0.95		
FPR= 0.041			FPR= 0.028			FPR= 0.018		
PPV=0.785			PPV=0.857			PPV=0.904		
ACC=0.956			ACC=0.942			ACC=0.976		

Table 6. Contingency matrixes.

The four outcomes can be formulated in a 2×2 contingency table. All contingency matrixes for each motion are shown in **Table 6**.

4. 3D modeling and manufacturing of prosthetic hand

4.1. 3D modeling of prosthetic hand via SolidWorks

In order to develop a multifunctional prosthetic hand model, the structural characteristics of the human hand must first be determined. In other words, it is necessary to determine the number of joints, the number of links, the fingers and the length and width parameters of each finger. In order to obtain a prosthetic hand the same size as a human hand, the hand characteristics of an adult male were recorded as in **Table 7** for the purposes of this study [42–44].

	First link		Second link		Third link	
	Length (mm)	Width (mm)	Length (mm)	Width (mm)	Length (mm)	Width (mm)
Thumb	70	30	45	30	40	30
Index	55	30	40	25	30	25
Middle	55	30	50	25	40	25
Ring	55	30	40	25	30	25
Pinky	30	30	40	25	30	25
Palm	130	120				

Table 7. Part of the hand.

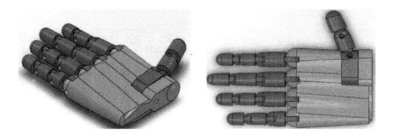

Figure 5. SolidWorks images of prosthetic hand.

Using the parameter values in **Table 5**, the prosthetic hand 3D model is designed with the help of the SolidWorks program as shown in **Figure 5**.

4.2. Manufacturing of prosthetic hand via 3D printer

The prototype of the prosthetic hand was produced with the help of the EDISON 3D printer manufactured by 3D Design Company. The necessary adjustments for the production (e.g., resolution, amount of fullness, amount of support) were made using the Simplify 3D program, which was offered by the same company as the software program. After a hand of 16 parts was produced, it was assembled as shown in **Figure 6**.

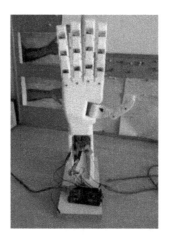
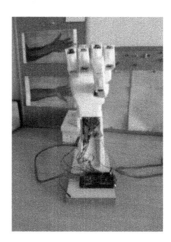

Figure 6. Prototype hand.

5. Prosthetic hand simulator design

5.1. Mechanical design of prosthetic hand simulator via SimMechanics

SimMechanics used in the realization of simulations of mechanical systems [45, 46]. By transferring the 3D CAD model of the prosthetic hand developed in the SolidWorks program to the Matlab SimMechanics program, a chain structure containing each joint and link of the prosthetic hand was obtained as shown in **Figure 7**. Five fingers connected to the palm, three rotary hinges forming each finger, and three connecting links are arranged in series to form the hand SimMechanics model.

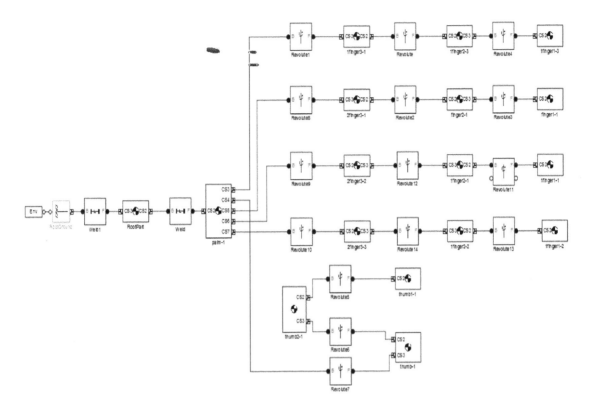

Figure 7. Prosthetic hand SimMechanics model.

As shown in **Figure 7**, when SolidWorks solid model is transferred to Matlab Program, a chain structure composed of revolute and link parts is obtained.

5.2. Modeling of the DC motor

In this study, it was decided to use a DC servo motor for movement of each joint in the prosthetic hand. The equivalent circuit of the DC servo motor is given in **Figure 8** [47–49].

Modeling equations of DC motor were expressed in terms of the Laplace variable s as Eqs. (11)–(13).

$$s(Js + B)\theta(s) = K_t I(s) \tag{11}$$

$$(Ls + R)I(s) = V(s) - K_e s\theta(s) \tag{12}$$

We arrive at the following open-loop transfer function by eliminating $I(s)$ between the two equations above, where the rotation is considered the output and the armature voltage is considered the input.

$$\frac{\theta(s)}{V(s)} = \frac{K}{s\left((Ls + R)(Js + b) + K^2\right)} \tag{13}$$

Using the mathematical model of the DC servo motor, the Matlab/Simulink model is constructed as shown in **Figure 9**.

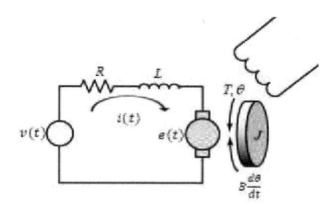

Figure 8. DC motor electrical and mechanical model.

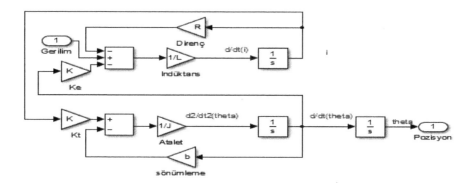

Figure 9. DC motor Matlab/Simulink model.

6. Controller design

Position of ultra-nano DC servomotors connected to joints is controlled using a PID controller. The controller's proportional gain coefficient (Kp), integral gain coefficient (Ki), and derivative gain (Kd) values are determined by Genetic Algorithm [11, 50–52] to ensure that the system quickly reaches a steady state without overshooting as shown in **Table 8**. The PID controller has an input-output relationship with input e (t) and output u (t) [53–55].

$$u(t) = K_p \cdot e(t) + K_i \cdot \int_0^t e(\tau).d\tau + Kd.\frac{de(t)}{dt} \qquad (14)$$

	K_p	K_i	K_d
All DC motors connected the each finger joints	0.42176	0.75724	0.0048566

Table 8. PID parameters.

7. Graphical and numerical results

Electromyography is used to measure EMG signals, which are extracted from the forearm muscles and classified with the help of four surface electrodes. The type of motion that one wishes to perform is the perceived and designed three-dimensional prosthetic hand simulator and the five-fingered and 15-jointed hand. These movements were made in real time on the prototype. Each joint of the prosthetic hand is moved with one ultra-nano servomotor, and the position control of the motors is provided by the designed PID.

The prosthetic hand was made with hand closure, hand opening, thumb-index touch, hand opening, thumb-middle touch, hand opening, thumb-ring touch, hand opening, thumb-pinkie touch, and hand opening movements. The hand opening movement is performed after the hand closing movement and touch movement.

1. EMG signals were taken from four channels, four groups of muscles simultaneously, as shown in **Figures 10–13**, and preprocessed. First, the signal amplitude was scaled from 0 to 10 V and then filtered.

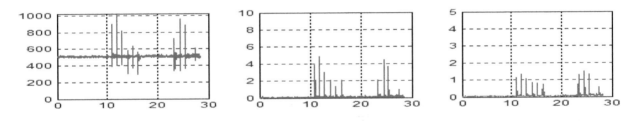

Figure 10. Preprocessing step graphics of EMG signal recorded Channel 1.

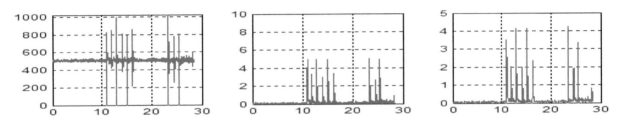

Figure 11. Preprocessing step graphics of EMG signal recorded Channel 2.

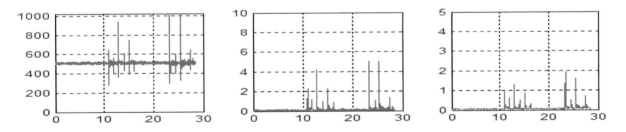

Figure 12. Preprocessing step graphics of EMG signal recorded Channel 3.

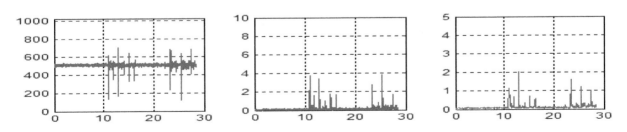

Figure 13. Preprocessing step graphics of EMG signal recorded Channel 4.

2. As shown in **Figures 14–17**, the energy, maximum, effective, mean, and variance attribute values of the respective signals were calculated.

3. Motion pattern was determined by motion classification algorithm.

4. The specified type of motion information was input to the simulator and the prototype.

5. According to the recognized hand pattern, the reference joint angles in **Table 9** were applied as the control input signal, and the closed loop position control of the DC servo-motors was performed according to feedback information from sensors connected to the simulator joints.

Position control of the finger joints for six hand patterns was provided by the PID controllers as shown in **Figures 18–23**.

For all finger joints, PID performance is shown in **Table 10**.

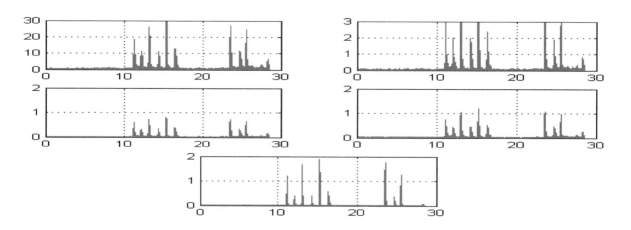

Figure 14. Features graphics of EMG signal recorded Channel 1.

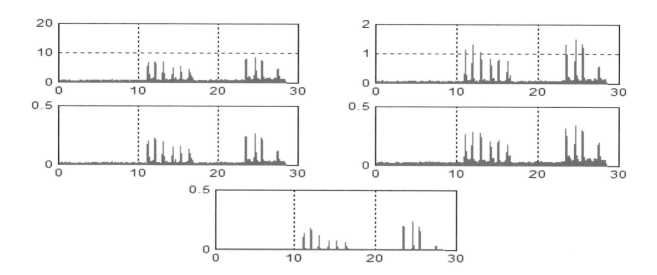

Figure 15. Features graphics of EMG signal recorded Channel 2.

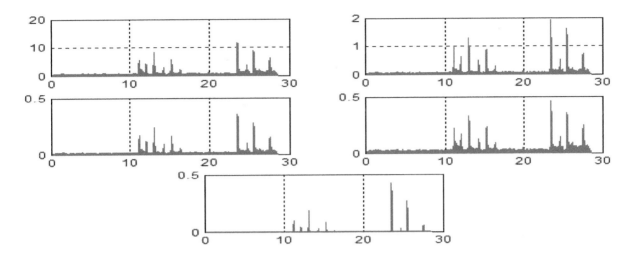

Figure 16. Features graphics of EMG signal recorded Channel 3.

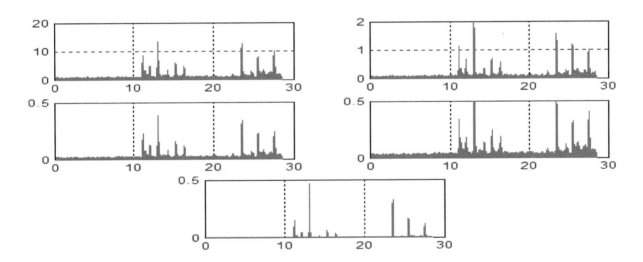

Figure 17. Features graphics of EMG signal recorded Channel 4.

		Index			Middle			Ring			Pinkie			Thumb		
		θ_1	θ_2	θ_3	θ_1	θ_2	θ_3	θ_1	θ_2	θ_3	θ_1	θ_2	θ_3	θ_1	θ_2	θ_3
1	Motion 1	90	90	90	90	90	90	90	90	90	90	90	90	90	90	90
2	Motion 2	0	0	0	0	0	0	0	0	0	0	0	0	0	0	0
3	Motion 3	90	30	30	0	0	0	0	0	0	0	0	0	70	15	5
4	Motion 4	0	0	0	90	25	25	0	0	0	0	0	0	87	5	5
5	Motion 5	0	0	0	0	0	0	90	25	10	0	0	0	105	15	5
6	Motion 6	0	0	0	0	0	0	0	0	0	90	30	5	125	15	5

Table 9. Reference value for each finger joints.

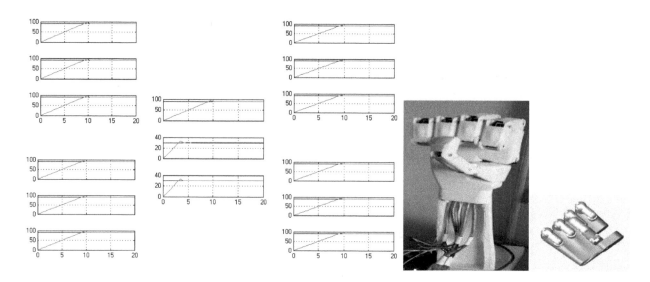

Figure 18. PID response graphics of five fingers for hand close and prosthetic hand photograph.

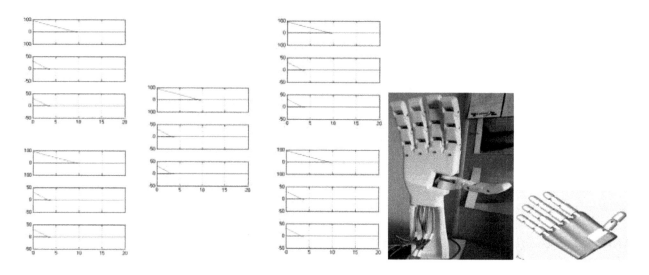

Figure 19. PID response graphics of five fingers for hand opening and prosthetic hand photograph.

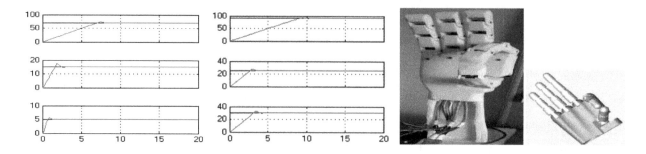

Figure 20. PID response graphics of five fingers for thumb-index touch and prosthetic hand photograph.

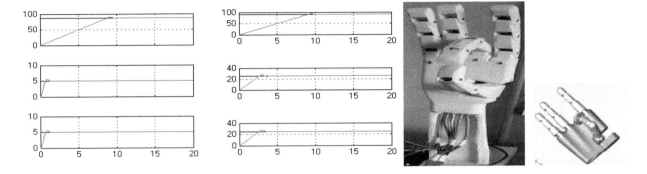

Figure 21. PID response graphics of five fingers for thumb-middle touch and prosthetic hand photograph.

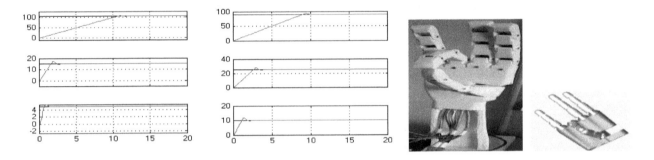

Figure 22. PID response graphics of five fingers for thumb-ring touch and prosthetic hand photograph.

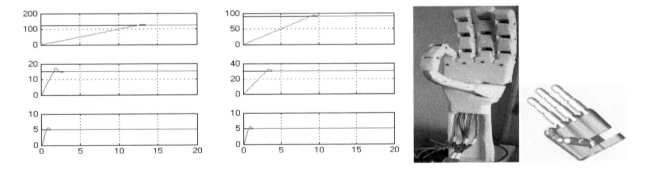

Figure 23. PID response graphics of five fingers for thumb-pinkie touch and prosthetic hand photograph.

Finger	Joint no		Motion 1	Motion 2	Motion 3	Motion 4	Motion 5	Motion 6
Thumb finger	1	Overshoot (deg.)	2.835	0.2932	2.137	2.936	3.025	3.655
		Steady state time (s)	9.8084	13.413	8.8084	9.988	10.8084	12.8084
		Steady state error (deg.)	0.046	0.041	0.037	0.027	0.021	0.024
	2	Overshoot (deg.)	2.755	0.3265	0.652	0.252	0.652	0.652
		Steady state time (s)	4.415	2.883	1.952	0.752	1.952	1.952
		Steady state error (deg.)	0.0052	2.6e-3	0.0001	0.0001	0.0001	0.0001
	3	Overshoot (deg.)	2.754	0.2696	0.357	0.357	0.357	0.357
		Steady state time (s)	4.524	1.972	0.956	0.956	0.956	0.956
		Steady state error (deg.)	0.0053	1.5e-3	1.5e-3	1.5e-3	1.5e-3	1.5e-3

Finger	Joint no		Motion 1	Motion 2	Motion 3	Motion 4	Motion 5	Motion 6
Index finger	1	Overshoot (deg.)	2.835	0.3299	2.835	0	0	0
		Steady state time (s)	9.915	9.71	9.915	0	0	0
		Steady state error (deg.)	0.045	10e-4	0.045	0	0	0
	2	Overshoot (deg.)	2.835	0.0368	2.349	0	0	0
		Steady state time (s)	9.915	4.555	7.0725	0	0	0
		Steady state error (deg.)	0.047	0.0183	0.0219	0	0	0
	3	Overshoot (deg.)	2.835	0.348	0.377	0	0	0
		Steady state time (s)	9.915	4.535	7.429	0	0	0
		Steady state error (deg.)	0.047	0.0202	0.0255	0	0	0
Middle finger	1	Overshoot (deg.)	2.8356	0.3244	0	2.8368	0	0
		Steady state time (s)	10.5022	10.279	0	10.52	0	0
		Steady state error (deg.)	0.0474	1e-3	0	0.0475	0	0
	2	Overshoot (deg.)	2.8356	0.3244	0	2.812	0	0
		Steady state time (s)	10.5022	10.279	0	3.437	0	0
		Steady state error (deg.)	0.0474	1e-3	0	0.0036	0	0
	3	Overshoot (deg.)	2.8356	0.3244	0	2.7812	0	0
		Steady state time (s)	10.5022	10.279	0	3.9265	0	0
		Steady state error (deg.)	0.0474	1e-3	0	0.0036	0	0
Ring finger	1	Overshoot (deg.)	2.8356	0.3244	0	0	2.8368	0
		Steady state time (s)	9.922	9.907	0	0	9.914	0
		Steady state error (deg.)	0.047	1e-3	0	0	0.047	0
	2	Overshoot (deg.)	2.8356	0.3244	0	0	2.781	0
		Steady state time (s)	9.915	9.9075	0	0	3.412	0
		Steady state error (deg.)	0.047	1e-3	0	0	0.0035	0
	3	Overshoot (deg.)	2.8357	0.3244	0	0	2.545	0
		Steady state time (s)	9.9055	9.906	0	0	1.884	0
		Steady state error (deg.)	0.047	1e-3	0	0	0.0005	0
Pinkie finger	1	Overshoot (deg.)	2.8356	0.3244	0	0	0	2.8368
		Steady state time (s)	9.9094	9.9122	0	0	0	9.29
		Steady state error (deg.)	0.0475	1e-3	0	0	0	0.0475
	2	Overshoot (deg.)	2.8357	0.3244	0	0	0	2.7883
		Steady state time (s)	9.9094	9.9122	0	0	0	4.8174
		Steady state error (deg.)	0.0475	1e-3	0	0	0	0.0052
	3	Overshoot (deg.)	2.8357	0.3244	0	0	0	2.636
		Steady state time (s)	9.9094	9.9122	0	0	0	1.3391
		Steady state error (deg.)	0.0475	1e-3	0	0	0	0

Table 10. PID performance value for each joint.

8. Conclusion

The main factor in increasing the functionality of the prosthetic hand to the extent of imitating biological hand functions is the movement of the fingers. The greater the number of movements the fingers can do independently of each other, the greater the ability of the prosthetic hand to move and the more successfully it can mimic the biological hand. Within the scope of this thesis, the function of the prosthetic hand is improved by six different finger movements. Bioelectrical signals of two separate users were recorded from the forearm muscles (the flexor pollicis longus, flexor carpi radialis, brachioradialis, extensor carpi radialis, extensor digiti minimi, and extensor carpi ulnaris) with the help of four surface electrode groups. Thus, a broad bioelectrical signal database was created. The recorded bioelectrical signals were subjected to a series of preprocessing and feature extraction processes to calculate the maximum, effective, mean, variance, and energy values of the EMG signals. An FL classification algorithm was developed to create an effective cognitive interaction network, and 90% classification success was obtained from these algorithms. The identified bioelectrical signals were applied to the designed three-dimensional prosthesis handheld simulator. The five-fingered and 15-jointed prosthetic hand prototypes produced with a 3D printer, and the positional control of the prosthetic finger joints was performed with the designed controllers. Each finger of the prosthetic hand was moved by an ultra-nano DC motor, and the position controls of the motors were provided by the designed PID. Thus, a cognitive interface and communication network were established between the person and the prosthetic hand with great success.

Acknowledgements

The subject of this chapter, which is Beyda TAŞAR's doctoral thesis, was supported by TÜBİTAK under the Domestic Doctoral Scholarship Program for Priority Areas in 2211 C. In addition, the study was supported by Fırat University Scientific Research Projects Management Unit within the scope of PhD Thesis Project number MF-14.25.

Author details

Beyda Taşar[1]* and Arif Gülten[2]

*Address all correspondence to: btasar@firat.edu.tr

1 Firat University, Engineering Faculty, Department of Mechatronics, Elazig, Turkey

2 Firat University, Engineering Faculty, Department of Electrical and Electronics, Elazig, Turkey

References

[1] Boostani R, Moradi MH. Evaluation of the forearm EMG signal features for the control of a prosthetic hand. Institute of Physics Publishing Physiological Measurement. Physiological Measurement. 2003;24:309-319. PII: S0967-3334(03)38946-4

[2] Nishikawa D, Yu W, Yokoi H, Kakazu Y. On-line supervising mechanism for learning data in surface electromyogram motion classifiers. Journal and Communication in Japan. 2002;**33**:14, pp. 2634-2643

[3] Arieta AH, Katoh R, Yokoi H, Wenwei Y. Development of multi-DOF electromyography prosthetic system using the adaptive joint mechanism. Applied Bionics and Biomechanics. 2006;**3**:101-112

[4] Zhao J, XIie Z, Jing L, Cai H, Hong L, Hırzınger G. EMG control for a five-fingered prosthetic hand based on wavelet transform and autoregressive model. International Conference on Mechatronics and Automation, China; 2006.

[5] Carrozza MC, Cappiello G, Stellin G, Zaccone F, Vecchi F, Micera S, Dario P. On the development of a novel adaptive prosthetic hand with compliant joints: Experimental platform and EMG control. In: Proceedings of the IEEE/RSJ International Conference on Intelligent Robots and Systems; April 2005. pp. 3951-3956

[6] Hocaoğlu E. Data acquisition and feature extraction for classification of prehensile SEMG signal for control of a multifunctional prosthetic hand [Master thesis]. Istanbul: Sabanci University, Mechanical Engineering; 2010.

[7] Carozza M, Cappiello G, Stellin G, Zaccone F, Vecchi F, Micera S, Dario P., On the development of a novel adaptive prosthetic hand with compliant joints: Experimental platform and EMG control, Intelligent Robots and Systems, 2005.(IROS 2005). pp. 1271–1276, 2-6 August 2005, 10.1109/IROS.2005.1545585

[8] Taylor Cl, Schwarz RJ. The anatomy and mechanics of the human hand. Artificial Limbs 2.2. 1955:**22**.

[9] Rakibul H, Vepar SH, Hujijbert H. Modeling and control of the Barrett hand for grasping. In: 15th International Conference on Computer Modelling and Simulation; 10–12 April 2013; Cambridge University.

[10] Hasan R, Rahideh A, Shaheed H. Modeling and interactional of the multifingered hand. In: Proceedings of the 19th International Conference on Automation & Computing. Brunel University, Uxbridge, UK; 2013.

[11] Michalewicz, Z. Genetic Algorithms + Data Structures = Evolution Programs. Berlin Heidelberg, New York: Springer-Verlag; 1999.

[12] Widhiada W, Douglas SS, Jenkinson ID, Gomm JB. Design and control of three fingers motion for dexterous assembly of compliant elements. International Journal of Engineering, Science and Technology. 2011;**3**(6):18–34

[13] Al-Assaf Y, Al-Nashash H. Surface myoelectric classification for prostheses control. Journal of Medical Engineering & Technology. 2005;**29**(5):203–207

[14] Parker P, Englehart K, Hudgins B. Myoelectric signal processing for control of powered limb prostheses. Journal of Electromyography and Kinesiology. 2006;**16**:541–548

[15] Englehart K, Hudgins B. A robust, real-time control scheme for multifunction myoelectric control. IEEE Transactions on Biomedical Engineering. 2003;**50**(7):848–854

[16] Hudgins B, Parker P, Scott RN. A new strategy for multifunction myoelectric control. IEEE Transactions on Biomedical Engineering. 1993;**40**(1):82–94

[17] Asghari Oskoei M, Hu H. Myoelectric control systems - a survey. Biomedical Signal Processing and Control. 2007;**4**(4):275–294

[18] Lamounier E, Soares A, Andrade A, Carrijo R. A virtual prosthesis control based on neural networks for EMG pattern classification. In: Proceedings of the Artificial Intelligence and Soft Computing; Canada; 2002

[19] Chu J, Moon I, Kim S, Mun M. Control of multifunction myoelectric hand using a real time EMG pattern recognition. In: Proceedings of the IEEE/RSJ International Conference on Intelligent Robots and Systems; China; 2005. pp. 3957–3962

[20] Mohammadreza AOI, Huosheng H. Review: Myoelectric control systems: A survey. Biomedical Signal Processing and Control. 2007;**2**:275–294

[21] Zhao Z, Chen X, Zhang X, Yang J, Tu Y, Lantz V, Wang K. Study on Online Gesture SEMG Recognition, Advanced Intelligent Computing Theories and Applications. With Aspects of Theoretical and Methodological Issues. 2007:1257–1265

[22] Mahdi K, Mehran J. A novel approach to recognize hand movements via sEMG patterns. Engineering in Medicine and Biology Society. In: 29th Annual International Conference of the IEEE; 2007.

[23] Zhizeng L, Xiaoliang R, Yutao Z. Multi-pattern recognition of the forearm movement based on SEMG, Information Acquisition. In: Proceedings of the International Conference on IEEE; 21–25 June 2004. DOI: 10.1109/ICIA.2004.1373391

[24] Roberto M. Electromyography Physiology, Engineering and Noninvasive Applications. IEEE Press, John Wiley & Sons Inc.; 2004, New Jersey, Canada

[25] De Luca CJ. Electromyography. Encyclopedia of Medical Devices and Instrumentation, John Wiley Publisher; 2006. pp. 98–109, New York City, United States, DOI: 10.1002/0471732877.emd097

[26] Hargrove L, Englehart K, Hudgins B. The effect of electrode displacements on pattern recognition based myoelectric control. In: IEEE Annual International Conference on Engineering in Medicine and Biology Society; 2006. pp. 2203–2206

[27] De Luca CJ. The use of surface electromyography in biomechanics. Journal of Applied Biomechanics. 1997;**1**(2):135–163

[28] SENIAM EMG protocol. Available from: http://www.seniam.org/(Download date: 21.03.2014)

[29] Daud WMBW, Yahya AB, Horng CS, Sulaima MF, Sudirman R. Features extraction of electromyography signals in time domain on biceps brachii muscle. International Journal of Modeling and Optimization. 2013;**3**(6)

[30] Yazıcı İ. EMG İşaretlerinin İşlenmesi Ve Sınıflandırılması [Master thesis]. Sakarya: Sakarya University, Institute of Science and Technology; 2008

[31] Taşan D. Protez Denetimi İçin Elektromiyografi (EMG)de Örüntü Tanıma, Yüksek Lisans Tezi, Ege Universty, Institute of Science and Technology, İzmir, 2008

[32] Akgün G, Demetgül M, Kaplanoğlu E. EMG Sinyallerinin Öznitelik Çıkarımı ve Geri Yayılımlı Yapay Sinir Ağı, Algoritması İle Sınıflandırılması, Otomatik Kontrol Ulusal Toplantısı, TOK2013, Malatya 26–28 Eylül 2013.

[33] Chen WT, Wang Z, Ren X. Characterization of surface EMG signals using improved approximate entropy. Zhejiang University Science B. 2006;7(10): 844–848

[34] Chu J, Moon I, Mun M. A real-time EMG pattern recognition system based on linear-non-linear feature projection for a multifunction myoelectric hand. IEEE Transactions on Biomedical Engineering. 2006;53:2232–2238

[35] Chan F, Yong-Sheng Y, Lam F, Yuan-Ting Z, Parker P. Fuzzy EMG classification for prosthesis control. IEEE Transactions on Rehabilitation Engineering. 2000;8(3)

[36] Yaraş B, Hüseynov R, Namazov M, ÇeliKKale İE, Şeker M. Fuzzy control and sliding mode fuzzy control of DC motor. Journal Of Engineering And Natural Sciences Mühendislik Ve Fen Bilimleri Dergisi, Sigma. 2014;32:97–108

[37] Ajiboye A, Weir R. A heuristic fuzzy logic approach to EMG pattern recognition for multifunction prosthesis control. IEEE Transactions on Biomedical Engineering. 2005;52 (11): 280–291

[38] Karlik B, M.O., T., & M., A. A fuzzy clustering neural network architecture for multifunction upperlimb prosthesis. IEEE Transactions on Biomedical Engineering. 2003;50:1255–1261

[39] Vuskovic M, Du SJ. Classification of prehensile EMG patterns with simplified fuzzy ARTMAP networks. In: Proceedings of the International Joint Conference on Neural Networks; 2002, 3, pp. 2539–2544

[40] Khzeri M, Jahed M, Sadati N. Neuro-fuzzy surface EMG pattern recognition for multifunctional hand prosthesis control, Industrial Electronics. In: IEEE International Symposium; 2007

[41] Zheng L, He X. Classification techniques in pattern recognition. In: WSCG, Conference Proceedings; 2005, ISBN 80-903100-8-7

[42] Taşar B, Yakut O, Gülten A. Object detection and grip force control via force sensor for EMG based prosthesis hand, E205. In: International Conference on Electrical and Electronics Engineering (ICEEE); 27–28 Nisan 2015; Ankara

[43] Taşar B, Gülten A, Yakut O. Modeling controlling and simulation of 15 DOF multifunctional prosthesis hand using SimMechanics, C201. In: International Conference on Automatic Control (ICOAC); 27–28 Nisan 2015; Ankara

[44] Taşar B, Gülten A, Yakut O. Kinematic analysis of the human hand for desing prosthetic hand. In: 3rd International Congress on Natural and Engineering Sciences; September 9–13, 2015; Sarajevo, Bosnia and Herzegovina: International University of Sarajevo

[45] Dung LT, Kang HJ, Ro YS. Robot manipulator modeling in Matlab SimMechanics with PD control and online Gravity compensation. IFOST Proceedings. 2010

[46] Fedák V, Durovsky F, Üveges R. Analysis of robotic system motion in SimMechanics and MATLAB GUI Environment. MATLAB Applications for the Practical Engineer. Chapter 20. 2014

[47] Bencsik AL. Appropriate mathematical model of DC servo motors applied in SCARA robots. Acta Polytechnica Hungarica. 2004;1(2):2004–2099

[48] Matlan Tuturial, DC Motor Position Simulink Model. Available from: Dowload:http://ctms.engin.umich.edu/CTMS/index.php?example=MotorPosition&section=Simulink-Modeling

[49] Meier R. Modeling DC servo motors control systems, Tech Note, Milwaukee School of Engineering 1025 North Broadway, Milwaukee. https://faculty-web.msoe.edu/meier/ee3720/technotes/dcservo.pdf

[50] Haupt Randly L, Haupt Sue E. Practical Genetic Algorithms. USA: A Wiley-Interscience Publication; 1998

[51] Davis L. Handbook of Genetic Algorithms. New York, NY: Van Nostrand; 1991

[52] Wook C, Ramakr Shna RS. Elitism-based compact genetic algorithms. IEEE Transactions on Evolutionary Computation. 2003;7(4):367–385

[53] Astrom KJ, Hagglund T. PID Controllers: Theory, Design and Tuning. Instrument Society of America; 1995. p. 343, Research Triangle Park, North Carolina, 1995

[54] Taguchi H, Araki M. Two-degree-of-freedom PID controllers. Proceedings of the IFAC Workshop on Digital Control: Past, Present and Future of PID Control; Elsevier; pp. 91–96. 5-7 April 2000, Terrassa, Spain

[55] Bennett S. A History of Control Engineering, Peter Peregrinus; 1993. pp. 28–69, London, United Kingdom

10

ANFIS Definition of Focal Length for Zoom Lens via Fuzzy Logic Functions

Bahadir Ergün, Cumhur Sahin and Ugur Kaplan

Abstract

The digital cameras have been effected from systematical errors which decreased metric quality of image. The digital cameras have been effected from systematical errors that decreases metric quality of image. The aim of this chapter is to explore usability of fuzzy logic on calibration of digital cameras. Therefore, a 145-pointed planar test field has been prepared in the laboratories of Department of Geodesy and Photogrammetric Engineering at the Gebze Technical University. The test field has been imaged from five points of view with the digital camera Nikon Coolpix-E8700 within maximum (71.2 mm) and minimum (8.9 mm) focal length. The input-output data have been determined from 10 calibration images obtained for fuzzy logic process. These data have also been used and formed for the space resection process. Adaptive neuro-fuzzy inference system (ANFIS) functions have been used for fuzzy process at MATLAB 7.0, and the results of these two distinct methods have been compared. Finally, the most convenient (least squares average error) or the most useful ANFIS "*Trimf, trapmf, gbellmf, gaussmf, gauss2mf, pimf, dsigmf and psigmf*" functions are determined and compared for space resection method for the conventional bundle adjustment process.

Keywords: ANFIS, zoom lens calibration, focal distance, MATLAB

1. Introduction

Fuzzy inference system (FIS) is a process of mapping from given inputs to outputs by using the theory of fuzzy sets [1]. FIS derives an output by using an inference engine, which is based on a form of **IF-THEN** rules. There are two well-established types of FIS [2–4]. While Mamdani FIS uses the technique of defuzzification of a fuzzy output, Sugeno FIS uses weighted average to compute the crisp output [4]. In fact, adaptive neuro-fuzzy inference system (ANFIS) structure is composed of a representation as a network structure, which has the neural learning ability of Sugeno-type fuzzy systems. This network is made of a combination of nodes, which are placed as layers in order to perform specific functions [5, 6].

Among the neuro-fuzzy models most used nowadays, the adaptive neuro-fuzzy inference system (ANFIS), which was proposed in 1992 by J.S Roger in his Ph.D. thesis, must be highlighted [7–9]. ANFIS adapts its parameters according to training data by using the hybrid learning algorithm. The algorithm consists of the gradient descent for tuning the non-linear antecedent parameters and the least square for tuning the linear consequent parameters [1]. Most of the success of ANFIS comes from its implementation in the MATLAB Fuzzy Logic Toolbox, with an excellent graphical interface personally developed by J.S. Roger in collaboration with N. Gulley, incorporating also diverse fuzzy logic pattern classification algorithms for the definition and dimensioning of the input membership functions (mf) [9, 10].

In the literature, there are several examples of the ANFIS, which enable it to achieve great success in a wide range of scientific applications. The advantageous features of an ANFIS include easy implementation, fast and accurate learning, strong generalization abilities, excellent explanation facilities through fuzzy rules, and easy to incorporate both linguistic and numeric knowledge for problem solving [11]. ANFIS models have recently gained much popularity not only for calibrating non-linear relationships because they offer more advantages over conventional modeling techniques, which include the ability to handle large amounts of noisy data from dynamic and non-linear systems, especially where the underlying physical relationships are not fully understood, but also for solving linear systems which include the interpolation modeling such as time series. Literature shows that lots of ANFIS and FIS methods were proposed for the determination of the uncertainty of pattern recognition, image matching, and three-dimensional (3D) position definition studies in computer vision applications. For instance, color recognition ANFIS model study for robust vision system has worked in Ref. [12]. Another application for ANFIS method is suggested for appropriate calibration method of stereo camera system used for non-intrusive distance measurement in [13]. Another example for ANFIS method in remote sensing study, functions for serving and prediction from satellite images of Prionace Glauca for pattern recognition in (Backpropagation network, RBF, functional separability network) and the neuro-diffuse networks (ANFIS) [14]. In Ref. [15], a new hybrid method of performing eye-to-hand coordination and manipulation to produce a working robot named COERSU. The method is an optimized combination of two neuro-fuzzy approaches developed by the authors: direct fuzzy servoing and fuzzy correction. The fuzzy methods are tuned by the adaptive neuro-fuzzy inference system (ANFIS). Human action recognition is an important research area in the field of computer vision having a great number of real-world applications. In Ref. [16], ANFIS controller method has been suggested for path tracking, a virtual field strategy for obstacle avoidance and path planning, and multiple sensors (an ultrasonic array, a thermal sensor, and a video streaming system) for obtaining information about the environment. In Ref. [17], development of a virtual robot tele-operation platform based on hand gesture recognition has been evolved from visual information by ANFIS and support vector machines (SVM). In Ref. [18], a multi-view action recognition framework that extracts human silhouette clues from different cameras was presented with fuzzy rule-based system for analyzing scene dynamics and interpreting human behaviors. The interaction tool has been located in 3D space then the 3D model has obtained by means of a structured light system which is calibrated using only the vanishing points extracted from a simple planar surface. Then, an immersive interaction technique was used to manipulate the 3D model using a fuzzy technique with the advantages of a low memory usage, real-time operation, and low positioning errors as compared to classical solutions in [19]. Quantitative analysis of the error in the reconstruction of a 3D scene, which has been captured with synthetic aperture integral imaging system, has been worked for two-dimensional (2D) images which was captured within unknown camera parameters with adaptive neuro-fuzzy inference system (ANFIS) in [20].

In this chapter, an ANFIS approach has been developed for the detection of effective camera focal distance parameters with additional parameters, which help the measurement of image coordinates that provide the basis for three-dimensional modeling obtained from two-dimensional images, which are similar to [19, 20] studies. Thus, the photogrammetric studies, which benefit from self-calibration conventional model, will be more usable with different cameras and different time points.

The main logic of this chapter is to process the selected radial distances via ANFIS functions and to obtain a focus distance value for each of the images. It is seen that ANFIS functions of optical distortion law can be validated by its effect on data sets. This also proves that ANFIS functions validate a physical reality and describe it in a highly reliable way. As a result of the research, it is seen that the approach of fuzzy logic can be used for the calibration process of digital cameras. Thus, it is concluded that it would be beneficial to use and study the fuzzy logic approach more in photogrammetric applications [21].

Information about fuzzy systems is described in the second part of this chapter. Third part of this chapter is the experimental application part. Test field has been photographed from five different angles with Nikon Coolpix-e8700 digital camera with maximum (71.2 mm) and minimum (8.9 mm) focal distances in the application. Input and output data are determined with the resulting 10 images; space resection approach is created and studied by using ANFIS functions on MATLAB 7.0 software. Trimf, trapmf, gbellmf, gaussmf, gauss2mf, pimf, dsigmf, and psigmf functions in Fuzzy Interface System (FIS), which are used for creating a relation between fuzzy sets, under anfisedit menu in fuzzy logic tools on MATLAB 7.0 software, are studied in terms of space resection approach, and the most appropriate functions are determined for the detection of focal distance. The fourth part presents the results and their interpretations.

2. Fuzzy logic and main principles

Fuzzy logic is based on the logic of clustering and determination of membership degrees depending of this clustering. Membership degrees generate rule-based work systematic which constitutes the rules of fuzzy systems. Fuzzy cluster sections which are placed in the inlets and outlets of the fuzzy rules express an approximation for each. In this respect, all expressions like "approximately 3," "nearly 9," "over 5 and approximate" always express a fuzzy number. Each of these approximations corresponds to a fuzzy cluster. It cannot be possible to solve mathematical operations with these fuzzy numbers. The operations are made with fuzzy numbers by defining some restrictions. In order for a fuzzy number to exist, fuzzy cluster of this needs to have an interval of normal, convex, limited support and at section of membership degree, closed and finite. For the fuzzy numbers to be normal, membership degree of at least one of the real numbers in the fuzzy expression must be 1.

Generally, two fuzzy numbers as a triangle and trapezoid are in question. Mathematical expression of a triangle fuzzy number showed with a fuzzy cluster is given as Eq. (1):

$$mf(x) = mf(x; a, b, c) = \begin{bmatrix} (x-a)/(b-a) & a \leq x \leq b \\ (c-x)/(c-b) & b \leq x \leq c \\ 0 & x > c \quad \text{or} \quad x < a \end{bmatrix} \tag{1}$$

In the expression of mf(x;a,b,c), a and c show the lower and upper limit values relatively and b shows the single number with full membership. Similarly, trapezoid fuzzy numbers are expressed with four full whole numbers as a, b, c, d. Here a and d show lower and upper limit values of trapezoid fuzzy numbers; b and c show the limits of the cluster of the trapezoid numbers whose membership degree is full between these two numbers. Mathematical indication of trapezoid fuzzy number is like Eq. (2):

$$mf(x) = mf(x; a, b, c, d) = \begin{bmatrix} (x-a)/(b-a) & a \leq x \leq b \\ 1 & b \leq x < c \\ (d-x)/(d-c) & c < x \leq d \\ 0 & x > d \quad \text{or} \quad x < a \end{bmatrix} \tag{2}$$

If we pay attention, when b = c, trapezoid fuzzy number is transformed into triangle fuzzy number. Graphical indication of these fuzzy numbers is as shown in **Figure 1**.

Generally, there are two reasons for the researchers to use fuzzy systems:

- Since the real-world incidents are very complicated, these incidents are not possible to be taken under control by being defined with specific equations. As a natural result of this,

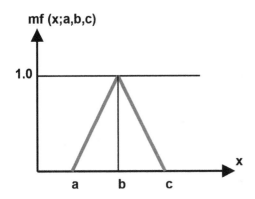
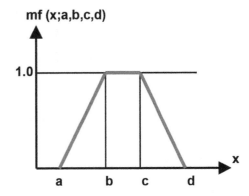

Figure 1. Fuzzy numbers: (a) triangle and (b) trapezoid.

the researcher always prefers applying to the methods that have approximate solubility even if not certain. As Einstein said, if it can be said that real-life incidents can be indicated with mathematical equations, either the accuracy of the equation cannot be mentioned or if the result that mathematical equations exactly depicts the reality is taken, then real-life incidents cannot be mentioned. So, the solutions are approximate to a certain extent in all studies conducted. Otherwise, many non-linear equations must be solved simultaneously which is known to lead to chaotic unspecified problems according to current information.

- All theories and equations in engineering express the real world approximately. Even though many real systems are not linear, every effort is given in order to accept the linearity in examination of these with classic methods. In order for the verbal data presented by people to be converted into numerical data and calculated by being perceived by computers and algorithms, fuzzy systems are needed.

Almost all of mathematical, stochastic, or conceptual systems so far are made up of three units given in **Figure 2**.

These are input unit, a transition function which converts this input to output and is called system behavior and output unit. In all of the units here, numerical data are processed. The difference of the fuzzy systems from the conventional systems is that the system behavior section is divided into two and there are four connected units between each other as shown in **Figure 3**.

Each of the units here has tasks, which are different but can be related to each other:

- **General information base unit:** It includes input variants to which the incident to be examined is subjected and all information about these. Because the it includes both numerical and/or textual data, the database is called as 'general database'.

Figure 2. Conventional system.

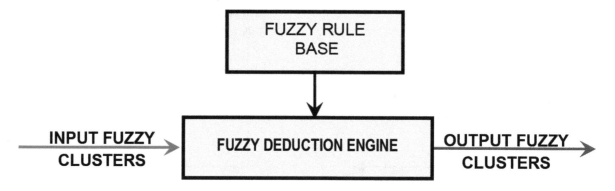

Figure 3. General fuzzy system.

- **Fuzzy rule base unit:** It includes all the rules which can be written in the type of logical **IF-THEN**, connecting the inputs in data base to output variants. In writing of these rules, the whole interval connections (fuzzy cluster) which can only be between input and output data are considered. Thus, each rule connects one piece of input space to the output space logically. All of these contexts form the base rule.

- **Fuzzy deduction engine unit:** It is a mechanism including the operations, which enable a system to behave as having one output by bringing the relations formed between input and output fuzzy clusters in a fuzzy rule base unit together. This engine serves for determination of what kind of output the whole system will give between the inputs by bringing deductions of each rule together.

- **Output unit:** It indicates the output values obtained as a result of the interaction of information and fuzzy rule bases with deduction engine.

Figure 3 represents a general fuzzy system. The point to be paid attention to here is information and outputs in the input; in other words, databases are fuzzy values. So each unit in **Figure 3** is made up of fuzzy clusters entirely. The most significant deficiency of basic fuzzy system is that numerical database cannot enter into such a fuzzy system and the outputs are not numerical, so they cannot be directly used in engineering designs.

In order to certainly eliminate the deficiencies of the general fuzzy system is extented to a new system which is proposed in Refs. [3, 22] This is called Takagi-Sugeno-Kank (TSK) fuzzy system. For each inputs and the outputs obtained as a result of operation of fuzzy rule and deduction engine are in the way of a function of inputs which are from input database. So like the input variants in rule base, it was thought that these variants are reflected to rule result section after THEN word as a linear function of these variants [21]. According to this, the rule is presented in the following part.

IF the speed of your car is high, **THEN** stepping on the gas force can be expressed as $y = ax$. For example, in the case that three input variants exist (x_1, x_2, and x_3), in one of fuzzy system, y as output variant generally; **IF** x_1 is little and x_3 is wide, **THEN** it can be expressed as $y = a_0 + a_1x_1 + a_2x_2 + a_3x_3$. Result sections of all rules are made up of a polynomial linear equation. Since in the fuzzy system which has such a structure output variants are not used in the deduction of fuzzy clustering, instead of fuzzy deduction unit in **Figure 3**, weighted deduction calculation unit comes as mainly the membership degrees calculated from the input section of each rule. This system is shown in **Figure 4**.

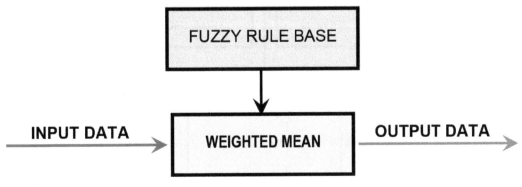

Figure 4. TSK fuzzy system.

Actually in such a fuzzy system, output space is represented as a function of the inputs for being a rule valid in each sub-space. Even in the case that the output surface is not linear, with TSK approach they are understood as modeled in the way of plain pieces of input variant kind on sub-spaces.

However, TSK fuzzy systems have deficiencies as there is a mathematical relation after **IF** part; output sections of the rules cannot model the verbal data given by human, and output sections of all rules, which are possible to be written between input and output variants cannot be written because they are fuzzy. In order to eliminate these deficiencies, fuzzy system, which is respectively blur, and clarification units are used in input and output units given in **Figure 5** [21].

Here, fuzzy rule base and deduction engine in a general fuzzy system remain as they are. In the case that the inputs are numerical, there are blurring agent unit, which is for blurring them with a process, and clarifying agent unit, which is for digitizing the fuzzy outputs. Blurring (fuzzification) and clarifying (defuzzification) mean, respectively, blurring the input numbers and digitizing the fuzzy numbers.

Among the main properties of fuzzy systems, multiple inputs, rule base, and conversion as single output by processing with deduction engine come as the most important issues. In some special situations, outputs may be more than one. Fuzzy system determines the behavior of the system by converting variants forming the inputs to output variant in a way of non-linear. By this way, it is possible to take the examined system under control in order to reach desired results by subjecting information base to non-linear conversions. Owing to the fuzzy systems, it becomes possible to process image, make guess based on time series, solve control problems, and perform applications on communication issues. Other than this, fuzzy systems can be used in many areas like engineering, medicine, sociology, psychology, business management, expert systems, artificial intelligence, signal processing, transportation, and signalization.

Exact numerical values are needed in practical applications particularly for sizing in engineering designs. In such cases, fuzzy information must be clarified in order for the required answers to be given by benefiting from information obtained or given as fuzzy. All processes made for conversion of fuzzy information to exact results are called clarification.

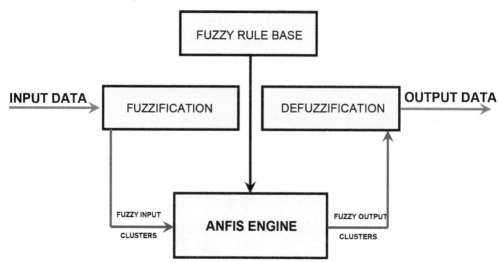

Figure 5. Fuzzy system with blurring-clarifying unit.

There are many clarification methods [23]. A few of them are presented below. In these processes, **z** indicates fuzzy deduction cluster, indicates components, and z* indicates clarified value.

- **The highest membership principle:** Another name of this process is height method. For this method to be used, fuzzy deduction clusters with peaks are needed. This method can be indicated with **Figure 6**.

- **Centroid method:** Another name of this method is center of gravity method. It could be the most common one of clarification methods. Mathematical expression is as shown in Eq. (3):

$$z^* = \frac{\int mf_C(z).zdz}{\int mf_C(z)dz} \tag{3}$$

Clarification is performed according to the center of gravity of fuzzy expression.

- **Weighted mean method:** In order for this method to be used, symmetric membership function (mf) is needed. Mathematical explanation is as shown in Eq. (4):

$$z^* = \frac{\sum mf_C(z).z}{\sum mf_C(z)} \tag{4}$$

Here Σ sign indicates algebraic sum. Graphical indication of this method is shown in **Figure 7**. Here, each membership function of fuzzy cluster constituting the output is multiplied with the highest membership degree value it has and their weighted mean is calculated. For instance, weighted mean (clarified value) of two fuzzy clusters in **Figure 7** is calculated as shown in Eq. (5).

$$z^* = \frac{a(0.5) + b(0.9)}{0.5 + 0.9} \tag{5}$$

Since this clarifying process is valid only for symmetric membership functions, a and b values are the mean of the figures they represent.

- **Averagely the highest membership degree method:** This method is also known as the mean of the highest ones. In this respect, it is very close to the first clarification principle. However, the position of the highest membership may not be singular. This means that the one having the highest membership degree in the membership function, mf (z) = 1, may exist in a plain section instead of a point.

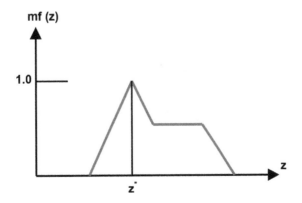

Figure 6. Clarification of the highest membership degree.

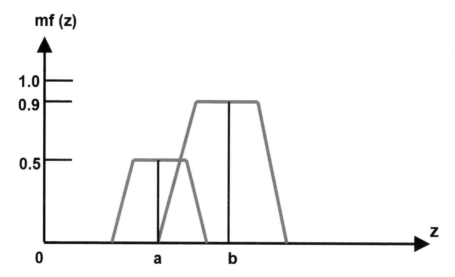

Figure 7. Clarification with weighted mean method.

Clarified value according to this method in graphical indication in **Figure 8** is as shown in Eq. (6):

$$z^* = \frac{a+b}{2} \tag{6}$$

- **Central management of the sums:** It is the fastest one among the clarification methods used. In this method, instead of combination of two fuzzy clusters, their algebraic sum is used. A deficiency of this is overlapping sections entering into the sum twice. Clarified value can be calculated as Eq. (7).

$$z^* = \frac{\int_z z \sum_{k=1}^{n} mf_c(z)\, dz}{\int_z \sum_{k=1}^{n} mf_c(z)\, dz} \tag{7}$$

In a way, this calculation form resembles weighted mean clarification. However, in the method of center of sums, weights are the areas of related membership functions. In the average weights method, this is a membership degree.

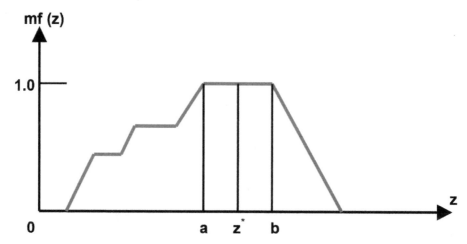

Figure 8. Averagely the highest membership clarification.

- **Center of the largest area:** If the outlet fuzzy cluster includes at least two convex fuzzy sub-clusters, center of gravity of the one with the biggest area of convex fuzzy clusters is used in clarification process. Mathematical indication of this method is as shown in Eq. (8):

$$z^* = \frac{\int mf_{Cm}(z)zdz}{\int mf_{Cm}(z)dz} \tag{8}$$

Here, $ü_{ebç}(z)$ indicates the sub-region where the convex fuzzy cluster with the biggest area dominates. This circumstance is used when all fuzzy deduction clusters are not convex; however, in the case that all deductions are convex, the result is the same with the one obtained with z^* centroid method.

- **The highest first and last membership degree method:** In this method, the lowest (or the highest) fuzzy cluster value with the highest membership degree in the fuzzy cluster that comes up as a combination of all outputs is selected. The equations below are valid for z^* value to be given by calculations. At first, the biggest height y_{eb} is determined in the combination of fuzzy cluster deduction, B.

$$y_{eb}(B) = \max\left[m\,f_B(z)\right] \tag{9}$$

Then, first highest value, z^* is found. Another way of this is to find the last highest fuzzy cluster value instead of the first one.

ANFIS name, which means fuzzy deduction system based on open adaptive networks or adaptive neural fuzzy detection system, is made of the first letters of adaptive network-based fuzzy interface system or adaptive neuro-fuzzy interface system. This network is the combination of the nodes, which are placed as layers for performing specific functions [5, 21]. ANFIS consists of six layers. This system is presented in **Figure 9**.

Node functions of each layers on ANFIS structure and the operations of layers are briefly explained [23, 24]:

- **First layer:** This is called the input layer. Input signals, which are taken from each of the nodes on this layer, are transferred into other layers.

- **Second layer:** This is called the fuzzification layer. Jang's ANFIS model uses the current Bell activation function as the membership function in order to divide input values into fuzzy sets. Here, output of each node is formed of input values, and membership degrees related to membership function and membership degrees, which are obtained from the second layer are shown as $\mu_{Aj}(x)$ and $\mu_{Bj}(y)$.

- **Third layer:** This is the rule layer. Each node in this layer expresses the rules and number of Sugeno fuzzy logic deduction system. Output of each rule node μ_i is the multiplication of membership degrees coming from second layer, and obtaining μ_i values are such as (j=1,2) and (i=1,....,n);

$$y_i^3 = \prod i = \mu_{A_j}(x)\,x\,\mu_{Bj}(y) = \mu_i \tag{10}$$

Here, y_i^3 represents the output values of the third layer and n represents the number of nodes in this layer.

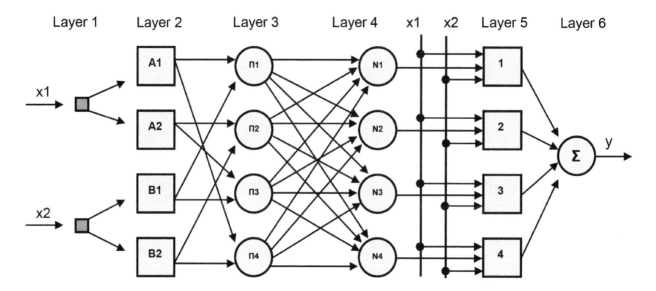

Figure 9. ANFIS network system.

- **Fourth layer:** This is the normalization layer. Each node in this layer assumes all the nodes coming from rule layer as the input value, and it calculates the normalized ignition level of each rule.

Calculation of normalized ignition level i μ is as shown in Eq. (11):

$$y_{i^A} = N_i = \frac{\mu_i}{\sum_{i=1}^{n} \mu_i} = \overline{\mu}, \ (i = 1, n) \tag{11}$$

- **Fifth layer:** This is the debugging layer. In this layer, weighted result values of a rule, which is given in each node, are calculated. Output value of i node in fifth layer is as shown in Eq. (12):

$$y_{i^5} = \overline{\mu}_i \big[p_i x_1 + q_i x_2 + r_i \big], \ (i = 1, n) \tag{12}$$

Here, (p_i, q_i, r_i) variables are result parameter set for i rule.

- **Sixth layer:** This is the sum layer. There is only one node in this layer, and it is tagged with Σ. Here, output values of each node in the fifth layer are added to each other, and a real value of ANFIS system is obtained. System output value y can be calculated with Eq. (13):

$$y = \sum_{i=1}^{n} \overline{\mu}_i \big[p_i x_1 + q_i x_2 + r_i \big] \tag{13}$$

3. Application

MATLAB is a software development instrument designed for technical calculations and the solutions of mathematical problems. MATLAB, which is the abbreviation of the words "MATrix LABoratory," works using matrixes as understood from its name or, in other words, using arrays. MATLAB, which is estimated to be used by over 500,000 academician, researcher, and students, is also described as the most advanced technical and scientific problem solving and application development instrument of the computer world with many interfaces it includes. MATLAB, particularly used in the analysis of the systems in engineering area, can perform the operations of data analysis and examination, visibility and image processing, generating algorithm prototype, modeling and simulation, programming and application development [25].

Application study consists of two basic steps. These are:

- Geometric camera calibration with conventional method

- Focal length calculation with ANFIS functions

In the application phase, geometric camera calibration study has been performed with bundle block adjustment method by using conventional method as the first step. In this study made by using zoom lens, camera calibration study has been preferred in both minimum and maximum focal lengths for Nikon Coolpix-E8700 camera whose focal length has been selected. The image of this camera is shown in **Figure 10**.

Figure 10. Nikon coolpix-E8700.

Images of test fields on which there are 145 points have been taken with Nikon Coolpix-E8700 digital camera from five angles in the situations of maximum (71.2 mm) and minimum (8.9 mm) focal length of the objective in the Photogrammetry Laboratory of Department of Geodesy and Photogrammetric Engineering of Gebze Technical University. This process is shown in **Figure 11**.

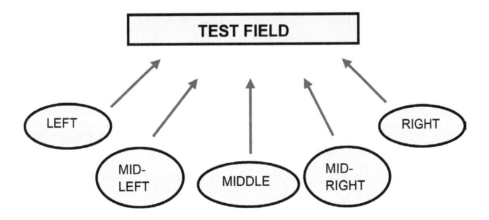

Figure 11. Test field shooting plan.

Coordinates of 145 points on test field were determined locally, and these values have been regarded as field coordinate (**ANNEX-1**). After that, 10 images obtained have been subjected to the evaluation in Topcon Pl-3000 software, and calibration parameters (inner orientation factors and distortion parameters) have been determined in situations of maximum focal length (71.2 mm) and minimum focal length (8.9 mm) of digital camera. These steps have been explained in **Figures 11** and **12** for both focal distances.

1	1.0000000e-002 1.0000000e-002 1.0000000e-002	73	4.3500000e-001 6.0500000e-001 1.0000000e-002
2	9.5000000e-002 1.0000000e-002 1.0000000e-002	74	4.3500000e-001 7.7500000e-001 1.0000000e-002
3	1.8000000e-001 1.0000000e-002 1.0000000e-002	75	4.3500000e-001 8.6000000e-001 1.0000000e-002
4	2.6500000e-001 1.0000000e-002 1.0000000e-002	76	4.3500000e-001 9.4500000e-001 1.0000000e-002
5	3.5000000e-001 1.0000000e-002 1.0000000e-002	77	4.3500000e-001 1.0300000e+000 1.0000000e-002
6	4.3500000e-001 1.0000000e-002 1.0000000e-002	78	4.3500000e-001 1.1150000e+000 1.0000000e-002
7	5.2000000e-001 1.0000000e-002 1.0000000e-002	79	4.3500000e-001 1.2000000e+000 1.0000000e-002
8	6.0500000e-001 1.0000000e-002 1.0000000e-002	80	5.2000000e-001 1.0000000e-002 1.0000000e-002
9	6.9000000e-001 1.0000000e-002 1.0000000e-002	81	5.2000000e-001 9.5000000e-002 1.0000000e-002
10	7.7500000e-001 1.0000000e-002 1.0000000e-002	82	5.2000000e-001 1.8000000e-001 1.0000000e-002
11	8.6000000e-001 1.0000000e-002 1.0000000e-002	83	5.2000000e-001 3.5000000e-001 1.0000000e-002
12	9.4500000e-001 1.0000000e-002 1.0000000e-002	84	5.2000000e-001 4.3500000e-001 1.0000000e-002
13	1.0300000e+000 1.0000000e-002 1.0000000e-002	85	5.2000000e-001 5.2000000e-001 1.0000000e-002
14	1.1150000e+000 1.0000000e-002 1.0000000e-002	86	5.2000000e-001 6.9000000e-001 1.0000000e-002
15	1.2000000e+000 1.0000000e-002 1.0000000e-002	87	5.2000000e-001 7.7500000e-001 1.0000000e-002
16	9.5000000e-002 1.0000000e-002 1.0000000e-002	88	5.2000000e-001 8.6000000e-001 1.0000000e-002
17	9.5000000e-002 9.5000000e-002 1.0000000e-002	89	5.2000000e-001 1.0300000e+000 1.0000000e-002
18	9.5000000e-002 1.8000000e-001 1.0000000e-002	90	5.2000000e-001 1.1150000e+000 1.0000000e-002
19	9.5000000e-002 2.6500000e-001 1.0000000e-002	91	5.2000000e-001 1.2000000e+000 1.0000000e-002
20	9.5000000e-002 3.5000000e-001 1.0000000e-002	92	6.0500000e-001 1.0000000e-002 1.0000000e-002
21	9.5000000e-002 4.3500000e-001 1.0000000e-002	93	6.0500000e-001 9.5000000e-002 1.0000000e-002
22	9.5000000e-002 5.2000000e-001 1.0000000e-002	94	6.0500000e-001 2.6500000e-001 1.0000000e-002
23	9.5000000e-002 6.0500000e-001 1.0000000e-002	95	6.0500000e-001 4.3500000e-001 1.0000000e-002
24	9.5000000e-002 6.9000000e-001 1.0000000e-002	96	6.0500000e-001 5.2000000e-001 1.0000000e-002
25	9.5000000e-002 7.7500000e-001 1.0000000e-002	97	6.0500000e-001 6.0500000e-001 1.0000000e-002
26	9.5000000e-002 8.6000000e-001 1.0000000e-002	98	6.0500000e-001 6.9000000e-001 1.0000000e-002
27	9.5000000e-002 9.4500000e-001 1.0000000e-002	99	6.0500000e-001 7.7500000e-001 1.0000000e-002
28	9.5000000e-002 1.0300000e+000 1.0000000e-002	100	6.0500000e-001 9.4500000e-001 1.0000000e-002
29	9.5000000e-002 1.1150000e+000 1.0000000e-002	101	6.0500000e-001 1.1150000e+000 1.0000000e-002
30	9.5000000e-002 1.2000000e+000 1.0000000e-002	102	6.0500000e-001 1.2000000e+000 1.0000000e-002
31	1.8000000e-001 1.0000000e-002 1.0000000e-002	103	6.9000000e-001 1.0000000e-002 1.0000000e-002
32	1.8000000e-001 9.5000000e-002 1.0000000e-002	104	6.9000000e-001 9.5000000e-002 1.0000000e-002
33	1.8000000e-001 1.8000000e-001 1.0000000e-002	105	6.9000000e-001 1.8000000e-001 1.0000000e-002
34	1.8000000e-001 3.5000000e-001 1.0000000e-002	106	6.9000000e-001 3.5000000e-001 1.0000000e-002

35	1.8000000e-001	4.3500000e-001	1.0000000e-002	107	6.9000000e-001	4.3500000e-001	1.0000000e-002
36	1.8000000e-001	5.2000000e-001	1.0000000e-002	108	6.9000000e-001	5.2000000e-001	1.0000000e-002
37	1.8000000e-001	6.0500000e-001	1.0000000e-002	109	6.9000000e-001	6.0500000e-001	1.0000000e-002
38	1.8000000e-001	6.9000000e-001	1.0000000e-002	110	6.9000000e-001	6.9000000e-001	1.0000000e-002
39	1.8000000e-001	7.7500000e-001	1.0000000e-002	111	6.9000000e-001	7.7500000e-001	1.0000000e-002
40	1.8000000e-001	8.6000000e-001	1.0000000e-002	112	6.9000000e-001	8.6000000e-001	1.0000000e-002
41	1.8000000e-001	1.0300000e+000	1.0000000e-002	113	6.9000000e-001	1.0300000e+000	1.0000000e-002
42	1.8000000e-001	1.1150000e+000	1.0000000e-002	114	6.9000000e-001	1.1150000e+000	1.0000000e-002
43	1.8000000e-001	1.2000000e+000	1.0000000e-002	115	6.9000000e-001	1.2000000e+000	1.0000000e-002
44	2.6500000e-001	1.0000000e-002	1.0000000e-002	116	7.7500000e-001	1.0000000e-002	1.0000000e-002
45	2.6500000e-001	9.5000000e-002	1.0000000e-002	117	7.7500000e-001	9.5000000e-002	1.0000000e-002
46	2.6500000e-001	2.6500000e-001	1.0000000e-002	118	7.7500000e-001	1.8000000e-001	1.0000000e-002
47	2.6500000e-001	4.3500000e-001	1.0000000e-002	119	7.7500000e-001	2.6500000e-001	1.0000000e-002
48	2.6500000e-001	5.2000000e-001	1.0000000e-002	120	7.7500000e-001	3.5000000e-001	1.0000000e-002
49	2.6500000e-001	6.0500000e-001	1.0000000e-002	121	7.7500000e-001	4.3500000e-001	1.0000000e-002
50	2.6500000e-001	6.9000000e-001	1.0000000e-002	122	7.7500000e-001	5.2000000e-001	1.0000000e-002
51	2.6500000e-001	7.7500000e-001	1.0000000e-002	123	7.7500000e-001	6.0500000e-001	1.0000000e-002
52	2.6500000e-001	9.4500000e-001	1.0000000e-002	124	7.7500000e-001	6.9000000e-001	1.0000000e-002
53	2.6500000e-001	1.1150000e+000	1.0000000e-002	125	7.7500000e-001	7.7500000e-001	1.0000000e-002
54	2.6500000e-001	1.2000000e+000	1.0000000e-002	126	7.7500000e-001	8.6000000e-001	1.0000000e-002
55	3.5000000e-001	1.0000000e-002	1.0000000e-002	127	7.7500000e-001	9.4500000e-001	1.0000000e-002
56	3.5000000e-001	9.5000000e-002	1.0000000e-002	128	7.7500000e-001	1.0300000e+000	1.0000000e-002
57	3.5000000e-001	1.8000000e-001	1.0000000e-002	129	7.7500000e-001	1.1150000e+000	1.0000000e-002
58	3.5000000e-001	3.5000000e-001	1.0000000e-002	130	7.7500000e-001	1.2000000e+000	1.0000000e-002
59	3.5000000e-001	4.3500000e-001	1.0000000e-002	131	8.6000000e-001	1.0000000e-002	1.0000000e-002
60	3.5000000e-001	5.2000000e-001	1.0000000e-002	132	8.6000000e-001	9.5000000e-002	1.0000000e-002
61	3.5000000e-001	6.9000000e-001	1.0000000e-002	133	8.6000000e-001	1.8000000e-001	1.0000000e-002
62	3.5000000e-001	7.7500000e-001	1.0000000e-002	134	8.6000000e-001	2.6500000e-001	1.0000000e-002
63	3.5000000e-001	8.6000000e-001	1.0000000e-002	135	8.6000000e-001	3.5000000e-001	1.0000000e-002
64	3.5000000e-001	1.0300000e+000	1.0000000e-002	136	8.6000000e-001	4.3500000e-001	1.0000000e-002
65	3.5000000e-001	1.1150000e+000	1.0000000e-002	137	8.6000000e-001	5.2000000e-001	1.0000000e-002
66	3.5000000e-001	1.2000000e+000	1.0000000e-002	138	8.6000000e-001	6.0500000e-001	1.0000000e-002
67	4.3500000e-001	1.0000000e-002	1.0000000e-002	139	8.6000000e-001	6.9000000e-001	1.0000000e-002
68	4.3500000e-001	9.5000000e-002	1.0000000e-002	140	8.6000000e-001	7.7500000e-001	1.0000000e-002
69	4.3500000e-001	1.8000000e-001	1.0000000e-002	141	8.6000000e-001	8.6000000e-001	1.0000000e-002
70	4.3500000e-001	2.6500000e-001	1.0000000e-002	142	8.6000000e-001	9.4500000e-001	1.0000000e-002
71	4.3500000e-001	3.5000000e-001	1.0000000e-002	143	8.6000000e-001	1.0300000e+000	1.0000000e-002
72	4.3500000e-001	4.3500000e-001	1.0000000e-002	144	8.6000000e-001	1.1150000e+000	1.0000000e-002
				145	8.6000000e-001	1.2000000e+000	1.0000000e-002

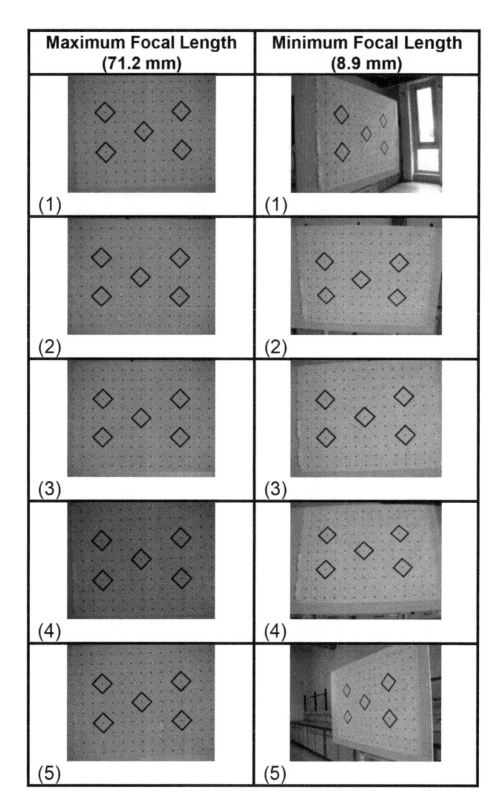

Figure 12. Camera calibration test field.

In **Figures 13** and **14**, focal length obtained with bundle block adjustment (conventional method), inner orientation parameters, and radial distortion parameters were summarized from Topcon PI-3000 software interface.

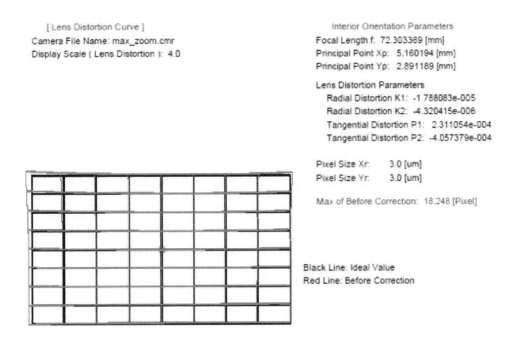

Figure 13. The one obtained by Topcon PI-3000 program in maximum focal length.

As the second step of the application, image coordinates measured over images have been indicated radially with Eq. (14) for maximum focal length and minimum focal length values of digital camera.

$$c_k = \frac{r^l}{\tan \tau} \tag{14}$$

c_k: calibrated focal length

r^l: radial distance

τ: distortion angle

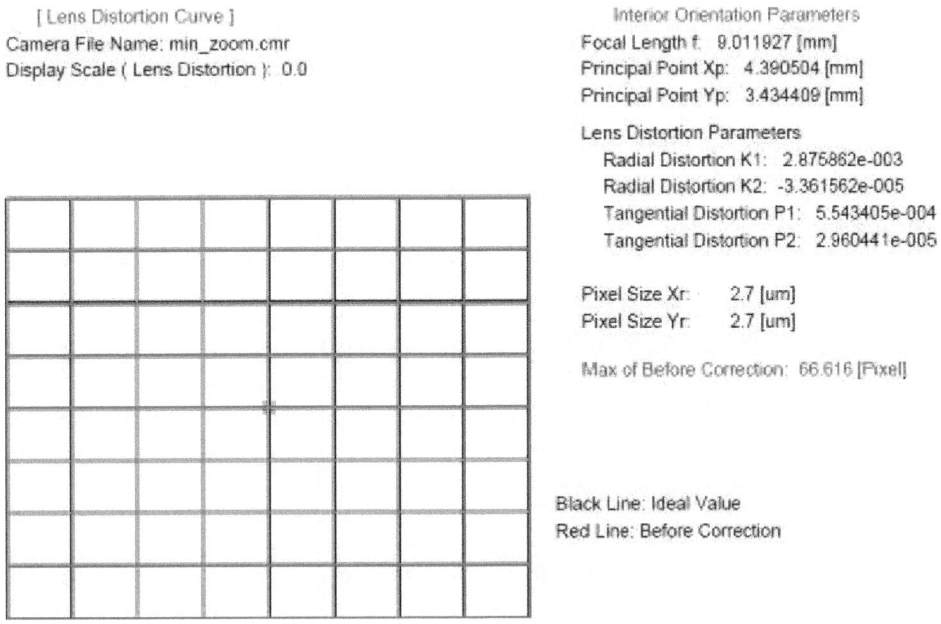

Figure 14. The one obtained by Topcon PI-3000 program in minimum focal length.

Twenty-three points have been selected and arranged in the format of training data (smalldata.dat) and remaining 122 points have been arranged in the format of test data (bigdata.dat) as shown in **Figure 15**. ANFIS data set which are used in fuzzification and defuzzification have been composed from equation process with radial distance and angle. This process has been repeated for the images taken from 10 different angles for each zoom distance. ANFIS data set has been composed from equation process with radial distance and angles.

In **Figure 15**, first and fourth columns indicate x values of image coordinates, second and fifth columns indicate y values, and third and sixth columns indicate focal lengths calculated radially.

After ANFIS data set has been generated, an ANFIS application stated below has been performed by using MATLAB software. The basic logic in this application is radial distances selected as input is processed with the help of ANFIS functions, and as a result, a focal length value for each image has been obtained. Algorithm figure determined for this method is indicated below. Here, it is seen that training algorithm determined for generation of ANFIS artificial neural network operates iteratively. Artificial neural network structure shaped with training data described as training data and consisting of 23 points gives result with the last iteration where 122 points are also included for getting the exact result. Thus, a calculation, which includes again the same quantity of measurement (145 radial values) corresponding to focal length distance, is determined with conventional method. For this reason, a logical measurement number equality has been enabled in comparison of ANFIS results with conventional method. In brief, the measurement values in the first and second steps are in the same quantity. This process has been explained in **Figure 16**.

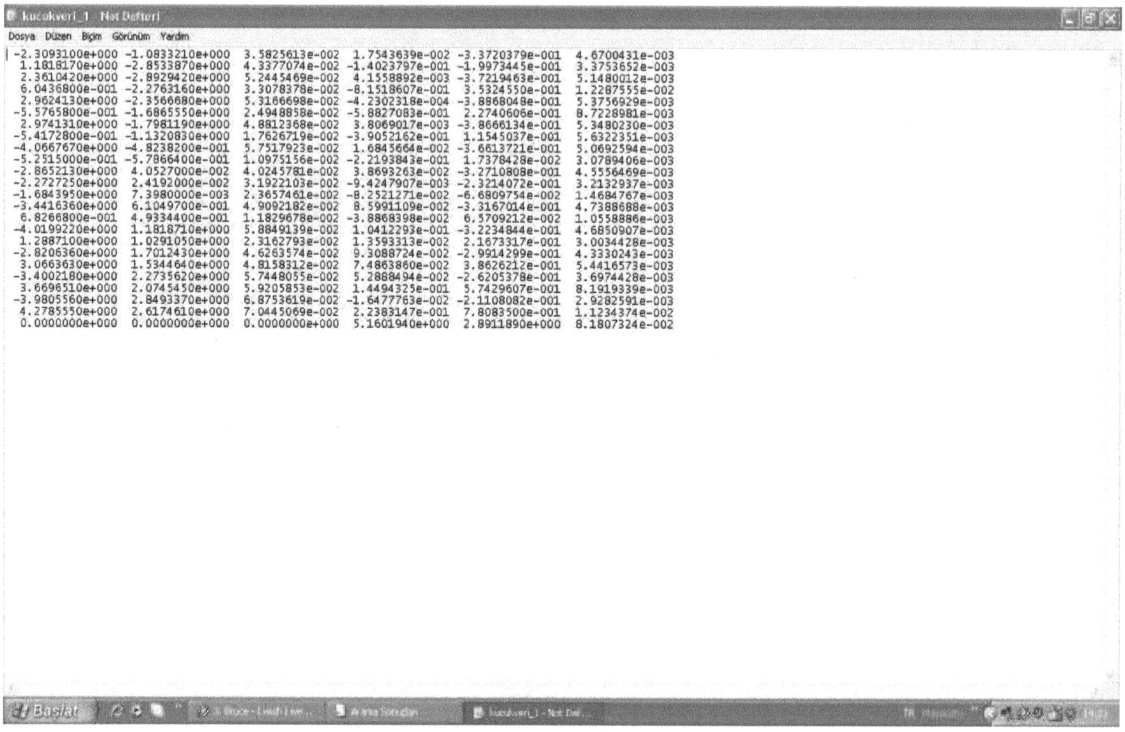
kucukveri_1 - Not Defteri

Dosya Düzen Biçim Görünüm Yardım

-2.3093100e+000	-1.0833210e+000	3.5825613e-002	1.7543639e-002	-3.3720379e-001	4.6700431e-003
1.1818170e+000	-2.8533870e+000	4.3377074e-002	-1.4023797e-001	-1.9973445e-001	3.3753652e-003
2.3610420e+000	-2.8929420e+000	5.2445469e-002	4.1558892e-003	-3.7219463e-001	5.1480012e-003
6.0436800e-001	-2.2763160e+000	3.3078378e-002	-8.1518607e-001	3.5324550e-001	1.2287555e-002
2.9624130e+000	-2.3566680e+000	5.3166698e-002	-4.2302318e-004	-3.8868048e-001	5.3756929e-003
-5.5765800e-001	-1.6865550e+000	2.4948858e-002	-5.8827083e-001	2.2740606e-001	8.7228981e-003
2.9741310e+000	-1.7981190e+000	4.8812368e-002	3.8069017e-003	-3.8666134e-001	5.3480230e-003
-5.4172800e-001	-1.1320830e+000	1.7626719e-002	-3.9052162e-001	1.1545037e-001	5.6322351e-003
-4.0667670e+000	-4.8238200e-001	5.7517923e-002	1.6845664e-002	-3.6613721e-001	5.0692594e-003
-5.2515000e-001	-5.7866400e-001	1.0975156e-002	-2.2193843e-001	1.7378428e-002	3.0789406e-003
-2.8652130e+000	4.0527000e-002	4.0245781e-002	3.8693263e-002	-3.2710808e-001	4.5556469e-003
-2.2727250e+000	2.4192000e-002	3.1922103e-002	-9.4247907e-003	-2.3214072e-001	3.2132937e-003
-1.6843950e+000	7.3980000e-003	2.3657461e-002	-8.2521271e-002	-6.6809754e-002	1.4684767e-003
-3.4416360e+000	6.1049700e-001	4.9092182e-002	8.5991109e-002	-3.3167014e-001	4.7388688e-003
6.8266800e-001	4.9334400e-001	1.1829678e-002	-3.8868398e-002	6.5709212e-002	1.0558886e-003
-4.0199220e+000	1.1818710e+000	5.8849139e-002	1.0412293e-001	-3.2234844e-001	4.6850907e-003
1.2887100e+000	1.0291050e+000	2.3162793e-002	1.3593313e-002	2.1673317e-001	3.0034428e-003
-2.8206360e+000	1.7012430e+000	4.6263574e-002	9.3088724e-002	-2.9914299e-001	4.3330243e-003
3.0663630e+000	1.5344640e+000	4.8158312e-002	7.4863860e-002	3.8626212e-001	5.4416573e-003
-3.4002180e+000	2.2735620e+000	5.7448055e-002	5.2888494e-002	-2.6205378e-001	3.6974428e-003
3.6696510e+000	2.0745450e+000	5.9205853e-002	1.4494325e-001	5.7429607e-001	8.1919339e-003
-3.9805560e+000	2.8493370e+000	6.8753619e-002	-1.6477763e-002	-2.1108082e-001	2.9282591e-003
4.2785550e+000	2.6174610e+000	7.0445069e-002	2.2383147e-001	7.8083500e-001	1.1234374e-002
0.0000000e+000	0.0000000e+000	0.0000000e+000	5.1601940e+000	2.8911890e+000	8.1807324e-002

Figure 15. ANFIS data set structure for radial distances.

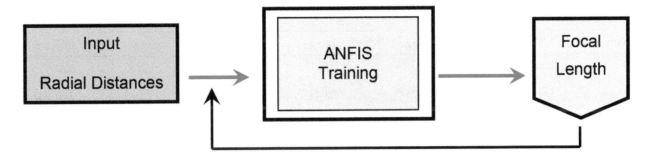

Figure 16. ANFIS algorithm.

Each data set has been subjected to process with eight different ANFIS functions (trimf, trapmf, gbellmf, gaussmf, gauss2mf, pimf, dsigmf, and psigmf) as indicated above and quadratic average error values of Artificial Neural Network and ANFIS functions have been obtained. Artificial neural network structure has been shown in **Figure 17** from MATLAB ANFIS interface.

Measured radial values and ANFIS artificial neural network structure have been indicated in **Figure 17**. Quadratic mean errors (standard deviation) of focal length differences related to radial lengths obtained for function structures used in forming artificial neural network have been generated for 10 images in total according to maximum focal length data as shown in **Table 1** and minimum focal length data as shown in **Table 2**. While there are standard deviation values here, focal length value obtained (with bundle block adjustment) in the first step has been used as exact value. At the end of the first step, inner orientation parameters obtained by conventional method will be considered as true, and they will constitute reference data to be used in comparison for the results obtained with second step in other word ANFIS.

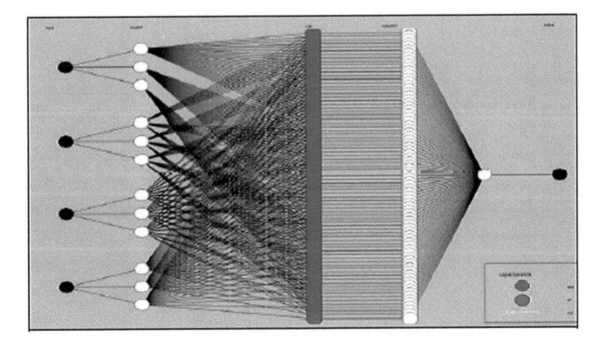

Figure 17. Artificial neural network structure generation.

Maximum focal length (71.9 mm)

Num.	ANFIS function	Image 1	Image 2	Image 3	Image 4	Image 5
1	Trimf	0.00179	0.00173	0.00210	0.00235	0.00190
2	Trapmf	0.00373	0.00382	0.00381	0.00319	0.00441
3	Gbellmf	0.00243	0.00261	0.00283	0.00218	0.00219
4	Gaussmf	0.00234	0.00229	0.00237	0.00210	0.00210
5	Gauss2mf	0.00347	0.00530	0.00515	0.00321	0.00307
6	Pimf	0.00512	0.00344	0.00488	0.00356	0.00342
7	Dsigmf	0.00306	0.00288	0.00452	0.00327	0.00277
8	Psigmf	0.00306	0.00288	0.00452	0.00327	0.00308

Table 1. Standard deviation values of maximum focal length obtained with ANFIS functions.

The result of determining focal distance with eight ANFIS functions, which are used in the application and square mean errors which are obtained with these functions, are compared to camera calibration values which are calculated with the conventional method (bundle block adjustment), and the differences of focal distances are illustrated image by image.

The results that eight ANFIS functions have given standard deviations for first image to fifth image depending on the maximum and minimum focal lengths have been detailed in the graphs in **Figures 18** and **19**. When ANFIS method is examined in terms of reliability and inner reliability parameters between selected functions with this application realized, it has been seen that it gives the most suitable results in determination of focal length of trimf and gaussmf functions.

Minimum focal length (8.9 mm)

Num.	ANFIS function	Image 1	Image 2	Image 3	Image 4	Image 5
1	Trimf	0.01814	0.02217	0.01626	0.02560	0.02326
2	Trapmf	0.02204	0.03220	0.02181	0.02701	0.04293
3	Gbellmf	0.01637	0.02047	0.01736	0.02276	0.03822
4	Gaussmf	0.01429	0.01982	0.01745	0.02221	0.03269
5	Gauss2mf	0.02195	0.03180	0.02524	0.02729	0.04476
6	Pimf	0.02528	0.03589	0.02648	0.02965	0.04609
7	Dsigmf	0.02323	0.03274	0.02448	0.02774	0.04494
8	Psigmf	0.02323	0.03274	0.02448	0.02774	0.04494

Table 2. Standard deviation values of minimum focal length obtained with ANFIS functions.

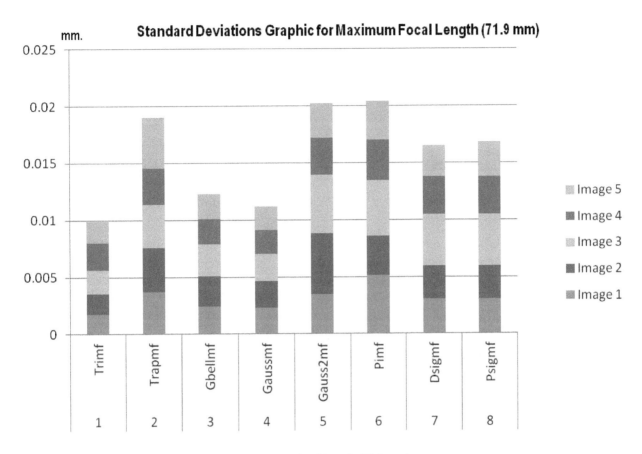

Figure 18. Standard deviations graphic for maximum focal length (71.9 mm).

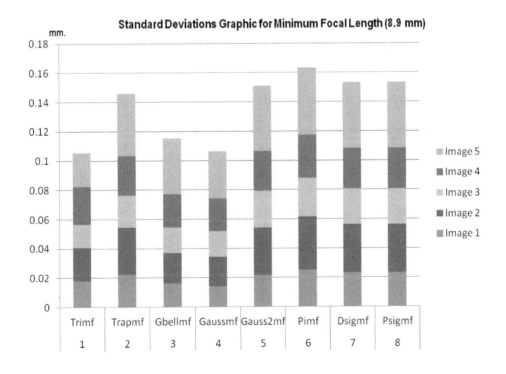

Figure 19. Standard deviations graphic for minimum focal length (8.9 mm)

4. Conclusion

When the results were obtained at the end of the application, it was seen that data with long focal lengths produce lower quadratic mean errors, and test data produced by using short focal length produce higher quadratic mean error values in the same ANFIS functions. When its mathematical structure is considered from radial distortion focal length graphics, it is seen that the shorter the focal length, the more radial distortion error happens. When this situation is considered, it is seen that radial distortion error directly influences the approach to ANFIS functions, and it has an influence on general error amount in data set. In other words, it has been seen that optical distortion law can be verified with the influence of ANFIS functions to data sets. This at the same time proves a physical fact in general table that it verifies ANFIS functions and depicts it in a very proper way.

When the graphics of the functions between each other are examined, it is seen that the most proper (with the least quadratic mean error) or the most usable ANFIS functions in a bundle block adjustment study to be modeled in ANFIS structure related to spatial resection structure are *"trimf, gbellmf and gaussmf."*

It is seen that ANFIS functions, which depict balancing as the weakest (with the highest quadratic mean error), are *"pimf, dsigmf and psigmf"* functions with this approach. When an assessment is made concerning the general of this study to make an approach of spatial resection by using ANFIS system, advantages and disadvantages below will occur for the calibration studies.

Advantages:

- There will be no need for generating a separate unreal algorithm for spatial resection step in bundle block adjustment.

- Study will be able to be made without the need of approximate rotation and reciprocation parameters.

- It will decrease iteration number for bundle block adjustment.

- Calibration will be able to be enabled during study not only in minimum and maximum focal lengths but also in all focal lengths.

Disadvantages:

- Data sets must be prepared for ANFIS sets. This requires additional time.

- It is not possible to reach approximate rotation and reciprocation parameters.

- Since the system will directly give result, focal length necessary for calibration will be known only as approximately depending on data number.

- It is verified for more than sufficient images that focal length found with additional transaction can be used as calibrated for certain.

- All images to be determined for the project must be taken from the same focal length.

As a result of the studies conducted, it has been seen that fuzzy logic approach can be used in the study of calibration of digital cameras. It was determined that the accuracy can be increased by increasing the data number of estimation model established with ANFIS method and estimation can be made benefiting from other artificial intelligence methods. For this reason, it was concluded that it will be more beneficial to use and search fuzzy logic approach more in photogrammetric applications.

Author details

Bahadır Ergün[1]*, Cumhur Sahin[1] and Ugur Kaplan[2]

*Address all correspondence to: bergun@gtu.edu.tr

1 Department of Geodesy and Photogrammetry, Gebze Technical University, Gebze, Turkey

2 Department of Mathematics, Gebze Technical University, Gebze, Turkey

References

[1] Kajornrit J, Wong KW, Fung CC. A comparative analysis of soft computing techniques used to estimate missing precipitation records. In: Proceedings of the 19th ITS Biennial Conference; 18-21 November 2012; Bangkok, Thailand.

[2] Mamdani EH, Assilian S. An experiment in linguistic synthesis with a fuzzy logic controller. International Journal of Human-Computer Studies. 1999;51(2):135-147. doi:10.1006/ijhc.1973.0303.

[3] Takagi T, Sugeno M. Fuzzy identification of systems and its applications to modeling and control. IEEE Transactions on Systems, Man and Cybernetics. 1985;15:116-132. WOS:A1985AFX0900011.

[4] Hamam A, Georganas ND. A comparison of mamdani and sugeno fuzzy inference systems for evaluating the quality of experience of hapto-audio-visual applications. In: Proceeding of the IEEE International Workshop on Haptic Audio Visual Environments and their Applications 18-19 October 2008; Ottawa, Canada. IEEE.

[5] Tsoukalas LH, Uhrig RE. Fuzzy and neural approaches in engineering (1st ed.). New York: John Wiley & Sons; 1996, 600 p. ISBN:0471160032.

[6] Citak E. Fuzzy logic approach to determine the factors affecting hand dexterity [thesis]. University of Cukurova; 2008.

[7] Roger JS, Sun C. Functional equivalence between radial basis function networks and fuzzy inference systems. IEEE Transactions on Neural Networks. 1993;4:156-159. doi:10.1109/72.182710.

[8] Roger JS. ANFIS: adaptive network based fuzzy inference systems. IEEE Transactions on Systems Man and Cybernetics. 1993;**23**(3):665-685. doi:10.1109/21.256541.

[9] Perez JA, Gonzalez M, Dopico D. Adaptive neurofuzzy ANFIS modeling of laser surface treatments. Neural Computing & Applications. 2010;**19**:85-90. doi:10.1007/s00521-009-0259-x.

[10] Roger JS, Gulley N. Matlab fuzzy logic toolbox. User#x2019;s guide. Natick: The MathWorks Inc.; 2007.

[11] Jang JSR, Sun CT, Mizutani E. Neuro-fuzzy and soft computing: a computational approach to learning and machine intelligence. Englewood Cliffs, NJ: Prentice-Hall; 1997.

[12] Sabzevari R, Masoumzadeh S, Ghahroudi MR. Employing anfis for object detection in robo-pong. In: Proceeding of 5th International Symposium on Mechatronics and its Applications (ISMA08); 27-29 May 2008; Amman, Jordan, pp. 707-712.

[13] Orghidan R, Danciu M, Vlaicu A, Oltean G, Gordan M, Florea C. Fuzzy versus crisp stereo calibration: a comparative study. In: Proceeding of 7th International Symposium on Image and processing and analysis (ISPA 2011); 4-6 September 2011; Dubrovnik, Croatia, pp. 627-632.

[14] Nuno AI, Arcay B, Cotos JM, Varela J. Optimisation of fishing predictions by means of artificial neural networks, anfis, functional networks and remote sensing images. Expert Systems with Applications. 2005;**29**:356-363. doi:10.1016/j.eswa.2005.04.008.

[15] Jafari S, Jarvis R. Robotic hand-eye coordination: from observation to manipulation. In: Proceedings of the Fourth International Conference on Hybrid Intelligent Systems (HIS'04); 5-8 December 2004; Kitakyushu, Japan. IEEE. doi:10.1109/ICHIS.2004.82.

[16] Gallardo A, Taylor J, Paolini C, Lee HK, Lee GK. An ANFIS-based multi-sensor structure for a mobile robotic system. In: Proceeding of Computational Intelligence in Control and Automation; 11-15 April 2011; Paris, France. IEEE. doi:10.1109/CICA.2011.5945755.

[17] Li C, Ma H, Yang C, Fu M. Teleoperation of a virtual iCub robot under framework of parallel system via hand gesture recognition. In: Proceeding of International Conference on Fuzzy Systems (FUZZ-IEEE); 6-11 July 2014; Beijing, China, pp. 1469-1474.

[18] Orazio TD, Leo M, Mazzeo PL, Spagnolo P. Soccer player activity recognition by a multivariate features integration. In: Proceeding of Seventh IEEE International Conference on Advanced Video and Signal Based Surveillance; 29 August 2010-1 September 2010; Boston, USA, pp. 32-39.

[19] Orghidan R, Gordan M, Danciu M, Vlaicu A. A prototype for the creation and interactive visualization of 3D human face models. Advanced Engineering Forum. 2013; **8-9**:45-54. doi:10.4028/www.scientific.net/AEF.8-9.45.

[20] Navarro H, Orghidan R, Gordan M, Saavedra G, Martinez-Corral M. Fuzzy integral imaging camera calibration for real scale 3D reconstructions. Journal of Display Technology. 2014;**10**(7): 601-608. doi:0.1109/JDT.2014.2312236.

[21] Ozbilge EU. An approach of matlab about calibration of digital cameras [thesis]. Gebze Institute of Technology; 2010.

[22] Sugeno M, Kang G. Structure identification of fuzzy model. Fuzzy Sets and Systems. 1988;**26**(1):15-33. doi:10.1016/0165-0114(88)90113-3.

[23] Ross TJ. Fuzzy logic with engineering applications. Chichester: McGraw-Hill; 1995, pp. 134-147. ISBN: 0-07-053917-0.

[24] Hocaoğlu FO, Kurban M. Adaptif ağ tabanlı bulanık mantık çıkarım sistemi ile Eskisehir bolgesi icin güneşlenme süreleri tahmini. Elektrik-Elektronik-Bilgisayar Mühendisliği 11. Ulusal Kongresi ve Fuarı, 22-25 Eylul 2005; Istanbul, Turkiye.

[25] Mathworks. 2017. Retrieved 25 January 2017, from https://www.mathworks.com/products/matlab.html.

11

Vibration Suppression Controller of Multi-Mass Resonance System Using Fuzzy Controller

Hidehiro Ikeda

Abstract

Vibration suppression control of the mechanical system is a very important technology for realizing high precision, high speed response and energy saving. In general, the mechanical system is modeled with a multi-mass resonance system, and vibration suppression control is applied. This chapter presents a novel controller design method for the speed control system to suppress the resonance vibration of two-mass resonance system and three-mass resonance system. The target systems are constructed by a motor, finite rigid shafts, and loads. The control system consists of a speed fuzzy controller and a proportional-integral (PI) current controller to realize precise speed and torque response. In order to implement the experimental system, the system is treated as the digital control. This chapter also utilizes a differential evolution (DE) to determine five optimal controller parameters (three scaling factors of the fuzzy controller and two controller gains of PI current controller. Finally, this chapter verified the effectiveness to suppress the resonance vibrations and the robustness of the proposed method by the computer simulations and the experiments by using the test experimental setup.

Keywords: multi-mass resonance system, vibration suppression control, fuzzy controller, differential evolution

1. Introduction

Recently, motor drive system, which consists of several motors, shafts, gears, and loads, is widely utilized in industrial fields. These mechanical systems are made a request the high-speed response, weight reduction, miniaturization, and high precision requirements for various industrial applications.

Hence, in industrial field, the system is treated as a multi-mass resonance system, which consists of several inertial moments, torsional shafts, and gear coupling. The first-order approximation model of multi-mass resonances model is two-mass resonance model. For instance, several control methods, which are PID control (Proportional plus Integral plus Derivative Control) with a resonance ratio control using the disturbance observer, coefficient diagram method (CDM), full state feedback control with the state observer, the pole placement method, fractional order PID_k control, and H_∞ control method, are effective to control for two-mass resonance system [1–3]. Ikeda et al. [4] have explained the effectiveness of the controller design technique using the pole placement method for the two-mass position control system.

However, the resonance system is required more high precision and high response speed control in recent years. Therefore, it is necessary to deal with a higher order model of the resonance system. For instance, the drive train of the electric vehicle is constructed the four-mass system. Likewise, the ball screw drive stage is typically four-mass system. The thermal power generation system composed of multiple turbines and generators is modeled as twelve-mass resonance system. Thus, several vibration suppression control methods on three-mass resonance system or more have been proposed [5, 6]. Here, modified-IPD speed controller using Taguchi Method has been proposed in Refs. [7, 8].

Meanwhile, the state equations of the controlled object and its parameters are required to design the control systems. Refs. [9, 10] previously proposed a controller gain tuning method for a vibration suppression-type speed controller using fictitious reference iterative tuning (FRIT) for single-input multi-variable control objects without knowledge of the system state equations and the parameters.

In contrast, a fuzzy control system can be assumed as one method for solving these problems. A fuzzy control system using a fuzzy inference is the embodiment of non-mathematical control algorithm, which is constructed by experience and intuition. Several applications brought in the fuzzy control system to motor drive system [11–14].

This chapter proposes a vibration suppression controller by using a fuzzy inference. The control system consists of a speed fuzzy controller and a proportional-integral (PI) current controller to realize precise speed and torque response on two or three inertial resonance system. In the control system, only motor side state variables are utilized for controlling the resonance system. Additionally, this chapter treats with the proposed control system as the digital control system. Here, the proposed control system is new system that I improved to apply the control system which I already proposed for simulation model in Refs. [13, 14] to experimental actual equipment.

The fuzzy controller has three scaling factors, and the PI current controller has two controller gains. In this chapter, a differential evolution algorithm (DE) is utilized the determination of these five controller parameters [13–18]. DE, which was proposed by Price and Storn, is one of the evolutionary optimization strategies. By using DE, it is easy and fast to determine the proper controller parameters.

Lastly, the validity of the controller design, the robustness, and the control effectiveness of the proposed method was verified using the simulations and the experiments by using the test experimental set up.

2. Multi-mass vibration suppression control system

2.1. 2-mass model

Figure 1 shows the two-mass resonance model. The model is configured of two rigid inertial masses with a torsional shaft, where ω_M, T_{dis}, ω_L, T_{in}, J_M, J_L, K_s, and T_L denote the motor angular speed, the torsional torque, the load angular speed, the input torque, the inertia of motor, the inertia of load, the shaft torsional stiffness, and the load torque, respectively.

If all the state variables can be observed by several sensors and all the system parameters are known or identified, it is easy to construct the optimal control system. However, in general, it is difficult to measure the state variables of the load side due to constraints on scarce measurement environment and sensor installation location. Therefore, in this chapter, we use only the motor side variables. Furthermore, we contemplate for the current minor control in order to compensate torque response. Eq. (1) shows the continuous state equation of two-mass resonance model, where the viscous friction is not considered.

$$\frac{d}{dt}\begin{pmatrix} \omega_M \\ \omega_L \\ T_{dis} \end{pmatrix} = \begin{pmatrix} 0 & 0 & -\frac{1}{J_M} \\ 0 & 0 & \frac{1}{J_L} \\ K_s & -K_s & 0 \end{pmatrix}\begin{pmatrix} \omega_M \\ \omega_L \\ T_{dis} \end{pmatrix} + \begin{pmatrix} \frac{1}{J_M} \\ 0 \\ 0 \end{pmatrix}T_{in} + \begin{pmatrix} 0 \\ -\frac{1}{J_L} \\ 0 \end{pmatrix}T_L \tag{1}$$

Eq. (2) shows the transfer function of two-mass model, which input signal is T_{in} and output signal is ω_M.

$$\frac{\omega_M}{T_{in}} = \frac{s^2 + \omega_a^2}{J_M s(s^2 + \omega_r^2)} \tag{2}$$

where ω_r is a resonance frequency and ω_a is an anti-resonance frequency. Here, we use the DC servo motor as the driving motor. Eq. (3) is the voltage equation of dc servo motor, where R_a is the armature resistance, L_a is the armature inductance, K_e is the back-emf constant, and K_0 is the converter gains of the DC power supply. Input torque is calculated by $T_{in} = K_t i_a$, where K_t is the torque constant.

$$L_a\frac{di_a}{dt} + R_a i_a = K_0 u_c - \omega_M \tag{3}$$

Figure 2 is indicative of the block diagram of the two-mass resonance system.

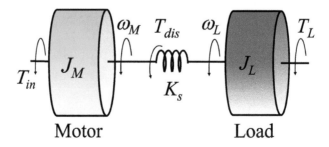

Motor   Load

Figure 1. 2-mass model.

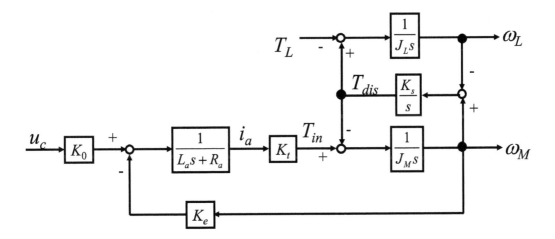

Figure 2. Block diagram of two-mass resonance model.

The inertia ratio R of two-mass model is given by Eq. (4), where J_{Mn} and J_{Ln} represent the nominal values of the motor and load inertias, respectively.

$$R = \frac{J_{Ln}}{J_{Mn}} \tag{4}$$

2.2. Three-mass model

Similarly to two-mass resonance model, **Figure 3** reveals the three-mass model. The model consists of three rigid inertias and two shafts. Here, J_c and J_L are the load 1 inertia moment and the load 2 inertia moment, respectively. Furthermore, ω_c, ω_L, T_{dis1}, T_{dis2}, K_{s1}, and K_{s2} denote load 1 angular speed, load 2 angular speed, shaft 1 torsional torque, shaft 2 torsional torque, the shaft 1 stiffness, and the shaft 2 stiffness, respectively.

$$\frac{d}{dt}\begin{pmatrix} \omega_M \\ \omega_M \\ \omega_M \\ T_{dis} \\ T_{dis} \end{pmatrix}\begin{pmatrix} \omega_M \\ \omega_L \\ T_{dis} \end{pmatrix} = \begin{pmatrix} 0 & 0 & 0 & -\dfrac{1}{J_M} & 0 \\ 0 & 0 & 0 & \dfrac{1}{J_c} & -\dfrac{1}{J_c} \\ 0 & 0 & 0 & 0 & \dfrac{1}{J_L} \\ K_{s1} & -K_{s1} & 0 & 0 & 0 \\ 0 & K_{s2} & -K_{s2} & 0 & 0 \end{pmatrix}\begin{pmatrix} \omega_M \\ \omega_M \\ \omega_M \\ T_{dis} \\ T_{dis} \end{pmatrix} + \begin{pmatrix} \dfrac{1}{J_M} \\ 0 \\ 0 \\ 0 \\ 0 \end{pmatrix}T_{in} + \begin{pmatrix} 0 \\ 0 \\ -\dfrac{1}{J_L} \\ 0 \\ 0 \end{pmatrix}T_L \tag{5}$$

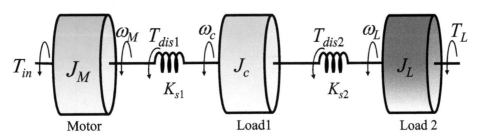

Figure 3. Three-mass model.

The state equation of three-mass resonance model is shown in Eq. (5). Then, Eq. (6) shows the continuous transfer function of three-mass resonance model, which input signal is T_{in} and output signal is ω_M.

$$\frac{\omega_M}{T_{in}} = \frac{(s^2 + \omega_{a1}^2)(s^2 + \omega_{a2}^2)}{J_M s(s^2 + \omega_{r1}^2)(s^2 + \omega_{r2}^2)} \tag{6}$$

In this equation, ω indicates the angular frequency, where ω_{r1}, ω_{r2}, ω_{a1}, and ω_{a2} are the resonance frequencies, and anti-resonance frequency, respectively. Then, the block diagram realized by using above equations is shown in **Figure 4**.

2.3. Experimental set up

This chapter confirms the effectiveness and performance of the proposed method by experiments using the experimental equipment.

Figure 5 is the appearance of the experimental system constructed in this research. The two-mass resonance system is simulated by utilizing the dc servo motor and the dc generator with a finite rigid coupling. The controller is realized on a digital signal processor, which calculates the PWM signal to a four-quadrant dc chopper.

The DSP board (PE-PRO/F28335 Starter Kit, Myway Plus Corp.) consists of the DSP (TMS320F28335PGFA), a digital input/output (I/O), ABZ counters for encoder signals, analog-to-digital (AD) converters and digital-to-analog (DA) converters [19]. The motor and load angles and angular speeds are detected using 5000 pulses-per-revolution encoders. The current of dc servo motor is measured by the current sensor and AD converter.

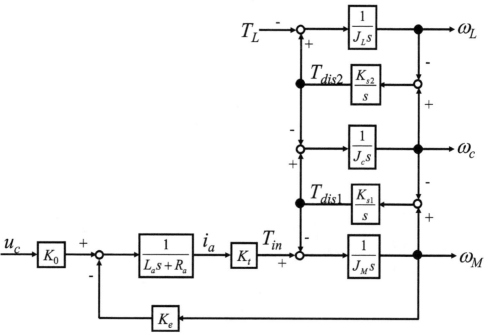

Figure 4. Block diagram of three-mass model.

Figure 5. Experimental apparatus.

The control frequency and the detection frequency of the encoder are both 1 ms, and the detection period for the current is 10 μsec. The design language used was C. Then, while considering the application of the system to specific apparatus, we constructed a digital control system that contains a discrete controller. In addition, we used MATLAB/Simulink software for the proposed off-line tuning process based on simulation and constructed the fuzzy control system as a continuous system [20]. The disturbance is added to the dc generator as the torque by using the electric load device on constant current mode. **Figures 6** and **7** show the apparatus of the two-mass model and three-mass model used in the experimental set up, respectively. **Figure 8** shows the experimental system configuration. For reference, the nominal parameters

Figure 6. Photograph of two-mass resonance model.

Figure 7. Photograph of three-mass resonance model.

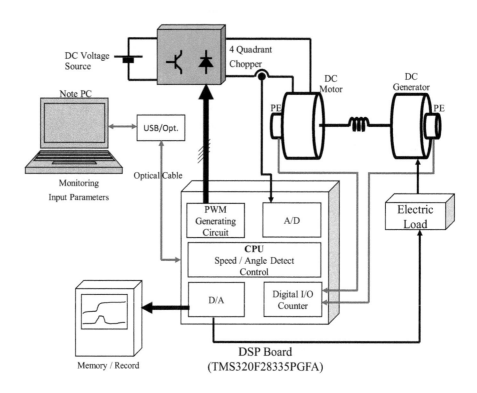

Figure 8. Configuration of experimental system (two-mass resonance model).

of the experimental two-mass model and three-mass model are given in **Tables 1** and **2**, respectively.

Figure 9 shows an example of experimental result using two-mass model. These step waves are the motor and load angular speeds with direct current voltage input. Similarly, **Figure 10** shows an example of experimental result using three-mass model, which are the motor and

Symbol	Parameter	Value
J_{Mn}	Motor inertia	2.744×10^{-4} (kgm^2)
J_{Ln}	Load inertia	2.940×10^{-4} (kgm^2)
K_{sn}	Shaft stiffness	18.5 (Nm/rad)

Table 1. Nominal parameters of two-mass experimental model.

Symbol	Parameter	Value
J_{Mn}	Motor inertia	2.744×10^{-4} (kgm^2)
J_{cn}	Load 1 inertia	1.112×10^{-4} (kgm^2)
J_{Ln}	Load 2 inertia	2.940×10^{-4} (kgm^2)
K_{s1n}	Shaft stiffness 1	18.5 (Nm/rad)
K_{s2n}	Shaft stiffness 2	18.5 (Nm/rad)

Table 2. Nominal parameters of three-mass experimental model.

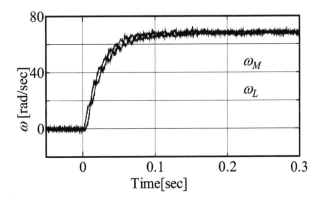

Figure 9. Angular speeds (ω_M and ω_L) of the step responses to a DC voltage input (two-mass model).

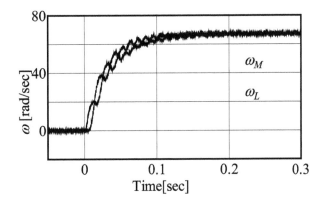

Figure 10. Angular speeds (ω_M and ω_L) of the step responses to a DC voltage input (three-mass model).

load angular speeds with same above condition. In these figures, the resonance vibrations can be observed. The purpose of this research is to suppress these resonance vibrations.

3. Proposed fuzzy control system

3.1. Fuzzy speed controller

Fuzzy controller, which is executed by the fuzzy set and the fuzzy inference, can control for nonlinear systems or uncertain model. **Figure 11** indicates the proposed fuzzy speed controller in this chapter. The speed controller is based on fuzzy control. The current controller is typical PI controller. Furthermore, the load side state variables are not utilized for control, where S_1, S_2, and S_3 are the parameters to determine the scale of the membership function, which are called scaling factors or scaling coefficient. K_{pc} and K_{ic} are the current PI controller gains. Eq. (7) shows the transfer function of current PI controller. Additionally, this chapter uses the discrete control system.

$$u_c(k) = \left(K_{pc} + \frac{1}{s} K_{ic} \right) e(k) \tag{7}$$

Figure 12 is indicative of the membership function for the premise variables. This membership function is a shape of triangle with a dense center. **Figure 13** indicates the membership

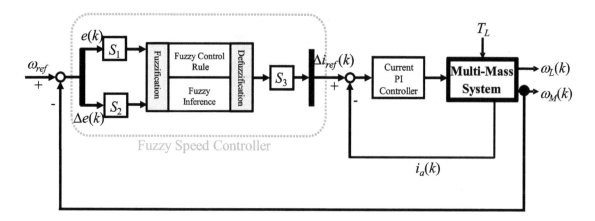

Figure 11. Block diagram of the proposed control system.

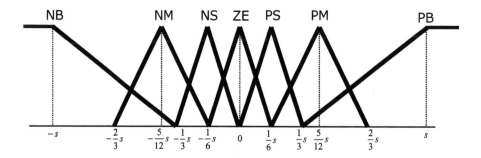

Figure 12. Membership functions of the antecedence.

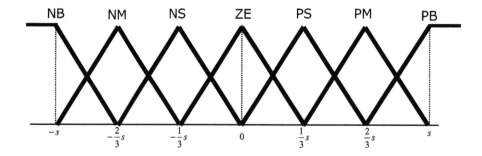

Figure 13. Membership functions of the consequence.

function, which is formed uniformly triangle for the consequent variable. Here, the s denotes the scaling factor. PB, PM, PS, ZE, NS, NM, and NB are the linguistic variables of the fuzzy control where, PB indicates positive big, PM indicates positive medium, PS indicates positive small, ZE indicates zero, NS indicates negative small, NM indicates negative medium, and NB indicates negative big, respectively. The premise variables are $e_{\omega M}(k)$ and $\Delta e_{\omega M}(k)$.

$$e_{\omega M}(k) = \omega_{ref} - \omega_M(k) \qquad (8)$$

$$\Delta e_{\omega M}(k) = e_{\omega M}(k) - e_{\omega M}(k-1) \qquad (9)$$

Then, the consequence variable is the variation width of the current input $\Delta i_{ref}(k)$. Therefore, the proposed fuzzy controller is nearly same as the proportional-derivative (PD) type controller.

Figure 14 is indicative of the fuzzy rule table. The rule is included the rising correction of the angular speed response.

e \ Δe	NB	NM	NS	ZE	PS	PM	PB
NB				NB	NM		
NM				NM			
NS				NS	ZE		PM
ZE	NB	NM	NS	ZE	PS	PM	PB
PS	NM			ZE	PS		
PM				PM			
PB			PM	PB			

Figure 14. Control rule table.

3.2. Design method of controller parameters by differential evolution

In this chapter, five parameters (S_1, S_2, S_3, K_{pc} and K_{ic}) of the proposed controller have to be designed. However, it is difficult to determine them by trial and error or some. Therefore, this chapter proposes the differential evolution (DE) to search the optimal controller parameters. Here, DE is one of evolutionary optimized solution search methods. DE is the optimization method-based multi-point search method. In particular, basic GA expresses parameter by binary coding, whereas DE uses the parameters by real variable vector. The DE design is conducted by the initial population, the mutation, the crossover, and the selection. The design flow of DE is shown in **Figure 15**. In this chapter, DE/rand/1/bin design strategy is used for the determination of five controller parameters.

where D is the number of design parameter vectors, NP is the number of members in each population. Each parameter vector is represented by the parameter vector (target vector) $x_{i,G}$, where G denotes one generation. The mutation vector $v_{i,G}$ is calculated by Eq. (10). From this equation, F indicates the step width (scaling factor) of DE design, and CR indicates of the crossover rate, where r_1, r_2, and r_3 are different values.

$$v_{i,G+1} = x_{r1,G} + F(x_{r1,G} - x_{r3,G}), \quad r_1 \neq r_2 \neq r_3 \neq i \tag{10}$$

$$u_{j,G+1} = \begin{cases} v_{j,G+1} & \text{rand} \leq CR \text{ or } j = ST \\ x_{j,G} & \text{rand} > CR \text{ or } j \neq ST \end{cases} \tag{11}$$

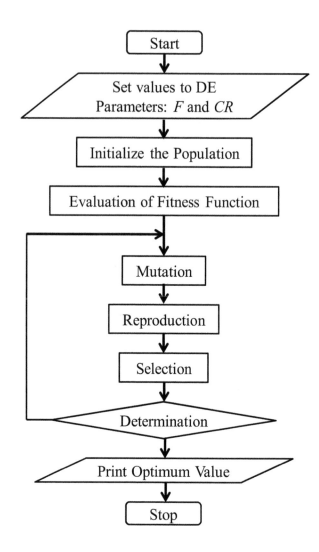

Figure 15. Flow of DE algorithm.

In Eq. (11), $u_{j,G+1}$ is the vector of trial parameter, the rand is random value, and ST indicates the start point. The selection is utilized next algorithm,

$$x_{i,G+1} = \begin{cases} u_{i,G+1} & \text{if } y(u_{i,G+1}) > y(x_{i,G}) \text{ for maximaization problems} \\ x_{i,G} & \text{otherwise} \end{cases} \quad (12)$$

As previously described, the proposed method uses five control parameters (S_1, S_2, S_3, K_{pc}, and K_{ic}). The population size is 2000, the order of each vector is 20, and the coefficient of membership function F is 0.5. Moreover, the rate of crossover CR is 0.9. Then, the performance index function is shown in Eq. (13). Meanwhile, this chapter utilizes the inverse of y as a fitness function.

$$y = \int_0^\infty t\sqrt{(\omega_{ref} - \omega_L)^2}dt \quad (13)$$

4. Simulation and experimental results

4.1. Verification results of computer simulation

Next, the simulation results of the proposed method are demonstrated by computer simulation.

Table 3 shows the results of design parameter using the proposed method for two-mass model. **Figure 16** is indicative of the transition of the maximum fitness function. In this simulation design, the step response and the disturbance response have been evaluated. Furthermore, the inertia ratio R is 1.07, and the stiffness of shaft K_{sn} has been set to 18.5 Nm/rad in the simulation design.

S_1	S_2	S_3	K_{pc}	K_{ic}
8.486	0.4802	0.4001	4.678	1.0×10^{-6}

Table 3. Results of design parameter calculated by DE.

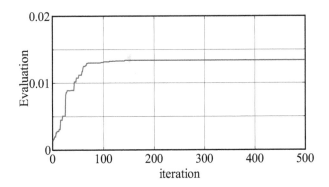

Figure 16. Convergence of index function y.

Figures 17 and **18** show the step responses that were obtained for the motor and load angular speeds, and armature current when using the proposed method. In this chapter, ω_{ref} is 30 rad/s, the DC voltage input is 25 V, and the disturbance input T_L is changed from 0 to 20% at $t = 0.3$ s. As shown by these figures, good waves are observed for the reference-following, vibration

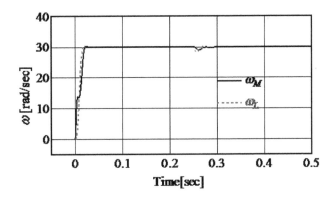

Figure 17. Simulation results ω_M and ω_L (two-mass, $R = 1.07$, $K_{sn} = 18.5$ Nm/rad).

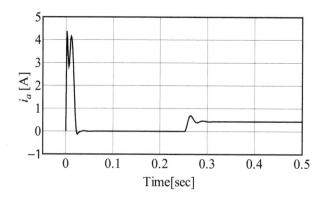

Figure 18. Simulation results i_a (two-mass, $R = 1.07$, $K_{sn} = 18.5$ Nm/rad).

suppression, and the disturbance performance. **Figure 19** is indicative of the search process of the S_1 vector. Similarly, **Figures 20–23** show the transition of the S_2 vector, S_3 vector, K_{pc} vector and K_{ic} vector, respectively. In particular, from **Figure 23** and **Table 3**, K_{ic} is 1.0×10^{-6} of the design limitation value. Therefore, integral gain of the current PI controller can be omitted for this control object.

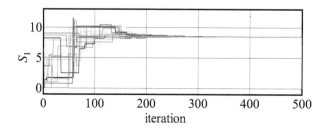

Figure 19. Transition of scaling factor S_1.

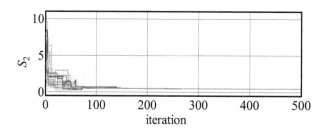

Figure 20. Transition of scaling factor S_2.

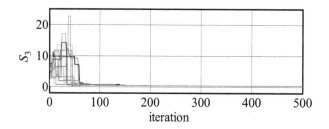

Figure 21. Transition of scaling factor S_3.

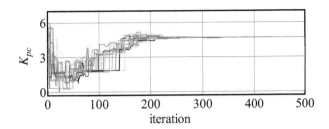

Figure 22. Transition of current proportional gain K_{pc}.

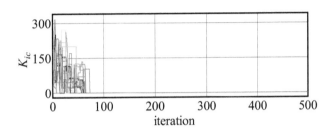

Figure 23. Transition of current integral gain K_{ic}.

4.2. Experimental results

4.2.1. 2-mass model

Next, the experimental results by using the proposed method are illustrated in this section. **Figures 24** and **25** show the experimental results of two-mass model using the proposed method, where the condition ($R = 1.07$, $K_{sn} = 18.5$ Nm/rad) is same as the above simulation results shown in **Figures 17** and **18**. From these figures, it is observed that the resonance vibrations between the motor and the load angular speed (ω_M and ω_L) have been suppressed very well. Furthermore, after inputting disturbance, it can be seen that the angular speeds immediately have followed the reference speed ω_{ref} without resonance vibrations. Hence, the validity of the control system, which consists of the proposed method, can be confirmed.

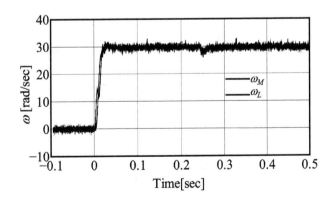

Figure 24. Experimental results for ω_M and ω_L obtained using the proposed method (two-mass, $R = 1.07$, $K_{sn} = 18.5$ Nm/rad).

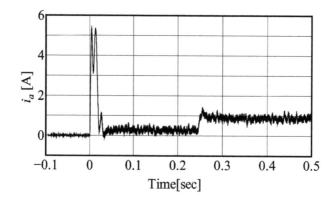

Figure 25. Experimental results for i_a obtained using the proposed method (two-mass, $R = 1.07$, $K_s = 18.5$ Nm/rad).

5. Effects of parameter variation

Next, it is described the effectiveness of robustness by the proposed design method. This section evaluates the robustness to variations in the ratio of inertia and the stiffness of the rigid shaft based on a nominal value.

Figures 26 and **27** show the experimental results of the motor and load angular speeds obtained for the inertia ratio variation when using the same controller gains that were designed using the

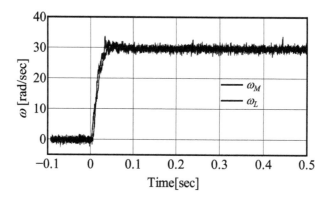

Figure 26. Robustness verification results (two-mass, $R = 0.42$, $K_{sn} = 18.5$ Nm/rad).

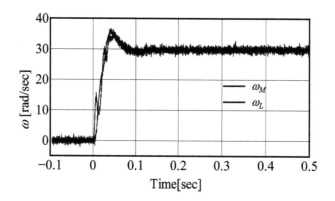

Figure 27. Robustness verification results (two-mass, $R = 2.67$, $K_{sn} = 18.5$ Nm/rad).

proposed method, when R = [0.42, 2.65], where the disturbance torque input was skipped. From these figure, although it can be observed some overshoot and resonance vibration, the good results can be confirmed that were obtained for the design condition.

Figure 28 shows the experimental results of the motor and load angular speeds obtained for the stiffness of shaft variation using the same controller gains, when K_{sn} = 70.7. From this figure, it can be seen some resonance vibrations. However, the vibrations rapidly have been suppressed well.

Similarly, **Figure 29** shows the experimental results when K_{sn} = 3.1. As can be seen, the motor and load angular speeds oscillated and overshot. Therefore, if the stiffness of shaft of the experimental model is less than the design value, the settling time to suppress the resonance vibration becomes longer, although the proposed control system is not unstable. In addition, **Figure 30** shows the experimental result when the control parameter redesigned with the stiffness of shaft K_{sn} as the nominal value of experimental model. Good responses can be observed in this figure.

Furthermore, the proposed fuzzy control system is applied to a three-mass resonance model. **Figure 31** shows the experimental results of the motor and load angular speeds when using the same controller gains designed for two-mass model (R = 1.07, K_{sn} = 18.5 Nm/rad, where the nominal parameters of the three-mass experimental setup are J_{Mn} = 2.774 × 10^{-4} kgm², J_{Ln} = 2.940 × 10^{-4} kgm², K_{s1n} = 18.5 Nm/rad, K_{s2n} = 18.5 Nm/rad. From this figure, the effectiveness of the proposed method can be confirmed in a similar manner to the two-mass model case.

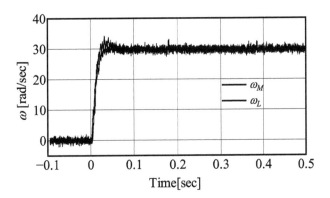

Figure 28. Robustness verification results (two-mass, R = 1.07, K_{sn} = 70.7 Nm/rad).

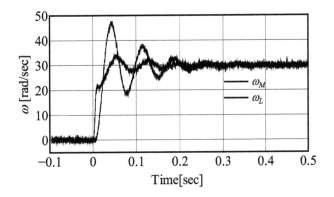

Figure 29. Robustness verification results (two-mass, R = 1.07, K_{sn} = 3.1 Nm/rad).

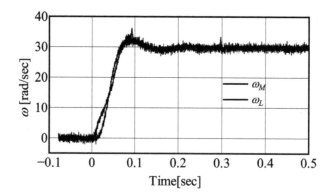

Figure 30. Experimental results for ω_M and ω_L redesigned using the proposed method (two-mass, $R = 1.07$, $K_{sn} = 3.1$ Nm/rad).

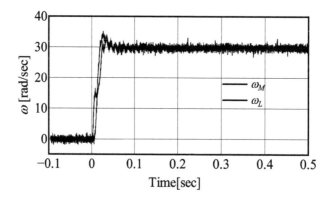

Figure 31. Robustness verification results (three-mass, $J_{Mn} = 2.774 \times 10^{-4}$ kgm^2, $J_{cn} = 1.112 \times 10^{-4}$ kgm^2, $J_{Ln} = 2.940 \times 10^{-4}$ kgm^2, $K_{s1n} = 18.5$ Nm/rad, $K_{s2n} = 18.5$ Nm/rad).

6. Conclusions

This chapter proposed the speed control system to suppress the resonance vibration of multi-inertial model, especially two-mass system and three-mass system. The controller has been constructed with the digital fuzzy controller for speed control and the digital PI controller for current control. In the control system, only motor side state variables have been used for controlling the resonance system. Additionally, this chapter utilized the DE to determine these five controller parameters. Finally, the validity of the controller design, the robustness, and the control effectiveness of the proposed method has been verified using the simulations and the experiments by using the test experimental set up.

Author details

Hidehiro Ikeda

Address all correspondence to: ikeda@nishitech.ac.jp

Nishinippon Institute of Technology, Kitakyushu, Japan

References

[1] Hori Y, Sawada H, Chun Y. Slow resonance ratio control for vibration suppression and disturbance rejection in torsional system. IEEE Transactions on Industrial Electronics. 1999;**46**(1):162–168

[2] Kwang-Ho Yoon, Jong-Kwang Lee, Ki-Ho Kim, Byung-Suk Park, Ji-Sup Yoon. Hybrid robust controller design for a two mass system with disturbance compensation. In: Proc. ICCAS 2008, pp. 1367–1372

[3] Szabat K, Kowalska TO. Vibration suppression in a two-mass drives system using PI speed controller and additional feedbacks – comparative study. IEEE Transactions on Industrial Electronics, 2007;**54**(2):1193–1206

[4] Ikeda H, Hanamoto T, Tsuji T, Tanaka Y. Position control of 2-mass systems with speed minor loop designed by pole placement method. IEEJ Transactions on Industry Applications. 1999;**119-D**(4):544–545

[5] Zhang G, Furusho J. Control of three-inertia system by PI/PID control. Transactions of IEE Japan. 1999;**119-D**(11):1386–1392

[6] Eker I, Vural M. Experimental online identification of a three-mass mechanical system. Proceedings of 2003 IEEE Conference. 2003;**1**:60–65

[7] Ikeda H, Hanamoto T, Tsuji T. Design of multi-inertia digital speed control system using Taguchi method. In: Proceedings of ICEM 2008, Paper ID 1167, PB.3.9; 2008. pp. 1–6

[8] Ikeda H, Hanamoto T, Tsuji T, Tomizuka M. Design of vibration suppression controller for 3-inertia systems using Taguchi method. In: Proceedings of SPEEDAM 2006, Mechatronic Systems, S10-19 to S10-25; 2006.

[9] Ikeda H, Hanamoto T. Design of vibration suppression controller for 2-inertia system by fictitious reference iterative tuning. In: Proceedings of ICEE 2015, ICEE15A-123; 2015. p. 6

[10] Ikeda H, Ajishi H, Hanamoto T. Application of fictitious reference iterative tuning to vibration suppression controller for 2-inertia resonance system. In: Proceedings of IECON 2015, TS-48, YF-008451; 2015. pp. 1825–1830

[11] Malhotra R, Kaur T, Deol GS. DC motor control using fuzzy logic controller. International Journal of AEST. 2011;**8**(2):291–296

[12] Chakravorty J, Sharma R. Fuzzy logic based method of speed control of DC motor. International Journal of ETAE. 2013;**3**(4):64–66

[13] Ikeda H, Hanamoto T. Fuzzy controller of multi-inertia resonance system designed by differential evolution. In: Proceedings of ICEMS 2013, MC-1883; 2013. pp. 2291–2295

[14] Ikeda H, Hanamoto T. Fuzzy controller of three-inertia resonance system designed by differential evolution. Journal of International Conference on Electrical Machines and Systems. 2014;**3**(2);184–189

[15] Yadav JS, Patidar NP, Singhai J. Controller design of discrete system by order reduction technique employing differential evolution optimization algorithm. International Journal of IMS. 2010;**6**(1):43–49

[16] Yamaguchi S. An automatic control parameters tuning method for differential evolution. Transactions of IEE Japan. 2008;**128-C**(11):1696–1703

[17] Brest J, et al. Self-adapting control parameters in differential evolution: A comparative study on numerical benchmark problems. IEEE Transactions on Evolutionary Computation. 2006;**10**(6):646–657

[18] Ikeda H, Hanamoto T. Design of m-IPD controller of multi-inertia system using differential evolution. In: Proceedings of IPEC-Hiroshima 2014 – ECCE ASIA, 21J1-2; 2014. pp. 2476–2482

[19] Myway Plus Corporation, https://www.mayway.co.jp/, Yokohama, Japan.

[20] The Mathworks, https://www.mathworks.com, Massachusetts, U.S.A.

Permissions

All chapters in this book were first published in MFCSIA, by InTech Open; hereby published with permission under the Creative Commons Attribution License or equivalent. Every chapter published in this book has been scrutinized by our experts. Their significance has been extensively debated. The topics covered herein carry significant findings which will fuel the growth of the discipline. They may even be implemented as practical applications or may be referred to as a beginning point for another development.

The contributors of this book come from diverse backgrounds, making this book a truly international effort. This book will bring forth new frontiers with its revolutionizing research information and detailed analysis of the nascent developments around the world.

We would like to thank all the contributing authors for lending their expertise to make the book truly unique. They have played a crucial role in the development of this book. Without their invaluable contributions this book wouldn't have been possible. They have made vital efforts to compile up to date information on the varied aspects of this subject to make this book a valuable addition to the collection of many professionals and students.

This book was conceptualized with the vision of imparting up-to-date information and advanced data in this field. To ensure the same, a matchless editorial board was set up. Every individual on the board went through rigorous rounds of assessment to prove their worth. After which they invested a large part of their time researching and compiling the most relevant data for our readers.

The editorial board has been involved in producing this book since its inception. They have spent rigorous hours researching and exploring the diverse topics which have resulted in the successful publishing of this book. They have passed on their knowledge of decades through this book. To expedite this challenging task, the publisher supported the team at every step. A small team of assistant editors was also appointed to further simplify the editing procedure and attain best results for the readers.

Apart from the editorial board, the designing team has also invested a significant amount of their time in understanding the subject and creating the most relevant covers. They scrutinized every image to scout for the most suitable representation of the subject and create an appropriate cover for the book.

The publishing team has been an ardent support to the editorial, designing and production team. Their endless efforts to recruit the best for this project, has resulted in the accomplishment of this book. They are a veteran in the field of academics and their pool of knowledge is as vast as their experience in printing. Their expertise and guidance has proved useful at every step. Their uncompromising quality standards have made this book an exceptional effort. Their encouragement from time to time has been an inspiration for everyone.

The publisher and the editorial board hope that this book will prove to be a valuable piece of knowledge for researchers, students, practitioners and scholars across the globe.

List of Contributors

Danil Dintsis
Educational Private organization "Specialist", Moscow, Russian Federation

Anatoly D. Khomonenko, Sergey E. Adadurov, Alexandr V. Krasnovidow and Pavel A. Novikov
Petersburg State Transport University, St. Petersburg, Russia

Mao Li
The University of Birmingham, Birmingham, UK

Junmin Li, Jinsha Li and Ruirui Duan
School of Mathematics and Statistics, Xidian University, Xi'an, PR China

Dušan Krokavec and Anna Filasová
Department of Cybernetics, Artificial Intelligence, Faculty of Electrical Engineering, Informatics, Technical University of Košice, Košice, Slovakia

Brandon Cook
NASA Ames Research Center, Moffett Field, CA, USA
Department of Aerospace Engineering and Engineering Mechanics, University of Cincinnati, Cincinnati, OH, USA

Tim Arnett and Kelly Cohen
Department of Aerospace Engineering and Engineering Mechanics, University of Cincinnati, Cincinnati, OH, USA

Wafa Gritli, Hajer Gharsallaoui and Mohamed Benrejeb
National Engineering School of Tunis, Tunis, Tunisia

Longzhi Yang and Zheming Zuo
Department of Computer and Information Sciences, Northumbria University, Newcastle, UK

Fei Chao
School of Information Science and Engineering, Xiamen University, Xiamen, PR China

Yanpeng Qu
Information Science and Technology College, Dalian Maritime University, Dalian, PR China

Beyda Taşar
Firat University, Engineering Faculty, Department of Mechatronics, Elazig, Turkey

Arif Gülten
Firat University, Engineering Faculty, Department of Electrical and Electronics, Elazig, Turkey

Bahadir Ergün and Cumhur Sahin
Department of Geodesy and Photogrammetry, Gebze Technical University, Gebze, Turkey

Ugur Kaplan
Department of Mathematics, Gebze Technical University, Gebze, Turkey

Hidehiro Ikeda
Nishinippon Institute of Technology, Kitakyushu, Japan

Index

Printed in the USA
CPSIA information can be obtained
at www.ICGtesting.com
JSHW051431221024
72173JS00006B/1433